The Politics of Blood

D1765773

How best to manage risk involving multi-valued human biological materials is the overarching theme of this book, which draws on the sourcing and supply of blood as a case study. Blood has ethical, social, scientific and commercial value. This multi-valuing process presents challenges in terms of managing risk, therefore making it ultimately a matter for political responsibility. This is highlighted through an examination of the circumstances that led to HIV blood contamination episodes in the USA, England and France, as well as their consequences. The roles of scientific expertise and innovation in managing risks to the blood system are also analysed, as is the increased use of precautionary and legal strategies in the post-HIV blood contamination era. Finally, consideration is given to a range of policy and legal strategies that should underpin effective risk governance involving multi-valued human biological materials.

ANNE-MAREE FARRELL is Associate Professor of Law at the Faculty of Law, Monash University, Melbourne. Her research expertise lies broadly within the area of health law and policy, with a particular interest in the regulatory governance of human biological materials. She previously practised as a lawyer for over ten years, specialising in medical-related litigation.

Cambridge Bioethics and Law

This series of books was founded by Cambridge University Press with Alexander McCall Smith as its first editor in 2003. It focuses on the law's complex and troubled relationship with medicine across both the developed and the developing world. In the past twenty years, we have seen in many countries increasing resort to the courts by dissatisfied patients and a growing use of the courts to attempt to resolve intractable ethical dilemmas. At the same time, legislatures across the world have struggled to address the questions posed by both the successes and the failures of modern medicine, while international organisations such as the WHO and UNESCO now regularly address issues of medical law.

It follows that we would expect ethical and policy questions to be integral to the analysis of the legal issues discussed in this series. The series responds to the high profile of medical law in universities, in legal and medical practice, as well as in public and political affairs. We seek to reflect the evidence that many major health-related policy debates in the UK, Europe and the international community over the past two decades have involved a strong medical law dimension. Organ retention, embryonic stem cell research, physician-assisted suicide and the allocation of resources to fund health care are but a few examples among many. The emphasis of this series is thus on matters of public concern and/or practical significance. We look for books that could make a difference to the development of medical law and enhance the role of medico-legal debate in policy circles. That is not to say that we lack interest in the important theoretical dimensions of the subject, but we aim to ensure that theoretical debate is grounded in the realities of how the law does and should interact with medicine and health care.

General Editors
Professor Margaret Brazier, *University of Manchester*
Professor Graeme Laurie, *University of Edinburgh*

Editorial Advisory Board
Professor Richard Ashcroft, *Queen Mary, University of London*
Professor Martin Bobrow, *University of Cambridge*
Dr Alexander Morgan Capron, *Director, Ethics and Health, World Health Organization, Geneva*
Professor Jim Childress, *University of Virginia*
Professor Ruth Chadwick, *Cardiff Law School*
Dame Ruth Deech, *University of Oxford*
Professor John Keown, *Georgetown University, Washington, DC*
Dr Kathy Liddell, *University of Cambridge*
Professor Alexander McCall Smith, *University of Edinburgh*
Professor Dr Mónica Navarro-Michel, *University of Barcelona*

Marcus Radetzki, Marian Radetzki, Niklas Juth
Genes and Insurance: Ethical, Legal and Economic Issues

Ruth Macklin
Double Standards in Medical Research in Developing Countries

Donna Dickenson
Property in the Body: Feminist Perspectives

Matti Häyry, Ruth Chadwick, Vilhjálmur Árnason, Gardar Árnason
The Ethics and Governance of Human Genetic Databases: European Perspectives

Ken Mason
The Troubled Pregnancy: Legal Wrongs and Rights in Reproduction

Daniel Sperling
Posthumous Interests: Legal and Ethical Perspectives

Keith Syrett
Law, Legitimacy and the Rationing of Health Care

Alastair Maclean
Autonomy, Informed Consent and the Law: A Relational Change

Heather Widdows, Caroline Mullen
The Governance of Genetic Information: Who Decides?

David Price
Human Tissue in Transplantation and Research

Matti Häyry
Rationality and the Genetic Challenge: Making People Better?

Mary Donnelly
Healthcare Decision-Making and the Law: Autonomy, Capacity and the Limits of Liberalism

Anne-Maree Farrell, David Price, Muireann Quigley
Organ Shortage: Ethics, Law and Pragmatism

Sara Fovargue
Xenotransplantation and Risk: Regulating a Developing Biotechnology

John Coggon
What Makes Health Public?: A Critical Evaluation of Moral, Legal, and Political Claims in Public Health

Anne-Maree Farrell
The Politics of Blood: Ethics, Innovation and the Regulation of Risk

The Politics of Blood

Ethics, Innovation and the
Regulation of Risk

Anne-Maree Farrell

CAMBRIDGE
UNIVERSITY PRESS

University Printing House, Cambridge CB2 8BS, United Kingdom

Cambridge University Press is part of the University of Cambridge.

It furthers the University's mission by disseminating knowledge in the pursuit of education, learning and research at the highest international levels of excellence.

www.cambridge.org
Information on this title: www.cambridge.org/9781107474796

© Anne-Maree Farrell 2012

First published 2012
First paperback edition 2014

A catalogue record for this publication is available from the British Library

Library of Congress Cataloguing in Publication data
Farrell, Anne-Maree, 1964–
    The politics of blood : ethics, innovation, and the regulation of risk / Anne-Maree Farrell.
        p.   cm. – (Cambridge Bioethics and Law)
    Includes bibliographical references and index.
    ISBN 978-0-521-19318-4 (hardback)
    1. Blood banks–Government policy.   2. Blood products–Safety measures.   3. Blood–Moral and ethical aspects.   4. Blood–Social measures.   I. Title.
    RM172.F37 2012
    362.17′84–dc23
    2012003509

ISBN 978-0-521-19318-4 Hardback
ISBN 978-1-107-47479-6 Paperback

This book is dedicated to my father, Gerard Farrell

Ar dheis Dé go raibh a anam uasal

Contents

Acknowledgements   *page* x
Chronological table of cases   xii
Chronological table of legislation   xiii
List of abbreviations   xvi

1   Introduction   1

2   The governance of the blood system   24

3   Revisiting the gift relationship   56

4   Professional beliefs and scientific expertise   76

5   Risk and innovation   99

6   The rise of the recipient   124

7   The politics of precaution   166

8   Regulating risk   198

9   Conclusion   222

Bibliography   230
Index   257

Acknowledgements

This book has been a long time coming. My initial interest in the subject matter of the book had its origins in my previous work as a lawyer in the field of blood-related litigation. Much of the in-depth reading that was required as a prelude to the writing of the book took place while I was in receipt of a Leverhulme Trust Research Fellowship, and the Trust's support is gratefully acknowledged. I also benefited greatly from a period of research leave provided by the School of Law, University of Manchester, during the writing up phase of the book. Further impetus and stimulation has been provided through my involvement in a number of research collaborations, including the Economic and Social Research Council (ESRC) research grant: *Risk, Safety and Consent in Contemporary Blood Services in the UK: Perspectives from Sociology and Law* (RES-062-23-2751) and the University of Manchester Wellcome Strategic Programme: *The Human Body: its Scope Limits and Future*. Chapter 8 drew on research done whilst in receipt of an ESRC seminar series grant: *European Law and New Health Technologies* (RES-451-26-0764). The support of both the Wellcome Trust and the ESRC is gratefully acknowledged.

I would also like to acknowledge the support and assistance I have received from Cambridge University Press in the preparation and completion of the book, in particular Finola O'Sullivan, Elizabeth Spicer and Richard Woodham. The encouragement of Margaret Brazier and Graeme Laurie, the commissioning editors for Cambridge University Press's Law, Medicine and Ethics series, was also much appreciated.

I would like to thank the anonymous reviewer who provided helpful feedback on the draft manuscript, as did colleagues including Helen Busby, John Coggon, Sarah Devaney, Julie Kent and Michael Moran. Thanks must also go to the Peek-Farrell families, colleagues and friends for their continuing support while I was writing the book, as well as to my sons Tom and Josh for always being delightful and welcome distractions. Last but not least, this book would never have been completed without the unwavering support, patience and proofing skills of my husband, Ron – I could not have done it without you, schatje.

Chronological table of cases

ENGLAND

Re HIV Haemophiliac Litigation (1990) 41 BMLR 171 (Court of Appeal, Civ. Div)   138, 139
A v. *National Blood Authority* [2001] 3 All ER 289   163
The Queen (on the application of Andrew Michael March) v. *The Secretary of State for Health* [2010] EWHC 765 (Admin), Case No. CO/9344/09   142

EUROPEAN UNION

Humanplasma GmbH v. *Republik Österreich*, Case C - 421/09 [2011] OJC 55/13   212

FRANCE

Cour de cassation, Chambre criminelle, 22 juin 1994 (Bull. crim, n° 248, p. 604)   146
Cour de cassation, Chambre criminelle, 18 juin 2003 (Bull. n° 127)   148

UNITED STATES

Perlmutter v. *Beth David Hospital*, 308 NT 100, 123 NE 2d 192 (1954)   155
Fogo v. *Cutter Laboratories*, 68 Cal. App. 3d 744, 137 Cal. Rptr. 417 (1977)   154
United Blood Services v. *Quintana* 827 P. 2d 509 (Colorado, 1992)   154
Wadleigh v. *Rhone Poulenc Rorer Inc.* No. 93 C 5969 (N.D. Ill., filed Sept 30, 1993)   156
In the matter of Rhone-Poulenc Rorer Inc. 51 F 3d 1293 (7th Cir. 1995)   157
Christopher v. *Cutter Laboratories*, 53 F 3d 1184 (11th Cir. 1995)   154
In the matter of Rhone-Poulenc Rorer Inc. 51 F 3d 1293 (7th Cir. 1995), *cert. denied, Grady* v. *Rhone-Poulenc Rorer Inc.* 516 U.S. 867 (1995)   157
In re Factor VIII or IX Concentrate Blood Products Litigation, MDL 986, No. 93 C 7452   156
In re Factor VIII or IX Concentrate Blood Products Litigation, No. 96 C 5024   157

xii

Chronological table of legislation

COUNCIL OF EUROPE

Council of Europe, Convention on the Elaboration of a European
Pharmacopoeia, Strasbourg, 2VI1.1964, ETS No. 50, as amended
by the Protocol to the Convention on the Elaboration of a European
Pharmacopoeia. ETS No. 134, in force 1 November 1992   47
Recommendation No. R (95) 15 of the Committee of Ministers to Member
States on the Preparation, Use and Quality Assurance of Blood
Components (adopted by the Committee of Ministers on 12 October
1995 at the 545th meeting of the Ministers' Deputies)   47

EUROPEAN UNION

Council Directive 89/381/EEC of 14 June 1989 extending the scope of
Directives 65/65/EEC and 75/319/EEC on the approximation of
provisions laid down by law, regulation or administrative action relating
to medicinal products and laying down special provisions for proprietary
medicinal products derived from human blood or human plasma
(repealed)   214, 215
98/463/EC Council Recommendation of 29 June 1998 on the suitability of
blood and plasma donors and the screening of donated blood in the
European Community, OJ L 203, 21.7.1998   12, 204
Directive 2001/83/EC of the European Parliament and of the Council of 6
November 2001 on the Community code relating to medicinal products
for human use, OJ L 311, 28.11.2001   48, 120, 215, 216
Directive 2002/98/EC of the European Parliament and of the Council of 27
January 2003 setting standards of quality and safety for the collection,
testing, processing, storage and distribution of human blood and
blood components and amending Directive 2001/83/EC, OJ L 33,
8.2.2003   12, 50, 71, 204
Commission Directive 2003/63/EC of 25 June 2003 amending Directive
2001/83/EC of the European Parliament and of the Council on the
Community code relating to medicinal products for human use, OJ L
159, 27.6.2003   48, 120, 216
Commission Directive 2003/94/EC of 8 October 2003 laying down the
principles and guidelines of good manufacturing practice in respect

of medicinal products for human use and investigational products for human use, OJ L 262, 14.10.2003   215

Commission Directive 2004/33/EC of 22 March 2004 implementing Directive 2002/98/EC of the European Parliament and of the Council as regards certain technical requirements for blood and blood components, OJ L 91, 30.3.2004   204, 206

Regulation (EC) No. 726/2004 of the European Parliament and of the Council of 31 March 2004 laying down Community procedures for the authorisation and supervision of medicinal products for human and veterinary use and establishing a European Medicines Agency, OJ L 136, 30.4.2004   50

Commission Directive 2005/61/EC having regard to Directive 2002/98/EC of the European Parliament and of the Council of 27 January 2003 setting standards of quality and safety for the collection, testing, processing, storage and distribution of human blood and blood components and amending Directive 2001/83/EC, OJ L 256, 1.10.2005   204, 206, 207

Commission Directive 2005/62/EC of 30 September 2005 implementing Directive 2002/98/EC of the European Parliament and of the Council as regards Community standards and specifications relating to a quality system for blood establishments, OJ L 256, 1.10.2005   204, 206, 207

Regulation (EC) No. 1394/2007 of the European Parliament and of the Council of 13 November 2007 on advanced therapy medicinal products and amending Directive 2001/83/EC and Regulation (EC) No. 726/2004   4

Commission Directive 2009/135/EC allowing temporary derogations to certain eligibility criteria for whole blood and blood components laid down in Annex III to Directive 2004/33/EC in the context of a risk of shortage caused by the Influenza A(H1N1) pandemic, OJ L 288, 4.11.2009   205

FRANCE

Loi n° 91-1406 du 31 décembre 1991 portant diverses dispositions d'ordre social (1), JORF n° 3 du 4 janvier 1992, p. 178   144

UNITED KINGDOM

Equality Act 2010, c. 15   188

UNITED STATES

Food, Drug and Cosmetics Act, 21 U.S.C. § 301 et seq.   35

Ryan White Comprehensive AIDS Resources Emergency (CARE) Act of 1990 Ryan White Care Act, Ryan White, Pub. L. 101–381, 104 Stat. 576   152

Ricky Ray Hemophilia Relief Fund of 1998, Secs. 101–108 of Pub. L. 105–369, 112 Stat. 3368   152

WORLD HEALTH ORGANIZATION

Constitution of the World Health Organization   44
World Health Organization. Twenty-Eighth World Health Assembly.
Utilization and supply of human blood and blood products, WHA28.72, 1975
World Health Organization. Fifty-Eighth World Health Assembly.   42, 65
Blood safety: Proposal to establish World Blood Donor Day, WHA58.13,
     2005   42

Abbreviations

AABB	American Association of Blood Banks
ABC	America's Blood Centers
ABRA	American Blood Resources Association
ACT-UP	AIDS Coalition to Unleash Power
ACBSA	Advisory Committee on Blood Safety and Availability (USA)
AFH	Association Française des Hémophiles (Haemophilia Association of France)
AHF	Anti-haemophiliac factor
AIDS	Acquired immune deficiency syndrome
AP	Association des Polytransfusés (Multi-Transfused Association, France)
ARC	American Red Cross
BOTS WG	Blood, Organ and Tissue Safety Working Group (USA)
BPAC	Blood Products Advisory Committee (FDA-US)
BPL	Blood Products Laboratory (UK; later known as Bio Products Laboratory)
BRN	Blood Regulators Network (WHO)
BSE	Bovine spongiform encephalopathy
BSP	Biological Standardisation Programme (Council of Europe)
BWP	Biologics Working Party (EMA–EU)
CDC	Centers for Disease Control (USA; now called Centers for Disease Control and Prevention)
DGS	Direction Générale de la Santé (Department of Health, France)
DG SANCO	Directorate General for Health and Consumers (EU)
DHSS	Department of Health and Social Security (UK)
EBA	European Blood Alliance
EC	European Community

ECBS	Expert Committee on Biological Standardisation (WHO)
EDQM	European Directorate for the Quality of Medicines and HealthCare (Council of Europe)
EHC	European Haemophilia Consortium
EMA	European Medicines Agency (EU)
EPAR	European Public Assessment Reports (EMA–EU)
EU	European Union
FDA	Food and Drug Administration (USA)
GCBS	Global Collaboration on Blood Safety (WHO)
GDP	Gross domestic product
GM	Genetically modified
GMP	Good Manufacturing Practice
HBV	Hepatitis B virus
HCV	Hepatitis C virus
HHV-8	Human herpesvirus-8
HIV	Human immunodeficiency virus
HPC	Haematopoietic progenitor cell
HTLV-III	Human T-lymphotropic virus-type III
ICH	International Conference on Harmonisation
IFBDO	International Federation of Blood Donor Organizations
IFRC	International Federation of Red Cross and Red Crescent Societies
IOM	Institute of Medicine (USA)
IPFA	International Plasma Fractionation Association
IPOPI	International Patient Organisation for Primary Immunodeficiencies
IQPP	International Quality Plasma Program
ISBT	International Society of Blood Transfusion
MASAC	Medical and Scientific Advisory Council (NHF-US)
MDL	Multi-District Litigation
MP	Member of Parliament (UK)
MSM	Men who have sex with men
NANB	Non-A non-B (hepatitis)
NAT	Nucleic acid amplification technology
NHF	National Hemophilia Foundation (USA)
NHS	National Health Service (UK)
NHSBT	National Health Service Blood and Transplant (UK)
OECD	Organisation for Economic Co-operation and Development

OMCL	Official Medicines Control Laboratories (Council of Europe)
OPEC	Organization of the Petroleum Exporting Countries
PDG	Pharmacopoeial Discussion Group (Council of Europe)
PhEur	European Pharmacopeia (Council of Europe)
PMF	Plasma Master File
PPTA	Plasma Protein Therapeutics Association
PRT	Pathogen reduction technology
PWA	People with AIDS
PWH	People with haemophilia
QALY	Quality-adjusted life years
QSEAL	Quality Standards of Excellence, Assurance and Leadership
rFVIII	Recombinant factor VIII
SaBTO	Advisory Committee on the Safety of Blood Tissues and Organs (UK)
SAC	Special Assistance Council (NHF–US)
SHOT	Serious Hazards of Transfusion (UK)
TFEU	Treaty on the Functioning of the European Union (EU)
TTI	Transfusion-transmitted infection
UK	United Kingdom
UKHCDO	United Kingdom Haemophilia Centre Doctors' Organisation (UK)
USA	United States
vCJD	Variant Creutzfeldt–Jakob disease
VNRBD	Voluntary non-remunerated blood donation
WFH	World Federation of Hemophilia
WHO	World Health Organization
WTO	World Trade Organization

1 Introduction

Throughout human history, blood has been imbued with many social and cultural meanings. It has also been used to identify and classify human beings, as well as structure social relationships.[1] The twentieth century saw a revolution in the use of blood, with scientific discoveries transforming its role in modern medicine. The sourcing and supply of blood became organised on a national basis in developed countries, underpinned by the notion of the gift relationship which promoted altruistic, non-remunerated blood donation in the context of an anonymous relationship between donors and recipients.[2] Scientific and technological developments led to the industrial production of plasma-derived medicinal products (plasma products),[3] which were predominantly sourced from individuals who received financial compensation for providing their blood (paid donors).[4] In turn, this facilitated the development of a global blood market in such products.[5]

---

[1] D. Nelkin, 'Cultural perspectives on blood', in E. A. Feldman and R. Bayer (eds.), *Blood Feuds: AIDS, Blood, and the Politics of Medical Disaster* (New York: Oxford University Press, 1999), pp. 274–92.

[2] R. M. Titmuss, *The Gift Relationship: From Human Blood to Social Policy* (London: George Allen & Unwin, 1970).

[3] Plasma is the straw-coloured fluid in which blood cells are suspended. It contains a high concentration of various proteins. Through a treatment process known as fractionation, plasma proteins are separated into fractions of more or less purified proteins with different properties. Plasma products often require thousands of donations in order to manufacture a single batch. For further details, see P. Hagen, *Blood Transfusion in Europe: A 'White Paper'* (Strasbourg: Council of Europe, 1993), pp. 188–90.

[4] For the purposes of this book, the term 'paid donor' is used, although I acknowledge that the for-profit plasma products industry prefers the term 'compensated donor' on the grounds that the individual is being compensated for their time and effort in undertaking plasma donation. See Plasma Protein Therapeutics Association (PPTA), *The Facts about Plasma Collection* (www.pptaglobal.org).

[5] For an overview of the early development of the plasma products industry, see P. Hagen, *Blood: Gift or Merchandise? Towards an International Blood Policy* (New York: Alan R. Liss Inc., 1982).

In the 1980s, the acquired immune deficiency syndrome (AIDS) emerged as an epidemic in the developed world. The infectious agent responsible for the disease, which later became known as the human immunodeficiency virus (HIV), was found to be transmissible by blood.[6] Once HIV testing became available, large numbers of individuals were also found to have been infected with the virus through the use of blood. In the 1990s, revelations about the circumstances that had led to HIV blood contamination episodes caused political scandals in a number of developed countries, where it became clear that the response by those with responsibility for the blood system had been inadequate. These scandals were characterised by adverse media reaction, protracted litigation in the courts, state-sponsored tribunals of inquiry, as well as institutional and regulatory reform of national blood systems.[7] For those deemed responsible for the contamination episodes, the consequences included public excoriation and on occasion the imposition of criminal sanctions. For those individuals who were infected with HIV through blood, it was a deeply personal tragedy, resulting in serious disability and/or loss of life.[8]

Risk, public health and human biological materials

Risk governance in public health is not new, but we now live in an era of globalisation where such risks may have a rapid and wide-ranging impact with deleterious social, economic and political consequences. This is particularly true in relation to risks to public health posed by infectious diseases. In recent years, it has been recognised that there is

[6] The human immunodeficiency virus (HIV) is the virus that causes the acquired immune deficiency syndrome (AIDS). A person may be infected with the virus, but will only be considered to have AIDS once there is severe immune deficiency, or s/he is diagnosed with illnesses associated with such deficiency.

[7] For the purposes of this book, the use of the term 'blood system' is intended to refer to the collection and supply of blood components; the manufacture and supply of plasma products; and policy and regulatory processes involved in these activities. When reference is made to the term 'blood supply', it is confined to collection and supply issues involving blood and plasma products, primarily at national level.

[8] For an overview, see L. Leveton, H. C. Sox and M. A. Stoto (eds.), *HIV and the Blood Supply: An Analysis of Crisis Decisionmaking* (Committee to Study HIV Transmission through Blood and Blood Products, Division of Health Promotion and Disease Prevention) (Washington, DC: National Academy Press, 1995); The Honourable Mr Justice H. Krever, *Commission of Inquiry on the Blood System in Canada*, 3 vols (Ottawa: Canadian Government Publishing, 1997); E. A. Feldman and R. Bayer (eds.), *Blood Feuds: AIDS, Blood, and the Politics of Medical Disaster* (New York: Oxford University Press, 1999); The Right Honourable Lord Archer of Sandwell QC, N. Jones and J. Willetts, *Independent Public Inquiry Report on NHS Supplied Contaminated Blood and Blood Products* (2009).

a need for more effective global governance in this area.[9] In turn, this has fed into new initiatives in risk governance at national and regional levels to address the issue.[10] Risks to public health may often require governing entities to balance competing considerations in seeking to protect citizens' health. These may include the need to balance individual rights or entitlements to freedom of choice and liberty of the person against the need to protect the collective well-being of the population. At state level, the recognition of public health risks within national boundaries, such as those posed by infectious diseases, may result in the need to implement restrictive measures with regard to the movement of persons and goods, in order to prevent the spread of the disease. While this may have an adverse economic impact on trade and the daily lives of citizens, it is also likely to have significant political repercussions at global level.[11]

The need to engage in a similar balancing act has emerged in recent years in the context of risk governance involving the use of human biological materials, where the need to protect public health may be at stake. As a result of scientific research and technological innovation, their use in medico-scientific settings has expanded rapidly in recent years. While there has been significant political support for promoting innovation and the commercial potential of new health technologies that may result from these developments, there has also been a need in political terms to manage ethical tensions that have arisen in the public domain over their use. The aim of this book is to explore these issues in detail through examining the inter-relationship between politics, ethics and law in risk governance involving human biological materials, drawing on an in-depth qualitative study of the sourcing and supply of blood.

There are a number of reasons for choosing this case study. First, blood has socio-cultural, scientific and commercial value, and it is this multi-valuing that is likely to present challenges in terms of facilitating effective risk governance. Blood has long been recognised as

---

[9] L. O. Gostin, 'Meeting the survival needs of the world's least healthy people: a proposed model for global health governance', *Journal of the American Medical Association*, 298 (2007), 225–8.

[10] For example, the European Union (EU) created a legal competence in the field of public health in 1999 (see Article 152(4)(a) of the European Community (EC) Treaty, now Article 168(4)(a) of the Consolidated Version of the Treaty on the Functioning of the European Union, OJ C 83, 30.3.2010 (TFEU)). Since such time, the EU has adopted a number of policy initiatives, as well as regulatory regimes, in the field. For further details, see http://ec.europa.eu/health/index_en.htm.

[11] D. P. Fidler and L. O. Gostin, 'The new International Health Regulations: an historic development for international law and public health', *Journal of Law, Medicine and Ethics*, 34 (2006), 85–94 at 91–3.

having significant socio-cultural and religious value.[12] Family and kinship were traditionally structured by blood ties, which were in turn intertwined with both individual and national identity.[13] Scientific and technological developments in the twentieth century, however, led to both the medicalisation and the industrialisation of blood and its components.[14] Blood transfusion, as well as the infusion of plasma products, became widely used therapies in clinical settings, with significant patient benefit.[15] When combined with the legacy of socio-cultural value ascribed to blood, this altered characterisation brought about by scientific research and technological developments has led to ethical complexity, policy conundrums and regulatory tensions in risk governance, as was evidenced by HIV blood contamination episodes and their aftermath. Findings from an examination of how risk was managed in this context are therefore likely to have broader implications for risk governance involving multi-valued human biological materials, particularly given their use in a range of new health technologies including cellular therapies and tissue-engineered products.[16]

Second, two of the main legacies of HIV blood contamination episodes in developed countries are the increased use of the precautionary principle to manage risk, as well as a much stronger patient-centred approach to promoting safety and achieving good clinical outcomes.[17]

---

[12] P. Camporesi, *The Juice of Life: The Symbolic and Magical Significance of Blood*, trans. R. R. Barr (New York: Continuum Publications, 1996), pp. 14–32.

[13] D. M. Schneider, 'What is kinship all about?', in R. Parkin and L. Stone (eds.), *Kinship and Family: An Anthropological Reader* (Oxford: Blackwell Publishing, 2003), pp. 257–74; Nelkin, 'Cultural perspectives on blood', pp. 285–6.

[14] For an historical overview of such developments, see D. Starr, *Blood: An Epic History of Medicine and Commerce* (New York: Alfred A. Knopf, 1998).

[15] C. D. Hillyer, N. Blumberg, S. A. Glynn *et al.*, 'Transfusion recipient epidemiology and outcomes research: possibilities for the future', *Transfusion*, 48 (2008), 1530–7 at 1531.

[16] *Cellular therapies* involve the transplantation of human cells to replace or replenish damaged tissue and/or cells. Bone marrow, umbilical cord blood and peripheral blood stem cell transplants are examples of this type of therapy. The cells used in transplantation include haematopoietic progenitor cells (HPCs) (see www.aabb.org/resources/bct/therapyfacts/pages/default.aspx). *Tissue-engineered products* contain or consist of engineered cells or tissues which can be administered to human beings with a view to regenerating, repairing or replacing human tissue. Such products may contain cells or tissues of human or animal origin, or both, and cells or tissues may be viable or non-viable: see, for example, Article 1(b), Regulation (EC) No. 1394/2007 of the European Parliament and of the Council of 13 November 2007 on advanced therapy medicinal products and amending Directive 2001/83/EC and Regulation (EC) No. 726/2004.

[17] Hillyer *et al.*, 'Transfusion recipient epidemiology and outcomes research', p. 1531; R. E. Davis, C. A. Vincent and M. F. Murphy, 'Blood transfusion safety: the potential role of the patient', *Transfusion Medicine Reviews*, 25 (2011), 12–23; J. L. Callum, Y. Lon, A. Lima *et al.*, 'Transitioning from "blood" safety to "transfusion" safety: addressing the single biggest risk of transfusion', *ISBT Science Series*, 6 (2011), 96–104.

While there has been a significant level of policy and academic debate about the use and limits of the precautionary principle,[18] as well as its application in the public health context,[19] a detailed examination of the aftermath of the HIV blood contamination episodes provides a concrete example of how, and to what extent, the precautionary principle may be said to work in practice, taking account of institutional and resource implications involving the blood system.[20] In addition, it also offers an opportunity to reflect more broadly on the effectiveness (or otherwise) of precautionary strategies in the management of risks to public health.

Finally, the focus on examining risk governance involving the blood system has been an under-researched aspect of the existing sociolegal academic literature on blood-related issues.[21] An early seminal work in the field was Richard Titmuss's *The Gift Relationship*, which was first published in 1970. He conceptualised the gift relationship as involving altruistic, non-remunerated blood donation to anonymous

[18] Various perspectives have been offered on the usefulness (or otherwise) of a precautionary approach to risk governance in relation to the environment, as well as more recently in the area of public health. For example, it has been suggested that we are witnessing a convergence of an approach to precaution between the USA and Europe: see D. Vogel, 'The hare and the tortoise revisited: the new politics of consumer and environmental regulation in Europe', *British Journal of Political Science*, 33 (2003), 557–80. Conversely, it has been suggested that no general statement of convergence can be made between the USA and Europe because it is dependent on the policy sector at issue: see J. B. Wiener and M. Rogers, 'Comparing precaution in the United States and Europe', *Journal of Risk Research*, 5 (2002), 317–49. Sunstein views the application of the precautionary principle as being incoherent and argues for the adoption of an alternative approach to managing risk in the context of uncertainty; see C. Sunstein, *Laws of Fear: Beyond the Precautionary Principle* (Cambridge University Press, 2005). For a detailed examination of the issue, see Chapter 7.

[19] Much of what has been written about the use of the precautionary principle has been in relation to managing environmental risks. In recent years, there has been a more explicit focus in policy terms on its application in the public health context: see C. Raffensperger and J. Tickner (eds.), *Protecting Public Health and the Environment: Implementing the Precautionary Principle* (Washington, DC: Island Press, 1999). Under EU law, the precautionary principle is now viewed as an autonomous legal principle applicable to the environment and public health: see N. de Sadeleer, 'The precautionary principle in EC environmental and health law', *European Law Journal*, 12 (2006), 139–72.

[20] The advantages and disadvantages of the application of the precautionary principle to transfusion safety have been examined by various commentators within the transfusion medicine literature. See, for example, K. Wilson and M. N. Ricketts, 'The success of precaution? Managing the risk of transfusion transmission of variant Creuzfeldt-Jakob disease', *Transfusion*, 44 (2004), 1475–8; K. Wilson, 'A framework for applying the precautionary principle to transfusion safety', *Transfusion Medicine Reviews*, 25 (2011), 177–83.

[21] For historical, journalistic-style overviews of blood, including sourcing, supply and contamination issues, see the following: Hagen, *Blood: Gift or Merchandise?*; Starr, *Blood*.

patient-recipients. He justified its importance on ethical, economic and safety grounds and argued more broadly for its importance in promoting social solidarity in industrial societies.[22] Titmuss's arguments provoked a lively debate across a range of academic disciplines.[23] Over the last ten years, academic interest by social scientists in blood-related issues has focused on examining the political dynamics which structured HIV blood contamination scandals.[24] There has also been renewed interest in examining the continuing relevance of the gift relationship in genetics research;[25] the expanding economy in human tissue;[26] and the organisational procurement of blood and organs.[27] The role of the law in risk governance involving the blood system has also been an under-researched issue within this literature. What examination of the law that has taken place has most often focused on issues of liability in the wake of blood contamination episodes.[28] While my own research has sought to make a contribution in this regard,[29] this book addresses the

[22] Titmuss, *The Gift Relationship*.

[23] For example, see K. Arrow, 'Gifts and exchanges', *Philosophy and Public Affairs*, 4 (1972), 343–62; P. Singer, 'Altruism and commerce: a defence of Titmuss against Arrow', *Philosophy and Public Affairs*, 2 (1973), 312–20; H. M. Sapolsky and S. N. Finkelstein, 'Blood policy revisited: a new look at "the gift relationship"', *Public Interest*, 46 (1977), 15–27; R. Plant, 'Gifts, exchanges and the political economy of health care. Part 1: Should blood be bought and sold?', *Journal of Medical Ethics*, 3 (1977), 166–73; A. W. Drake, S. N. Finkelstein and H. M. Sapolsky, *The American Blood Supply* (Cambridge, MA: MIT Press, 1982).

[24] For an examination of the social, legal and political aspects of HIV blood contamination episodes and scandals in a range of developed countries, see Feldman and Bayer (eds.), *Blood Feuds*. For a specific examination of the dynamics of policy-making in relation to HIV blood contamination episodes/scandals in a number of countries, see M. Bovens, P. Hart and B. G. Peters (eds.), *Success and Failure in public Governance: A Comparative Analysis* (Cheltenham: Edward Elgar, 2001).

[25] R. Tutton, 'Gift relationships in genetics research', *Science as Culture*, 11 (2002), 524–42; D. Dickenson, 'Consent, commodification and benefit-sharing in genetic research', *Developing World Bioethics*, 4 (2004), 109–24; H. Busby, 'Biobanks, bioethics and concepts of donated blood in the UK', *Sociology of Health and Illness*, 28 (2006), 850–65.

[26] C. Waldby and R. Mitchell, *Tissue Economies: Blood, Organs, and Cell Lines in Late Capitalism* (Durham, NC: Duke University Press, 2006).

[27] K. Healy, *Last Best Gifts: Altruism and the Market for Human Blood and Organs* (Chicago University Press, 2006), pp. 15–22.

[28] E. A. Feldman, 'Blood justice: courts, conflict and compensation in Japan, France and the United States', *Law and Society Review*, 34 (2000), 651–701; A. Rueda, 'Rethinking blood shield statutes in view of the hepatitis C pandemic and other emerging threats to the blood supply', *Journal of Health Law*, 34 (2001), 419–58; R. Goldberg, 'Paying for bad blood: strict product liability after the Hepatitis C litigation', *Medical Law Review*, 10 (2002), 165–200.

[29] A. M. Farrell, 'Is the gift still good? Examining the politics and regulation of blood safety in the European Union', *Medical Law Review*, 14 (2006), 155–79; A. M. Farrell, 'The politics of risk and EU governance of human material', *Maastricht Journal of European and Comparative Law*, 16 (2009), 41–64.

need for a more detailed examination of the role of law and its contextual relationship with ethics and politics in risk governance involving human biological materials.

I acknowledge that there are a range of different subject areas, institutions, techno-scientific developments and sub-systems of governance that could be covered in relation to the chosen case study.[30] A number of deliberate choices have been made, however, with respect to limiting the parameters of examination involving the sourcing and supply of blood, with a view to developing a focused narrative in line with the key arguments made in the book. While such narrative has a broad focus on the management of risk relating to transfusion-transmitted infections (TTIs) through the blood supply,[31] it draws specifically on an in-depth analysis of HIV blood contamination episodes and their aftermath in selected developed countries. Such analysis is limited to an examination of risk governance relating to the sourcing and supply of blood and its components by national blood services, as well as plasma products which are manufactured and supplied by the global for-profit

---

[30] These issues have been the subject of examination in published literature and include (but are not limited to) the following: non-infectious risks (e.g. H. G. Klein, D. R. Spahn and J. L. Carson, 'Red blood cell transfusion in clinical practice', *Lancet*, 370 (2007), 415–26); donor selection and protection (e.g. A. Eder, M. Goldman, S. Rossmann *et al.*, 'Selection criteria to protect the blood donor in North America and Europe: past (dogma), present (evidence) and future (hemovigilance)', *Transfusion Medicine Reviews*, 23 (2009), 205–20); haemovigilance (e.g. D. Stainsby, H. Jones, D. Asher *et al.*, 'Serious hazards of transfusion: a decade of haemovigilance in the UK', *Transfusion Medicine Reviews*, 20 (2006), 273–82); the optimal use of blood components (e.g. K. Berger, H. G. Klein, R. Seitz *et al.*, 'The Wilbad Kreuth initiative: European current practices and recommendations for optimal use of blood components', *Biologicals*, 39 (2011), 189–93); the role of patients in transfusion safety (e.g. Davis *et al.*, 'Blood transfusion safety: the potential role of the patient'); the use of blood in less developed countries (e.g. D. J. Roberts, J.-P. Allain, A. D. Kitchen *et al.*, 'Blood transfusion in a global context', in M. F. Murphy and D. H. Pamphilon (eds.), *Practical Transfusion Medicine*, 3rd edn (Oxford: Wiley-Blackwell, 2009), pp. 251–65); and the expanded use of cellular therapies (e.g. M. Strong, A. Farrugia and P. Rebulla, 'Stem cell and cellular therapy developments', *Biologicals*, 27 (2009), 103–7; K. Devine, 'Risky business? The risks and benefits of umbilical cord blood collection', *Medical Law Review*, 18 (2010), 330–62; H. Busby, 'The meanings of consent to the donation of cord blood stem cells: perspectives from an interview-based study of a public cord blood bank in England', *Clinical Ethics*, 5 (2010), 22–7).

[31] Although there has been an increased focus on non-infectious risks involved in blood transfusion in recent years (see fn. 30 above), TTIs have certainly garnered most of the attention in political, regulatory, scientific and technological terms over the past twenty-five years. HIV blood contamination episodes in developed countries have provided the focus for much of this attention and, to a lesser extent, hepatitis C (HCV) blood contamination episodes.

plasma products industry, in particular factor concentrates used in the treatment of haemophilia.[32]

National HIV blood contamination episodes and their aftermath provide an opportunity to examine and learn from how a serious public health risk was assessed and managed within and across national boundaries, as well as the ethical, legal and political consequences that flowed from the perceived failure to manage such risk. In addition, risk governance involving the blood system in developed countries such as the United States (USA), France and England will be drawn on by way of example. The reason for choosing these three countries is that while they are similar in the sense that they are all liberal democratic and resource-rich states with long-established national blood services, there were significant differences between them with respect to the sourcing, manufacture and supply of blood components and plasma products, as well as in their political responses to managing the consequences of the risk posed by HIV. Such differences will inform the key arguments presented in this book.

Risk governance of human biological materials: politics, ethics and law

The key objective of this book is to develop an understanding of what constitutes effective risk governance involving multi-valued human biological materials, such as blood. Governance is used here as an overarching term to describe how governing entities engage in policy-making and regulation to meet new and challenging circumstances in situations of complexity and uncertainty, where there is a need to develop new ways of collaboration and decision-making.[33] This

---

[32] Haemophilia is a genetic disorder that is carried by females, but affects – with rare exceptions – male offspring. The disorder results in a (severe, moderate or mild) deficiency of clotting factors VIII or IX. Factor concentrates are plasma products that have been sourced from thousands of donors in order to extract a concentrated form of the clotting factors which are lacking in those with haemophilia. Factor concentrates can be administered at home to stop internal bleeding episodes (depending on their severity), thus avoiding the need for regular hospital attendance (see Krever, *Commission of Inquiry on the Blood System*, pp. 26–7).

[33] G. Stoker, 'Designing institutions for governance in complex environments: normative, rational choice and cultural institutional theories explored and contrasted', *ESRC Fellowship Paper No. 1* (University of Manchester, 2004). For further details on theories of governance, see J. Pierre (ed.), *Debating Governance: Authority, Steering and Democracy* (Oxford University Press, 2000); J. Pierre and B. G. Peters, *Governance, Politics and the State* (Basingstoke: Palgrave Macmillan, 2000); B. Kohler-Koch and B. Rittberger, 'The governance turn in EU studies', *Journal of Common Market Studies*, 44 (2006), 27–49; V. Chotray and G. Stoker, *Governance Theory: A Cross-Disciplinary Approach* (Basingstoke: Palgrave Macmillan, 2008).

description aptly captures both the opportunities and the difficulties confronting those with responsibility for managing risks to public health at both national and supranational levels. It is also important to be clear about how risk is conceptualised, given that risk governance involving the blood system will be the subject of particular examination in this book.

Within the relevant socio-legal literature, risk has been defined in varying ways and there has been extensive academic debate on its interpretation and application. Risk is often used as a term to describe situations where behaviour is known and where a probabilistic value or calculation can be assigned to outcomes. This needs to be distinguished from uncertainty, where important parameters of circumstances are known, but not the probability of outcomes.[34] Risk analysis to assess the probability of outcomes has traditionally been structured around a tripartite approach comprising risk assessment, risk management and risk communication. While risk assessment has been viewed as the domain of scientific experts who interpret the available empirical data and provide advice on likely outcomes, risk management is seen as ultimately a matter for those in political leadership.[35]

The role of science and politics in risk governance has also attracted significant academic debate. Those with scientific expertise demand that the science–politics divide be maintained in the interests of maintaining integrity and objectivity in the process of risk assessment. Conversely, claims to scientific objectivity and exclusive expertise in risk assessment have been called into question, particularly where sensitive ethical and social issues are at stake.[36] In simple terms, there are those who view risk as an objective and knowable phenomenon which can be measured, whereas for others it is socially constructed and influenced by cultural, institutional and political contexts. From this latter viewpoint, risk is a subjective and reflexive phenomenon, indicative of broader social changes in line with the emergence of what has been described as the

[34] B. Wynne, 'Uncertainty and environmental learning: reconceiving science and policy in the preventative paradigm', *Global Environmental Change*, 2 (1992), 111–27 at 114.

[35] For an overview, see O. Renn, 'Three decades of risk research: accomplishments and new challenges', *Journal of Risk Research*, 1 (1998), 49–71.

[36] For an overview and sociological critique of arguments made regarding the interrelationship between science, society and politics in risk assessment, see R. E. Kasperson, O.Renn, P. Slovic *et al.*, 'The social amplification of risk', *Risk Analysis*, 8 (1988), 177–87; S. Jasanoff, *The Fifth Branch: Science Advisers as Policymakers* (Cambridge, MA: Cambridge University Press, 1990); U. Beck, *Risk Society: Towards a New Modernity* (London: Sage, 1992); S. Krimsky and D. Golding (eds.), *Social Theories of Risk* (Westport, CT: Praeger Publishers, 1992); B. Wynne, 'Creating public alienation: expert cultures of risk and ethics on GMOs', *Science as Culture*, 10 (2001), 445–81.

'risk society' in advanced post-industrial democracies.[37] There has been criticism of such 'grand narratives' on risk, however, particularly by those who are interested in examining how risk is assessed and managed in institutional and regulatory environments on a day-to-day basis. It is argued that such narratives are not sufficiently nuanced to deal with variability of interpretation and implementation in different policy sectors, as well as across particular national legal and cultural settings.[38]

The politicisation of risk

For the purposes of this book, risk is conceptualised as a socio-cultural construct that is influenced by public perception and necessitates a political response where the protection of public health is at stake. In adopting this perspective, I draw on sociological interpretations of risk with an emphasis being placed on how the political context structures risk governance. In particular, I focus on what happens when a risk to public health becomes politicised, drawing on an examination of the circumstances that led to HIV blood contamination episodes, as well as their aftermath. What such examination reveals is that one of the main features of this politicisation of risk is heightened sensitivity on the part of governing entities to the potential for adverse public reaction resulting from any perceived failure to manage risks to public health. This heightened sensitivity leads to responses by governing entities to emerging risks that are focused on enhancing political credibility and justifying the legitimacy of their preferred course of action.[39] This may result in the subordination of traditional scientific risk assessment and

---

[37] M. Douglas, *Risk Acceptability According to the Social Sciences* (London: Routledge, 1985); A. Giddens, *The Consequences of Modernity* (Stanford University Press, 1990); U. Beck, *Risk Society*; M. Douglas, *Risk and Blame* (London: Routledge, 1992); P. Slovic, 'Perceived risk, trust, and democracy', *Risk Analysis*, 13 (1993), 675–82; S. Jasanoff, 'Citizens at risk: cultures of modernity in the US and EU', *Science as Culture*, 11 (2002), 363–80.

[38] C. Hood, H. Rothstein and R. Baldwin, *The Government of Risk: Understanding Risk Regulation Regimes* (Oxford University Press, 2001); Wiener and Rogers, 'Comparing precaution in the United States and Europe'; M. J. Smith, 'Mad cows and mad money: problems of risk in the marking and understanding of policy', *British Journal of Politics and International Relations*, 6 (2004), 312–32, at 312, 315–16. For an examination of the impact of national legal cultures and institutions on risk regulation, see E. Fisher, *Risk Regulation and Administrative Constitutionalism* (Oxford: Hart Publishing, 2007); S. Jasanoff, *Designs on Nature: Science and Democracy in Europe and the United States* (Princeton University Press, 2005).

[39] There are varying interpretations that can be offered as to what constitutes legitimacy of action, as opposed to legitimating actions, particularly in terms of regulatory governance. My preferred view is that in order to realise legitimacy in the political context, there is a need to achieve a sufficient degree of consensus among relevant stakeholders, as well as in the public domain. This may involve making use

cost–benefit analysis to political concerns, as well as increased recourse to precautionary and regulatory strategies to legitimate policy decisions, assuage ethical concerns and enhance public trust.[40] Although these may not be the only effects resulting from the politicisation of risk, they are particularly important for developing a more in-depth understanding of risk governance involving the use of multi-valued human biological materials.

Managing ethical concerns

Ethical argumentation regarding the sourcing and supply of blood is well rehearsed within the relevant academic literature;[41] however, it is not my intention to undertake a detailed critique of such arguments in this book. Instead, I propose a different approach to examining this issue which focuses on how ethical concerns have operated as important policy frames, which in turn have informed the approach taken to risk governance. How policy is framed is important because it affects not only how issues or problems are perceived but also the design and implementation of governance initiatives in a given policy sector.[42] Ethical concerns have loomed large in policy-making processes involving the use of multi-valued human biological materials, and the ability to manage such concerns has become an important legitimising aspect of risk governance in the field.

of a number of strategies (ethical, policy, regulatory) to achieve such consensus. For a further examination of this issue, see R. Brownsword, *Rights Regulation and the Technological Revolution* (Oxford University Press, 2008), pp. 9–11, who refers to I. Ayres and J. Braithwaite, *Responsive Regulation: Transcending the Deregulation Debate* (Oxford University Press, 1992).

[40] I note that variations of this phenomenon have been described by a number of academic commentators working within the field of regulatory governance: see, for example, the tendency towards 'hyper-innovation' in the wake of policy and regulatory failure (M. Moran, *The British Regulatory State: High Modernism and Hyper-Innovation* (Oxford University Press, 2003), pp. 6–7); and institutional risk management to deal with threats created by 'delivery failure, budget overruns, liabilities and loss of reputation' (H. Rothstein, M. Huber and G. Gaskell, 'A theory of risk colonization: the spiralling regulatory logics of institutional and societal risk', *Economy and Society*, 35 (2006), 91–112 at 92).

[41] See, for example, T. Murray, 'Gifts of the body and the needs of strangers', *Hastings Center Report*, 17 (1987), 30–8; J. Keown, 'The gift of blood in Europe: an ethical defence of EC Directive 89/381', *Journal of Medical Ethics*, 23 (1997), 96–100; D. Archard, 'Selling yourself: Titmuss's argument against a market in blood', *Journal of Ethics*, 6 (2002), 87–102; T. C. Voo, 'The social rationale of the gift relationship', *Journal of Medical Ethics* 27 (2011), 663–7.

[42] Jasanoff, *Designs on Nature*, p. 23; see also D. A. Snow, E. B. Rochford, S. K. Worden *et al.*, 'Frame alignment processes, micromobilization and movement participation', *American Sociological Review*, 51 (1986), 464–81 at 464.

In the case of blood, ethical concerns have largely centred on what should be recognised as the preferred method of blood donation and the extent to which this contributes to patient-recipient safety.[43] Opposing stakeholder views on whether blood should be viewed as a gift or a commodity (colloquially known as the 'gift versus commodity debate') became entrenched in the wake of revelations concerning the exploitation of donors and higher rates of TTIs, which accompanied the development and global expansion of the for-profit plasma products industry from the late 1960s onwards.[44] On one side of the debate were those in charge of national blood services who supported voluntary non-remunerated blood donation (VNRBD), as exemplified in Titmuss's conception of the gift relationship.[45] While he offered a range of arguments in support of the gift relationship in blood donation, he suggested on safety grounds that the altruistic motivation of VNRBD made it much more likely that they would provide blood that was free from disease that would harm the patient-recipient.[46] As a result of the arguments Titmuss put forward in this regard, the gift relationship became the predominant factor in determining blood safety within many national blood services in developed countries, as well as operating as the general guiding principle in both national and supranational blood policy.[47] On the opposing side of the debate were those who were in favour of paying individuals to provide their blood. Support for this method of donation came largely from the for-profit plasma products industry, which sourced its products predominantly from paid donors

[43] R. Bayer and E. A. Feldman, 'Understanding the blood feuds', in Feldman and Bayer (eds.), *Blood Feuds*, pp. 7–10.

[44] Farrell, 'Is the gift still good?', pp. 159–62.

[45] A widely accepted definition of voluntary non-remunerated blood donation (VNRBD) is as follows: a donation is considered voluntary and non-remunerated 'if the person gives blood, plasma or cellular components of his/her own free will and receives no payment for it, either in the form of cash or in kind which could be considered a substitute for money. This would include time off work other than that reasonably needed for the donation and travel. Small tokens, refreshments and reimbursements of direct travel costs are compatible with voluntary, non-remunerated donations'; see paragraph 9(d) of 98/463/EC Council Recommendation of 29 June 1998 on the suitability of blood and plasma donors and the screening of donated blood in the European Community, OJ L 203, 21.7.1998.

[46] Titmuss, *The Gift Relationship*, pp. 195–208.

[47] Directive 2002/98/EC of the European Parliament and of the Council of 27 January 2003 setting standards of quality and safety for the collection, testing, processing, storage and distribution of human blood and blood components and amending Directive 2001/83/EC, OJ L 33/30, 8.2.2003; Council of Europe, European Directorate for the Quality of Medicines and HealthCare, *Guide to the Preparation, Use and Quality Assurance of Blood Components*, 16th edn (Strasbourg: Council of Europe, 2010); World Health Organization, The Melbourne Declaration on 100% Voluntary Non-remunerated Donation of Blood and Blood Components (June 2009) (www.who.int).

in the USA. Unlike many developed countries, the USA did not ban payment for blood donation as it was deemed necessary in order to meet growing demand for plasma products.[48]

HIV blood contamination episodes complicated the debate over whether blood should be viewed as a gift or a commodity. It became clear in countries such as England and France, for example, that the gift relationship was not a guarantor of blood safety on its own. Instead, a range of factors needed to be taken into account to ensure effective risk governance.[49] Notwithstanding the need to reassess the importance of the gift relationship on safety grounds, support for it to be maintained as the preferred method of donation at national and supranational levels has remained high.[50] This is to be contrasted with the day-to-day reality in many developed countries where there are ongoing difficulties in meeting the growing demand for a range of plasma products through VNRBD. Problems in meeting such demand have been resolved by some countries through the importation of plasma products sourced predominantly from US paid donors, in circumstances where such products are marketed and distributed by the for profit plasma products industry on a global basis.[51]

While opposing views on whether blood should be viewed as a gift or commodity is a dichotomous framing that has much deeper and more complex roots in notions of reciprocity and exchange, as well as property and control,[52] it is conceptualised in this book as reflecting a

---

[48] Leveton et al., *HIV and the Blood Supply*, p. 30.

[49] Farrell, 'Is the gift still good?', p. 178.

[50] *Ibid.*, pp. 168–9. In addition, see European Opinion Research Group, *Le don de sang*, Eurobaromètre spécial, 1883–4/Vague 58.2 (Brussels: European Commission, 2003).

[51] It is very difficult to obtain up-to-date published data on the extent to which developed countries are dependent upon the importation of plasma products manufactured by the for-profit plasma products industry. This is no doubt due to a combination of commercial and political sensitivities. For example, it has been suggested that the for profit industry controls at least 50 per cent of the blood market in Europe (see Farrell, 'Is the gift still good?', p. 172). For an overview of the sourcing and supply of plasma products, see the website of the Plasma Protein Therapeutics Association (PPTA), the international representative body for the industry (www.pptaglobal.org).

[52] Although it is outside the scope of this book to examine these issues in detail, there is an extensive and wide-ranging academic literature dealing with these issues across a range of disciplines. For example, see fn. 40 in this chapter; M. Mauss, *The Gift: The Form and Reason for Exchange in Archaic Societies* (London: Routledge, 1990), translated by W. D. Halls from M. Mauss, 'Essai sur le don', *Sociologie et Anthropologie* (Paris: Presses Universitaires de France, 1950); S. Munzer, 'An uneasy case against property rights in body parts', *Social Philosophy and Policy*, 11 (1994), 259–86; M. Radin, *Contested Commodities: The Trouble with Trade in Sex, Children, Body Parts and Other Things* (Cambridge, MA: Harvard University Press, 1996); R. Gold, *Body Parts: Property Rights and the Ownership of Human Biological Materials*

broader tension between the social and the economic that has arisen in capitalist economies in the wake of techno-scientific innovation and market expansion involving the use of multi-valued human biological materials. How best to manage this tension has been the subject of considerable academic debate. In general terms, it has been suggested that any attempt to disembed the social from the economic will not resolve the tension between the two but will instead contribute to a 'counter-movement' aimed at its correction or the re-embedding of social relations in those of the market, whether in part or in full.[53] A distinction between the economic and the social has also been drawn within the regulatory governance literature. Regulatory intervention has traditionally been justified as a corrective to market failure or dysfunction, with a view to enhancing economic efficiency and consumer choice.[54] In contrast, issues defined as non-economic or otherwise related to broader socio-cultural concerns were viewed as being more appropriately dealt with in the context of democratic politics. It is a distinction that has been challenged in recent years, however, on the grounds that it is too simplistic to capture the diversity of regulatory purposes and activity across a range of policy sectors, particularly those involving healthcare or health technologies.[55]

In the case of blood, Titmuss advocated that the inter-relationship between the social and the economic in the context of sourcing and supply issues was to be resolved through the exclusion of the marketplace in favour of the promotion of important social values and community relations, as exemplified in the gift relationship in blood donation.[56] While his views in this regard proved to be highly influential in (regulatory)

(Washington, DC: Georgetown University Press, 1996); M. Ertmann and J. Williams (eds.), *Rethinking Commodification: Cases and Readings in Law and Culture* (New York University Press, 2005).

[53] I am drawing here on the Polanyian critique of the inter-relationship between social and economic relations in market societies; see F. Block, 'Introduction', in F. Block (ed.), K. Polanyi, *The Great Transformation: The Political and Economic Origins of Our Time*, 2nd edn (Boston, MA: Beacon Press, 2001), pp. 1–16; G. Grippner, M. Granovetter, F. Block *et al.*, 'Polanyi symposium: a conversation on embeddedness', *Socio-Economic Review*, 2 (2007), 109–35; A. Ebner, 'Transnational markets and the Polanyi problem', in C. Joerges and J. Falke (eds.), *Karl Polanyi, Globalisation and the Potential of Law in Transnational Markets* (Oxford: Hart Publishing, 2011), pp. 19–40.

[54] See, for example, A. I. Ogus, *Regulation: Legal Form and Economic Theory* (Oxford: Hart Publishing, 2004).

[55] T. Prosser, *The Regulatory Enterprise: Government, Regulation and Legitimacy* (Oxford University Press, 2010), pp. 1–22; P. Vincent-Jones, 'Embedding economic relationships through social learning? The limits of patient and public involvement in healthcare governance in England', *Journal of Law and Society*, 38 (2011), 215–44.

[56] Titmuss, *The Gift Relationship*, pp. 210–42.

governance involving the blood system, it needs to be kept in mind that such views were grounded in empirical research conducted over forty years ago, when blood testing and related technologies were fairly rudimentary and the market for plasma products both within and across national borders was in the early stages of development and expansion. Such views now require a critical reassessment in the light of such developments, as well as taking into account the seismic effect of HIV blood contamination episodes in developed countries on risk governance involving the blood system.

Such episodes made clear that to privilege the social to the exclusion of the economic through the use of a dichotomous policy framing of gift versus commodity does not fully account for the complexity of risk governance involving multi-valued human biological materials, such as blood. What is needed instead is a more holistic approach to risk governance in the field in which the inter-relationship between the social and the economic is made more explicit and transparent in policy and regulatory processes. Achieving optimum safety for patient-recipients should operate as the predominant policy frame in the field, with the ethico-social commitment to the gift relationship acting as a legitimising device in political terms, rather than being necessarily linked to blood quality and safety. This would allow for flexibility in risk governance involving the blood system, rather than any rigidity in approach brought about by a priori ethical, professional or commercial commitments with respect to blood sourcing and supply issues.

The role of law

Law was influential in the construction of, as well as the consequences resulting from, the politicisation of risk involving the blood system in the wake of HIV blood contamination episodes in developed countries. For present purposes, the term 'law' is broadly defined to include both soft and hard law such as guidelines, recommendations, principles, case law and regulation, as well as legal institutions such as tribunals and the courts.[57] In making use of this definition, I draw a distinction between the terms 'law' and 'regulation'. Black has provided a useful definition of regulation as involving the 'sustained and focused attempt to alter the behaviour of others according to standards and goals with the intention of producing a broadly defined outcome or outcomes,

---

[57] I agree with Brownsword that 'while law and regulation intersect with one another, they are not co-extensive' (see Brownsword, *Rights, Regulation, and the Technological Revolution*, pp. 7–8).

which may involve mechanisms of standard setting, information gathering and behaviour modification'.[58] Such a definition is adopted for the purposes of this book as it captures in particular the more 'decentred' approach to regulatory governance involving the blood system that is to be found at supranational level.[59] While the role of regulation involving the blood system at both national and supranational levels is the subject of detailed analysis in the book, how individuals who were infected with HIV through blood and plasma products made strategic use of the law outside these organised processes of governance is also examined. It is for this reason that the broader term 'law' is used in this book.

The role and impact of law on risk governance involving the blood system can be discerned in a number of ways. First, one of the key triggers which led to the development of HIV blood contamination scandals in a number of developed countries was the fact that those infected with HIV as a result of the use of blood and plasma products saw law, in the form of legal action in the courts and demands for state-sponsored tribunals of inquiry, as a way in which they were able to hold those responsible for the episodes to account, as well as to obtain financial compensation for the harm they had suffered.[60] In this way, law became a strategy for seeking redress and accountability where there was a perceived failure to engage in effective risk governance in the field. Second, heightened sensitivity on the part of those responsible for the blood system in the wake of national HIV blood contamination episodes has resulted in increased recourse to the use of both soft and hard law, including the precautionary principle and risk regulation, with a view to enhancing blood safety.[61] In this context, law has been used strategically to serve a number of purposes: to prevent and/or manage emerging

[58] J. Black, 'What is regulatory innovation?', in J. Black, M. Lodge and M. Thatcher (eds.), *Regulatory Innovation: A Comparative Analysis* (Cheltenham: Edward Elgar, 2005), pp. 1–15 at 11.

[59] A point made in general terms by R. Baldwin, M. Cave and M. Lodge, 'Introduction: Regulation – the field and the developing agenda', in R. Baldwin, M. Cave and M. Lodge (eds.), *The Oxford Handbook of Regulation* (Oxford University Press, 2010), pp. 3–16 at 12.

[60] For an overview of the use of law by recipients of HIV-contaminated blood and plasma products in various developed countries, see Feldman and Bayer (eds.), *Blood Feuds*; Starr, *Blood*.

[61] M. A. Stoto, 'The precautionary principle and emerging biological risks: lessons from swine flu and HIV in blood products', *Public Health Reports*, 117 (2002), 546–52; K. Wilson, M. Wilson, P.C. Hébert *et al.*, 'The application of the precautionary principle to the blood system: the Canadian blood system's vCJD donor deferral policy', *Transfusion Medicine Reviews*, 17 (2003), 89–94; E. Hergon, G. Moutel, N. Duchange *et al.*, 'Risk management in transfusion after the HIV blood contamination crisis in France: the impact of the precautionary principle', *Transfusion Medicine Reviews*, 19 (2005), 273–80.

risks; to control and bring about behaviour modification amongst key stakeholders; to enhance political credibility and public trust; and to legitimate governance initiatives.[62]

These examples identify the strategic role law can play in facilitating effective risk governance involving multi-valued human biological materials. For risk governance to be effective in this context, however, a full range of legal strategies for facilitating redress and accountability should be made available to individuals who have suffered harm as a result of a failure to manage risk in this context. This should be supported not only on the grounds of promoting restorative justice,[63] but also because it incentivises a proactive approach to risk governance by those with institutional, professional and political responsibilities in the field. This feeds into, and should work in conjunction with, the use of legal strategies within organised processes of governance at both national and supranational levels to enhance public health protection resulting from the use of human biological materials.

Constituting effective risk governance

A key question to be addressed in this book is what constitutes effective risk governance involving multi-valued human biological materials, such as blood. Facilitating effectiveness is important for legitimating risk governance initiatives in circumstances where public trust is vital to the successful sourcing and supply of blood and plasma products. In simple terms, assessing effectiveness can be determined by reference

---

[62] It has been argued that the turn to the regulatory mode at state level has resulted in the politicisation of policy sectors that had previously operated below the political radar; see Moran, *The British Regulatory State*, pp. 6, 21. By analogy, it could be argued that this phenomenon is observable in the case of the blood policy sector in the wake of HIV blood contamination episodes. For a supranational (EU) perspective on such developments, see Farrell, 'Is the gift still good?', pp. 169–77; Farrell, 'The politics of risk', pp. 49–52.

[63] Although recent use of the concept has focused on its application in the criminal justice context, the underlying principles should be viewed as having a much wider application, extending to confronting and resolving injustice in any arena. One key aspect of the concept involves acknowledging the importance of accepting responsibility towards those who have suffered harm unjustly at the hands of another. Acceptance of responsibility can take numerous forms, such as the offering of apologies and explanations; repairing harm that has been caused; and accepting accountability through mechanisms of public and private governance. Where the state is involved, there is a particular responsibility for facilitating the accountability of restorative justice processes, which should be underpinned by respect for, as well as access to, the rule of law for those involved. This may include interpretation and representation by legal professionals in order to ensure that rights and due process are protected. For an overview of the concept, see J. Braithwaite, *Restorative Justice and Responsive Regulation* (Oxford University Press, 2002).

to the extent to which patient-recipients do not suffer any harm as a result of the administration of blood or plasma products. The more difficult question to be addressed is how best to achieve this outcome. In this regard, account needs to be taken of regulatory design, particularly with regard to standard setting; the extent to which there is stakeholder compliance, or conversely resistance, to governance initiatives; whether such initiatives have resulted in appropriate behaviour modification by stakeholders with a view to enhancing safety; and what accountability mechanisms are in place at both national and supranational levels in order to evaluate the effectiveness of such initiatives post-implementation. This book focuses in particular on the use of the precautionary principle and risk regulation in order to examine whether current risk governance involving the blood system could be said to be effective by reference to the criteria outlined above. Increased recourse to these two strategies was viewed as the great political panacea for redressing the loss of political and regulatory credibility, as well as public trust, that occurred in the wake of HIV blood contamination episodes in developed countries. However, what evidence is available in relation to the implementation of such strategies presents a complicated picture with regard to assessing their effectiveness.[64]

Path dependencies created by the politicisation of risk which occurred in the wake of such contamination episodes have contributed to policy and regulatory processes that are underpinned by public and political expectations of zero-risk, particularly with regard to TTIs.[65] While the achievement of zero-risk is seen as largely unachievable by stakeholders,[66] it has nevertheless contributed to problems in interpreting the nature and scope of (emerging) risks to the blood system. It has been

[64] I note that the precautionary principle is recognised as a legal principle in some jurisdictions, but not in others. For a more detailed examination of its (legal) status, see Chapter 7.

[65] 'Path dependency' is a term used within historical institutional theory to explain how and why certain policy processes persist over time and space within institutional settings, notwithstanding the need for innovation or change. See K. Thelen and S. Steinmo, 'Historical institutionalism in comparative politics', in S. Steinmo, K. Thelen and F. Longstreth (eds.), *Structuring Politics: Historical Institutionalism in Comparative Perspective* (Cambridge University Press, 1992), pp. 1–32; P. Pierson, 'The limits of design: explaining institutional origins and change', *Governance*, 13 (2000), 475–99.

[66] For a medico-scientific perspective on the implications of public and political expectations of zero-risk in relation to blood safety, see H. Klein, 'Will blood transfusion ever be safe enough?', *Journal of the American Medical Association*, 284 (2000), 238–40. For a perspective on problems that have been encountered in implementing risk regulation in relation to blood quality and safety at EU level, see Farrell, 'The politics of risk', pp. 51–2, 60–1.

suggested that this has led to inconsistency and uncertainty with regard to the appropriate use of the precautionary principle to deal with such risks.[67] This has been compounded by the adoption of a limited, rather than an expansive, approach to dealing with what constitutes risk for the purposes of regulating blood quality and safety,[68] a situation that is particularly apparent in relation to the regime that has been established at EU level.[69]

What is troubling about problems identified with the use of preferred techniques of legitimation in the post-HIV blood contamination era, such as the precautionary principle and risk regulation, is their potential to compromise the effectiveness of initiatives designed to enhance blood safety. In order to facilitate effective risk governance involving the blood system in the collective public interest, it is therefore suggested that policy-makers and regulators need to pay particular attention to regulatory design in order to facilitate comprehensiveness involving 'vein-to-vein' risk management,[70] as well as ensuring the adoption of a holistic approach to incorporating both the social and economic aspects of blood sourcing and supply in and across national boundaries. Regular and detailed evaluation is also required as to the costs and benefits of using particular legal and other strategies to enhance blood safety, given finite financial, administrative and institutional resources. Although the availability of informational and deliberative accountability mechanisms may be important for facilitating transparency in risk governance involving the blood system,[71] the politicisation of risk that occurred in the wake of national HIV blood contamination episodes also makes it imperative for the purposes of maintaining public trust that monitoring of such governance is undertaken by institutions and/or individuals subject to electoral mandate. Where this is not possible at

---

[67] J. Stein, J. Besley, C. Brook et al., 'Risk-based decision-making for blood safety: preliminary report of a consensus conference', Vox Sanguinis 101 (2011) 277–81 at 277–8.

[68] Lee has identified the tendency towards using the term 'risk' in a restrictive and technical manner in regulatory governance involving technologies, as this enables decision-makers to exclude consideration of difficult questions raised by social, ethical and political concerns related to their use. See M. Lee, 'Beyond safety? The broadening scope of risk regulation', Current Legal Problems, 62 (2009), 242–85 at 242–3.

[69] The EU risk regulation regime is examined in more detail in Chapter 8.

[70] A 'vein-to-vein' approach involves an approach to risk management from blood donation to the transfusion of blood to a recipient (and beyond); see Stein et al., 'Risk-based decision-making for blood safety', p. 3.

[71] Within the academic literature on regulation, a range of mechanisms have been identified as important for facilitating accountability in decision-making processes; see J. Black, 'Proceduralizing regulation: part I', Oxford Journal of Legal Studies, 20 (2000), 597–614 at 597–9; Prosser, The Regulatory Enterprise, p. 7.

supranational level,[72] then arrangements need to be made to ensure that this takes place on a periodic basis at national level. In the final analysis, risk governance involving multi-valued human biological materials, such as blood, should be seen as ultimately a matter for those in political leadership in circumstances where law, as well as ethics, science and commerce, all play a role but are not determinative.

Organisation of the book

The chapters of the book have been organised around an examination of both the construction and the consequences of dealing with the politicisation of risk involving the blood system. Having identified the key themes and arguments to be made in the book in this introductory chapter, an overview is provided of historical and current governance arrangements involving the blood system at national, regional and global levels in Chapter 2, focusing on the collection and supply of blood components and plasma products. In mapping the key institutional, policy and regulatory arrangements that comprise the governance of the blood system, the aim is to 'set the scene' for what is discussed in subsequent chapters. In order to facilitate a more effective approach to the management of risk, it is suggested in this chapter that a more holistic and flexible approach to governance is required, which acknowledges the inter-relationship between the social and the economic in the context of the multi-valuing of blood that has occurred in the wake of techno-scientific developments. This needs to be underpinned by the primary objective of ensuring patient-recipient safety.

Chapter 3 revisits the arguments made by Richard Titmuss in *The Gift Relationship*, with a particular focus on examining the arguments he put forward to support the gift relationship in blood donation on safety grounds. The use of the gift relationship as a predominant factor in assessing the risk posed by HIV to the blood system is examined, drawing on the approach taken in the USA, England and France, by way of example. Such examination shows that the gift relationship proved to be an inadequate frame of reference on its own for assessing and managing risk involving the blood system. In the circumstances, it is suggested that the ethico-social commitment to the gift relationship

---

[72] On the difficulties of facilitating accountability in the context of regulatory governance at supranational level, see J. Black, 'Constructing and contesting legitimacy and accountability in polycentric regulatory regimes', *Regulation & Governance*, 2 (2008), 137–64 at 137–9; K. Yeung, 'The regulatory state', in R. Baldwin, M. Cave and M. Lodge (eds.), *The Oxford Handbook of Regulation* (Oxford University Press, 2010), pp. 64–83 at 80.

should be used primarily as a legitimising device in political terms, rather than being linked to blood safety. Given the multi-valuing of blood, it is argued that what is required is flexibility in risk governance which draws on a range of factors to facilitate patient-recipient safety, rather than any rigidity in approach brought about by a priori ethical, scientific or professional commitments to the gift relationship.

Chapter 4 analyses the relationship between scientific expertise and risk governance, focusing on the role and influence of experts in transfusion medicine in national and supranational blood policy and regulation. The chapter examines the emergence of transfusion medicine as an independent specialty, as well as the development of the core professional beliefs of the group. Such beliefs included a commitment to the gift relationship as a guarantor of blood safety and the achievement of national self-sufficiency in blood and plasma products sourced through this method of donation. The consequences of national HIV blood contamination episodes highlighted the inadequacy of reliance on such beliefs in relation to risk governance involving the blood system. Notwithstanding such outcome, it is argued that transfusionists' core professional belief in the link between the gift relationship and blood safety appears resistant to change and continues to be influential in national and supranational blood policy and regulation. In the circumstances, it is suggested that ensuring patient-recipient safety should instead operate as the main policy framing device in order to facilitate effective risk governance, rather than one that is skewed to fit the core professional beliefs of one group of blood experts.

Chapter 5 analyses the relationship between risk and innovation, drawing on an examination of the production and supply of factor concentrates used in the treatment of haemophilia by the for-profit plasma products industry. It provides an historical overview of the emergence of the industry in the USA, which in turn led to the development of the global market for plasma products. Such developments occurred in circumstances where there was inadequate regulation of the industry and its activities, where it existed at all. An examination is then provided of the impact of such developments on the assessment and management of the risk posed by HIV in countries such as the USA, England and France, in addition to exploring the industry's response to high levels of HIV infection resulting from the use of its factor concentrates. While innovation by the industry in the post-HIV blood contamination era has significantly reduced the rate of TTIs in plasma products, such as factor concentrates, it is argued that the loss of public trust that occurred in the wake of such episodes requires that innovation in this context, as well as the markets for such products, are subject to stringent regulatory governance in order to enhance blood safety. At a minimum, this requires regulatory cooperation and harmonisation at both national and supranational levels involving the use of standard setting for quality and safety, as well as the establishment of legally binding risk regulation regimes, where possible.

Chapter 6 examines the emergence of haemophilia activism in countries such as the USA, England and France, in the wake of national HIV blood contamination episodes. In examining this phenomenon, there is a particular focus on the inter-relationship between law and the political mobilisation of haemophilia groups. Although the contingent nature involved in the use of legal tactics in specific national political and legal environments meant that some haemophilia groups enjoyed more success than others in realising their mobilisation goals, it is argued that a full range of legal mechanisms for redress and accountability should be made available where there has been a failure to manage public health risks, such as those involving the sourcing and supply of blood. This is for two main reasons: first, to facilitate choice on the part of those individuals who have suffered harm as a result of such failure with regard to pursuing claims for financial compensation or other forms of redress; and second, to incentivise governing entities to adopt a proactive approach to the management of risk involving the blood system.

Chapters 7 and 8 examine the increased use of the precautionary principle and risk regulation as legitimating techniques to redress the loss of political credibility and public trust that occurred in the wake of national HIV blood contamination episodes. In Chapter 7, the key elements of the precautionary principle are described and its interpretation in policy, case law and regulation are analysed, drawing on examples from the USA and Europe. The particular challenges faced by those in charge of national blood services in meeting public and political expectations of zero-risk are examined in the context of a broader evaluation of the usefulness of a precautionary approach to risk governance in the field. Until it can be established that public trust in the safety of the blood system has been regained in the wake of the fallout from national HIV blood contamination episodes, it is suggested that the use of a precautionary approach will dominate risk governance in the field. This is likely to take place at times to the detriment of traditional scientific risk assessment and cost–benefit analysis, particularly with regard to the implementation of new technologies to minimise TTIs. It is argued that acceptance of this political reality should not obscure the fact that there is a need for greater clarity and transparency as to both the interpretation and application of the principle in the context of managing risks to the blood system. This needs to be underpinned by regular evaluation of the effectiveness of measures adopted in line with the principle.

The effectiveness of risk regulation as a preferred technique of legitimation in the post-HIV blood contamination era is examined in Chapter 8, drawing on a case study of EU risk regulation of blood and plasma products. In assessing what constitutes effectiveness in risk regulation, it is argued that an expansive, non-limiting approach to interpreting risk is needed in which regulatory design is focused on the setting of standards to achieve optimum patient-recipient safety. It is suggested that this offers the best way forward with regard to achieving a comprehensive vein-to-vein approach to regulating risk, as well as ensuring that the social and economic aspects involved in blood sourcing and supply are made transparent and incorporated into a holistic approach to regulatory design and implementation. While informational and deliberative accountability mechanisms are important for ensuring transparency with regard to determining whether risk regulation has been effective, it is suggested that the politicisation of risk that occurred in the wake of national HIV blood contamination episodes makes it imperative for the purposes of maintaining public trust that such regulation is also monitored by institutions and/or individuals that are subject to electoral mandate.

Chapter 9 sets out the key findings from the book. Drawing on such findings, the chapter concludes with a final word on the key elements that should underpin risk governance involving multi-valued human biological materials.

2   The governance of the blood system

The aim of this chapter is to present an overview of historical and current developments in relation to the governance of the blood system which have taken place at national, regional and global levels. A number of arguments are made by reference to such overview.

First, governance in the field has developed over time, from being quite minimal (where it existed at all) to the current state of affairs where there has been a noticeable upsurge in the adoption of norms, standards, guidelines, recommendations and regulation.[1] This has been particularly noticeable at national and regional (EU) levels, leading to the adoption of 'hard' (legally binding) law and enhanced regulatory oversight.[2] It is a change which has its origins primarily in the need on the part of those with responsibility for blood safety in developed countries to regain political credibility and restore public trust in the wake of the fallout from national HIV blood contamination episodes.[3]

---

[1] It has been observed that there has been a general upsurge in the scope and breadth of regulatory governance across a diverse range of policy sectors at both national and supranational levels over the past twenty years. See J. Jordana and D. Levi-Faur, 'The politics of regulation in the age of governance', in J. Jordana and D. Levi-Faur (eds.), *The Politics of Regulation: Institutions and Regulatory Reforms for the Age of Governance* (Cheltenham: Edward Elgar, 2004), pp. 1–28 at 1; M.-L. Djelic and K. Sahlin-Andersson, 'Introduction: A world of governance: the rise of transnational regulation', in M.-L. Djelic and K. Sahlin-Andersson (eds.), *Transnational Governance: Institutional Dynamics of Regulation* (Cambridge University Press, 2006), pp. 1–28 at 1.

[2] In the case of the EU, for example, the main way in which it exercises control and seeks to enhance its legitimacy is through the use of regulation, leading to it being described as having the hallmarks of a 'regulatory state'; see G. Majone (ed.), *Regulating Europe* (London: Routledge, 1996). In the case of blood policy, an increase in regulatory demands and oversight has also been observed by a range of stakeholders; see A. Farrugia, 'The regulatory pendulum in transfusion medicine', *Transfusion Medicine Reviews*, 16 (2002), 273–82; T. Burnouf, 'Modern plasma fractionation', *Transfusion Medicine Reviews*, 21 (2007), 101–17; and I. von Hoegen and M. Gustafson, 'The importance of greater regulatory harmonization', *Pharmaceuticals Policy and Law*, 7 (2006), 171–6.

[3] Moran has observed that there has been an upsurge in the use of regulation in the context of the decline of trust in developed countries more generally; see M. Moran, 'From command state to regulatory state', *Public Policy and Administration*, 15 (2000),

Second, global regulatory governance involving the blood system can best be described as 'decentred', characterised by fragmentation, complexity and heterarchy.[4] Although nation-states are represented, such governance is largely fostered through networks comprised of experts, regulators and industry representatives. Decision-making takes place in stable institutional environments,[5] which are largely insulated from the vagaries of democratic politics and accountability mechanisms that operate at national and regional (EU) levels.[6] Against a background of limited legal competence, the regulatory order that has developed at global level primarily involves the use of 'soft' (non-legally binding) law[7] – the adoption of norms, guidelines, recommendations and standards – underpinned by a drive towards greater technical harmonisation and cooperation.[8] Such 'patchwork' regulatory development underlines the fact that in order to gain a more rounded understanding of the governance of the blood system,[9] there is a need to take account of

1–13 at 10. The political and regulatory reforms that were undertaken to address issues such as loss of credibility and public trust in the wake of national HIV blood contamination episodes are examined in more detail in Chapters 7 and 8.

[4] J. Black, 'Decentring regulation: understanding the role of regulation and self-regulation in a "post-regulatory" world', *Current Legal Problems*, 54 (2001), 103–47 at 104.

[5] For a detailed examination of how such networks operate at global level, see R. O. Keohane and J. S. Nye Jr, 'Introduction', in J. S. Nye Jr and J. D. Donahue (eds.), *Governing in a Globalizing World* (Washington, DC: Brookings Institution, 2000), pp. 1–41 at 37; J. N. Rosenau, 'Governance in a new global order', in D. Held and A. McGrew (eds.), *Governing Globalization: Power, Authority and Global Governance* (Cambridge: Polity Press, 2002), pp. 70–86 at 77. For an examination of the phenomenon at EU level, see G. Skogstad, 'Legitimacy and/or policy effectiveness?: Network governance and GMO regulation in the European Union', *Journal of European Public Policy*, 10 (2003), 321–38.

[6] The problem of how best to facilitate political accountability of decision-making by institutions, actors and states at supranational level has been noted as an ongoing problem within the relevant academic literature. See R. O. Keohane, 'Governance in a partially globalized world', in D. Held and A. McGrew (eds.), *Governing Globalization: Power, Authority and Global Governance* (Cambridge: Polity Press, 2002), pp. 325–47 at 339; Black, 'Decentring regulation', pp. 337–9; S. Picciotto, *Regulating Global Corporate Capitalism* (Cambridge University Press, 2011), p. 20.

[7] This shift from hard law at national level to soft law at global level has been observed as a more general phenomenon across a range of policy sectors; see W. Mattli and N. Woods, 'In whose benefit? Explaining regulatory change in global politics', in W. Mattli and N. Woods (eds.), *The Politics of Global Regulation* (Princeton University Press, 2009), pp. 1–43 at 3.

[8] The existence and development of standards have become a prominent aspect of global order in order to facilitate cooperation and coordination, as well as to exert a measure of control in the absence of legally binding regulatory mandates to take action in a given policy sector (see N. Brunsson and B. Jacobsson, 'The contemporary expansion of standardization', in N. Brunsson, B. Jacobsson and Associates (eds.), *A World of Standards* (Oxford University Press, 2000), pp. 1–17 at 1).

[9] The term 'patchwork' has been used to describe the diverse approaches taken to regulatory governance of (bio) technology at global level; see Brownsword, *Rights,*

the specific historical trajectories that have influenced developments at this level; the specific roles, influence and activities of both state and non-state actors, in particular the role of experts;[10] and the interaction in and across governance systems operating at national, regional and global levels.[11]

Finally, the governance of the blood system across all three levels has been characterised by the increasing need to manage the tension between the social and the economic in the context of the multi-valuing of blood, which has occurred in the wake of techno-scientific innovation and market expansion involving plasma products from the latter half of the twentieth century onwards. The most obvious manifestation of this tension has been the development of differing sub-systems of governance involving not-for-profit national blood services, which are predominantly involved in the collection and supply of blood and its components on the one hand;[12] and that involving the for-profit plasma products industry, which manufactures and supplies a range of products in the global marketplace on the other hand. This bifurcated approach has evolved over time, despite the fact that each sub-system deals with much of the same source material, which potentially raises similar issues

Regulation, and the Technological Revolution, p. 296. It is also a useful descriptor for the way in which regulatory governance involving the blood system has developed at global level.

[10] The role of experts has also been identified as a major element of global governance across a range of policy sectors. The relevant literature has characterised the role of experts in different ways, in addition to examining the advantages and disadvantages of their role in policy-making and regulatory processes beyond the nation-state (see, for example, P. M. Haas, 'Introduction: Epistemic communities and international policy coordination', *International Organization*, 46 (1992), 1–35; B. Jacobsson, 'Standardization and expert knowledge', in N. Brunsson, B. Jacobsson and Associates (eds.), *A World of Standards* (Oxford University Press, 2000), pp. 40–9; M.-L. Djelic and S. Quack, 'Transnational communities and governance', in M.-L. Djelic and S. Quack (eds.), *Transnational Communities: Shaping Global Economic Governance* (Cambridge University Press, 2009), pp. 3–36 at 19–20). A much more detailed examination of the literature in this area, as well as its relevance for understanding the role of transfusionists as a key expert group involved in the governance of the blood system, is provided in Chapter 4.

[11] For example, it has been observed that the use of the term 'global regulation' focuses on where regulation takes place, but this does not mean that there has been a wholesale shift of regulatory processes in a given policy sector to global level. In many cases, there will still be a need to take account of such processes at national or regional levels as well; see Djelic and Sahlin-Andersson, 'Introduction: A world of governance', p. 18; Mattli and Woods, 'In whose benefit?', pp. 2–3.

[12] I accept that there are a number of not-for-profit organisations that have traditionally been aligned with national blood services and which are involved in the manufacture and supply of plasma products. In such cases, there appears to be some historical and/ or national variation as to which sub-system of governance they are identified with. The evolution and role of these organisations is discussed in more detail later in this chapter.

in risk governance in the political context. If a more effective approach to risk governance in the field is to evolve at supranational level, however, it is vital that the relationship between the social and the economic is made much more explicit in (regulatory) governance processes. This also involves acknowledging the multi-valuing of blood, whilst at the same time remaining focused on the primary objective of achieving optimum patient-recipient safety.

In order to examine the governance of the blood system, the first section of the chapter provides an historical overview of the evolution of governance arrangements involving national blood services. The organisation of blood services necessarily reflects specific national socio-cultural and political traditions, making it difficult to present a 'one size fits all' overview. As such, key elements are identified and specific examples are provided from France, England and the USA. Thereafter, an overview is provided of the development of the for-profit plasma products industry and its governance arrangements. Finally, the role and influence of key regulatory and other institutions with governance responsibilities for blood components and plasma products are identified, as are key stakeholder organisations which are involved in policy-making and regulatory processes in the field.

Blood as a medico-scientific resource: an historical overview

Prior to the twentieth century, many diseases afflicting human beings were considered to result from an imbalance of key 'humours', which included phlegm, choler, bile and blood. This line of thinking had been passed down from the Ancient Greeks who viewed the body as a reflection of nature. As all natural phenomena were considered to result from the interplay of four elements – air, fire, water and earth – the assumption was made that four analogous humours govern the body. The secret to good health was to maintain a balance of the humours. Blood was considered to be the key humour and was linked to Galen's theory of vitalism: blood represented the spiritual essence of human beings. It was a theory that proved to be highly influential and received significant support from Christian Churches.[13] Bloodletting, which involved cutting the vein of a human being to drain blood, was also practised for hundreds of years as a curative approach to disease. Although this was underpinned by the notion that the disease had resulted from an

---

[13] Starr, *Blood*, pp. 5–7.

imbalance of the humours, there was little evidence of any therapeutic benefit resulting from the practice.[14]

In the 1600s, a series of blood transfusion experiments and blood-related scientific research in France and England, as well as a growing interest in anatomy and dissection more generally, led to greater scientific questioning about the role of blood in the human body. The circulatory system for blood was identified, as well as flow and volume, and this undermined mystical and spiritual conceptions concerning blood. Following the death of a number of people from transfusions, both the medical establishment and the Pope banned the practice throughout Europe, and a century and a half passed before further experimentation with human-to-human blood transfusion took place.[15] In 1818, James Blundell, an English physician, performed a human-to-human blood transfusion, although the patient subsequently died. Thereafter, he transfused a series of patients, over half of whom survived. In the absence of any scientific understanding of blood groups and compatibility issues at the time, he nevertheless argued that human-to-human blood transfusion was a pragmatic and effective tool in clinical therapy.[16]

It was not until the early part of the twentieth century that medical and scientific research advanced to the point that discoveries were made with respect to different blood types. This took place in lock-step with techniques that were developed to collect, store and transfuse blood. In 1900, Karl Landsteiner, a Viennese scientist, discovered the presence of isoagglutinins in human blood which reacted with the red cells of certain other human subjects. As a result of this discovery, he went on to identify four main blood groups – A, B, AB and O. Further research revealed that blood was in fact composed of plasma and several cellular elements, which included red cells, five kinds of white cells and platelets. By 1940, Landsteiner and two other scientists, Stetson and Levine, had discovered the Rhesus system, which meant that eight different blood groups could now be distinguished.[17]

Blood was urgently needed to treat the wounded in World War Two and this led to the systematic organisation of the collection and supply of blood and its components at national level. At the time, the choice with regard to treating the wounded with blood was to use either whole blood or liquid plasma. Whole blood had to be used within a week

---

[14] *Ibid.*, p. 17.   [15] *Ibid.*, pp. 3–13.

[16] P. Borzini, P. Nembri and F. Biffoni, 'The evolution of transfusion medicine as a stand alone discipline', *Transfusion Medicine Reviews*, 11 (1997), 200–8 at 202.

[17] Hagen, *Blood: Gift or Merchandise?*, pp. 12–13; Leveton *et al.*, *HIV and the Blood Supply*, p. 27.

of collection, so there were logistical problems in getting the blood to the war front in time. Liquid plasma had a longer shelf-life than whole blood, but it was easily contaminated and was therefore also problematic.[18] It was in response to the need for a quick, safe and efficient way of providing the necessary blood components to deal with the wounded that the US government retained the services of Dr Edwin Cohn, a protein chemist based at Harvard University. Cohn had developed a technique whereby various proteins or fractions could be separated from plasma. As a result of this technique, Cohn was able to make albumin. Albumin proved to be extremely useful in the treatment of severe blood loss and shock suffered by wounded soldiers. It kept blood vessels dilated and was able to restore volume in blood vessels. In addition, it could also be stored for long periods before use. This technique came to be known as the Cohn fractionation method and it provided the basis for subsequent developments with respect to blood component therapy in the latter half of the twentieth century.[19]

In order to make the best use of the Cohn fractionation method, multiple units of whole blood and blood components were required. Charitable organisations, such as the Red Cross, as well as other government-sponsored organisations, were subsequently drafted into the war effort with the specific aim of collecting enough blood donations to meet the demand for both freeze-dried plasma and albumin at the war front. As a result of these developments with respect to the collection and supply of blood in World War Two, blood became a 'growth industry'.[20] Organisations charged with the collection of blood focused on the recruitment and retention of donors, the supply of whole blood and the increasing demand for blood components, such as platelets, red cells and clotting factors, especially factors VIII and IX. Clotting factors are those elements contained within the blood that are activated when a blood vessel wall is damaged and platelets begin adhering to the break. Deficiency in any of these factors leads to spontaneous internal bleeding, requiring the administration of blood products containing those clotting factors to stop it. Once they were discovered, Roman numerals were used by the scientific community to describe each of the clotting factors. Clotting factors VIII and IX were the most common factors found to be deficient in males who suffered from the genetic disorder haemophilia[21] (see Figure 2.1).

---

[18] Starr, *Blood*, pp. 101–2.
[19] *Ibid.*, pp. 102–4.   [20] *Ibid.*, p. 187.
[21] Krever, *Commission of Inquiry on the Blood System*, p. 17.

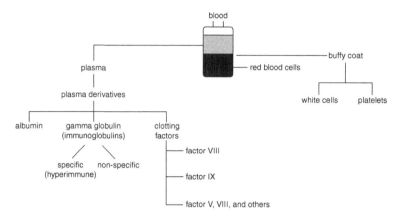

Figure 2.1: Blood components and plasma products.
Source: Krever, *Commission of Inquiry on the Blood System*, p. 16.

National blood services: policies, institutions and regulation

Following the end of World War Two, many governments in developed countries formalised the arrangements for the collection, organisation and supply of blood. In some countries, the Red Cross undertook this task, while in other countries governments created state executive agencies to manage national blood systems. Coexisting with such arrangements, independent and hospital blood banks were established in a range of countries as well. The decision as to how a national blood supply was to be organised often turned on the peculiarities of national historical and social developments, rather than any specific economic considerations.[22] For example, the Red Cross had played a seminal role in the collection and supply of blood during World War Two. As a result, the organisation was asked by several national governments to formally organise and run the national blood supply once the war ended. In other cases, the organisation of the national blood supply was subsumed within a wider reorganisation and restructuring of national health services in the post-war period. By the 1970s, governments in several developed countries, including England and France, also provided financial and institutional support for the development of not-for-profit manufacturing

---

[22] Hagen, *Blood: Gift or Merchandise?*, p. 74.

facilities, with a view to meeting growing consumer demand for plasma products.

The gift relationship and national self-sufficiency

VNRBD underpins the collection of blood by national blood services, as well as the manufacture of plasma products in state-sponsored manufacturing facilities in the majority of developed countries.[23] As mentioned in Chapter 1, Richard Titmuss had conceptualised this as the gift relationship: the donation of blood by voluntary, altruistic individuals to anonymous patient-recipients with no expectation of financial or other reward. Although Titmuss's arguments in support of the gift relationship in blood donation are examined in much more detail in Chapter 3, it is important to note for present purposes that his conceptualisation of the gift relationship had become an integral part of national and supranational blood policy, achieving the status of 'international orthodoxy' by the 1980s.[24] For those in charge of national blood services and not-for-profit manufacturing facilities for plasma products, the gift relationship also became an important part of their professional beliefs. The development and impact of such professional beliefs on risk governance, particularly during the time that HIV posed a risk to the blood supply, is discussed in much more detail in Chapter 4.

By the 1980s, the gift relationship in blood donation had become inextricably linked to the achievement of self-sufficiency in blood and plasma products in national blood policy, and was seen as an important objective to be realised on ethical, economic and safety grounds. Although varying definitions have been offered as to what was meant by self-sufficiency, it was generally considered to entail 'the provision of blood and blood products from within a population to satisfy the clinical needs of that population'.[25] It was not made clear as to how and when self-sufficiency in a given national setting would be deemed to have been achieved. In reality, the achievement of self-sufficiency remained illusory in many developed countries, particularly in the context of growing demand for factor concentrates which had brought about a revolution in treatment of haemophilia during this period.[26]

---

[23] For a definition of voluntary non-remunerated blood donation, see fn. 45, Chapter 1.
[24] Bayer and Feldman, 'Understanding the blood feuds', pp. 7–9.
[25] Hagen, *Blood: Gift or Merchandise?*, p. 190.
[26] For a definition of haemophilia, see fn. 32, Chapter 1.

England and France

Prior to the 1980s, national regulation of the blood system was fragmented and dysfunctional in many developed countries. In countries such as France and England, for example, the reasons for this state of affairs were attributable to a number of factors. In both countries, blood services had been organised on a regional basis following World War Two and national Departments of Health exercised weak and ineffective oversight of their activities.[27] Such departments were under-resourced in financial and administrative terms, as well as being heavily reliant on advice received from those in charge of blood services with respect to the management of the blood system in general, as well as in relation to safety issues in particular. The lack of independent and centralised institutional management of blood services in these two countries created dysfunction and inefficiency in the management of supply and demand for blood and plasma products, leading to oversupply in some areas and undersupply in others. Where regulatory powers did exist to facilitate risk governance in relation to blood and plasma products, such powers were either poorly used, or not used at all.[28]

It was against this background of institutional and regulatory dysfunction and inefficiency, as well as difficulties in meeting growing consumer demand for plasma products that HIV emerged as a risk to national blood supplies in the early 1980s. Despite attempts at achieving national self-sufficiency in relation to such products, both countries had been forced to resort to the importation of factor concentrates sourced from US paid donors that had been manufactured and supplied by the for-profit plasma products industry. Although it was estimated that between 10 and 30 per cent of factor concentrates used in France during this period were imported,[29] the level of importation in England was much higher at between 50 and 70 per cent.[30]

---

[27] M. Steffen, 'The nation's blood: medicine, justice and the state', in Feldman and Bayer (eds.), *Blood Feuds*, pp. 95–126 at 100; R. Freeman, 'HIV and the blood supply in the United Kingdom: professionalism and pragmatism', in Bovens *et al.* (eds.), *Success and Failure in Public Governance*, pp. 567–81 at 569.

[28] J. Cash, 'The blood transfusion service and the National Health Service', *British Medical Journal*, 295 (1987), 617–19; A. M. Casteret, *L'Affaire du sang contaminé* (Paris: Éditions La Decouverte, 1992), p. 21; J. P. Geronimi, F. Henry-Bonnot, A. Feltz *et al.*, *Les Collectes de sang en milieu pénitentiare*, ISGJ RMT 1392 IGAS Code Mission SA07 No. 92 119 (Paris: Inspection Générale des services judiciaires, 1992), pp. 116–17; M. Moran, *Governing the Health Care State: A Comparative Study of the United Kingdom, the United States and Germany* (Manchester University Press, 1999), pp. 155–6.

[29] Casteret, *L'Affaire du sang contaminé*, pp. 30–1.

[30] P. Jones, 'Factor VIII: supply and demand', *British Medical Journal*, 280 (1980), 1531–2.

When HIV testing became available, it became clear that there was a high rate of HIV infection among national haemophilia populations in both England and France. In the case of England, this was primarily attributable to the use of imported factor concentrates, whereas in France it was a combination of both imported and local factor concentrates.

In examining the circumstances that contributed to the failure in risk governance, particularly in relation to national haemophilia populations in both countries, it became clear that the commitment to the gift relationship could no longer be viewed as a guarantor of blood safety on its own. Instead, a more complex assessment of risk was required in relation to risks to the blood supply; one which took account of a range of institutional, epidemiological, economic and regulatory factors.[31] Although the specific problems encountered with managing the risk posed by HIV is examined in more detail in subsequent chapters, it is important to note that the political fallout from HIV blood contamination episodes in developed countries such as England and France was considerable.[32] It led to widespread institutional reform of national blood services, as well as the adoption of a more stringent approach to risk governance involving the blood system more generally.

United States

Prior to the 1980s, the governance of the blood system in the USA was markedly different and indeed much more complex in both organisational and regulatory terms than that of other developed countries. In unpicking this complexity, it is important to distinguish between developments in relation to the collection and supply of whole blood on the one hand, and plasma collection and the manufacture of plasma products on the other hand. In the case of the whole blood sector, demand had increased dramatically following World War Two. A range of organisations proliferated to meet this growing demand, including community, independent and hospital blood services and laboratory support services. There were two key organisations that sought to control the direction of whole blood collection and supply in the USA: the American Red Cross (ARC) and the American Association of Blood Banks (AABB). The ongoing tensions between the two organisations over a range of issues would account in large part for the lack of a unified

---

[31] Farrell, 'Is the gift still good?', pp. 162–9.
[32] Feldman and Bayer (eds.), *Blood Feuds*; Bovens *et al.* (eds.), *Success and Failure in Public Governance*.

national approach to whole blood collection in the decades immediately following World War Two, which was compounded by a lack of political will or interest at federal level in adopting such an approach.

The ARC had been actively involved in the collection and supply of blood during World War Two. Following the war, it took the decision that it would commit itself to establishing a dominant national presence in blood collection and supply. Given that many independent blood banks had already been established under the control of local physicians, the ARC took the strategic decision to only establish local ARC blood banks where it was invited to do so. The ARC took the view that non-medically qualified personnel could be involved in the management of blood collection, along with physician support. It also supported centralised, rather than localised, control over the management of blood collection. It promoted the gift relationship as the core principle underpinning the donation of whole blood, emphasising community responsibility with no demands being placed on patient-recipients. It sought to engender public support for blood donation through reliance on American patriotism, a strategy which had proved successful during the war years.

Many of the independent or community blood banks run by physicians were represented by the AABB, a national body that had been formed in 1947 to represent their interests. Following the war, many physicians had organised their own blood banks in local hospitals and operated independently. They were unhappy about attempts by the ARC to establish a dominating national presence in the field, as well as by moves to usurp the role of physicians in performing various medical functions associated with blood collection and supply. They placed much more emphasis on local autonomy and professional control of the process. They also operated a philosophy of individual responsibility whereby individual patient-recipients of blood were expected to contribute towards the replacement and/or cost of the blood they had received. The AABB established a National Blood Clearinghouse where hospitals and local blood banks traded blood and blood credits with repayment being in the form of money or blood.[33]

By the early 1970s, there were over 5,400 organisations involved in blood collection and supply in the USA. It was estimated that the ARC collected about half of the whole blood supply, followed by community or independent blood centres and hospital blood banks.[34] The post-war

[33] Starr, *Blood*, pp. 174–6.
[34] Drake *et al.*, *The American Blood Supply*, pp. 6–7; R. E. Domen, 'Paid-versus-volunteer blood donation in the United States: a historical overview', *Transfusion Medicine Reviews*, 10 (1995), 53–9 at 53.

years had seen increasing rivalry and disputation between the ARC and the AABB as they battled for control of the national blood policy agenda, in circumstances where there was dysfunctional national regulatory oversight of blood quality and safety.[35] Institutional and regulatory dysfunction also contributed to a paucity of good quality data tracking the supply and demand for blood, resulting in over- and undersupply across different regions. This lack of coordination was estimated to have resulted in the loss of between 10 and 30 per cent of blood due to outdating.[36] This began to change in the early 1970s, given Titmuss's damning indictment of the dysfunction and inefficiencies of the American blood system in *The Gift Relationship*. Inspired by Titmuss's work, the then Nixon administration embarked upon the reform of governance arrangements involving the blood system. This led to the promulgation of a national blood policy which set out a series of goals to be achieved.[37] In addition, the Food and Drug Administration (FDA), the national regulatory agency responsible for medicines (amongst other things), was made responsible for national regulatory oversight of blood and plasma products in 1973.[38]

The FDA's regulatory mandate in the field was facilitated through amendments to its governing legislation, the Food, Drug and Cosmetics Act.[39] As a result of such amendments, the FDA's regulatory powers in relation to blood were now substantial and covered all areas of blood procurement, as well as the system of production of blood and its components into various products.[40] By the mid 1970s, the FDA had published regulations defining good manufacturing practices (GMP); devised licensing arrangements for those organisations involved in blood collection and supply; and required that both whole blood and plasma donations be tested for the presence of the hepatitis B virus (HBV). In 1978, the FDA also mandated that whole blood and plasma be labelled as sourced from either paid or volunteer donors. In the case of the former, it was to be accompanied by a warning that blood from paid donors was associated with a higher risk of transmitting hepatitis.[41] This action resulted in the rapid elimination of the use of paid donors in

[35] Domen, 'Paid-versus-volunteer blood donation in the United States', pp. 56–7; Starr, *Blood*, pp. 176, 189.
[36] Titmuss, *The Gift Relationship*, pp. 48–63.
[37] Starr, *Blood*, p. 251.
[38] *Ibid.*, pp. 226–9.
[39] Food, Drug and Cosmetics Act, 21 U.S.C.§301 et seq.
[40] Farrugia, 'The regulatory pendulum in transfusion medicine', p. 274.
[41] Domen, 'Paid-versus-volunteer blood donation in the United States', p. 57; Starr, *Blood*, p. 257.

whole blood collection, with a consequent drop in HBV infection rates through blood transfusion as a result.[42]

When HIV emerged as a risk to the blood supply in the early 1980s, the FDA had extensive regulatory powers at its disposal to address such risk. Although it could have adopted a leadership role which brought together a range of stakeholders involved in the national blood system to create a unified approach to dealing with the risk, this did not take place. At an institutional level, the FDA was engaged in an ongoing 'turf war' with the Centers for Disease Control (CDC) over which national public health agency should take charge of managing the emerging AIDS epidemic. In addition, many officials within the FDA were sceptical about the CDC's claims about the spread and likely impact of the new disease on the blood supply. At a seminal meeting held at the CDC in January 1983, which was attended by FDA officials and other key stakeholders, the CDC attempted to reach a consensus on a unified approach to be taken to addressing the risk posed by HIV. There was a failure to reach consensus at the meeting and stakeholder organisations were left to issue their own guidelines and take action as they saw fit to deal with the risk.[43] Although the FDA did promulgate guidelines in March 1983, they were not made mandatory and their legal status remained unclear.[44] It would be a further two years before the FDA issued an updated policy position, setting out its guidelines for the introduction of HIV testing on whole blood and plasma donations.[45]

In addition, there were also structural and institutional cultural problems within the FDA itself which adversely affected the way in which it approached the management of the risk posed by HIV to the blood system. During this period, the FDA was institutionally disposed to adopting a 'collegial' approach to decision-making processes, working towards achieving a position of consensus on policy and regulatory issues. Over time, this had resulted in actions being taken on a more informal basis in relation to (regulatory) governance involving the national blood system.[46] In its evaluation and regulation activities, the FDA had always made extensive use of scientific advisory committees. The use of advisory committees also fitted with its collegial approach to decision-making and it was heavily reliant on advice received from such committees. In

[42] Starr, *Blood*, p. 257.
[43] R. Shilts, *And the Band Played On: Politics, People and the AIDS Epidemic* (New York: Penguin Books, 1987), pp. 221–3; R. Bayer, 'Blood and AIDS in America: science, politics and the making of an iatrogenic catastrophe', in Feldman and Bayer (eds.), *Blood Feuds*, pp. 20–58 at 23–4.
[44] Leveton *et al.*, *HIV and the Blood Supply*, p. 146.
[45] *Ibid.*, p. 59.   [46] *Ibid.*, pp. 138–40.

the case of blood, its main advisory committee at the time was the Blood Products Advisory Committee (BPAC). A retrospective evaluation of the advice provided by BPAC to the FDA during the period when HIV posed a risk to the blood supply showed that the Committee had by and large adopted a reactive and conservative approach in relation to a range of policies designed to reduce the risk posed by the virus.[47] Nevertheless, the FDA had invariably adopted BPAC's recommendations as official policy. Instead of adopting a proactive approach to dealing with the risk, the FDA had elected to make use of 'standard operating procedures' in relation to its regulatory oversight of the blood system.[48] The problems with the approach taken by the FDA became clear once HIV testing was available in 1985 and it was evident that the US blood supply had been heavily contaminated by the virus.[49]

Revelations concerning the FDA's shortcomings with regard to facilitating effective regulatory oversight of the blood system;[50] increasing levels of patient activism and legal action in the courts;[51] and a government-sponsored inquiry into the circumstances that had led to the HIV blood contamination episode in the USA[52] led to regulatory and institutional reforms to the management of the national blood system in the 1990s. As a result of such reforms, the FDA adopted a much more proactive approach to managing risks involving the blood system. This led to the reorganisation of the charter and membership of BPAC to facilitate a more rigorous and inclusive approach to providing advice on a range of issues impacting upon blood safety.[53] In addition, the FDA introduced GMP standards for blood services, thus broadening their application beyond the pharmaceutical sector. Although this produced an initial adverse reaction from those involved in managing blood services, such standard setting has now become embedded within the national blood system.[54] An analysis of whether the FDA's proactive approach to blood safety has led to more effective risk governance in the field is the subject of more detailed examination in Chapter 7.

[47] *Ibid.*, pp. 45, 149.   [48] *Ibid.*, pp. 138–54.
[49] *Ibid.*, pp. 19–21.
[50] G. Gaul, 'The blood brokers: the loose way the FDA regulates blood industry', *Philadelphia Inquirer*, 25/9/89.
[51] S. Resnik, *Blood Saga: Hemophilia, AIDS and the Survival of a Community* (Berkeley, CA: University of California Press, 1999), pp. 146–90.
[52] Leveton *et al.*, *HIV and the Blood Supply.*
[53] M. A. Friedman, Lead Deputy Commissioner, Food and Drug Administration, Testimony on FDA's regulation of blood, blood products, and plasma, before the House Committee on Government Reform and Oversight, Subcommittee on Human Resources and Intergovernmental Relations, 5 June 1997 (www.hhs.gov/asl/testify/t970605a.html).
[54] Farrugia, 'The regulatory pendulum in transfusion medicine', p. 275.

The development of the global plasma products industry

The USA is the global leader in the industrial manufacture and supply of plasma products. As mentioned previously, the development of the industry had quite a different historical trajectory to the whole blood sector. It is therefore important to identify and map this trajectory in order to understand the evolution of national and global governance regimes in relation to such products. In the early 1940s, the first industrial manufacturing plant for plasma products was established in the USA by a company known as Cutter, although the plant's operations at the time were limited.[55] The use of the Cohn fractionation method, a series of advances in blood research and the development of the technique of plasmapheresis, led to the rapid expansion of the industry by the end of the 1960s. Plasmapheresis is a procedure which enables plasma to be extracted from a donor, with red cells then being returned to the donor's body. As the donor suffers no loss of vital red blood cells, it is possible to repeat the procedure frequently. The procedure enabled the burgeoning industry to collect plasma from individuals on a weekly basis which could result in up to fifty litres of plasma being taken from a single donor on an annual basis.[56] In 1965, Judith Graham Pool, an American scientist, discovered that if plasma was frozen and then slowly thawed, a thick white residue of clotting factor VIII remained. This residue, which became known as cryoprecipitate, had ten times the clotting power of plasma on its own. Depending on the severity of a bleed, people with haemophilia (PWH) who had a deficiency in this clotting factor needed between one and ten bags of cryoprecipitate to treat a bleed. Each bag corresponded to one blood donation.

Cryoprecipitate – or 'cryo' as it became colloquially known – proved to be the starting point for research conducted by two American scientists, Brinkhous and Shanbrom. Using large pools of individual units of plasma, the cryoprecipitate was dissolved again and then treated with chemicals, as well as filtered and centrifuged, to produce a white crystalline powder of pure highly concentrated clotting factor VIII.[57] The purified clotting factor VIII powder, which became known as factor VIII concentrate, was freeze-dried during processing and kept in glass vials. It could then be dissolved in sterile water for use in the treatment of clotting disorders, especially haemophilia.[58] Large pools of plasma

---

[55] Hagen, *Blood: Gift or Merchandise?*, p. 113.
[56] *Ibid.*, pp. 18, 114.   [57] Starr, *Blood*, pp. 222–4.
[58] Krever, *Commission of Inquiry on the Blood System*, p. 22.

were needed for the manufacture of the product and the companies involved in the industry moved to secure sufficient supplies of the required source material. They established their own plasmapheresis programmes which involved individuals providing their plasma on a regular basis in return for financial compensation, as well as seeking out a range of other supply sources both within and outside the USA. Payment for both whole blood and plasma was not prohibited in the USA in the decades immediately following World War Two. The whole blood sector ceased to collect blood from paid donors in the mid to late 1970s but payment for donation via plasmapheresis continued. This seems to have been accepted by US policy-makers and regulators on the basis that a sufficient supply of source material would not be obtained for the manufacture of plasma products, if the practice of payment for plasma donation was not allowed to continue.[59] As a result, the USA has long enjoyed national self-sufficiency in whole blood and plasma products, unlike the situation in many other developed countries.

Companies involved in the industry adopted various strategies to obtain regular and adequate supplies of plasma. First, they either bought up, or entered into contracts with, suppliers who owned plasmapheresis centres in the USA. The plasma that they obtained from these centres was known as source plasma. Second, they arranged to purchase recovered plasma which had been separated from the donation of whole blood and other components by blood banks. Third, they entered into what were known as 'short supply agreements' with hospital blood banks in order to obtain further supplies of recovered plasma. Fourth, they regularly purchased plasma from plasma brokers who were individuals or companies that bought and sold plasma on what became known as the international 'spot market'.[60] Apart from the recovered plasma obtained from blood banks and hospitals who used VNRBD, the companies usually obtained source plasma from groups such as college students, prison inmates and those from poor or what became known as 'skid row' neighbourhoods. Donors such as prison inmates and gay men were also considered to be a valuable and regular source of plasma, particularly as their plasma often contained HBV antibodies, which was needed in the manufacture of the HBV vaccine.[61]

During the 1970s, the international traffic in plasma grew dramatically, with cities such as Montreal and Zurich becoming hubs for what became known in the industry as 'spot markets'. Self-styled plasma

[59] Leveton et al., HIV and the Blood Supply, p. 30.
[60] Krever, Commission of Inquiry on the Blood System, p. 371.
[61] Leveton et al., HIV and the Blood Supply, p. 30; Starr, Blood, p. 265.

'brokers' used these cities as their base for selling large quantities of plasma on the open market to the highest bidders. Companies involved in the industry established, or otherwise encouraged third parties to establish, plasmapheresis centres in a number of developing countries, including Lesotho, Belize, Dominican Republic, Costa Rica, Nicaragua, El Salvador and Colombia. This was in addition to a series of centres which were established along the US border with Mexico. Mexicans were then able to cross the border relatively easily to provide plasma and therefore there was no need to meet any import requirements for the plasma collected. In the face of growing condemnation by the Red Cross and the World Health Organization (WHO), the industry eventually closed down its plasma collection operations in these countries by the end of the 1970s. From this point on, the industry claimed it would only collect plasma from centres in the USA and, to a lesser extent, in Europe.[62] By the 1980s, the USA had come to be known as the 'OPEC of plasma',[63] with the US-based plasma products industry developing a flourishing and lucrative export market, particularly in relation to factor concentrates used in the treatment of haemophilia. By the 1980s, the industry was meeting approximately 60 per cent of market demand for factor concentrates in Europe alone, in circumstances where it was often able to charge triple the amount that was charged in the US market.[64]

Although the US-based companies that were supplying factor concentrates to the European market during this period were required to have licences to market their products, national regulators had little direct control over the quality and safety of the source material used. They were essentially reliant upon the industry itself vouchsafing the safety of the products, as well as upon the ability of the US regulator, the FDA, to ensure that appropriate quality and safety standards were met. As previously discussed, the industry was collecting plasma from what would turn out to be HIV high-risk donor groups, in circumstances where the FDA's approach to regulating quality and safety was dysfunctional and ineffective during this period.

Once HIV testing was instituted in the mid 1980s, it became apparent that there were high rates of HIV infection among national haemophilia populations where factor concentrates manufactured by the industry had been used. In the wake of the political fallout from national HIV blood contamination episodes, the industry has since focused on enhancing the safety of its plasma products; improving the quality of

---

[62] Starr, *Blood*, pp. 233–7; 246–7.
[63] *Ibid.*, p. 240.   [64] *Ibid.*, p. 241.

its source plasma; and promoting greater transparency in relation to its plasma collection operations. Although concerns remain over the safety of sourcing plasma from paid donors,[65] the industry claims it has made significant strides in enhancing the safety of its products, a detailed examination of which is undertaken in Chapter 5.

Global governance of the blood system

Up until relatively recently, national regulation of the blood system has been the norm. Global governance in the field has developed in a piece-meal and incremental fashion, largely grounded in the development of non-legally binding norms, technical standard-setting, guidelines and recommendations. The development of regulatory governance in the field at global level has for the most part focused on the content, manu-facture and supply of plasma products, although there are some not-able exceptions which are discussed below. The manufacture of plasma products is undertaken by companies that form a distinct niche within the larger global pharmaceutical industry. There are longstanding governance arrangements in place at supranational level covering the pharmaceutical industry within which global governance in relation to the smaller plasma products industry is situated.

Such governance has largely been driven by the need to promote technical harmonisation measures at global level in order to facilitate trade and/or markets for the plasma products industry. This has led to the development of cooperative arrangements supported by global and regional institutions, industry, regulators and scientific experts to develop harmonisation on a range of technical matters pertaining to medicines for human use, which includes plasma products. The adop-tion of such harmonisation measures has largely taken place in closed technocratic, expert-driven environments. It is a governance regime that operates largely beyond the democratic oversight of individual nation-states, although there is clearly benign state support for the work done at supranational level. This is evidenced by the representation of national regulators, civil servants and experts across a range of advisory and decision-making bodies within global and regional institutions in the field, such as the WHO, the Council of Europe and the EU. While at EU level, there is some degree of democratic accountability which operates in relation to dealing with blood quality and safety issues,[66]

---

[65] C. L. van der Poel, E. Seifried and W. P. Schaasberg, 'Paying for blood donations: still a risk?', *Vox Sanguinis*, 83 (2002), 285–93.
[66] For further details, see Chapter 8.

the global governance regime that operates through institutions such as the WHO and the Council of Europe does so with little or no recourse to such accountability mechanisms. The political legitimacy of governance initiatives concerning blood quality and safety which take place in these institutional environments therefore remains problematic.

World Health Organization

The WHO has a longstanding commitment to promoting quality, safety and access issues in relation to blood and plasma products. Although it lacks binding regulatory powers in the area, it has nevertheless focused on information gathering and dissemination, establishing norms and standards, as well as promoting global collaboration between blood experts and Member States. The WHO also supports VNRBD (from low-risk donor populations) as a guiding principle for the sourcing of whole blood and blood components by national blood services. Its commitment to this principle has its historical origins in concerns regarding exploitative practices engaged in by the plasma products industry in developing countries in the 1970s, which led to the adoption of a unanimous resolution at its World Assembly in 1975 condemning such practices and affirming its commitment to VNRBD.[67]

Although the WHO promotes VNRBD as its preferred approach for ensuring blood safety, it acknowledges that well over 50 per cent of blood collected on a global basis comes from paid and replacement donors.[68] In recent years, it has developed guidelines as well as offering expert and institutional support to countries wishing to establish national blood services based on VNRBD. Its initiatives in this area were supported by a resolution adopted by the World Health Assembly in 2005, which established a World Blood Donor Day.[69] It takes place on 14 June each year in order to raise awareness about the importance of VNRBD and to encourage individuals to donate blood on a regular basis. In June 2009, WHO organised a global consultation meeting

---

[67] World Health Organization. Twenty-Eighth World Health Assembly. *Utilization and supply of human blood and blood products*, WHA28.72, 1975.

[68] Based on data it has collected, WHO estimates that forty-five countries collect more than 75 per cent of their blood supplies from family, replacement and paid blood donors; 37 per cent of all donations in developing countries and 26 per cent in transitional countries are collected from family/replacement and paid blood donors; see World Health Organization, *Global Blood Safety and Availability: Key Facts and Figures, 2010* (www.who.int/worldblooddonorday/media/en).

[69] World Health Organization. Fifty-Eighth World Health Assembly. *Blood safety: Proposal to establish World Blood Donor Day*, WHA58.13, 2005.

which brought together a range of blood experts, policy-makers and non-government organisations from thirty-eight countries. It led to the adoption of the Melbourne Declaration, which called on 'all governments to achieve 100% voluntary non-remunerated donations by 2020 as the cornerstone of their blood policies'.[70]

In addition to emphasising the importance of VNRBD for enhancing blood safety, WHO supports the adoption of a nationally coordinated and government supported blood service as the optimum organisational approach. There has been considerable debate about the efficacy of this approach. On the positive side, it has been suggested that centralised blood collection systems contribute significantly to blood safety. Dealing with large volumes of blood in one place is more cost-effective and also leads to better trained and experienced staff. It also means that more attention can be given to recruiting a sufficient number of low-risk donors to meet local needs.[71] On the negative side, the WHO's preferred approach has been criticised for failing to take account of particular local contexts in developing countries. It has been argued that a significant amount of national healthcare budgets in developing countries would be taken up with implementing such an approach in circumstances where a centralised national blood service would probably only be able to provide for the needs of the capital city and which would in any case be at odds with other aspects of national healthcare systems. It also assumes that countries have a sufficiently developed internal infrastructure to make a centralised national blood service workable on a day-to-day basis. It has been suggested that it would be better if the WHO opted for a differential approach which was more in line with specific local conditions in developing countries.[72]

Although the WHO has been involved in governance initiatives in the field of blood for many years, its prioritisation of global blood safety in recent years has led to it becoming a key global player in promoting norms and standards in relation to the quality and safety of blood and its components, as well as that of plasma products.[73] In addition to collecting global data on blood safety on a regular basis,[74] it also convened the Global Collaboration on Blood Safety (GCBS) between 2000 and

[70] World Health Organization, The Melbourne Declaration on 100% Voluntary Non-remunerated Donation of Blood and Blood Components.
[71] B. Fraser, 'Seeking a safer blood supply', *Lancet*, 365 (2005), 559–60.
[72] M. Larkin, 'WHO's blood-safety initiative: a vain effort?', *Lancet*, 355 (2000), 1245.
[73] M. McCarthy, 'What's going on at the World Health Organization?', *Lancet*, 360 (2002), 1108–10 at 1109.
[74] World Health Organization, Blood Transfusion Safety, Global Database on Blood Safety (www.who.int/bloodsafety/global_database/en).

2010. The GCBS's main objective was the harmonisation of activities to promote global safety and it involved a voluntary partnership of internationally recognised organisations, institutions, associations, agencies and experts from both developed and developing countries.[75] In 2011, the WHO reorganised its work in the field and established two new groups: the WHO Global Forum for Blood Safety and the WHO Global Blood Safety Network. The former group has primarily focused to date on patient blood management, as well as patient health and safety. The latter group has focused on developing an organised global network of WHO collaborating centres, experts and non-government organisations in order to promote blood safety.[76]

One of the WHO's specific constitutional functions is 'to develop, establish and promote international standards with respect to … biological, pharmaceutical and similar products'.[77] In this regard, it has long been active in developing and promoting norms, standards and guidance to promote access, technical harmonisation and the safety of biological medicines, such as plasma products. The WHO develops norms and sets standards based on an international consensus derived from broad consultation among professional, pharmaceutical, regulatory and other stakeholder groups. In relation to the manufacture of plasma products, the WHO commissioned expert groups, such as the Expert Committee on Biological Standardization (ECBS), to develop detailed recommendations and guidelines for the manufacturing, licensing and control of plasma products, among a range of other products and testing technology.[78] In the case of plasma products, the ECBS has been specifically involved in the development of international reference preparation materials with a view to promoting best practice in the manufacture of plasma products, as well as supporting the introduction of testing technologies designed to minimise and/or eradicate TTIs from plasma products.[79] At the recommendation of the ECBS, WHO also supported the establishment of a global Blood Regulators Network (BRN). Its membership comprises leading international regulators

[75] World Health Organization, Blood Transfusion Safety, Global Collaboration for Blood Safety (2000–2010) (www.who.int/bloodsafety/gcbs/en).
[76] World Health Organization, Blood Transfusion Safety, Collaboration and Partnerships (www.who.int/bloodsafety/collaboration/en/index.html).
[77] Article 2(u), Constitution of the World Health Organization.
[78] World Health Organization, Expert Committee on Biological Standardization (www.who.int/biologicals/expert_committee/en/index.html).
[79] World Health Organization, Expert Committee on Biological Standardization. Recommendations for the production, control and regulation of human plasma for fractionation (Technical Report Series – 941, Annex 4, 2006).

with responsibility for blood and plasma products. The BRN facilitates information exchange among its members on blood-related issues, as well as exploring options for regulatory cooperation on a range of issues involving blood safety.[80]

Council of Europe

Since 1949, the Council of Europe has been actively involved in developing policies and guidelines in the field of blood transfusion. The Council has promoted its overarching policy commitments and activities in the field predominantly through the adoption of formal recommendations by the Committee of Ministers, which is its key decision-making body. Although recommendations are not binding on Member States, the Committee of Ministers can require that Member States provide information on the extent to which there has been compliance with recommendations at national level. The subject matter of recommendations adopted in the field has been wide-ranging and includes protection of the health of donors and recipients; responsibilities of health authorities in the field of blood transfusion; introduction of pathogen inactivation procedures for blood components; traceability of blood and plasma products; clinical trials involving the use of blood components or fractionated blood products; and screening of blood donors for AIDS markers.[81]

In developing recommendations in the field of blood transfusion, the Committee of Ministers draws on two expert committees: the Committee on Quality Assurance in Blood Transfusion Services (Expert Committee) (GTS) and the European Committee on Blood Transfusion (Steering Committee) (CD-P-TS). The Committees' members are drawn primarily from those involved in, or otherwise connected to, national blood services in Member States.[82] While the former committee focuses primarily on quality assurance issues, the European Committee on Blood Transfusion has a broader remit that includes providing assistance to Member States on improving blood transfusion services and promoting the principle of VNRBD; defining and promoting the implementation of quality and safety standards in blood and blood components collection, storage, distribution and use; developing ethical, safety and quality standards with respect to

[80] World Health Organization, Blood Products and Related Biologicals, Blood Regulators Network (www.who.int/bloodproducts/brn/en).
[81] For a full list of recommendations adopted by the Council of Europe in the field of blood transfusion, see www.coe.int/t/dg3/health/recommendations_en.asp#blood.
[82] Hagen, *Blood Transfusion in Europe*, p. 15.

professional practice in the field; ensuring the transfer of knowledge and expertise through training and networking; monitoring practices in Europe and assessing epidemiological risks linked to blood and its components;[83] promoting quality assurance; and ensuring the availability of rare blood products.[84]

The work of the Council of Europe in the field of blood transfusion is currently managed by one of its internal Directorates, namely the European Directorate for the Quality of Medicines and HealthCare (EDQM). The EDQM was formally established in 1996 and has a range of responsibilities, including the coordination of activities, programmes and policies linking the quality of medicines to the quality and safety of their use in the fields of pharmaceutical practice and care, risk prevention, counterfeiting and the classification of medicines, blood transfusion, organ transplantation, pharmaceuticals and pharmaceutical care. This involves a significant amount of liaison, as well as harmonisation activities with a range of regional and international bodies on behalf of the Council of Europe.[85] In the field of blood transfusion, EDQM plays a central role in the development of regional and international norms and standards, as well as contributing expert advice and support in relation to EU regulation in the field. EDQM has identified three main principles as underpinning its work in the field of blood transfusion: the non-commercialisation of substances of human origin provided on the basis of VNRBD; the realisation of the goal of self-sufficiency; and the protection of both donors and recipients.[86] It has also focused in recent years on promoting the optimal use of blood components and plasma products.[87]

---

[83] On this aspect of its work, the European Committee on Blood Transfusion appointed a working group (TS057) to monitor current practices, evaluate scientific data and define a harmonised approach to establishing donor deferral policies with respect to risks associated with sexual behaviour. At the time of writing, the report setting out the findings of the working group was yet to be published. It was anticipated that such findings would provide the basis for a Council of Europe resolution on the matter (www.edqm.eu). See Chapter 7 for a detailed examination of the approach taken to such donor deferral policies in the USA and the UK.

[84] Council of Europe, European Directorate for the Quality of Medicines and HealthCare. Terms of Reference of the European Committee (Partial Agreement) on Blood Transfusion (CD-P-TS) Factsheet, 1076th Meeting – 3–4 February 2010 (www.edqm.eu).

[85] Council of Europe, European Directorate for the Quality of Medicines and HealthCare (EDQM) (www.edqm.eu).

[86] *Ibid.*

[87] In April 2009, the Council of Europe sponsored the Kreuth symposium on the optimal clinical use of blood components. This symposium had its roots in an initial meeting also held in Wildbad Kreuth in 1999 that had been organised under the German Presidency of the EU, which represented an initial attempt to agree on a common approach in the area. The 2009 symposium brought together over one hundred

One of EDQM's key activities in the field is the updating of guides dealing with the preparation, use and quality assurance of blood components.[88] The origins of the guide lie in work done by the Select Committee of Experts on Quality Assurance in Blood Transfusion Services, which first published proposals on quality assurance in the field in the 1980s. This subsequently led to the publication of a guide on blood components in 1995 in line with Recommendation No. R (95) 15 of the Committee of Ministers.[89] This Recommendation provides for the guide to be updated on a regular basis by the European Committee on Blood Transfusion (CD-P-TS) with assistance from leading experts in the field. The guide contains recommendations on blood collection, blood components, technical procedures, transfusion practices and quality systems for blood establishments. It has been crucial in informing the approach taken to setting technical standards for blood quality and safety in EU regulation in the field.[90]

In addition to its work in the field of blood transfusion, EDQM is responsible for a range of activities related to quality and safety issues involving medicines such as plasma products. One of EDQM's core activities involves the management of the European Pharmacopoeia (PhEur). The PhEur is a single reference work which sets out quality control of medicines in Europe. The EDQM's legal competence to undertake such management is to be found in the Council of Europe's Convention on the Elaboration of a European Pharmacopoeia which came into force in 1964.[91] Under the terms of the Convention, a European Pharmacopoeia Commission was established and is overseen by the Council's Public Health Committee. Contracting parties

experts in blood transfusion medicine from thirty-eight countries, together with a range of other stakeholders. The aim of the symposium was to develop recommendations on how to optimise the clinical use of blood and blood components based on the best available clinical evidence (www.edqm.eu/medias/fichiers/Kreuth_Symposium. pdf).

[88] Council of Europe, European Directorate for the Quality of Medicines and HealthCare, *Guide to the Preparation, Use and Quality Assurance of Blood Components*, 16th edn (Strasbourg: Council of Europe, 2010) (www.edqm.eu).

[89] Recommendation No. R (95) 15 of the Committee of Ministers to Member States on the Preparation, Use and Quality Assurance of Blood Components (adopted by the Committee of Ministers on 12 October 1995 at the 545th meeting of the Ministers' Deputies).

[90] Council of Europe, European Directorate for the Quality of Medicines and HealthCare, *Guide to the Preparation, Use and Quality Assurance of Blood Components*.

[91] Council of Europe, Convention on the Elaboration of a European Pharmacopoeia, Strasbourg, 2VII.1964, ETS No. 50, as amended by the Protocol to the Convention on the Elaboration of a European Pharmacopoeia. ETS No. 134, in force 1 November 1992.

to the Convention undertake to engage in the progressive development of the PhEur; to take all necessary measures to ensure that the monographs which make up the PhEur are completed and correct; and to ensure that standards in the field are applied at national level, whether through direct or indirect implementation under national law. The Commission allocates work on monographs to specifically constituted groups of experts and working parties. Membership of these groups is comprised of representatives from national regulatory agencies, official medicines control laboratories, pharmaceutical companies, universities and research institutions. The PhEur is also incorporated into and relied upon in relevant pharmaceutical legislation adopted at EU level.[92]

The EDQM is actively involved in promoting international harmonisation in this area, viewing it as an important part of its work in the field of pharmaceuticals. As a result of a trilateral agreement signed in 1990, the EDQM engages in formal liaison with the other major Pharmacopoeias based in Japan and the USA through the Pharmacopoeial Discussion Group (PDG), which meets on a regular basis. The meetings of the PDG usually coincide with those of the International Conference on Harmonisation (ICH), with the PDG reporting on its activities to the ICH. The overarching aim is to reduce the overall cost of pharmaceutical research on a global basis; to avoid the duplication of work; and to reduce the time required for medicines to reach the market. Activities to promote harmonisation include the selection of specific monographs and general methods of analysis for the purposes of developing convergence and harmonisation between the three pharmacopoeias. When engaging in harmonisation activities, the PDG aims to consult with relevant experts, regulatory agencies and other interested stakeholders. Following on from such consultation, harmonisation of pharmacopoeial documentation occurs once common agreement has been reached by

---

[92] Directive 2001/83/EC of the European Parliament and of the Council of 6 November 2001 on the Community code relating to medicinal products for human use, OJ L 311, 28.11.2001; Commission Directive 2003/63/EC of 25 June 2003 amending Directive 2001/83/EC of the European Parliament and of the Council on the Community code relating to medicinal products for human use, OJ L 159, 27.6.2003. These Directives incorporate European Pharmacopoeia specifications on medicines for marketing authorisation applications through the European Medicines Agency. These specifications concern the qualitative and quantitative composition of these medicines; the tests to be carried out on them; as well as on the raw materials used in production and the intermediates of synthesis. All producers of medicines or substances for pharmaceutical use must apply the quality standards of the European Pharmacopoeia for the marketing and use of these products in Europe (www.edqm.eu).

the relevant expert bodies of each pharmacopoeia.[93] In terms of regional harmonisation, EDQM is responsible for the management of a common sampling and testing programme for centrally authorised products by agreement with the European Medicines Agency (EMA), as well as the European network of Official Medicines Control Laboratories (OMCL) by agreement with the European Commission.

The EDQM also has specific responsibilities with respect to the management of the European Biological Standardisation Programme (BSP). With respect to biologicals, the main aims of the BSP are to establish European reference substances and working standards; to develop standardisation in relation to testing methods for quality control purposes; to set out alternative methods for quality control; and to contribute to international harmonisation in the field. One of the key objectives in promoting the BSP within Europe is to enable both national regulatory agencies and pharmaceutical manufacturers to avoid costly duplication of effort and work, which could in turn lead to disagreement and prevent mutual recognition between countries. In 1991, an agreement was reached between the Council of Europe and what was then the Commission of the European Communities (now European Commission) that the predecessor to, and now the EDQM, would provide logistical and scientific assistance for activities related to the testing of biological medicines, in particular plasma products. Wherever possible, European studies with respect to the BSP are coordinated with those being carried out, or otherwise planned, by the WHO and the FDA.

European Union

One notable exception to the non-legally binding approach to supranational governance of the blood system is to be found at regional (EU) level. The impetus for the adoption of an EU-wide regulatory regime for blood and its components was the political fallout from HIV blood contamination episodes in a number of Member States in the late 1980s and 1990s.[94] The legal basis for regulation in the area is to be found in Article 168(4)(a) TFEU and the parameters of the regulatory

[93] Council of Europe, European Directorate for the Quality of Medicines and HealthCare, Pharmacopoeial Discussion Group. International Harmonisation: Statement of Harmonisation Policy (2003); Council of Europe, European Directorate for the Quality of Medicines and HealthCare, Working Procedures of the Pharmacopoeial Discussion Group (PDG), Revised Version (June 2010) (www.edqm.eu).

[94] A. M. Farrell, 'The emergence of EU governance in public health: the case of blood policy and regulation', in M. Steffen (ed.), Health Governance in Europe (London: Routledge, 2005), pp. 134–51 at 135.

framework are set out in legislation known as the Blood Directive.[95] The Blood Directive was adopted at EU level in 2003 and was required to be transposed into national law by Member States by 2005. The Blood Directive sets minimum standards for quality and safety in relation to the use of blood and blood components. Although problems have been experienced in relation to various aspects of its implementation,[96] it represents the first and only example of legally binding supranational risk regulation in the field.[97]

Companies engaged in the manufacture of plasma products which circulate within the EU are required to comply with the quality and safety standards set out in the Blood Directive in relation to the source material used in their products. In addition, they need to ensure compliance with standards and requirements set out in a range of other EU legislation dealing with 'medicinal products derived from human blood or plasma'.[98] In order to understand the totality of EU governance in the field, therefore, it is important to take account of separate policy-making and regulatory processes involving plasma products, which are largely overseen by the European Medicines Agency (EMA). The precursor to the EMA was established in the mid 1990s to facilitate an integrated approach to the licensing and marketing of pharmaceutical products within the EU.[99] Within the EMA, the Committee for Medicinal Products for Human Use (CHMP) is responsible for preparing opinions on all questions concerning the use of such products within its legal remit.[100] The CHMP's work covers risk governance issues that may arise in the case of plasma products. In terms of managing risk issues that may arise in relation to medicines for human use such as plasma products, the CHMP is generally empowered to engage in pharmacovigilance activities; issue 'urgent safety restriction' notices to healthcare professionals in the event of an emergent risk; and

[95] Directive 2002/98/EC of the European Parliament and of the Council of 27 January 2003 setting standards of quality and safety for the collection, testing, processing, storage and distribution of human blood and blood components and amending Directive 2001/83/EC, OJ L 33/30, 8.2.2003.

[96] E. A. E. Robinson, 'The European Union Blood Safety Directive and its implications for blood services', *Vox Sanguinis*, 93 (2007), 122–30 at 129; Farrell, 'The politics of risk', p. 51.

[97] Farrell, 'Is the gift still good?', p. 178.

[98] *Ibid.*, p. 174.

[99] The precursor to the EMA was the European Agency for the evaluation of Medicinal Products (EMEA). D. Vogel, 'The globalization of pharmaceutical regulation', *Governance: An International Journal of Policy and Administration*, 11 (1998), 1–22 at 7.

[100] Regulation (EC) No. 726/2004 of the European Parliament and of the Council of 31 March 2004 laying down Community procedures for the authorisation and supervision of medicinal products for human and veterinary use and establishing a European Medicines Agency, OJ L 136, 30.4.2004.

to cooperate with other regulators such as the FDA and other supra-national bodies (of which previous mention has been made) with regard to the harmonisation of requirements for the manufacture and supply of plasma products.[101] A detailed examination of EU risk regulation of blood and plasma products is provided in Chapter 8.

Key stakeholders

There are a range of stakeholder groups which play an influential role in the governance of the blood system, including companies that manu-facture plasma products; transfusionists involved in national blood ser-vices; and representative groups for donors and recipients. The role played by transfusionists in policy and regulatory processes in the field is discussed further in Chapters 3 and 4. Key organisations rep-resenting their interests include the AABB and the ARC in the USA, the European Blood Alliance (EBA) in Europe and the International Society of Blood Transfusion (ISBT) at global level. In relation to the plasma products industry, there are two main representative organisa-tions: the Plasma Protein Therapeutics Association (PPTA) and the International Plasma Fractionation Association (IPFA). Although the PPTA's head office is in the USA, it also maintains regional offices in Europe and Japan. It represents manufacturers engaged in for-profit activities involving the manufacture and supply of plasma products and recombinant therapies,[102] as well as plasma source collectors.[103] In 2008 alone, PPTA plasma source collectors collected over 20 million plasma donations through 408 licensed and industry-certified centres in the USA, Canada and Europe.[104] Although a niche industry, PPTA mem-bers maintain strong corporate and institutional links with the wider global pharmaceutical industry, thus contributing to its financial and political influence. The use of the term 'plasma protein' reflects the fact that the industry is engaged in the collection and use of a range of plasma proteins contained in blood. These proteins are subsequently used in the manufacture of products designed to treat a range of 'orphan diseases', including primary immunodeficiency, haemophilia and other

[101] For further details, see European Medicines Agency, Committee for Medicinal Products for Human Use (CHMP) (www.ema.europa.eu).
[102] Recombinant therapies are derived from genetically adapted cell cultures, where an original cell is modified or reprogrammed to produce specific proteins. These proteins are then harvested for use in a range of therapies, in particular for those with bleeding disorders such as haemophilia. For further details, see Plasma Protein Therapeutics Association (PPTA) (www.pptaglobal.org).
[103] Plasma Protein Therapeutics Association (PPTA), *The Facts about Plasma Collection* (www.pptaglobal.org).
[104] *Ibid.*

bleeding disorders. This is in addition to the manufacture and supply of other well-known plasma products, such as immunoglobulin and albumin.[105] The role and influence of the for-profit plasma products industry are examined in detail in Chapter 5.

As previously mentioned, the other organisation with interests in plasma products manufacture is the IPFA, which represents the interests of not-for-profit manufacturers of plasma products. Originally more narrowly focused to represent such manufacturers in Europe, its membership now covers non-European manufacturers as well. Not-for-profit manufacturers tend to be linked to national blood services and may receive some form of state (financial) support. The work of the IPFA is closely linked to that of the EBA, particularly in relation to representation in blood policy and regulatory processes at European level. The IPFA distinguishes its activities from that of the PPTA on both philosophical and industry model grounds. IPFA members are committed to sourcing their products through VNRBD and engaging for the most part in the manufacture and supply of plasma products on a not-for-profit basis. IPFA also promotes the importance of diversity in the sourcing and manufacture of such products, given the small integrated network of companies involved in the for-profit industry.[106]

Another important group of stakeholders are donor organisations. They tend to be nationally based, although the International Federation of Blood Donor Organizations (IFBDO/FIODS) represents their interests at supranational level. Donor organisations are particularly strong and influential in Europe, although such organisations exist in various Asian, African and Latin American countries as well. The IFBDO is firmly committed to promoting VNRBD and the not-for-profit manufacture of plasma products. It aims to facilitate the development of national donor organisations, as well as to promote information exchange between them. It represents the interests of donors in various international organisations, such as the Council of Europe, the EU and WHO, with the aim of providing a counterbalancing perspective on blood sourcing and supply issues to that of other stakeholders in the blood system, such as blood services and the plasma products industry.[107]

---

[105] Plasma Protein Therapeutics Association (PPTA), *The Facts about Plasma Used to Produce Life-Saving Therapies* (www.pptaglobal.org).

[106] International Plasma Fractionation Association (IPFA), *IPFA Position Statement: Towards a Safe, Secure and Sufficient National Supply of Plasma Products*. Executive Summary, EB-2009–06, July 2009.

[107] The International Federation of Blood Donor Organizations (FIODS) (www.fiods.org).

Another representative organisation with global reach that also supports and promotes VNRBD and the not-for-profit manufacture of plasma products is the International Federation of Red Cross and Red Crescent Societies (IFRC) (formerly known as the League of Red Crescent Societies). As mentioned previously, the involvement of the Red Cross in blood sourcing and supply has its historical origins in the early role it played in this regard during World War Two. Following the war, the Red Cross continued this role in certain countries at the behest of national governments. The Federation's secretariat is based in Geneva and it has long maintained strong links with the WHO regarding blood quality and safety issues, as well as with the IFBDO and other organisations that support VNRBD.[108] The Federation has a broader remit than just dealing with the governance of the blood system, however, providing support in relation to the Red Cross's involvement in humanitarian work and response to large-scale emergencies on a global basis.

There are also a range of patient-recipient groups which have had, or continue to have, some degree of influence in governance processes involving the blood system. Representative groups have been formed on an ad hoc basis to represent the interests of patient-recipients in cases where they have suffered harm through blood contamination episodes (such as those involving HIV and hepatitis C virus (HCV)). They do not have the profile and continuity, however, of the more established user groups of plasma products with orphan or rare diseases. In governance terms, there has been a significant increase in the number of these types of representative groups at regional and global level in recent years. These include national organisations dealing with primary immune deficiencies, as well as their international representative body, the International Patient Organisation for Primary Immunodeficiencies (IPOPI).[109] There are also more long-standing groups representing people with haemophilia (PWH) which operate at national level and regional levels (European Haemophilia Consortium – EHC),[110] as well as at global level (World Federation of Hemophilia – WFH).[111] More recently, there has been a move towards establishing representative platforms to advocate for the interests of

---

[108] International Federation of Red Cross and Red Crescent Societies (IFRC) (www.ifrc.org).
[109] International Patient Organisation for Primary Immunodeficiencies (IPOPI) (www.ipopi.org).
[110] European Haemophilia Consortium (EHC) (www.ehc.eu).
[111] World Federation of Hemophilia (WFH) (www.wfh.org).

users of plasma products more generally.[112] A detailed examination of the role of national PWH groups in mounting political campaigns to seek redress for the harm caused to their members as a result of HIV blood contamination episodes that occurred in the USA, England and France is provided in Chapter 6.

Conclusion

This chapter examined key developments that have shaped current governance arrangements involving the blood system; core guiding principles in national and supranational blood policy; and the role and influence of leading institutions and stakeholder groups in the field. This examination revealed that the governance of the blood system has evolved from particular national historical and socio-cultural contexts, institutional preferences, as well as national and supranational regulatory regimes. It was also shown that policy and regulatory processes in the field have been strongly influenced by a number of key issues including the merits or otherwise of sourcing blood through VNRBD or paid donation; whether blood should be collected in a for-profit or not-for-profit environment; and the need to achieve national self-sufficiency in relation to both blood and plasma products.

While the use of legally binding regulatory regimes to enhance blood quality and safety has become more prominent at national level in recent years in the wake of the political fallout from national HIV blood contamination episodes, the use of informal or soft governance mechanisms such as guidelines, standards and recommendations features more prominently at supranational level, with the exception of the regulatory regime that has been adopted at EU level. This reflects the limits of legal competence, as well as the emphasis placed by influential global institutions such as the WHO and the Council of Europe, on technical harmonisation with a view to addressing access, market and safety concerns, particularly in relation to plasma products. Such an institutional emphasis derives in large part from the historical embedding of governance processes involving plasma products within the broader regime for pharmaceuticals at supranational level. This has resulted in the creation of two sub-systems of governance: one which

---

[112] Key representative groups include the Plasma Users Coalition and the American Plasma Users Coalition. For an example of their recent activity in the field, see B. O'Mahony and A. Turner, 'The Dublin Consensus Statement 2011 on vital issues relating to the collection and provision of blood components and plasma-derived medicinal products', *Vox Sanguinis* 102 (2012), 140–3.

deals with blood and its components sourced and supplied by national blood services on the one hand; and one which deals with plasma products involving and manufactured and supplied by the plasma products industry on the other hand.

There are a number of problems with the current approach to the governance of the blood system. First, it contributes to the perpetuation of an exclusionary approach between the social and the economic, as exemplified in the dichotomous framing of blood as either gift or commodity. What is needed instead is the adoption of a more holistic approach to governance processes at both national and supranational levels which focuses on the need to achieve optimum patient-recipient safety, in addition to taking account of both the social and economic aspects involved in blood sourcing and supply. Second, the politicisation of risk that occurred in the wake of national HIV blood contamination episodes now makes it imperative that governance processes involving blood safety are subject to regular monitoring by democratically accountable institutions and mechanisms. If this is not possible at supranational level, then arrangements need to be made for this to take place on a periodic basis at national level.

3   Revisiting the gift relationship

The gift relationship has been characterised as the altruistic donation of blood to an anonymous patient-recipient without expectation of financial reward. This method of sourcing the blood supply was given public and political prominence in the early 1970s following publication of Titmuss's seminal work in the field, *The Gift Relationship*. For those involved in the governance of the blood system, it is now more formally known as voluntary non-remunerated blood donation (VNRBD) and has become a core principle underpinning the collection and supply of whole blood and blood components in developed countries.[1] The aim of this chapter is to revisit Titmuss's key arguments in favour of the gift relationship in blood donation with a view to examining its impact on the development of national and supranational blood policy, as well as to critically examine its continuing relevance to the governance of the blood system in the twenty-first century.

Given that the overarching theme of the book is to examine risk governance involving human biological materials, such as blood, this chapter examines the arguments Titmuss put forward to support the gift relationship in blood donation on safety grounds and how this came to frame the assessment and management of the risk posed by HIV to national blood systems in countries such as France, England and the USA in the 1980s. The consequences of relying on the gift relationship as a key frame of reference for risk governance in these circumstances are also critically analysed. What such examination reveals is that the gift relationship in blood donation provides an inadequate

---

[1] For a definition of VNRBD, see fn. 45, Chapter 1. For the purposes of this chapter, I use the term 'gift relationship' to refer to the ethico-social commitment to altruistic, unpaid blood donation as espoused by Titmuss. I use the term 'VNRBD' in the context of stakeholder debates about the merits of paid over unpaid blood donation and risk governance involving the blood system, which is examined in the latter half of the chapter. VNRBD is used to cover terms that have been used elsewhere in the relevant academic and policy literature, such as 'voluntary, unpaid donors'; 'unpaid donors'; 'volunteer donors' and 'voluntary donors'.

frame of reference on its own for assessing and managing risk. In the circumstances, it is argued the ethico-social commitment to the gift relationship in national and supranational blood policy should be used primarily as a legitimising device in ethico-political terms, rather being linked to blood safety.

Given the multi-valuing of blood that has occurred in the wake of techno-scientific developments, what is now required is flexibility in risk governance that draws on a range of factors to facilitate patient-recipient safety, rather than any rigidity in approach brought about by a priori ethical, scientific or professional commitments to the gift relationship. In order to examine these arguments in detail, this chapter provides a brief overview of the key arguments put forward by Titmuss to support the gift relationship in blood donation, with a particular focus on those offered on safety grounds. Thereafter, the arguments Titmuss made regarding the gift relationship and the link to blood safety are re-examined in the light of the circumstances that led to HIV blood contamination episodes in the USA, England and France in the 1980s. The final section of the chapter critically analyses the continuing relevance of the gift relationship in risk governance involving the blood system in the wake of such episodes.

The gift relationship in blood donation

The Gift Relationship was first published in 1970, following several years of data collection and research on blood donation and transfusion by Richard Titmuss. Although he published data from a range of countries, much of his arguments drew on a comparative analysis of the blood systems operating in England/Wales and the USA. His interest in the field derived in part from a perceived need to respond to the growing prominence of conservative economic policies in England. This was exemplified in the work undertaken by the Institute for Economic Affairs, which had been advocating the establishment of a market-based blood system.[2] In addition, it enabled him to expand more fully on what has been described as his overarching moral philosophy: namely that a 'competitive, materialistic society based on hierarchies of power and privilege ignores at its peril the life-giving impulse towards altruism which is needed for welfare in the most fundamental sense'.[3]

[2] M. H. Cooper and A. J. Culyer, *The Price of Blood* (London: Institute of Economic Affairs, 1968).
[3] A. Oakley and J. Ashton, 'Introduction to the new edition', in A. Oakley and J. Ashton (eds.), R. M. Titmuss, *The Gift Relationship: From Human Blood to Social Policy* (London: LSE Books, 1997), pp. 3–13 at 7.

Ethics and the gift relationship[4]

Titmuss decided to examine the dynamics of blood donation and supply on the grounds that it provided one of the most basic indicators of social values and human relationships,[5] in addition to exemplifying where the social began and the economic ended. If human blood was to be treated either in practice or in law as a tradable commodity, then he argued that it was likely to lead to a slippery slope whereby human hearts, kidneys, eyes and other organs of the body would be treated as commodities to be bought and sold in the marketplace.[6] He went on to suggest that the burden of trading human body parts or substances as commodities would fall disproportionately upon the most socially and economically disadvantaged individuals in society and would therefore be exploitative in practice.[7]

Titmuss conceptualised the gift relationship as the anonymous altruistic donation of blood without financial reward by one person to another in need of blood for the treatment of an injury or other medical condition.[8] Those involved in blood donation expressed such an act in moral terms, structured by social relations in a community context.[9] In such circumstances, engaging in blood donation was a moral act that went beyond the economic: there was a moral choice at stake that could not be solved through technological means, nor be removed from its social context.[10]

In drawing on the notion of gift-giving, Titmuss was influenced by the work of scholars such as Mauss who had earlier examined the importance of reciprocity in social relations through gift-giving in pre-industrial societies. For Mauss, reciprocity as provided in gift exchange provided the basis for building and maintaining social relations in such societies.[11] Titmuss identified the importance of gift-giving for the promotion of social relations, but suggested that the voluntary, altruistic donation of blood without any expectation of reciprocity could be described as gift-giving in its 'purest form'.[12] He argued that the gift

---

[4] As stated in the introductory chapter, it is outside the scope of the book to engage in a detailed examination of the merits (or otherwise) of ethical argumentation that has been offered in relation to the gift relationship. For a detailed examination in this regard, see references set out in fns. 23 and 41, Chapter 1.

[5] Titmuss, *The Gift Relationship*, p. 198.

[6] *Ibid.*, p. 158.   [7] *Ibid.*, p. 201.

[8] *Ibid.*, pp. 210–25.   [9] *Ibid.*, p. 237.   [10] *Ibid.*, pp. 241–3.

[11] Mauss, *The Gift: The Form and Reason for Exchange in Archaic Societies*.

[12] Oakley and Ashton, 'Introduction', p. 8. Mary Douglas pointed out that Mauss would have disagreed with Titmuss's interpretation of gift-giving in the context of blood donation, as it represents a form of non-reciprocal altruism (see M. Douglas 'Foreword: no free gifts', in Mauss, *The Gift: The Form and Reason for Exchange in Archaic Societies*, pp. vii–ix).

relationship emphasised the importance of the social obligations that existed between members of a community. Within such a community, space needed to be made available to ensure that this form of gift-giving was allowed to develop. Allowing financial reward for blood donation would reduce and/or eradicate opportunities for altruism to flourish. This would serve to undermine the social values and bonds of a community and should therefore not be permitted. In effect, he was arguing that there were certain communal activities to which no financial or commodity value should be attached.[13]

Economics and the gift relationship

Titmuss also argued that a blood system sourced through the gift relationship was likely to be much more economically efficient than one that was sourced from paid donors. His argument in this regard was based on empirical research conducted in the mid to late 1960s, drawing primarily on a comparison between the blood system in England and the USA. He characterised the English blood system as being based on the gift relationship, whereas the US system was predominantly based on viewing blood as a tradable commodity, to be bought and sold in the marketplace. He argued that the US system showed a much higher degree of waste; chronic and acute shortages; and significant external costs. It was also administratively inefficient in that it resulted in more bureaucracy and involved higher overheads. According to Titmuss, such wastage and inefficiencies resulted in the cost per unit of blood being five to fifteen times higher in the USA, when compared to England.[14]

Titmuss's arguments that a blood system based on the gift relationship was to be preferred to a market-based approach elicited a strong response from those working in the field of economics. His arguments challenged the established orthodoxy that markets enhance freedom to choose, as well as being the most efficient mechanism for producing and distributing quality goods and services.[15] Although a detailed examination of the academic critique in relation to the arguments put forward by Titmuss on economic grounds is outside the scope of this book,[16] it is useful for present purposes to briefly summarise the

---

[13] Titmuss, *The Gift Relationship*, pp. 198–9.   [14] *Ibid.*, p. 205.
[15] E. J. Emmanuel, 'Is health care a commodity?', *Lancet*, 350 (1997), 1713–14 at 1714.
[16] For a more recent analysis and critique of Titmuss's arguments in this regard, see J. Le Grand, 'Afterword', in A. Oakley and J. Ashton (eds.), R. M. Titmuss, *The Gift Relationship: From Human Blood to Social Policy* (London: LSE Books, 1997), pp. 333–9.

response to Titmuss's arguments by a then leading economist, Kenneth Arrow. He argued that it was wrong to substitute ethics for self-interest. He suggested that the promotion of ethical behaviour as characterised by the gift relationship in blood donation should instead be confined to those very limited circumstances where there is a breakdown in the market system and the price mechanisms associated with it.[17] Much of the academic debate that ensued following the publication of *The Gift Relationship* has focused on the ethical and economic arguments put forward by Titmuss. The arguments he put forward in support of the gift relationship on safety grounds, however, have been subject to much less critical examination and it is this aspect to which I now turn in the next section of the chapter.

Risk and the gift relationship

In *The Gift Relationship*, Titmuss devoted a whole chapter to considering matters of risk involving the transfusion of blood. He acknowledged that the transfusion of blood could potentially be a 'highly dangerous act'.[18] This was particularly with regard to the transmission of diseases, such as hepatitis, syphilis and malaria, which at the time were regarded as the most serious transmissible risks. He argued that the patient was ultimately the 'laboratory for testing the quality of "the gift"' and would therefore be more often than not required to bear the adverse consequences of transmission of such diseases.[19] In the circumstances, he argued for the importance of maintaining high standards in the selection of donors. In particular, knowledge of donors' state of health, health history and social habits were crucial where identification of transmissible diseases was not possible through testing on blood donations. It was for this reason that ensuring the truthfulness of the donor was vital and that trust was maintained between patient-recipients and their doctors, as well as between doctors and donors.[20]

Focusing on the problem of transmission of serum hepatitis through blood transfusion, Titmuss then reviewed published medical and scientific evidence emanating mainly from the USA, which showed that the risk of serum hepatitis from transmission was six to ten times greater where the blood came from paid donors, such as those from Skid Row, prisons and intravenous drug users, when compared to blood donated

---

[17] Arrow, 'Gifts and exchanges'.
[18] Titmuss, *The Gift Relationship*, p. 25.
[19] *Ibid.*, p. 143.   [20] *Ibid.*, pp. 143–4.

by unpaid donors.[21] The problem was compounded where plasma from paid donors was used in large pools to manufacture plasma products.[22] He argued that the evidence showed that time and time again the truthfulness of paid donors was at issue and that they were much more likely to lie about their medical and social history. He went on to suggest that this was likely to be particularly problematic when dealing with 'coloured donors', whose poor level of education and background meant that they would be unable to understand the medical history questions put to them.[23]

The poor level of regulation with respect to the collection and supply of blood, as well as the significant increase in the number of profit-making hospitals, were additional factors that Titmuss identified as having contributed to the growth in the use of paid donors in the USA during this time.[24] He suggested that the only solution to poor quality, high-risk blood was to eliminate the paid donor entirely, against a background where governmental systems of licensing, inspection and quality validation appear 'helpless to control private markets in blood and blood products'.[25] He concluded by suggesting that the commercialisation of blood was discouraging and downgrading the voluntary principle, and that both the sense of community and the expression of altruism were being silenced. The adverse social costs involved in applying the values of the marketplace to human blood included a much greater risk of ill health, disability and death to patient-recipients; it was potentially more dangerous to donors' health; and it was likely to involve much greater shortages of blood in the long run.[26]

Titmuss also acknowledged the importance of the relationship between the donor and patient-recipient in terms of the need to protect the health and welfare of both. He presented a stark contrast between the paid and the unpaid donor in terms of the relative risk posed to the patient-recipient. The patient-recipient was presented as vulnerable, ignorant and reliant on the donor and their treating doctors. They had no alternative but to trust that they would receive safe blood in circumstances

---

[21] *Ibid.*, pp. 146–7. The use of the term 'Skid Row' donors refers to those individuals who lived in conditions of poverty and/or homelessness, who used drugs and engaged in other 'unsanitary practices'. The practice of using prisoners as captive blood donor populations was common in a number of developed countries. It was a practice that did not cease in the USA until the mid 1980s; see Leveton *et al.*, *HIV and the Blood Supply*, p. 30. The practice continued in France up until at least the end of the 1980s (see Geronimi *et al.*, *Les Collectes de sang*). This practice, as well as its impact on rates of HIV contamination of national blood supplies, is discussed in more detail in Chapter 6.

[22] Titmuss, *The Gift Relationship*, p. 149.

[23] *Ibid.*, pp. 151–2.   [24] *Ibid.*, p. 151.

[25] *Ibid.*, p. 154.   [26] *Ibid.*, p. 157.

where they would have to bear the socio-economic and medical burdens brought about by the consequences of receiving contaminated blood.

In this regard, Titmuss suggested that it was the payment mechanism in the context of the operation of a private, unregulated market that accounted for the greatly increased risk of transmissible diseases to patient-recipients. His emphasis on ensuring that the donor was truthful and free from disease through severing the link with payment proved highly influential in national and supranational blood policy. This led to an over-reliance being placed by those in charge of national blood services on the gift relationship as the key to facilitating blood safety. Titmuss's analysis of the role played by the payment mechanism in managing risk would be seriously challenged as a result of the circumstances that led to HIV blood contamination episodes in various developed countries in the 1980s, where both paid *and* unpaid donors were implicated as sources of transmission of the virus.

Because of Titmuss's focus on the payment mechanism as the main source of the risk of transmissible disease, he omitted to examine in detail other relevant issues such as the importance of understanding the epidemiology of donor populations, or the problems created by the fragmented and dysfunctional approach to regulating both blood institutions and blood safety generally during this time in the USA. Although the Nixon administration moved relatively quickly towards reforming national blood regulation and administration in the early to mid 1970s,[27] the absence of a more unified, national approach to the blood system in the years preceding these reforms had enabled a range of organisations and individuals to engage in practices such as the systematic recruitment of high-risk donors, and this clearly had an adverse impact on blood safety.[28] To argue, as Titmuss did, that the US government was 'helpless' in the face of the development of such practices, however, should perhaps be viewed as a rhetorical flourish and no more. Prior to the Nixon administration, there was simply a lack of political will to bring about the necessary institutional and regulatory reforms at national level that would have led to the development of a safer blood system.

A number of commentators have taken issue with Titmuss's specific arguments regarding the link between the gift relationship and blood safety, as well as what they saw as his misrepresentation of the US blood system. They argued that the collection and supply of blood in the USA was not dominated by commercial arrangements, underpinned by paid

[27] Starr, *Blood*, pp. 250–7.
[28] See Chapter 2; Titmuss describes such practices in detail in Chapters 6, 8 and 9 of *The Gift Relationship*.

donors. On the contrary, there was in fact strong and consistent support for the gift relationship, particularly in the context of whole blood donation.[29] They also considered that Titmuss had glossed over the complex inter-relationship of politics, science and institutional dysfunction that had contributed to the firm association being made between hepatitis, blood transfusion and the paid donor in the post-war period in the USA, against a background of diverse arrangements with respect to the collection and supply of blood.[30] The political dimension to the debate over the merits (or otherwise) of unpaid over paid donation in the 1960s and 1970s had also served to drown out calls for a more detailed examination of what constituted high-risk donors in the USA.[31]

Blood: gift or commodity?

The merits (or otherwise) of VNRBD, as opposed to paid blood donation, had long been a matter of debate for those involved in the collection and supply of blood, one which preceded the publication of *The Gift Relationship*. While it became fairly settled in the pre-World War Two period in countries such as England that unpaid donors would be used,[32] a mixture of both sourcing methods was used during World War Two and in the immediate post-war period in other countries. In France, for example, it would take until the 1950s before it was enshrined in law that VNRBD was to be the preferred method of sourcing the national blood supply.[33] In the case of both England and France, VNRBD had become inextricably linked to the war effort, representing an affirmation of all that was good about bonds and obligations of citizenship, whilst at the same time having its historical roots in nineteenth-century thinking about the relationship between blood, race and nationhood.[34] While such associations were also made during the same period in the USA, the absence of a unified national approach to the organisation and regulation of blood collection and supply had allowed a proliferation of

---

[29] Sapolsky and Finkelstein, 'Blood policy revisited'; Drake *et al.*, *The American Blood Supply*; Bayer, 'Blood and AIDS in America', p. 20.

[30] Domen, 'Paid-versus-volunteer blood donation in the United States', p. 57.

[31] D. B. Johnson (ed.), *Blood Policy: Issues and Alternatives*. Proceedings of a Conference sponsored by the Center for Health Policy Research of the American Enterprise Institute for Public Policy Research (Washington, DC: American Enterprise Institute, 1977), referred to in Domen, 'Paid-versus-volunteer blood donation in the United States', p. 57; Sapolsky and Finkelstein, 'Blood policy revisited', p. 18.

[32] Starr, *Blood*, pp. 53–7.

[33] Casteret, *L'Affaire du sang contaminé*, p. 20; M.-A. Hermitte, *Le sang et le droit* (Paris: Éditions du Seuil, 1996), p. 129.

[34] P. Rabinow, *French DNA – Trouble in Purgatory* (Chicago University Press, 1999), p. 84; Waldby and Mitchell, *Tissue Economies*, p. 4.

both commercial and non-commercial arrangements to develop in relation to the collection of whole blood, as well as in the industrial manufacture of plasma products.[35]

What Titmuss did in *The Gift Relationship*, however, was to mount a
forceful set of arguments in favour of promoting the gift relationship
in blood donation on ethical, economic and safety grounds. The political and scientific prominence given to such arguments, particularly
in the USA, only served to further polarise academic, policy and stakeholder views regarding whether human biological materials, such as
blood, should be viewed as a gift or a commodity. While there has been
much debate within the relevant academic literature on this issue,[36] its
implications for risk governance involving the blood system have been
much less examined.[37] It is this relationship that I now wish to examine
further in this chapter, with a particular focus on how the parameters
of the 'gift versus commodity' debate were interpreted and applied by
those who had responsibility for the collection and supply of blood and
plasma products.

The main protagonists in this debate were, and indeed continue to
be, transfusionists who work within national blood services and not-
for-profit manufacturers of plasma products on the one hand; and
those involved in for-profit source plasma collection, as well as the
plasma products industry, on the other hand. Transfusionists' support
for VNRBD has been longstanding and Titmuss's arguments in favour
of this sourcing method simply provided further support for what had
become one of their core professional beliefs. In the 1970s, their commitment to VNRBD had been further strengthened in the wake of
revelations concerning the plasma collection practices that had been
undertaken by the (largely) US-based plasma products industry, which
had resulted in unregulated black markets for the buying and selling
of plasma. This was in addition to transfusionists' concerns about the
exploitation of socio-economically disadvantaged and 'captive' plasma
donor populations both within the USA and in a number of developing countries. Although the for profit industry had by and large closed

---

[35] Titmuss, *The Gift Relationship*, Chapters 4, 8 and 9.

[36] It is outside the scope of this book to explore the extensive multi-disciplinary literature which examines the arguments regarding whether blood and/or other human
biological materials should be viewed as a gift or a commodity. A useful definition of
commodification has been provided by Radin, which is adopted for the purposes of
this book: it describes a particular social construction of things people value. With
this in mind, commodification should be viewed as the social process by which some-
thing comes to be apprehended as a commodity, as well as to the state of affairs once
this process has taken place; see Radin, *Contested Commodities*, p. xi.

[37] Cf. Farrell, 'Is the gift still good?'

down its operations in developing countries by the end of the 1970s in the wake of international condemnation of its plasma collection practices,[38] the association between paid donation, donor exploitation and high-risk blood had now been firmly established within the minds of transfusionists.[39]

By the 1980s, the link between VNRBD and blood safety had also become firmly entrenched within the transfusionists' professional belief system, in addition to supporting Titmuss's arguments in favour of this method of donation on both ethical and economic grounds. They also considered that it encouraged long-term loyalty on the part of donors, which led to repeated donations over time.[40] This enabled regular tests to be conducted on donors, as well as their blood, and ensured continuity in supply. Notwithstanding any claims to alleged improvements in the evaluation and testing of paid donors by the for-profit industry, transfusionists argued that it remained the case that it was much more likely that new transmissible diseases would appear first, and in much greater numbers, in this donor population.[41] Transfusionists also remained committed to the realisation of the 'aspirational' goal of (global) sufficiency of blood and plasma products through VNRBD, primarily on the grounds of enhanced quality and safety.[42] However, it was not exactly clear how and when such a goal would be deemed to have been achieved in the light of changing clinical needs; innovation in blood-related technology; and longstanding reliance on the for-profit industry to meet consumer demand for plasma products.[43]

---

[38] Starr, *Blood*, p. 247; see also World Health Organization, Twenty-Eighth World Health Assembly, Resolution 28.72 adopted in 1975.

[39] Farrell, 'Is the gift still good?', p. 161.

[40] A recently published study revealed that plasmapheresis donors in a VNRBD environment valued the increased frequency of donation because it established routine; fostered the relationship between blood services staff and donors; and provided a regular source of self-esteem for donors given the perceived preferential treatment received from such staff. See L. L. Bove, T. Bednall, B. Masser *et al.*, 'Understanding the plasmapheresis donor in a voluntary, nonremunerated environment', *Transfusion* 51 (2011), 2411–24.

[41] R. Beal and W. van Aken, 'Gift or good? A contemporary examination of the voluntary and commercial aspects of blood donation', *Vox Sanguinis*, 63 (1992), 1–5.

[42] P. Flanagan, 'ISBT Board response to the Dublin consensus statement', *Vox Sanguinis*, 100 (2011), 250–1 at 250.

[43] The for-profit plasma products industry estimates that '80 percent of the current global requirements for high quality plasma derivatives are covered by source plasma. The requirements, however, are defined by the population in the developed world that accounts for 20 percent of the world population, leaving 80 percent of the population (in transitional and developing countries) to be covered by only 20 percent of plasma for fractionation from recovered plasma'; see S. Beck, 'Blood centers and plasma centers: mutual benefit', *The Source* (Summer 2011), 12–15 at 13.

As a result of scientific developments and innovation in technology from the 1960s onwards, as well as the fact that payment for plasma donation had always been permitted in the USA,[44] it became possible to engage in the industrial manufacture of plasma products, leading to the creation of a global market for such products.[45] As demand for such products grew, national blood services in many developed countries found it difficult to meet such demand through the use of local donors.[46] In Europe, for example, several countries took the decision to import US-sourced plasma products in order to address the growing gap between demand and supply. By the 1990s, it was estimated that plasma products sourced through paid donors accounted for well over 50 per cent of the European market.[47] This was the case despite the commitment to promoting VNRBD in both national and European blood policy.[48] The rationale for this apparent contradiction lay in the fact that this was viewed by those in charge of national blood services, civil servants and political leaders as being a short-term solution, pending the realisation of self-sufficiency in blood and plasma products. This was to be achieved through an increase in government financial investment, the implementation of strategies to increase the number of donors and the establishment of not-for-profit facilities for the industrial manufacture of plasma products.[49] Reality proved to be somewhat different, however, with the importation of US-sourced plasma products instead becoming the long-term solution to the growing gap between supply and demand in the European context.

For those in favour of the use of paid donors to address this growing gap, the apparent contradiction between the ethical commitment to the gift relationship and the day-to-day reality of reliance on the importation of plasma products sourced from paid donors represented 'hypocrisy' of the worst sort. In such circumstances, it was argued that 'moral misgivings' concerning paid donors were simply 'transferred across national borders' rather than being resolved.[50] It was further argued

---

[44] Leveton et al., HIV and the Blood Supply, p. 30.

[45] Starr, Blood, pp. 240–1, 264–5.

[46] Leveton et al., HIV and the Blood Supply, pp. 170–1.

[47] S. Lewis, 'EC Commission and blood self-sufficiency', Lancet, 342 (1993), 1228.

[48] Commission of the European Communities, Communication on Blood Safety and Self-Sufficiency in the Community, COM (94) 652 final, 21.12.1994. The commitment to promoting the use of VNRBD within the EU remains ongoing; see Commission of the European Communities, Report from the Commission to the Council and the European Parliament on the promotion by Member States of voluntary, unpaid blood donations, COM (2006) 217 final, 17.5.2006.

[49] Farrell, 'Is the gift still good?', p. 163.

[50] P. R. del Pozo, 'Paying donors and the ethics of blood supply', Journal of Medical Ethics, 20 (1994), 31–5.

that there was clearly an urgent and justified consumer demand for plasma products that should be met, where possible. The solution was to avoid recourse to moral absolutes of the type propagated by those who supported the gift relationship and to move instead towards the acceptance of a system that either permitted payment for the collection of plasma within national boundaries, or adopted a mixed national collection system involving the use of VNRBD for the donation of blood and its components and paid donation for source plasma.[51] Contrary to concerns expressed by transfusionists that the adoption of a mixed system would have a deleterious effect on blood donation through VNRBD,[52] it was argued by the industry that the available evidence pointed the other way.[53]

Whatever approach was to be adopted in order to meet growing consumer demand for plasma products, it was recognised that there was a need to implement quality control measures and, if necessary, regulation in order to ensure the highest possible levels of safety for such products.[54] Although it was conceded that there had been evidence of higher rates of transmitted infection in patient-recipients who had used plasma products in the past, the industry argued that it had learned from the problems that had arisen from such contamination episodes.[55] It claimed that stricter donor screening protocols, as well as more sophisticated testing and viral inactivation methods, had now made plasma products sourced from paid donation as safe as those sourced from unpaid donors.[56]

VNRBD and the risk posed by HIV

When HIV emerged as a risk to national blood systems in the 1980s, transfusionists largely relied on VNRBD as the main mechanism for assessing and managing such risk. The framing of risk in this way overrode an epidemiological assessment of high-risk groups in national donor populations and excluded consideration of the separate risk for patient groups such as people with haemophilia (PWH). Many PWH

---

[51] H. von Schubert, 'Donated blood – gift or commodity? Some economic and ethical considerations on voluntary vs commercial donation of blood', *Social Science and Medicine*, 39 (1994), 201–6; del Pozo, 'Paying donors', p. 34.

[52] Flanagan, 'ISBT Board response to the Dublin consensus statement', p. 250.

[53] Beck, 'Blood centers and plasma centers: mutual benefit'.

[54] del Pozo, 'Paying donors', pp. 33–4.

[55] Starr, *Blood*, p. 345; see also Chapter 5.

[56] R. Beal, 'Titmuss revisited', *Transfusion Medicine*, 9 (1999), 352–9 at 355; Farrugia, 'The regulatory pendulum in transfusion medicine', p. 276.

relied on the use of plasma products which had been sourced from US paid donors,[57] a significant number of whom were likely to come within high-risk categories for transmitting the virus through plasma donation.[58] The reasons for persisting with this approach to risk governance involving HIV was largely attributable to VNRBD operating as a core professional belief for transfusionists, which overrode scientific risk assessment criteria based on epidemiological data.[59]

In countries such as France it led to transfusionists holding fast to their professional beliefs in VNRBD and national self-sufficiency in blood and plasma products sourced through this method of donation, as providing the bulwarks against the risk posed by HIV. Although guidelines were issued with a view to screening out blood donors considered to be at high risk of transmitting the virus, such as homosexual men with multiple partners and intravenous drug users, there was a good deal of evidence to suggest that this screening protocol was not appropriately implemented in any consistent way, if at all.[60] Instead, transfusionists continued to collect blood from groups of donors that were likely to carry a higher risk of being infected with the virus on epidemiological grounds. For example, blood donation by prisoners was seen as an important act of social rehabilitation and therefore transfusionists continued to collect blood from this group. This was despite scientific data being available which pointed to them being a high-risk group for transmitting HIV, given widespread intravenous drug use within French prisons.[61] In addition, transfusionists opted to continue with mobile collections on the streets of Paris, in circumstances where the city had come to be known as the 'AIDS capital of Europe'.[62] Once HIV testing became available, France was shown to have one of the most HIV-contaminated blood supplies in the developed world with high levels of infection amongst both its haemophilia population and blood transfusion recipients.[63]

In England, transfusionists were also committed to both VNRBD and national self-sufficiency. During the time when HIV emerged as a risk to the blood supply in the early to mid 1980s, such commitment persisted notwithstanding the fact that a mixed public/private market operated in England with whole blood being sourced through VNRBD

[57] Farrell, 'Is the gift still good?', pp. 163–9.
[58] Leveton et al., HIV and the Blood Supply, p. 104.
[59] See Chapter 4 for a detailed examination of how the core professional beliefs of transfusionists impacted on the assessment and management of the risk posed by HIV to national blood systems.
[60] Casteret, L'Affaire du sang contaminé, pp. 79–86.
[61] Geronimi et al., Les Collectes de sang.
[62] Casteret, L'Affaire du sang contaminé, p. 85.
[63] Farrell, 'Is the gift still good?', pp. 167–8.

and plasma products, such as factor concentrates, being sourced from a mixture of VNRBD and US-based paid donors.[64] Those that were sourced from the latter group of donors accounted for over 50 per cent of the products used by PWH in England during this period.[65] For transfusionists, the ongoing importation of US-sourced products was viewed as a 'temporary aberration from ethical norms and a transient risk to blood safety pending the achievement of self-sufficiency'.[66] Such rationalisation led to a form of 'institutional and political blindness' to the realities of the risk posed by HIV to PWH and, as such, the risk was not effectively addressed by those responsible for blood safety.[67] Once HIV testing became available, a mixed picture emerged. There was evidence of low prevalence of the virus amongst patient-recipients where the blood had been sourced from the local donor population.[68] However, the rate of HIV infection in the national haemophilia population was comparatively high at 34 per cent and this was largely attributable to the use of US-sourced products. For those who used such products regularly, including persons with severe haemophilia, the rate of infection was even higher at 75 per cent.[69]

In the USA, the position with regard to the assessment and management of the risk posed by HIV to the blood system in the early to mid 1980s was complicated not only by the range of organisations involved in the collection and supply of blood and plasma products, but also by the number of government organisations that had some degree of responsibility for providing oversight and management of such risk.[70] Although an initial link was made between the disease and transmission of blood with reports of cases of AIDS in PWH who had used factor concentrates, as well as those that had occurred through blood transfusion,[71] there was a persistent failure over time to adopt a common position with regard to how to manage the risk posed by HIV.[72]

For organisations such as the ARC, the approach taken was to rely to a large extent on VNRBD as the main mechanism for reducing

[64] V. Berridge, *AIDS in the UK: The Making of Policy 1981–1994* (Oxford University Press, 1996), p. 38.
[65] Jones, 'Factor VIII: supply and demand', p. 1532.
[66] Farrell, 'Is the gift still good?', p. 163.
[67] *Ibid.*
[68] R. Cheingsong-Popov, R. Weiss, R. A. Dalgleish *et al.*, 'Prevalence of antibody to human T-lymphotropic virus type III in AIDS and AIDS-risk patients in Britain', *Lancet*, ii (1984), 477–80.
[69] C. R. Rizza, R. J. D. Spooner, P. Giangrande *et al.*, 'Treatment of haemophilia in the UK: 1981–1996', *Haemophilia*, 7 (2001), 349–59.
[70] Leveton *et al.*, *HIV and the Blood Supply*, pp. 34–53.
[71] Shilts, *And the Band Played On*, pp. 165, 206–7.
[72] See Chapter 2.

the risk posed by HIV. The ARC was wary of upsetting or alarming its much valued volunteer donors and it was also concerned about the cost of having to recruit new donors in the event of being forced to adopt stricter AIDS donor screening protocols. Whilst it was prepared to implement donor screening that encouraged self-exclusion by identified high-risk groups, including homosexual men with multiple partners and intravenous drug users, it was not prepared to question donors about whether they engaged in any potential high-risk behaviour.[73] Notwithstanding the implementation of such donor screening, it sought to emphasise to the American public that the risk of transmission of HIV through blood transfusion was remote in any case, quoting a figure of 'one in a million'.[74] Despite growing epidemiological evidence that the risk was much greater than this figure, this remained the ARC's public position of the assessment of the risk posed by HIV for a further two years until testing became available to detect the virus in blood donations.[75] Once such testing did become available, it became apparent that the 'one in a million' claim represented a serious underestimate of the risk and that VNRBD on its own was no guarantor of blood safety.[76] For PWH, who had largely been reliant on factor concentrates sourced from paid donors, the position was dire: approximately 63 per cent of the national haemophilia population had been infected with the virus.[77] For those with severe haemophilia who used the products on a regular basis, the rate was much higher at 96 per cent.[78]

VNRBD and risk governance of the blood system

The fallout from HIV blood contamination episodes in countries such as the USA, England and France revealed the inadequacy of employing VNRBD as the main frame of reference for assessing and managing risks to national blood systems. What the episodes highlighted was the 'contingent' nature of risk governance involving the blood system: while VNRBD may have been one factor to take into account, what mattered most was the extent to which this category of donors overlapped with

---

[73] Leveton et al., HIV and the Blood Supply, p. 71.
[74] Bayer, 'Blood and AIDS in America', p. 26.
[75] Leveton et al., HIV and the Blood Supply, pp. 75–6.
[76] Ibid., p. 21.
[77] Ibid.
[78] B. K. Kroner, P. S. Rosenberg, L. M. Aledort et al., 'HIV-1 infection incidence among persons with hemophilia in the United States and Europe', Journal of Acquired Immune Deficiency Syndromes, 7 (1994), 279–86 at 281.

high-risk donor populations.[79] More importantly, a range of factors needed to be taken into account in order to facilitate effective risk governance in the field, including the following: epidemiological profiling of high-risk donors in local and foreign donor populations; the need for national coordinated management and appropriate government financing of national blood services and the manufacture of plasma products; an assessment of the costs and benefits of achieving national self-sufficiency; and well-targeted risk regulation regimes.[80]

Notwithstanding the findings from national HIV blood contamination episodes, transfusionists' core professional belief in VNRBD has remained largely intact, although it is now emphasised that such donation should be sought from low-risk populations as far as possible.[81] Given transfusionists' ongoing influence in national and supranational blood policy, this has ensured that VNRBD remains the predominant ethical principle underpinning the collection and supply of blood at national level. It also continues to be viewed as a key factor in minimising the risk of TTIs through blood,[82] as well as contributing to the avoidance of exploitation of individuals involved in the provision of blood in developing countries.[83] VNRBD continues to attract significant public support in many developed countries,[84] with local donors remaining committed to its underlying rationale of altruism and helping other members of the community in need.[85] This is despite the fact

---

[79] Healy, *Last Best Gifts*, p. 92.

[80] Farrell, 'Is the gift still good?', pp. 164, 167.

[81] P. Sullivan, 'Developing an administrative plan for transfusion medicine – a global perspective', *Transfusion*, 45 (2005), 224S–40S. In making this point, Sullivan relies upon a study which reviewed 28 published datasets regarding the relative safety of blood donations sourced from either paid or unpaid donors; see van der Poel *et al.*, 'Paying for blood donations: still a risk?'. It should be noted that Sullivan, as well as van der Poel *et al.*, were linked at the time of publication of these articles to national blood services in England (Sullivan), The Netherlands (van der Poel) and Germany (Seifried). For a critique of the methodology and findings of this article, see V. Kretschmer, M. Weippert-Kretschmer, J. Slonka *et al.*, 'Perspectives of paid whole and plasma donation', in G. N. Vyas and A. E. Williams (eds.), *Advances in Transfusion Safety* (Basel: Karger, 2005), pp. 101–11 at 102.

[82] For example, in the Recital to Directive 2002/98/EC (Blood Directive), it is noted at paragraph 23 that 'voluntary and unpaid blood donations are a factor which can contribute to high safety standards for blood and blood components and therefore to the protection of human health'. For a more detailed examination of the EU Blood Directive, see Chapter 8.

[83] See, World Health Organization, *Global Consultation, 100% Voluntary Non-Remunerated Donation of Blood and Blood Components* (Geneva: WHO, 2009).

[84] See, for example, studies conducted within the EU: INRA Europe, *Europeans and Blood, Eurobarometer 41.0* (Brussels: European Commission, 1995); European Opinion Research Group (EEIG), *Le don de sang*.

[85] C. Waldby, M. Rosengarten, C. Treloar *et al.*, 'Blood and bioidentity: ideas about self, boundaries and risk among blood donors and people living with Hepatitis C', *Social*

that some (or indeed much) of the blood they donate feeds into increasing complex networks of collection and supply that operate within and across national boundaries.[86] For national blood services facing ongoing restrictions on blood donation due to new transmissible disease risks, as well as the spectre of blood shortages,[87] the gift relationship as exemplified in VNRBD remains, at the very least, an important framing device at national level to facilitate organised opportunities for giving within a moral order of exchange.[88] This is said to engender an ongoing sense of loyalty on the part of local donor populations, which in turn contributes to sufficiency in supply.

The ongoing professional, institutional and public support for VNRBD has important implications for its level of influence in governance regimes involving the blood system at both national and supranational levels. This high level of support means that those in political leadership, who have ultimate responsibility for such regimes, are unlikely to discard VNRBD as the predominant policy framing for promoting blood donation, at least in the short to medium term. In the context of this framing, exchange based on the moral order of gift-giving is likely to be given more prominence in the political context. This is likely to operate to the detriment of any acknowledgement of the ways in which blood has become commodified through a diverse range of collection and supply arrangements, which have been underpinned by technological innovation and facilitated by market processes. So while it may rightly be suggested that the framing of blood as either gift or commodity offers an inadequate conceptualisation of current processes involving the collection and supply of blood and plasma products,[89] it nevertheless remains a politically attractive option and a publicly supported activity in the context of democratic politics. In institutional environments operating at supranational level that are largely insulated from the vagaries of such politics, there is more scope to accommodate and deal with the diverse and complex arrangements involving such processes. It has enabled the framing of governance initiatives involving the blood system in terms of technical

Science and Medicine, 59 (2004), 1461–71; M. Alessandrini, 'Community volunteerism and blood donation: altruism as a lifestyle choice', *Transfusion Medicine Reviews*, 21 (2007), 307–16; H. Busby, 'Trust, nostalgia and narrative accounts of blood banking in England in the 21st century', *Health*, 14 (2010), 369–82.

[86] Waldby and Mitchell, *Tissue Economies*, p. 22; Healy, *Last Best Gifts*, pp. 20–1.

[87] T. W. Gillespie and C. D. Hillyer, 'Blood donors and factors impacting the blood donation decision', *Transfusion Medicine Reviews*, 16 (2002), 115–30.

[88] Healy, *Last Best Gifts*, p. 17.

[89] Waldby and Mitchell, *Tissue Economies*, p. 9.

harmonisation, thus avoiding to a large extent the ethico-political conflict that has dominated stakeholder, policy and regulatory debates over what should be recognised as the preferred sourcing method for blood and/or plasma donation.

The implications of this approach for managing the political conflict generated by the gift versus commodity debate are problematic, particularly with regard to facilitating effective risk governance involving the blood system. Reliance on VNRBD, as well as on the altruism and truthfulness of donors, clearly proved to be an inadequate approach for managing the risk posed by HIV to national blood systems. The focus on the individual altruist donor as a guarantor of blood safety served to obscure the risks faced by patient-recipients when confronted with the prevalence of transmissible disease in certain local and/or national donor populations, as well as the reality of mixed public–private blood markets that operate both within and across national boundaries. The problem with using VNRBD as a risk assessment tool in this context is that it worked to skew the donor–recipient relationship in favour of a donor-focused approach, which ultimately operated to the detriment of the patient-recipient in the event of a failure to manage risk.

Techno-scientific innovation and the development of interconnected transnational markets in human biological materials, such as blood, means acknowledging in the first instance that blood has ethical, as well as scientific and commercial, value. The value ascribed to it may also differ depending on one's position in the collection and supply chain. This multi-valuing involves a recognition of the inter-relationship between the social and the economic, rather than the privileging of one to the exclusion of the other as envisaged by Titmuss. Multi-valuing of human biological materials, such as blood, contributes to complexity in risk governance which cannot be addressed in terms of the dichotomous framing of blood as either a gift or a commodity. Neither can it be resolved in terms of creating bifurcated institutional and political arrangements for blood and its components on the one hand; and plasma products on the other hand. What needs to be kept in mind is that the same source material with the potential to transmit disease is the starting point in both cases, notwithstanding different processing arrangements.[90]

---

[90] Farrell, 'The politics of risk', pp. 62–3. The problems created by a bifurcated approach to the governance of blood and plasma products in the EU context is examined in detail in Chapter 8.

Conclusion

This chapter examined the arguments put forward by Titmuss in support of the gift relationship in blood donation, with a particular focus on the arguments presented to support the gift relationship on safety grounds. Titmuss argued that promotion of altruism in blood donation made it much more likely that donors would be truthful in disclosing their health status and therefore their donations were much less likely to transmit infections to patient-recipients. Paying individuals for their blood incentivised them to lie about their health status. He argued that those most likely to be attracted to such payment generally tended to come from socio-economically disadvantaged groups that were likely to have a higher rate of transmissible diseases. In support of these arguments, he drew largely on empirical research published in the 1960s about the relative rates of serum hepatitis found in volunteer and paid donor populations in the USA. Titmuss's arguments in this regard were challenged on the grounds that most of the blood collected in the USA was in fact through VNRBD; that the dysfunction he identified in relation to the governance of the US blood system reflected a lack of centralised institutional coordination and regulatory oversight, rather than a failure to promote the gift relationship in blood donation; and that blood safety depended not on the altruism and truthfulness of donors, but rather on the collection of blood from low-risk donor populations.

HIV blood contamination episodes in countries such as the USA, England and France revealed that while VNRBD may be supported on the grounds that it represents an ethically principled approach to blood donation, it was an inadequate frame of reference on its own for assessing and managing risks involving the blood system. The extent to which it facilitated blood safety turned on the extent to which blood collected through VNRBD was sourced from low-risk donor populations. It became clear that this method of donation should be considered as only one amongst a range of socio-cultural, epidemiological, scientific, economic and supply factors that should be taken into account with regard to facilitating effective risk governance of the blood system.

Public, professional and political support for the maintenance of VNRBD remains high. It is therefore likely to remain as a predominant policy frame, underpinning blood collection and supply, as well as blood policy and regulation at national and supranational levels, for the foreseeable future. While this may not be problematic on ethical grounds, the potential for it to continue to influence risk governance makes it so. For risk governance to be effective, it is important to acknowledge the multi-valuing of blood across ethical, social, economic and technological

domains. This multi-valuing contributes to complexity in risk governance which cannot be addressed either in terms of a dichotomous framing of blood as either a gift or a commodity, or by privileging social
relations embodied in gift-giving to the exclusion of market processes
involving the collection and supply of blood and plasma products. As was
made clear in HIV blood contamination episodes, the value ascribed to
safety must be given the greatest priority given the adverse consequences
resulting from a failure in risk governance for patient-recipients of blood
and plasma products. Governance involving the blood system needs to
take account of this multi-valuing process, as well as being centralised,
integrated and subject to democratically accountable institutions and
mechanisms at both national and supranational levels, regardless of
whether blood or plasma products are involved.

4   Professional beliefs and scientific expertise

In the previous chapter, the parameters of the longstanding academic and stakeholder debate on whether blood should be viewed as a gift or a commodity were examined. It highlighted the influential role played by transfusionists in promoting their core professional beliefs in the gift relationship and the goal of national self-sufficiency as dominant policy frames in both national and supranational governance processes involving the blood system. This chapter examines how and why this took place, in addition to exploring its impact on the way in which transfusionists assessed and managed the risk posed by HIV to national blood systems in the 1980s. This is undertaken with a broader aim in mind: namely, to analyse the relationship between scientific expertise and risk governance. Within the relevant academic literature, it has been argued that the process of constructing scientific expertise involves the development of 'paradigms' within a given scientific field over time.[1] This leads to the development of a commitment to various traditions, beliefs and techniques shared by members of a given scientific community,[2] as well as the 'blackboxing' of key ideas and concepts. While this 'blackboxing' is pursued in an attempt to bring clarity and certainty, it nevertheless obscures the messiness, incoherence and choice of preferences that may have structured such development in practice.[3]

---

[1] For an examination of the processes involved in the social construction of expertise, see B. Wynne, 'Risk and social learning: reification to engagement', in S. Krimsky and D. Golding (eds.), *Social Theories of Risk* (Westport, CT: Praeger Publishers, 1992), pp. 275–300 at 281–2; S. Jasanoff, 'Judgment under siege: the three-body problem of expert legitimacy', in S. Maasen and P. Weingart (eds.), *Democratization of Expertise? Exploring Novel Forms of Scientific Advice in Political Decision-Making – Sociology of the Sciences*, 24 (2005), 209–24 at 221; S. Maasen and P. Weingart, 'What's new in scientific advice to politics?', in S. Maasen and P. Weingart (eds.), *Democratization of Expertise? Exploring Novel Forms of Scientific Advice in Political Decision-Making – Sociology of the Sciences*, 24 (2005), 1–19 at 3.

[2] T. S. Kuhn, *The Structure of Scientific Revolutions*, 3rd edn (University of Chicago Press, 1998), pp. 11, 175.

[3] B. Latour, *Science in Action: How to Follow Scientists and Engineers through Society* (Cambridge, MA: Harvard University Press, 1987), pp. 2–7.

In seeking to carve out their expertise and promote their authority, those who claim expertise in a given scientific field also engage in 'boundary-work'. This involves promotion through demarcation of the work they do from what are deemed to be the non-scientific activities of others,[4] as well as those from other scientific disciplines where there is a cross-over in research interests or claims to authority.[5] This may be seen as an ideological endeavour aimed at defending professional autonomy, as well as increasing experts' perceived authority within specific domains of knowledge.[6] What this fails to acknowledge, however, is that expert knowledge may be either mediated by interaction with lay knowledge,[7] or that a range of personal, social or ethical values may inform both the construction of specific forms of expert knowledge and their assessment of risk.[8]

The core professional beliefs of transfusionists fitted within the key scientific paradigm that structured the emergence of the specialty of transfusion medicine, drawing on a mixture of ethical and social values, as well as scientific data. Such paradigm emerged following important scientific discoveries, such as ABO blood groups, in the early part of the twentieth century.[9] Over time, this contributed to medical and public acceptance of blood transfusion as beneficial, with blood being viewed as a valued resource: safe, available and essential for many aspects of modern medicine.[10] As transfusion medicine emerged as an independent specialty, the link between VNRBD and blood safety became black-boxed: raised to the level of a core professional belief and resistant to change.[11] It also served to create boundary lines with other (scientific)

---

[4] T. Gieryn, 'Boundary-work and the demarcation of science from non-science: strains and interests in professional ideologies of scientists', *American Sociological Review*, 48 (1983), 781–95 at 782.

[5] T. Pinch, 'The sun-set: the presentation of certainty in scientific life', *Social Studies of Science*, 11 (1981), 131–58 at 142–5.

[6] Gieryn, 'Boundary-work'.

[7] S. O. Funtowicz and J. R. Ravetz, 'Risk management as a postnormal science', *Risk Analysis*, 12 (1992), 95–7. B. Wynne, 'May the sheep safely graze? A reflexive view of the expert-lay knowledge divide', in S. Lash, B. Szerszynski and B. Wynne (eds.), *Risk, Environment and Modernity: Towards a New Ecology* (London: Sage, 1996), pp. 44–83.

[8] H. Otway and D. Winterfeldt, 'Expert judgment in risk analysis and management: process, context and pitfalls', *Risk Analysis*, 12 (1992), 83–93; P. Kitcher, *Science, Truth and Democracy* (Oxford University Press, 2001); H. Kincaid, J. Dupré and A. Wylie, *Value-Free Science?: Ideas and Illusions* (Oxford University Press, 2007); H. Douglas, *Science, Policy and the Value-Free Ideal* (University of Pittsburgh Press, 2009).

[9] M. A. Blajchman and H. G. Klein, 'Looking back in anger: retrospection in the face of a paradigm shift', *Transfusion Medicine Reviews*, 11(1) (1997), 1–5 at 3.

[10] *Ibid.*, p. 4.

[11] That groups of (scientific) experts can espouse values or hold beliefs that are resistant to change is a phenomenon that has been observed by a range of scholars (see

experts involved in the blood system, as well as with patient groups (lay experts), such as PWH, who were concerned to ensure both safety and availability of plasma products for the treatment of their condition. When HIV emerged as a risk to national blood systems in the early 1980s, these core professional beliefs served to skew transfusionists' assessment and management of the risk posed by the virus with adverse consequences for patient-recipients. The political fallout from these blood contamination episodes in countries such as the USA, England and France highlighted the inadequacy of reliance on such beliefs as tools in risk governance involving the blood system.

Although there is now less of a focus on the achievement of self-sufficiency by transfusionists, the political fallout from HIV blood contamination episodes has not altered their core professional belief in the link between VNRBD and blood safety. Given the continuing influential role of transfusionists as an 'epistemic community' in governance processes involving the blood system,[12] this core professional belief has continuing salience as a dominant policy frame at both national and supranational levels. As was pointed out in the introductory chapter, how policy is framed is important, as it affects not only how issues or problems are perceived but also the design and implementation of governance initiatives in a given policy sector.[13] Against a background where blood is multi-valued, the continuing prominence afforded to the gift relationship as exemplified in VNRBD in national

Kuhn, *Scientific Revolutions*, pp. 77–8). Within the advocacy coalition framework as developed by Paul Sabatier and others, the categories of beliefs that are likely to be resistant to change are elaborated upon in more detail. A hierarchical and tripartite structure is identified comprising deep core beliefs, policy core beliefs and beliefs regarding secondary aspects, such as problems and causes. It is argued that the first two sets of beliefs are resistant to change (see P. A. Sabatier, 'The advocacy coalition framework: revisions and relevance for Europe', *Journal of European Public Policy*, 5 (1998), 98–130 at 103–4). While I am not convinced that transfusionists, as a group of scientific experts, fit within an advocacy coalition framework, the insight regarding which types of (professional) beliefs are likely to be resistant to change is useful for present purposes.

[12] An 'epistemic community' has been defined as a network of professionals with recognised expertise and competence in a particular domain and an authoritative claim to policy-relevant knowledge within that domain or issue area. What this group of professionals have in common is a shared set of normative and principled beliefs which provide a value-based rationale for the social action of community members, shared causal beliefs, shared notions of validity and a common policy enterprise (see Haas, 'Introduction: Epistemic communities and international policy coordination', p. 3). It is interesting to note that Haas identifies similarities between how he defines epistemic communities and Kuhn's notion of a 'paradigm' and how it operates for communities of scientific experts. He argues that his definition is wider than that of Kuhn's, as it applies to both scientific and non-scientific experts; see fn. 4 in the article by Haas.

[13] Jasanoff, *Designs on Nature*, p. 23.

and supranational blood policy remains problematic in terms of facili-tating effective risk governance, given the findings from national HIV blood contamination episodes. What is required in the circumstances is a revised policy framing in which achieving optimum patient-recipient safety operates as the primary objective, rather than one that is skewed to fit the core professional beliefs of one particular group of experts involved in the blood system.

In order to examine these arguments in detail, a brief historical over-view is provided of the evolution of transfusion medicine as an inde-pendent specialty, together with an analysis of the role and influence of transfusionists in the development of national and supranational gov-ernance involving the blood system. Thereafter, transfusionists' role in the assessment and management of the risk posed by HIV to national blood systems in the 1980s is examined. The final section of the chapter investigates whether the political fallout from HIV blood contamin-ation episodes has brought about a paradigm shift in the specialty of transfusion medicine. It analyses the level of influence of transfusion-ists and their core professional beliefs in supranational regimes of gov-ernance involving the blood system, focusing in particular on how this has affected the management of risk.

From blood banking to transfusion medicine

It was not until the twentieth century that developments in scientific research made it possible to move towards a more systematic approach to the collection and supply of blood.[14] In England, Percy Lane Oliver, who had been involved with the work of the British Red Cross, estab-lished the Greater London Red Cross Blood Transfusion Service in 1921, as well as the world's first volunteer donor panel. Oliver had a par-ticular mission beyond simply organising the collection and supply of blood.[15] He was committed to developing a sense of community which he saw as exemplified in this new endeavour. Oliver's success in estab-lishing the first transfusion service in England led to the establishment of similar services in other developed countries in subsequent years.[16]

In France, Dr Arnault Tzanck established the first Emergency Blood Transfusion Service at the Hôpital St-Antoine in Paris. Like Oliver, he saw his work in the area of blood transfusion as being informed by eth-ical and humanitarian values and he wrote a number of philosophical

[14] See Chapter 2 for a detailed examination of such developments.
[15] Starr, *Blood*, p. 55.   [16] *Ibid.*, p. 57.

texts which expounded on the moral basis for the work he did. He trained a generation of physicians in the field who likewise became committed to espousing the importance of promoting wider community relations in the context of blood donation.[17] He went on to found the ISBT,[18] which continues to act as the international representative body for transfusionists working within national blood services.[19]

Notwithstanding Tzanck's work, both paid donation and VNRBD continued to be used in France throughout World War Two and this remained the case in the immediate post-war period.[20] Many of those involved in paid donation were associated with the discredited Vichy regime, which operated as a puppet government for the Nazis during the war. In contrast, those involved in VNRBD were associated with the Resistance and with the eventual liberation of France.[21] In the end, the Tzanck worldview embodied in the ethico-social commitment to VNRBD would prevail, but it is important to note that it was one that had to be fought for in terms of political recognition and legal sanction. This historical legacy no doubt accounts at least in part for the strong and enduring commitment in France to VNRBD on both ethical and safety grounds.[22]

In contrast, those involved in the development of a more organised approach to blood collection and supply in the USA differed from those who espoused support for the same ethical principles that guided the likes of Oliver in England and Tzanck in France. Those who supported VNRBD tended to be aligned with representative groups, such as the ARC and the AABB,[23] as well as having medical and/or scientific qualifications. In contrast, there were other individuals without these professional values or training but who nevertheless also became involved in blood collection and supply. They viewed it as a business and had no ethical or other qualms about paying, or otherwise providing financial incentives, for blood donation. The diversity in approach to blood collection in the USA reflected not only the absence of centralised political oversight and regulation of the activity during this period, but also deeply ingrained aspects of American culture, which included promoting an enthusiastic approach to capitalistic enterprise.[24] Indeed, it was

---

[17] W. H. Schneider, 'Arnault Tzanck, MD (1886–1954)', *Transfusion Medicine Reviews*, 24 (2010), 147–50 at 147.
[18] *Ibid.*   [19] For further details, see Chapter 2; www.isbtweb.org.
[20] Casteret, *L'Affaire du sang contaminé*, p. 20.
[21] Steffen, 'The nation's blood', p. 99.
[22] Hermitte, *Le sang et le droit*, pp. 96–109.
[23] For further details regarding the ARC and AABB, see Chapter 2.
[24] Starr, *Blood*, p. 57.

in the USA that the colloquial term of 'blood banker' came to be used to describe those individuals who were involved in the organised collection and supply of blood.[25]

Another group of individuals that became involved in the running of national blood services following World War Two included those who had been involved in similar activities during the wartime period. Some of them had relevant scientific and/or clinical qualifications, whereas others did not. What would prove invaluable when many developed countries moved towards establishing national blood services for the first time in the post-war period, however, was the practical experience and organisational skills such individuals had gained during wartime. In this brief overview of key individuals and types of persons who became involved in the organisation of blood collection and supply during the first half of the twentieth century, one of the key points to note is the diversity of backgrounds, professional orientations and values that they brought to their work. While those who engaged in such work and had scientific and/or medical qualifications may have viewed themselves as part of a larger professional group involved in the diagnosis and treatment of blood-related disorders or as providing expert advice on matters related to blood transfusion,[26] there were others who saw it simply as a business or who had a range of practical skills or experience that were useful in creating an organised approach to blood collection and supply.

Those who wished to develop their professional identity, and wanted what they did to be recognised as an independent scientific discipline, engaged in boundary-work to create demarcation lines between themselves and other scientific peers, as well as those with lay knowledge of the blood system. In relation to professional recognition by their peers, however, the group faced significant problems. There was a perception within the wider medico-scientific community that those who worked within national blood services were 'failed haematologists', who lacked the ability and/or skills to be involved in clinical practice.[27] In addition, their work was not initially viewed as forming part of an independent scientific discipline, but instead as providing practical support to clinicians involved in the treatment of patients.[28] The promotion of VNRBD

[25] *Ibid.*, p. 71. Starr notes that a certain Dr Bernard Fantus of Cook County Hospital began to use the term 'blood banking' to describe the system for collecting and supply of blood as it reflected the system of deposits and withdrawals which characterised financial banking activity.

[26] Borzini *et al.*, 'The evolution of transfusion medicine', p. 202.

[27] S. C. Davies, 'Editorial: Reforming England's blood transfusion service', *British Medical Journal*, 311 (1995), 1383–4 at 1383.

[28] Borzini *et al.*, 'The evolution of transfusion medicine', p. 202.

as the preferred sourcing method for national blood systems became an integral part of their professional beliefs. It was useful in creating a demarcation line between those in search of professional recognition as transfusionists and those who preferred to view the work of organised blood collection as a business in which individuals could be incentivised to donate through the payment of financial compensation.

A number of factors contributed to the shift towards the gift relationship becoming a core professional belief of transfusionists. The publication of Titmuss's *The Gift Relationship* in 1970 provided transfusionists with an ethically principled and risk-based set of arguments in support of this preferred source of blood donation, which at the same time was accompanied by political support for such an approach. Growing evidence of the exploitative plasma collection practices engaged in by the for-profit plasma products industry also served to intensify the importance of their professional belief in VNRBD, as well as emphasising the demarcation between those who worked within non-profit national blood services and those who worked within the for-profit industry. Such demarcation proved advantageous in political terms, as it enabled transfusionists to claim the moral high ground in the context of the use of a valued socio-cultural and medical resource. This in turn attracted public and political support, which subsequently proved useful in terms of positioning themselves as the dominant stakeholder group in blood governance processes at both national and supranational levels.

Following World War Two, transfusionists working within national blood services were primarily focused on establishing appropriate organisational mechanisms for collecting and supplying blood; in cultivating a suitable and sufficient local and national donor base; and in ensuring that appropriate laboratory and other checks were carried out on blood collected prior to it being forwarded on to hospitals and/or doctors for administration to patients. In practice, their primary allegiance lay with the (potential) donor population: on recruiting and retaining them in order to ensure a sufficient and safe supply, rather than on ensuring the safety of patient-recipients. In this regard, transfusionists viewed the treating doctor–patient relationship as the primary one dealing with patient-recipients' interests with respect to blood quality and safety issues.

While there was a category of patient-recipients who received blood as part of a one-off course of medical treatment, there were other groups such as PWH (and those with other bleeding disorders) who used plasma products on a regular basis. Their regular use of such products over an extended period in effect made them lay experts in the field, albeit still reliant on their treating doctors for expert advice on quality and safety issues. The creation by transfusionists of a division between themselves as experts in blood collection and supply and regular users of blood and plasma products[29] served to create a demarcation between expert and lay knowledge with respect to blood safety. This would in turn present problems with respect to the management of the risk posed by HIV to national blood systems, as well as in dealing with its consequences.[30]

The risk posed by HIV to the blood system

By the start of the 1980s, much of the early boundary-work engaged in by transfusionists had borne fruit in relation to control over the organised collection and supply of blood at national level. An ethically principled approach to blood donation based around VNRBD had become a core aspect of their professional belief system, linked to the goal of national self-sufficiency in blood and plasma products. The clinical, laboratory and administrative roles of transfusionists were coalescing into a growing recognition on the part of the established medico-scientific professions of the emerging specialty of transfusion medicine.[31] As this evolution was taking place, a new infectious disease, AIDS, emerged as a risk to national blood systems. Drawing on their shared professional beliefs, there was some degree of commonality in approach shown by transfusionists in different countries to this new risk to the blood system. Having said that, there was also a good degree of variation as well and this reflected the particular dynamics created by national socio-cultural, institutional and political contexts. The initial focus in this section of the chapter is on the response by US transfusionists to this new risk. The reason for this is that their response significantly influenced the approach subsequently adopted by transfusionists in countries such as England and France.

United States

As has already been discussed in Chapter 2, there was no single state-sponsored organisation responsible for the blood system in the USA.

---

[29] Healy emphasises how the embeddedness of organisational arrangements with respect to the collection and supply of blood could impact upon how staff in national blood services perceived their environment and made decisions. This included taking the view that their loyalties lay with one group over another (see Healy, *Last Best Gifts*, p. 88).

[30] How patient-recipient groups responded to boundary-work by transfusionists in the wake of HIV blood contamination episodes is examined in more detail in Chapter 6.

[31] M. A. Blajchman, 'Transfusion medicine – the coming of age of a new specialty', *Transfusion Medicine Reviews*, 1 (1987), 1–3; H. G. Klein, 'Transfusion medicine: the evolution of a new discipline', *Journal of the American Medical Association*, 258 (1987), 2108–9.

Instead, a diverse range of organisations, interest groups and individuals held an interest in blood collection and supply and there was a good deal of acrimony between various representative blood-related organisations.[32] As a result, reaching consensus on how best to approach the risk posed by HIV proved difficult and, in the end, each stakeholder group was essentially left to devise and implement their own response to the risk.[33] Transfusionists were largely unconvinced that this new infectious disease posed a significant risk to the US blood supply and remained primarily concerned that any action they decided to take would prove unduly alarming or upsetting to their volunteer donors. They wanted further monitoring of the situation, as well as scientific studies, to be done on the likely spread of the disease, before they were prepared either to take more drastic action to proactively exclude particular donor groups or to introduce surrogate testing on blood samples to identify donors likely to be at high risk of transmitting the disease.[34]

In the context of an ongoing turf war between the CDC and the FDA, as well as a general lack of political will to acknowledge that the emerging problem of AIDS represented a public health threat, there was an absence of both institutional and political leadership shown in responding to the threat.[35] This meant that US transfusionists were essentially able to devise their own set of donor screening guidelines that reflected their own concerns and professional beliefs, rather than having to take account of what was an overarching threat to national public health. As a consequence, they opted for an approach that focused on self-exclusion by donors based on information being provided to them about the risk posed by AIDS, rather than direct questioning. The decision was also taken that only gay men 'with multiple partners' would be asked to self-exclude from donation, although it was never made explicit exactly how many partners constituted a risk in terms of the risk of transmitting AIDS.[36] Potential donors were largely left to make such a determination themselves and to self-exclude, if appropriate.[37]

Having published their position on the threat posed by AIDS, transfusionists continued to assert that the risk of its transmission through blood transfusion remained very low, of the order of 'one case per million patients transfused'.[38] Such an assertion was not based on any scientific studies which had examined the risk posed by the disease at the time, but was made primarily to reassure the American public

---

[32] See Chapter 2.   [33] See Chapter 3.

[34] Shilts, *And the Band Played On*, pp. 220–2.

[35] *Ibid.*, pp. 222–3, 532; Leveton *et al.*, *HIV and the Blood Supply*, pp. 2–10.

[36] Leveton *et al.*, *HIV and the Blood Supply*, p. 71.

[37] *Ibid.*   [38] *Ibid.*, p. 74.

about the safety of the blood supply.[39] This essentially remained the publicly adopted position of transfusionists until HIV testing was introduced in 1985,[40] when it became apparent that the USA had the highest rate of transfusion-associated cases in the developed world on a per capita basis.[41]

England

Transfusionists in England had a great deal of autonomy with respect to assessing and managing the risk posed by HIV to the national blood system in the early 1980s.[42] A regionalised structure operated in relation to the collection and supply of blood during this period, in the absence of either a centralised management structure or effective regulatory oversight of blood quality and safety issues.[43] Although there was a commitment towards achieving the goal of national self-sufficiency, it was clear that it was not a political priority. Significant difficulties had been experienced in realising this goal, given dysfunctional management and financial structures and inadequate manufacturing facilities for plasma products.[44] The goal of self-sufficiency in plasma products therefore remained elusive during this period and it is debatable whether it was ever achieved in practice.[45]

Transfusionists were also hampered with respect to realising the goal of national self-sufficiency by the fact that they lacked control over the ordering and supply of plasma products. For example, haemophilia

---

[39] *Ibid.*, pp. 75–6.

[40] *Ibid.*, p. 128; Krever, *Commission of Inquiry on the Blood System*, pp. 284–92.

[41] S. Franceschi, L. Dal Maso and C. La Vecchia, 'Trends in incidence of AIDS associated with transfusion of blood and blood products in Europe and the United States, 1985–93', *British Medical Journal*, 311 (1995), 1534–6.

[42] M. Setbon, *Pouvoirs contre sida: de la transfusion sanguine au dépistage: decisions et pratiques en France, Grande-Bretagne et Suède* (Paris: Éditions du Seuil, 1993), p. 134.

[43] Editorial, 'The national blood transfusion service today', *British Medical Journal*, 281 (1980), 405–6 at 405.

[44] In England, the Blood Products Laboratory (BPL), as it was known during this period, was the state-sponsored manufacturing facility for plasma products in England. In 1980, it was declared 'unfit for manufacturing' following a government inspection. This forced the then Thatcher government to make a substantial financial investment in upgrading its facilities to a suitable standard. Such upgrading was not completed until 1987 (see Cash, 'The blood transfusion service', p. 618). Up until the early 1990s, the BPL retained Crown immunity in relation to the manufacture and supply of plasma products, such as factor concentrates used by PWH. This meant that it was not required to obtain licences from the national regulator for medicines in order to market and supply its products in England. Licensing would have required the BPL to provide data and justify the efficacy and safety of its products; see R. Lane, 'Letter: Safety levels of blood for haemophiliacs', *The Independent* (15/4/91).

[45] Archer *et al.*, *Independent Public Inquiry Report*, pp. 26–46.

doctors were able to take independent decisions about the type of factor concentrates that were administered to their patients. Given the ongoing problems with ensuring an adequate supply and level of quality of locally sourced factor concentrates, many such doctors opted to make arrangements for the importation of factor concentrates sourced from US-based donors and supplied by the for-profit plasma products industry. By the start of the 1980s, the importation of such products comprised well over 50 per cent of the total amount of products provided to PWH in England.[46] Notwithstanding the growing gap between transfusionists' core professional belief in achieving the goal of national self-sufficiency through VNRBD and the realities of the plasma products market in England, this state of affairs was viewed as a temporary aberration pending the realisation of the goal of self-sufficiency. In short, this core professional belief appeared resistant to change in the face of a persistent market reality to the contrary. This impacted on how transfusionists assessed and managed the risk posed by HIV to recipients of plasma products, in particular PWH who used US-sourced factor concentrates.[47]

Against a background of institutionally dysfunctional arrangements and fragmented regulation of quality and safety issues relating to the blood system, as well as adherence to core professional beliefs in the face of a contrary market reality, the implementation of AIDS donor screening guidelines was not uniform throughout England, where they were implemented at all. The guidelines adopted were essentially derived from the ones that had been adopted at an earlier stage by US transfusionists and included the identification of high-risk categories of donors, such as homosexual men with 'many different partners' and intravenous drug users.[48] They were set out in leaflets which were made available to donors from the latter half of 1983 onwards. The decision was taken that there would be no direct questioning and donors would be asked to self-exclude, based on their understanding of the guidelines. Although the Department of Health had been involved in the formal consultation and adoption of the guidelines, it was essentially left to transfusionists in regional blood services to implement them. In January 1985, the guidelines were revised and men who have sex with men (MSM) were permanently deferred from blood donation.[49]

---

[46] Jones, 'Factor VIII: supply and demand', p. 1532.
[47] Farrell, 'Is the gift still good?', p. 163.
[48] V. Berridge, 'AIDS and the gift relationship in the UK', in A. Oakley and J. Ashton (eds.), R. M. Titmuss, *The Gift Relationship: From Human Blood to Social Policy* (London: LSE Books, 1997), pp. 15–40 at 28.
[49] *Ibid.*

Notwithstanding the fact that HIV represented a serious public health threat, transfusionists adopted a highly cautious approach to implementing HIV testing on blood donations. They considered it important that such testing should be as accurate and as sensitive as possible, in order to ensure that undue distress was not caused to their donor base due to false positive or false negative results.[50] They were also resistant to what was perceived to be the 'premature' introduction of HIV testing in the USA, which was viewed as resulting from political pressure being exerted on American transfusionists, rather than on sound science.[51] As a result, transfusionists embarked on a six-month period of trialling different HIV test kits during the first half of 1985, which resulted in HIV testing on blood donations not being formally implemented on a national basis until October of that year.[52] While such testing revealed a low prevalence of the virus in the national donor population overall, higher rates were seen in certain cities, such as London. As has been mentioned previously, HIV testing on the haemophilia population in England revealed a different picture. While there was a relatively low rate of HIV infection among PWH who had used locally sourced products, the rate of infection among those who had used US-sourced factor concentrates on a regular basis was much higher, ranging between 50 per cent and 76 per cent on a regional basis.[53]

France

In France, the Minister for Health had political responsibility for the national blood system in the 1980s with wide-ranging legal powers to regulate the collection, manufacture and supply of blood and plasma products.[54] Much of the day-to-day oversight, however, came under the control of a directorate within the Ministry of Health known as the Direction générale de la santé (DGS). The DGS was a small and politically weak department within the French government and lacked the financial and administrative resources necessary to engage in effective management and regulation of the national blood system.[55] As in England, there was no national blood service in existence during this

---

[50] *Ibid.*, p. 30.
[51] J. Barbara, M. Contreras and P. Hewitt, 'AIDS: a problem for the transfusion service?', *British Journal of Hospital Medicine*, 36 (1986), 178–84 at 181.
[52] Berridge, 'AIDS and the gift relationship in the UK', p. 29.
[53] UK Haemophilia Centre Doctors' Organisation (UKHCDO) (AIDS group), 'Prevalence of HIV Antibody to HTLV-III in haemophiliacs in the UK', *British Medical Journal* 293 (1986), 175–6.
[54] Hermitte, *Le sang et le droit*, p. 136.
[55] Steffen, 'The nation's blood', p. 100.

period in France and transfusionists exercised a good deal of autonomy in relation to the management of over 160 regional blood services, as well as the seven manufacturing facilities which operated for the production and supply of plasma products.[56] The combination of a regionalised structure, dysfunctional financial reimbursement arrangements and a lack of appropriate political or institutional oversight meant that the blood system in France resembled a 'feudal system constituted by multiple baronies' during this period,[57] with no effective regulatory mechanisms for ensuring either the quantity or quality of blood and plasma products.[58]

As in England, VNRBD and the achievement of national self-sufficiency in blood and plasma products sourced through this method of donation were core professional beliefs for transfusionists in France. The gift relationship reflected an ethically principled commitment to altruism in blood donation which had been historically linked to the idea of all that was good about the French nation, as well as contributing to national social solidarity. Achieving self-sufficiency was also viewed in similar nationalistic terms. The core professional beliefs of transfusionists were also matched by a strong commitment on the part of the Socialist government in the early 1980s to achieving the goal of national self-sufficiency in blood and plasma products. To this end, transfusionists in charge of the Paris blood service and its plasma products manufacturing facility were made responsible for realising this goal as soon as possible. At the same time, they were also given monopoly decision-making powers with regard to the level of importation of plasma products that would be permitted in France.[59] Although transfusionists claimed that national self-sufficiency had been achieved by 1984, (clandestine) importation of largely US-sourced plasma products in fact continued in order to meet growing demand by PWH throughout this period and beyond.[60]

It was against this background that risk governance involving HIV was assessed and managed by transfusionists. Given the government

---

[56] Casteret, *L'Affaire du sang contaminé*, pp. 17–21.
[57] Geronimi *et al.*, *Les Collectes de sang*, p. 94.
[58] Setbon, *Pouvoirs contre sida*, pp. 78–83; Steffen, 'The nation's blood', p. 100.
[59] M. Lucas, *Transfusion sanguine et SIDA en 1985: chronologie des faits et de decisions pour ce qui concern les hémophiles* (Paris: Inspections Générales des Affaires Sociales, 1991), p. 6.
[60] It has been variously estimated that the level of importation of factor concentrates into France ranged between 10 per cent and 30 per cent throughout the 1980s. For further details, see Lucas, *Transfusion sanguine et SIDA*, p. 29; Casteret, *L'Affaire du sang contaminé*, pp. 30–1; J.-Y. Nau and F. Nouchi, 'Des produits sanguins ont été importés illégalement' *Le Monde* (13/2/92).

mandate which enabled them to control the ordering and supply of factor concentrates for PWH, as well as weak executive control, transfusionists in effect operated as the most influential stakeholder group
involved in national blood policy during this period.[61] With this level
of influence, transfusionists were able to frame and implement policies
to deal with the risk posed by HIV in line with their core professional
beliefs, for the most part unimpeded by institutional, political or cross-
specialty constraints. Like their English counterparts, French transfusionists also adopted for the most part the AIDS donor screening
guidelines that had been adopted earlier in the USA, in the absence of
testing being available to detect the disease in blood donations.

A circular was published in mid 1983, which was sent to all transfusionists in charge of regional blood services. It set out details of the risk
posed by this new disease, as well as recommendations for excluding
donors identified as being in high-risk categories for transmitting the
disease. Such categories included homosexuals and bisexuals with multiple partners; intravenous drug users; Haitians and those from equa-
torial Africa; and sexual partners of such persons. The circular also
explained that plasma from local donors was considered safe for use in
the manufacture of factor concentrates and steps were being taken to
reduce the level of importation of such products. Imported products
were seen to be at higher risk due to the fact that they were largely
sourced from US paid donors.[62] A donor leaflet was also prepared which
provided information regarding this new infectious disease, as well as
listing the high-risk donor categories. Following publication of the circular in mid 1983, very little in the way of strategic planning or review
of risk governance with respect to the risk posed by AIDS was undertaken by transfusionists, civil servants or political leaders for well over a
year. This was despite the fact that, during this same period, two PWH
were diagnosed with AIDS as a result of using only locally sourced factor concentrates and Dr Luc Montagnier, a well-known virologist based
in Paris, discovered the virus that caused AIDS.[63]

Notwithstanding accumulating evidence that whatever was causing
AIDS was likely to pose a substantial problem to the national blood
supply, transfusionists' core professional beliefs meant that they were
highly resistant to accepting that their volunteer donor base could be
a source of transmission of the disease, or that the pursuit of national

---

[61] Hermitte, *Le sang et de droit*, p. 136.
[62] Geronimi *et al.*, *Les Collectes de sang*, p. 100; Casteret, *L'Affaire du sang contaminé*,
pp. 79–80.
[63] Casteret, *L'Affaire du sang contaminé*, pp. 85–6.

self-sufficiency would need to be re-evaluated as a result. This was high-lighted at a national blood policy committee meeting held in June 1983, where the first case of AIDS in France involving a person with haemophilia was reported, as well as evidence being presented that a further six PWH were exhibiting signs and symptoms that were suggestive of AIDS. Of the six PWH, three had only used locally sourced factor concentrates, two had used a mixture of French and US-sourced products, and one had used only US-sourced products. Notwithstanding the evidence that locally sourced products were likely to have been contaminated with whatever was causing AIDS, the conclusion was reached that the main risk was US-sourced products. Caution was urged in relation to the use of such products both in order to reduce the risk of transmission of HIV and in the interests of achieving national self-sufficiency.[64] When a report was subsequently published about the six cases of AIDS involving PWH, all evidence implicating locally sourced products in the cases had been removed.[65]

Transfusionists' core professional belief in VNRBD as a guarantor of blood safety also persisted in relation to the potential risks faced by the regular blood collections that took place within French prisons. In socio-political terms, blood donation by prisoners was seen as an important aspect of social rehabilitation which was to be promoted in the interests of social solidarity. In addition, transfusionists viewed prison populations as an easy and consistent source of supply of blood donations and were happy for prison collections to continue. This combination of socio-cultural and supply aspects to prison collections in France meant that they continued long after they had ceased in many other developed countries. In the early 1980s, there had been a huge growth in intravenous drug use in French prisons, one of the recognised AIDS high-risk categories. Notwithstanding this growing risk, prison blood collections continued with the support of those in charge of the prison administration, who remained unaware of the steps being taken to reduce the risk of AIDS transmission elsewhere in relation to blood collection and supply.[66] This took place in the context of a failure on the part of regional directors of blood services to take account of, or otherwise implement, donor screening guidelines to exclude AIDS high-risk donors.[67]

[64] J.-P. Soulier, *Transfusion et sida: le droit à la verité* (Paris: Éditions Frison-Roche, 1992), p. 42.
[65] Casteret, *L'Affaire du sang contaminé*, pp. 71–2.
[66] Geronimi *et al.*, *Les Collectes de sang.*
[67] *Ibid.*, p. 107; Casteret, *L'Affaire du sang contaminé*, pp. 115–16.

By early 1985, transfusionists were becoming increasingly aware that the Parisian blood supply in particular was likely to be heavily contaminated with HIV.[68] This was highly problematic given that plasma from Parisian blood donors was being pooled with plasma received from regional blood services to manufacture factor concentrates at the Paris manufacturing facility. Such products were in turn distributed to PWH throughout France. The problem that this posed for the safety of PWH was only formally acknowledged by Dr Michel Garetta, the then head of the Parisian blood service, at a meeting held in May 1985 where he was recorded as admitting that it was likely that all lots of locally sourced factor concentrates were contaminated with HIV.[69] Notwithstanding such an admission, he took the decision that existing lots of locally sourced products would continue to be distributed to PWH until the inventory was exhausted, pending a formal decision to cease such distribution by the relevant government authorities.[70] Once HIV testing was implemented in October 1985, it became apparent that the national blood supply had been heavily contaminated by the virus. France was shown to have the highest rate of blood transfusion-associated HIV in Europe.[71] Subsequent studies showed that although prison blood collections accounted for only 0.37 per cent of all blood collected on a per annum basis, they accounted for at least 25 per cent of blood transfusion-associated HIV cases in 1985 alone.[72] Testing on the national haemophilia population revealed a rate of HIV infection of 38 per cent, although rates of infection varied on a regional basis. In Paris, the rate of infection was 75 per cent, whereas in the regional city of Lille it was only 10 per cent.[73]

Expertise, core professional beliefs and risk governance

The examination of how transfusionists in countries such as the USA, England and France dealt with the risk posed by HIV to national blood systems revealed the importance they attached to their core professional beliefs, such as VNRBD. In the case of transfusionists in France and England, the goal of national self-sufficiency also operated as a core belief, much more so than was the case for American transfusionists.

[68] The Pinon-Leibowitch study, which became available in early 1985, revealed that 5 out of every 1,000 blood donors in Paris were likely to be HIV positive. For further details, see Casteret, *L'Affaire du sang contaminé*, pp. 121–4.

[69] *Ibid.*, pp. 121–4.   [70] *Ibid.*, pp. 59, 171–7.

[71] Steffen, 'The nation's blood', p. 110.

[72] Geronimi *et al.*, *Les Collectes de sang*, pp. 55–68.

[73] *Ibid.*, p. 163.

Such beliefs operated as the predominant influence on risk assessment and were resistant to change. Such resistance operated in a number of ways. First, it meant that where there was a conflict between such beliefs and available scientific evidence concerning the extent of the risk posed by HIV, then such beliefs would override such evidence. What followed from this was that transfusionists across all three countries were not proactive in implementing and evaluating strategies to exclude donors identified as being at high risk for transmitting HIV through blood. Such an approach fitted with their core professional belief that VNRBD served to minimise, if not eradicate, the risk of transmission of infectious disease through the blood system. Their professional focus on cultivating an ongoing relationship with loyal volunteer donors also meant that they chose the least aggressive options of donor self-exclusion and no direct questioning, so as not to cause offence. They also expressed concern about the potential costs and supply consequences resulting from donor exclusion. In line with their core professional belief in VNRBD, the emphasis remained on transfusionists' primary relationship with their volunteer donor base.

Second, it meant that transfusionists rejected, or otherwise did not take account of, evidence from other scientific disciplines with respect to the assessment of the evidence risk posed by HIV to national blood systems. Professional isolation and the lack of recognition from the more established medico-scientific professions, as well as the institutional isolation of blood services generally within the wider health system, also operated as factors to reinforce the degree of commitment shown by transfusionists to their core professional belief in VNRBD. This led them to engage in essential boundary-work with other medico-scientific experts around the issue of risk governance involving the blood system. This could be seen in the way American transfusionists interpreted the epidemiological evidence presented to them regarding the risk posed by HIV to the blood supply. Their scepticism regarding such evidence would underpin the approach they subsequently took to the design and implementation of AIDS donor screening guidelines, which would in turn be adopted with little variation in many other countries. It was also apparent in the way in which French transfusionists failed to act on the epidemiological evidence made available to them which identified that the Parisian blood supply was likely to be heavily contaminated by HIV.

Third, the combination of scientific training, expertise in serology and practical experience predisposed transfusionists to seeking out particular forms of acceptable scientific data about the extent of the risk posed by HIV. Epidemiological evidence about such risk was clearly not sufficient for transfusionists; in line with their professional training, data from serological testing on blood donations to detect transmissible agents was much more acceptable. Transfusionists were used to playing a waiting game in relation to the development of serological testing for transmissible diseases. It had taken many years, for example, to develop a suitable serological test to detect serum HBV.[74] In the context of uncertainty about the extent of the risk posed by HIV to the blood system, transfusionists were professionally predisposed to wait until such uncertainty could be removed through suitable serological testing becoming available which would detect the virus in blood donations. Adopting this approach, it was only once such acceptable testing data, as well as longitudinal scientific studies, were available that a more informed approach to risk governance could then be taken by transfusionists to address the problem posed by HIV. In line with their core professional beliefs, it was a mindset which would not have seemed unreasonable in the circumstances at the time. However, it was an approach that would subsequently be criticised by a number of government-sponsored inquiries in the wake of HIV blood contamination episodes as being a reactive, slow and inappropriate response to the emerging risk posed by HIV under conditions of scientific uncertainty.[75] It is an issue that is examined in more detail in Chapters 6 and 7.

What was also apparent from the examination of how transfusionists dealt with the risk posed by HIV was that they were able to exercise a great deal of autonomy over both the assessment and the management of the risk, in the context of largely passive acquiescence by those in political leadership, as well as civil servants and regulators.[76] This was exemplified in a number of ways. First, notwithstanding the adoption of AIDS donor screening guidelines, they were unevenly implemented at local level, where this happened at all. Where civil servants became involved, they largely accepted advice received from transfusionists or otherwise allowed them to pursue their own approach to dealing with this new risk to the blood supply. This reflected not only the institutional isolation of blood services within the wider health system, but also the lack of political priority given to matters associated with risk governance involving the blood system. The absence of a proactive approach on

[74] Leveton et al., HIV and the Blood Supply, pp. 103–4.
[75] See generally: Lucas, Transfusion sanguine et SIDA; Geronimi et al., Les Collectes de sang; Leveton et al., HIV and the Blood Supply; Krever, Commission of Inquiry on the Blood System; A. Lindsay, Report of the Tribunal of Inquiry into the Infection with HIV and Hepatitis C of Persons with Haemophilia and Related Matters (Dublin: Government Publications, 2002); Archer et al., Independent Public Inquiry Report.
[76] Leveton et al., HIV and the Blood Supply, pp. 117, 121–8; Krever, Commission of Inquiry on the Blood System, pp. 208–96; Berridge, 'AIDS and the gift relationship in the UK', pp. 23–5; Lindsay, Report of the Tribunal of Inquiry, pp. 224–33.

the part of national governments and regulators to dealing with the risk posed by HIV prior to the availability of testing was also indicative of this longstanding political and institutional marginalisation. However, a more nuanced analysis is required in the case of national regulators. In the case of England, regulatory intervention and oversight was problematic, given the absence of overarching powers to regulate the blood system in the early to mid 1980s. In contrast, the Minister for Health in France had extensive regulatory powers in the field, as did the FDA in the USA. These powers were not used to facilitate a proactive approach to dealing with the risk posed by HIV, in the face of regulatory capture by those with expertise in blood and plasma products.[77]

A paradigm shift in the post-HIV blood contamination era?

The shift from blood banking to the recognition of transfusion medicine as an independent specialty accelerated in the 1980s.[78] This new specialty was viewed as being driven by the role of the transfusion consultant, who was involved in advising on the appropriate use of blood services, addressing the risk posed by transfusion-transmitted disease and reducing the risk to recipients of blood and its components.[79] The recognition of transfusion medicine as an independent specialty occurred at the same time as HIV emerged as a risk to national blood systems. It is clear that the political fallout from HIV blood contamination episodes served to galvanise the development and the expansion of transfusion medicine's role and functions within the wider healthcare context in subsequent decades.[80] From the perspective of transfusionists, it facilitated an important paradigm shift within their specialty in two key respects: first, it involved a shift in public and professional perceptions which viewed blood transfusion as beneficial and life-saving to it being considered a high-risk, life-endangering treatment; and second, it involved a change in the perception of blood donors as being a valu-

---

[77] In the USA, for example, it was found that the FDA had suffered regulatory capture by blood experts, given its preference for a consensus-based approach to decision-making processes involving the blood system; see Leveton et al., *HIV and the Blood Supply*, pp. 14–15, 135–40.

[78] Klein, 'Transfusion medicine', p. 2109.

[79] *Ibid.*

[80] Two leading North American transfusionists published a paper in 1997 in which they employed Kuhn's ideas concerning paradigm shifts in science to examine the impact of HIV blood contamination episodes on transfusion medicine; see Blajchman and Klein, 'Looking back in anger'.

able resource providing the gift of life, to viewing them as posing a risk of transmitting life-threatening disease to patient-recipients.[81]

In many ways, the paradigm shift which occurred in the wake of HIV blood contamination episodes could be seen as beneficial to the development of transfusion medicine as a fully-fledged independent specialty. It facilitated better transfusion practices in areas such as donor recruitment, the manufacture of plasma products, risk communication and the care of patient-recipients. It also led to greater awareness and emphasis being placed on risk management and quality control, as well as contributing to significant improvements in blood testing technology.[82] On the negative side, the impact of persistent negative media, government-sponsored inquiries, civil litigation and criminal prosecutions of individual transfusionists, as well as the imposition of stringent regulatory controls in the wake of such episodes, have also clearly taken their toll on the standing of the specialty and its collective professional identity.[83]

There is clearly an understanding on the part of transfusionists regarding the anger and loss experienced by those infected with HIV through blood, as well as recognition of the need to learn lessons from how and why the contamination episodes took place. At the same time, there is also a sense of bewilderment and anger at the extent to which they, both individually and collectively, have been held responsible by the media, the courts and politicians with regard to the harm caused as a result of such episodes. Transfusionists have expressed concern that retrospective analyses of the circumstances that led to such episodes failed to take sufficient account of the fact that as a group they acted in accordance with accepted practice at the time against a background of inadequate knowledge and a good deal of scientific uncertainty about the nature and scope of the risk posed by HIV to national blood systems. With this in mind, it has been argued that it is unhelpful and indeed unjust to assign responsibility to transfusionists, whether on an individual or collective basis, when there was an overarching institutional and political failure to generally deal with the risk posed by HIV to national blood systems.[84]

The paradigm shift claimed by transfusionists to have taken place in the wake of HIV blood contamination episodes is largely based on their

---

[81] *Ibid.*
[82] B. H. Shaz and C. D. Hillyer, 'Transfusion medicine as a profession: evolution over the past 50 years', *Transfusion*, 50 (2010), 2536–41 at 2537.
[83] Blajchman and Klein, 'Looking back in anger', pp. 3–4.
[84] *Ibid.*, pp. 2–4.

specialty's changing perceptions regarding risk involving the collection and supply of blood, as well as the need on their part to respond to this change. Kuhn viewed the shared beliefs of a given scientific community as an important constituent element in the development and maintenance of a given paradigm. Transfusionists' understanding of how the paradigm shift has occurred is interpreted as an external force structuring change within their specialty. Yet this interpretation does not appear to have been accompanied by a more critical analysis as to how their core professional beliefs, in particular the commitment to VNRBD and its link to blood safety, skewed their assessment and management of the risk posed by HIV. The analysis in the previous section of the chapter makes clear that the use of such beliefs, as the predominant mechanism structuring such risk governance, adversely impacted on blood safety in certain national contexts, given the existing prevalence of the disease in particular local and/or national donor populations.

A review of recent blood policy and regulatory documentation, as well as the relevant academic and practitioner literature in the field, reveals that transfusionists' commitment to VNRBD and its link to blood safety has proved to be largely resistant to change, notwithstanding HIV blood contamination episodes.[85] In that sense, the claim of a paradigm shift within the discipline is one based on a narrow, rather than an expansive, interpretation of what is involved in such a process. Understood in this way, it is a partial or incomplete shift. VNRBD remains a core professional belief, although transfusionists now acknowledge that blood collected in this way should as far as possible be sourced from low-risk donor populations.[86] It is acknowledged by transfusionists that the commitment to '100% VNRBD' remains an 'aspirational' goal given current demand, as well as the need to ensure availability where insufficient amounts of plasma are collected by national blood services for the manufacture of such products.[87] It has been acknowledged that advances in blood testing technology in recent years have meant that plasma products sourced from paid donors may be seen as just as safe as those sourced from VNRBD.[88] Concerns remain on the part of transfusionists that in the event of the emergence of a new infectious agent

---

[85] See, for example, Flanagan, 'ISBT Board response to the Dublin consensus statement'.

[86] Sullivan, 'Developing an administrative plan for transfusion medicine', p. 227S.

[87] World Health Organization, *Global Consultation, 100% Voluntary Non-Remunerated Donation of Blood and Blood Components*, p. 20; Flanagan, 'ISBT Board response to the Dublin consensus statement', p. 250.

[88] Beal, 'Titmuss revisited', p. 355.

for which no blood screening technology is available, it is still likely to appear first and in much greater numbers in the paid donor, as opposed to the VNRBD, population.[89]

The importance which transfusionists attached to realising the goal of national self-sufficiency also appears to have diminished in recent years. This has also been reflected in blood policy at both national and supranational levels. The emergence of new risks to national blood systems, such as variant Creutzfeldt–Jakob disease (vCJD) in countries such as England, necessitated a re-evaluation of the wisdom of maintaining such a policy. Adopting a precautionary approach in the wake of HIV blood contamination episodes, the decision was taken that plasma products manufactured for use in England would be sourced from US paid donors, given the low prevalence of vCJD in this national setting.[90] Sourcing and supply arrangements, whether derived from paid donors and/or VNRBD, are now much less straightforward, reflecting both developments in technology and complexity in risk governance. In these circumstances, the goal of national self-sufficiency no longer appears relevant or indeed appropriate in certain circumstances.[91]

Conclusion

This chapter examined the role of scientific expertise involved in risk governance of the blood system, drawing on an analysis of how the professional beliefs of transfusionists involved in national blood services have influenced, and indeed continue to influence, risk governance in the field. An examination of the circumstances that led to HIV blood contamination episodes in the USA, England and France revealed that these beliefs skewed transfusionists' assessment and management of the risk posed by HIV, leading to an inadequate response to the protection of recipients of blood and plasma products. Notwithstanding such findings, however, these core professional beliefs have appeared

[89] Beal and van Aken, 'Gift or good?', p. 3; van der Poel et al., 'Paying for blood donations: still a risk?', pp. 291–2; cf. Kretschmer et al., 'Perspectives of paid whole and plasma donation'.

[90] J. Barbara and P. Flanagan, 'Blood transfusion risk: protecting against the unknown', British Medical Journal, 316 (1998), 717–18; J. S. Cervia, S. O. Sowemimo-Coker, G. O. Ortolano et al., 'An overview of prion biology and the role of blood filtration in reducing the risk of transfusion-transmitted variant Creutzfeldt-Jakob Disease', Transfusion Medicine Reviews, 20 (2006), 190–206 at 197–8.

[91] A. Farrugia, 'International movement of plasma and plasma contracting', in G. N. Vyas and A. E. Williams (eds.), Advances in Transfusion Safety (Basel: Karger, 2005), pp. 85–96 at 93; O'Mahony and Turner, 'The Dublin Consensus Statement 2011', p. 2.

largely resistant to change. The role of transfusionists as an influential stakeholder group within the blood system has meant that such beliefs continue to operate as dominant framing devices in both national and supranational blood policy.

The adherence to the core professional belief of VNRBD and the maintenance of the (albeit now more nuanced) link to blood safety by transfusionists remains troubling in risk governance terms for a number of reasons. Despite the findings from national HIV blood contamination episodes that it should be viewed as one amongst a range of factors influencing blood safety, transfusionists' level of influence in governance processes involving the blood system means that VNRBD continues to be promoted as the preferred sourcing method on both ethical and safety grounds. While this remains well entrenched in national blood policy, it is also particularly noticeable in blood policy and associated initiatives undertaken by supranational organisations, such as the Council of Europe and the WHO. However, the fallout from national HIV blood contamination episodes has now created an environment in which risk governance involving the blood system is currently subject to ongoing political contestation and intervention, which may call such professional beliefs into question. This is less apparent at supranational level where transfusionists continue to operate as a highly influential epistemic community in a policy environment that is largely sealed off from such politicisation. In this context, transfusionists are more able to influence the framing of blood policy and associated governance initiatives, thus ensuring that VNRBD remains central to the framing of supranational blood policy.

If lessons are to be learned from national HIV blood contamination episodes, then it is clear that such an approach remains problematic. How policy is framed is important as it affects not only how issues or problems are perceived, but also the design and implementation of governance initiatives in a given policy sector. In such circumstances, the achievement of optimum patient-recipient safety should operate as the main framing device with respect to risk governance involving the blood system. Strategies should then be devised to ensure that every link in the donor–recipient chain, including the promotion of VNRBD where appropriate, is addressed in the light of such policy framing. What is required is a holistic and flexible approach to facilitating blood safety, rather than one that is skewed to fit the core professional beliefs of one, albeit influential, stakeholder group.

5   Risk and innovation

How the commitment to VNRBD has influenced risk governance involving the blood system was the subject of examination in the previous two chapters. In the context of an overarching examination of the relationship between risk and innovation, this chapter focuses on the sourcing and supply of factor concentrates to treat haemophilia[1] by the for-profit plasma products industry.[2] The industry is a mature one that has developed over the past fifty years. In the early decades of its development, risk governance involving the use of plasma products, such as factor concentrates, was structured by the dichotomous framing of blood as either a gift or a commodity. When HIV emerged as a risk to national blood systems in developed countries in the 1980s, this particular framing was subsequently shown to be problematic in terms of facilitating effective risk governance. High levels of HIV infection among people with haemophilia (PWH) who used factor concentrates manufactured by the industry acted as the catalyst for successive waves

[1] I note that factor concentrates are only one of several types of plasma products produced and supplied by the industry. The reason for focusing on this particular product in this chapter is because it was used by PWH and contributed to high rates of HIV infection among PWH in the 1980s. It therefore provides a useful case study on the relationship between risk and innovation, as well as providing important background information for the matters discussed in the following chapters. In this chapter, I also focus on issues of innovation in relation to factor VIII concentrate or recombinant factor VIII (rFVIII), as the majority of PWH have factor VIII deficiency.

[2] I acknowledge that a not-for-profit industry is also involved in the manufacture of factor concentrates. It has traditionally been aligned with national blood services and received some degree of state financial and other support. This sector has a different ethical and operational ethos to the for-profit industry and supports the sourcing of plasma products through VNRBD. In order to examine the dimensions of the gift versus commodity stakeholder debate more fully, I have chosen to focus on the for-profit industry in this chapter. In doing so, I recognise that obtaining detailed information about the industry is difficult. Much information is proprietary and therefore confidential, given that companies involved in the for-profit industry are in competition with each other, as well as with the non-profit sector (see Hagen, *Blood: Gift or Merchandise?*, p. 63; E. Nauenberg and S. D. Sullivan, 'Firm behavior in the U.S. market for Factor VIII: a need for policy?', *Social Science and Medicine*, 39 (1994), 1591–603 at 1598–9; Leveton *et al.*, *HIV and the Blood Supply*, p. 30).

of process and product innovation, with a view to enhancing product safety.[3]

Such innovation took place against the background of much greater regulatory oversight at both national and supranational levels. Innovation and regulation have traditionally been viewed separately within the relevant academic literature, with those interested in innovation being concerned with how new knowledge and discoveries are successfully transformed into marketable commodities.[4] The view was taken that regulation tends to impede, rather than facilitate innovation,[5] with its main aim being to promote a 'predictable and favourable regulatory environment' in order to bring about market success.[6] For those interested in regulation, the focus has been predominantly on standard setting and risk assessment in the context of managing innovation.[7] It is now recognised that the relationship between innovation and regulation is more complex,[8] particularly where ethico-social conflict converges around risks created by innovation in biotechnology, as well as the market processes that may emerge as a result.[9]

[3] Burnouf, 'Modern plasma fractionation', pp. 101–17.
[4] J. Abraham and T. Reed, 'Progress, innovation and regulatory science in drug development: the politics of international standard-setting', *Social Studies of Science*, 32 (2002), 337–69 at 337–8; L. Levidow, 'Biotechnology regulation as symbolic normalization', *Technology Analysis & Strategic Management*, 6 (1994), 273–90 at 273.
[5] J. Kent, A. Faulkner, I. Geesink *et al.*, 'Towards governance of human tissue engineered technologies in Europe: framing the case for a new regulatory regime', *Technological Forecasting and Social Change*, 73 (2006), 41–60 at 43; Organisation for Economic Co-operation and Development (OECD), *The OECD Innovation Strategy: Getting a Head Start on Tomorrow* (Paris: OECD, 2010), p. 10. For an exploration of this view in the context of the blood system, see Farrugia, 'The regulatory pendulum in transfusion medicine'; Burnouf, 'Modern plasma fractionation', p. 115; J. McCullough, 'Innovation in transfusion medicine and blood banking: documenting the record in 50 years of TRANSFUSION', *Transfusion*, 50 (2010), 2542–6 at 2544.
[6] Commission of the European Communities, Implementing the Community Lisbon Programme: Communication from the Commission to the Council, the European Parliament, the European Social and Economic Council and the Committee of the Regions, More Research and Innovation – Investing for Growth and Employment: A Common Approach, COM (2005) 488 final, 12.10.2005, p. 5.
[7] Abraham and Reed, 'Progress, innovation and regulatory science', p. 338.
[8] J. Grin and H. van de Graaf, 'Technology assessment as learning', *Science, Technology and Human Values*, 21 (1996), 72–99; Commission of the European Communities, Innovation Tomorrow: Innovation Policy and the Regulatory Framework (Brussels: DG Enterprise, 2002).
[9] S. Borrás, 'Legitimate governance of risk at the EU level? The case of genetically modified organisms', *Technological Forecasting and Social Change*, 73 (2006), 61–75 at 62–71; Kent *et al.*, 'Towards governance of human tissue engineered technologies', pp. 44–6; A. Webster (ed.), *New Technologies in Health Care: Challenge, Change and Innovation* (Houndmills: Palgrave Macmillan, 2006); A. Webster, *Health, Technology and Society: A Critique* (Houndmills: Palgrave Macmillan, 2007), pp. 1–50; A. Faulkner, *Medical Technology into Healthcare and Society: A Sociology of Devices, Innovation and Governance* (Houndmills: Palgrave Macmillan, 2009), pp. 1–9; H. Gottweis, B. Salter

The early years in the development of the for-profit plasma products industry were marked by dysfunctional regulation in relation to quality and safety aspects of collection, production and supply arrangements, where such regulation existed at all. While both product and process innovation by the industry in the wake of HIV blood contamination episodes have significantly reduced the rate of TTIs in plasma products, it is argued that innovation on its own should not be viewed as the great panacea for preventing or redressing failures to manage risk where multi-valued human biological materials are involved, such as blood and plasma products. Instead, the loss of public trust that occurred in the wake of such episodes now requires that innovation in this context, as well as markets in such products, should be subject to stringent regulatory governance which takes account of the relationship between the social and the economic in order to enhance blood safety and facilitate the protection of patient-recipients. At a minimum, this requires regulatory cooperation and harmonisation at both national and supranational levels, involving the use of standard setting for quality and safety, as well as the establishment of legally binding risk regulation regimes, where possible.

In order to examine these arguments in detail, the first section of the chapter provides an overview of the development of the for-profit plasma products industry in the USA in the decades immediately following World War Two. There is a particular focus on the scientific research and technological developments in the 1960s that led to the emergence of a global market in factor concentrates to treat haemophilia by the 1970s. The second section deals with how the risk of HIV contamination of factor concentrates was assessed and managed by manufacturers, regulators and those in charge of national blood services during the early to mid 1980s. The third section examines the successive waves of process and product innovation that followed in the wake of high levels of HIV infection among PWH who had used factor concentrates manufactured by the for-profit sector of the industry, as well as its subsequent impact on risk governance in the field. The penultimate section of the chapter examines how states, regulators and other key stakeholders have sought to manage the relationship between risk and innovation in the context of the manufacture and supply of plasma products, such as factor concentrates, in the post-HIV blood contamination era.

and C. Walby, *The Global Politics of Human Embryonic Stem Cell Science: Regenerative Medicine in Transition* (Houndmills: Palgrave Macmillan, 2009), pp. 2–23, 83–4; C. Davis and J. Abraham, 'Rethinking innovation accounting in pharmaceutical regulation: a case study in the deconstruction of therapeutic advance and therapeutic breakthrough', *Science, Technology and Human Values*, 36 (2011), 791–815.

The development of the plasma products industry

Plasma is a complex human biological material containing hundreds of proteins, which cover a range of physiological functions. Albumin and immunoglobulin represent approximately 80 per cent of all plasma proteins, with other proteins such as protease inhibitors and clotting factors VIII and IX contributing to the remaining 20 per cent.[10] Clotting factors are those elements contained within the blood that are activated when a blood vessel wall is damaged and platelets begin adhering to the break. Deficiency in any of these factors leads to spontaneous internal bleeding requiring the administration of products containing those clotting factors to stop it. Roman numerals are used by the scientific community to describe each of the clotting factors. Clotting factors VIII and IX are the most common factors found to be deficient in males who suffer from the genetic disorder haemophilia.[11]

The collection of plasma and the fractionation process

As was highlighted in Chapter 2, the need to find more efficient methods for the collection, storage and supply of blood and its components during World War Two contributed to innovation in blood-related technology, in the form of the development of the Cohn fractionation method for the production of plasma products.[12] It was the development of this fractionation technology that would prove crucial to the industrial manufacture of plasma products.[13] Although the first industrial fractionation plant to process blood components was opened in the early 1940s, its operations were limited.[14] However, a number of techno-scientific developments in the 1950s and 1960s made the large-scale industrial production of plasma products possible, including factor concentrates. The 1950s saw the development of the procedure then known as 'plasmapheresis', although it is more commonly referred to today as 'apheresis'. This was, and continues to be, a procedure which extracts plasma from the donor's blood through an automated process

---

[10] Burnouf, 'Modern plasma fractionation', p. 101. It has been 'estimated that there are in excess of 1000 proteins in plasma, of which 250 have been identified … of the identified proteins, approximately 10–15 per cent have commercial use as therapeutics', see E. Hutt, 'Specialised plasma products', *Pharmaceuticals Policy and Law*, 7 (2006), 67–73 at 67.

[11] See Figure 2.1.   [12] See Chapter 2.

[13] Companies or organisations which make use of this fractionation process are often referred to as 'fractionators'. For the purposes of this chapter, I use the terms 'companies' and 'industry'.

[14] Hagen, *Blood: Gift or Merchandise?*, p. 113.

(centrifugation, filtration or a combination of both), whereby the plasma is retained but other cellular components, such as red cells, are returned to the donor. As the donor suffers no loss of red cells, frequent donation is possible.[15] This means that a healthy adult donor could donate twice a week, with each donation taking between 60 and 90 minutes. Assuming that all relevant tests on the donor and the plasma itself were normal, the donor could provide up to 100 litres of plasma per annum.[16]

In the 1960s, it quickly became clear that the use of plasmapheresis was likely to become the main way in which sufficient amounts of plasma could be collected for the industrial manufacture of plasma products, in circumstances where between 1,000 and 20,000 (or more) plasma donations were needed to manufacture individual product lots.[17] In addition, pooling large numbers of plasma donations proved to be much more economical and efficient with respect to the manufacture of factor concentrates given that the relevant clotting factor proteins, such as factor VIII, were only found in very small quantities in the plasma.[18] The need to obtain large amounts of plasma for the industrial manufacture of plasma products, as well as the uncomfortable and lengthy donation procedure, led to political and regulatory acceptance in the USA that financial payment for plasma donation should be permitted.[19]

Although the development of plasmapheresis meant that it was possible to harvest high yields of plasma, the plasma products industry needed to ensure that it had a regular and adequate supply of this source material. As previously discussed in Chapter 2, the companies involved in the industry adopted a number of strategies to ensure supply from the 1960s onwards.[20] Plasma source collection in the immediate post-war decades in the USA was dominated by a range of 'untrained profiteers', who relied on socio-economically disadvantaged individuals to provide their plasma on a weekly basis in return for cash.[21] A large proportion of such individuals came from 'captive' populations including prisoners, inmates in mental institutions and soldiers.[22] By the 1970s, the donor base for source plasma had expanded to include students, housewives and gay men, as well as individuals in a range of developing countries where the industry had established plasma collection facilities.[23]

---

[15] *Ibid.*, p. 18.   [16] Leveton *et al.*, *HIV and the Blood Supply*, p. 30.
[17] *Ibid.*, p. 30.   [18] *Ibid.*, p. 31.
[19] *Ibid.*, p. 30.   [20] See Chapter 2, p. 39.
[21] Starr, *Blood*, p. 187; see also Chapter 3.
[22] Titmuss, *The Gift Relationship*, pp. 105–6, 119; Hagen, *Blood: Gift or Merchandise?*, p. 35.
[23] For more detailed information on the industry's plasma collection practices in developing countries in the 1970s, see Chapter 2, pp. 39–40.

During this period, both prisoners and gay men became valuable and regular sources of plasma, particularly as their plasma often contained HBV antibodies, which were needed in the manufacture of the HBV vaccine.[24]

It is important to note that plasma collections from prisoners became a particularly significant and valuable source for the industry from the 1960s onwards for a number of reasons. As previously mentioned, prisoners represented a captive population who could be incentivised to donate regularly in return for much needed cash or relief from their prison sentences. Prison plasma proved to be particularly useful for the manufacture of a plasma product known as gamma globulin. This is because medical procedures could be performed on prisoners which made it possible to produce a form of hyper-immune plasma that enabled the production of a highly concentrated and specific form of gamma globulin. By the 1960s, five prisons situated in the southern states of the USA were supplying plasma that accounted for 25 per cent of national demand for this type of product. Prison plasma collections largely took place in a regulatory vacuum and this meant that prisoners were exposed to unhygienic and risky procedures on a regular basis.[25] Prison plasma collections continued to take place in the USA right up until the early 1980s and only ceased when the industry belatedly recognised that such collections had become highly problematic in the wake of the AIDS epidemic.[26]

Research and innovation: haemophilia and factor concentrates

A key emerging market for the plasma products industry from the late 1960s onwards involved the manufacture and supply of factor concentrates for use in the treatment of haemophilia. As mentioned previously, haemophilia is a disorder mainly affecting males and involves excessive internal bleeding mainly in joints and organs. It is caused by an absence of one of two proteins in the blood, known as the coagulation factors VIII and IX, or by a deficiency in the functioning of those factors. Most people diagnosed with haemophilia suffer from a deficiency in clotting factor VIII. Haemophilia is classified as severe, moderate or mild, depending on the level of clotting factor in the blood. Prior to the latter half of the twentieth century, PWH suffered from inadequate or

---

[24] *Ibid.*; Starr, *Blood*, p. 265.   [25] Starr, *Blood*, pp. 210–11.

[26] Although companies began the process of closing down prison plasma collections in December 1982, it has been suggested that they did not in fact cease entirely in the USA until January 1984; see Leveton *et al.*, *HIV and the Blood Supply*, p. 30.

ineffective treatment of their bleeding episodes, leading to significant disability and death.[27] The only option for treatment was to administer blood transfusions, but this was not a targeted treatment as it contained very small amounts of the clotting factor needed to arrest bleeding.[28] Attendance and treatment at hospital was the norm and this often included prolonged inpatient admissions.

In the decades immediately following World War Two, scientific research by Kenneth Brinkhous and colleagues in the USA had shown that there were two main types of haemophilia: factor VIII and factor IX.[29] In the early 1960s, one US-based company, then known as Hyland Laboratories, began developing the prototype for what would become known as anti-haemophiliac factor (AHF) product (factor concentrate), with the first clinical trials of the product taking place during this period. Subsequently, Brinkhous took the decision to go into partnership with Hyland, viewing the commercialisation of the production of factor concentrates as congruent with the desirable outcome of improving the treatment and quality of life for PWH.[30] Brinkhous worked closely with a Hyland scientific researcher, Edward Shanbrom, to develop factor concentrates. By 1968, Hyland had obtained a licence from the FDA to market the product.[31]

During the 1960s another company, then known as Cutter Laboratories, was also collaborating with researchers at Stanford University in relation to the development of suitable product to treat haemophilia. There was a breakthrough in 1965 when one Stanford researcher, Dr Judith Graham Pool, discovered that after slowly thawing previously frozen plasma, a white residue that was rich in factor VIII could be collected. This residue had ten times the clotting factor of plasma and it could be made cheaply and easily by national blood services.[32] This residue became known as cryoprecipitate and it quickly became the treatment of choice for PWH with the clotting factor VIII form of the disorder.[33] With the licensing of Hyland's factor concentrate in the USA in 1968, other companies involved in the plasma products industry soon followed. The advent of factor VIII concentrates 'transformed' the treatment of haemophilia, leading to quick and effective treatment of bleeds. This enabled many PWH to enjoy a good quality of life, paid employment and increased life expectancy for the first time.[34]

[27] Krever, *Commission of Inquiry on the Blood System*, pp. 163–4.
[28] Resnik, *Blood Saga*, p. 41.   [29] *Ibid.*, p. 22.
[30] *Ibid.*, pp. 38–40.   [31] *Ibid.*, p. 53.
[32] Starr, *Blood*, p. 222.   [33] Resnik, *Blood Saga*, pp. 40–1.
[34] Krever, *Commission of Inquiry on the Blood System*, p. 164.

One potential downside of using factor concentrates, however, was the increased risk of contracting a range of viruses due to the pooling of large numbers of plasma donations in the manufacture of such products. It quickly became apparent that a high number of PWH had become infected with HBV, as well as with what was then known as hepatitis non-A, non-B (NANB) but is now known as HCV. In the USA, for example, it was estimated that 80 per cent of PWH who used factor concentrates were HBV positive by the mid 1970s, although the majority had not developed chronic disease. This chronic form of the infection was estimated to affect between 2.5 and 7.8 per cent of those infected. Many haemophilia doctors believed that their patients had developed immunity to HBV as a result of having been exposed to the virus.[35] Testing for HBV had become available in the early to mid 1970s resulting in a significant decrease in factor concentrates becoming contaminated with the virus; however, NANB hepatitis then emerged as the major hepatitis threat and infection with this virus accounted for between 80 and 90 per cent of cases involving PWH by the end of the 1970s.[36]

Viral activation

Given that it was well recognised that there was a substantial risk of transmission of hepatitis viruses to PWH through the use of factor concentrates, companies involved in the plasma products industry began to undertake research to identify methods that would inactivate such viruses in the factor VIII concentrates in the 1970s.[37] This included trialling the use of a detergent method to treat plasma before the manufacturing process took place. This method had been developed by Dr Edward Shanbrom, who had by now left Hyland and was self-employed. Shanbrom endeavoured to interest a number of companies, as well as regulators, in his detergent method, but neither showed much interest. For the industry, implementation of the method would have required the re-licensing of their factor concentrates and regulatory authorities did not see it as a priority at the time.[38]

Another promising method involved heat inactivation of factor concentrates. This involved making use of either 'dry' or 'wet' heat treating

---

[35] Leveton et al., HIV and the Blood Supply, p. 85.   [36] Ibid.

[37] The composition of factor IX concentrate made it more difficult to identify viral inactivation methods, without substantially reducing or destroying the concentrated clotting factor in the product. Therefore, the initial research on heat treatment methods focused mainly on factor VIII concentrates.

[38] Leveton et al., HIV and the Blood Supply, pp. 86–7.

of the product at a certain temperature over a number of hours (the methods employed varied with regard to the number of hours and dur-ation of time).[39] Although a number of US-based companies investi-gated the potential of heat inactivation during the mid to late 1970s, it would be the German-based company Behringwerke that moved for-ward with developing this particular method. By the start of the 1980s, the company was able to show that it could inactivate HBV in factor concentrates and was successful in obtaining a licence from the German regulatory authorities to market heat-treated factor concentrates in 1981. Notwithstanding Behringwerke's breakthrough, there was an ongoing debate between companies involved in the industry as to the efficacy of heat inactivation, given that the process reduced the potency of fac-tor VIII. Behringwerke claimed that the loss was 50 per cent, whereas other companies argued that their own research showed such loss to be of the order of 90 per cent, or more. In addition, this new heat-treated product was ten times more costly than the non-heat-treated product, due to the need to address the loss of potency.[40] Increased costs, doubts about the efficacy of viral inactivation methods, the regulatory bur-den involved in licensing such products and the existing complacency on the part of the industry, regulators and haemophilia doctors with respect to viral contamination of factor concentrates all contributed to a lack of urgency about the perceived need to innovate in the area.[41]

By the start of the 1980s, the plasma products industry operated as a niche within the much larger global pharmaceutical industry. At the time, there were six companies that controlled most of the world's plasma resources, the majority of which were based in the USA. Although a number of European companies would subsequently purchase these US-based companies, both plasma collection and the manufacture of plasma products nevertheless remained in the hands of a small group of companies. US plasma continued to be the main source for the industry's products which were distributed within the USA, as well as exported worldwide.[42] As HIV emerged as a risk to national blood sys-tems in the 1980s, the plasma products industry operated a tightly inte-grated network in a global market then worth an estimated US$1billion per annum.[43]

---

[39] *Ibid.*, p. 88.   [40] *Ibid.*, p. 87.   [41] *Ibid.*, pp. 93–6.
[42] Hagen, *Blood: Gift or Merchandise?*, pp. 97, 115. The companies which dominated the US market during this period were Alpha, Armour, Cutter and Baxter Travenol. Together with Behringwerke and Immuno, they also dominated the European market for factor concentrates.
[43] *Ibid.*, p. 64.

Factor concentrates and the risk posed by HIV

This section of the chapter focuses primarily on how the plasma products industry addressed the risk posed by HIV to factor concentrates in the USA. This is for two reasons: first, the AIDS epidemic first emerged in the developed world in the USA; and second, the majority of plasma collection, as well as the manufacture of factor concentrates for the global market, took place in the USA. Having said that, reference is also made to the impact of the approach taken by US-based plasma products manufacturers to the risk posed by HIV in countries such as England, given that there was a high level of importation of factor concentrates from the USA during this time.

In July 1982, the CDC published a report detailing the first three cases of *Pneumocystis carinii* pneumonia involving PWH, which was also associated with severe immune dysfunction. The cases matched others that had also been reported in gay men, intravenous drug users and Haitians. The CDC suggested that a transmissible agent in factor concentrates could have been responsible for the three cases.[44] Representatives from the industry subsequently attended a series of meetings sponsored by the FDA in the latter half of 1982 in which the risk to the blood system from what had come to be known as AIDS was discussed, as was the likely risk to PWH. In December 1982, the CDC issued a further report which detailed the rising number of cases of AIDS involving PWH and noted that they had all received large amounts of factor concentrates. The CDC suggested that the transmission routes for AIDS, as well as the other groups affected by the disease, bore a striking similarity to the way in which HBV was transmitted.[45]

Following these reports, representatives from the plasma products industry attended the meeting convened at the CDC in early January 1983 which had been called to discuss the risk posed by AIDS to the US blood system. As has been previously discussed in earlier chapters, no consensus was reached on a common approach to dealing with such risk at the CDC meeting.[46] In late January 1983, the American Blood Resources Association (ABRA), the then representative organisation for the plasma products industry, issued its recommendations for donor screening exclusion and deferral to reduce the risk of AIDS

[44] Centers for Disease Control, *Morbidity and Mortality Weekly Report*, July 16, 1982.
[45] Centers for Disease Control, *Morbidity and Mortality Weekly Report*, December 10, 1982.
[46] For further details concerning the CDC meeting held in January 1983, see Chapter 2, p. 36.

transmission in plasma products.[47] High-risk donor categories were identified, including gay men, intravenous drug users and persons who had been in Haiti. Donors were to be asked to read information provided by the companies at the time of plasma donation and indicate that they were not members of an identified high-risk group; if they were not willing to do so, then their plasma would be excluded. The publication of the ABRA recommendations was subsequently followed by the publication of FDA guidelines for all plasma collection centres and plasma product manufacturers which set out similar donor exclusion policies, as well as advising on particular practices to be followed in relation to the quarantining of high-risk plasma supplies.[48]

Neither the ABRA recommendations nor the FDA guidelines made clear what was to happen with the existing inventory of plasma products, including factor concentrates.[49] This was problematic given the fact that a significant proportion of the US plasma donor population was composed of gay men and prisoners and these groups had been identified as likely to be at high risk of transmitting the agent that was causing AIDS.[50] It was not clear that all companies involved in the plasma products industry moved quickly to exclude these two donor categories from the plasma pool,[51] particularly as prison collections did not fully cease in the USA until early 1984.[52] In terms of minimising the level of AIDS contamination in factor concentrates, further problems arose when the FDA took the decision in mid 1983 that there would be no automatic recall policy involving lots of factor concentrates, where such lots were associated with a donor who had been diagnosed with AIDS or had symptoms strongly suggestive of AIDS. This followed advice received from BPAC, its specialist advisory committee, that recalls should be considered on a case-by-case basis. The FDA also failed to make clear how this particular recall policy was actually going to work in practice and how the industry was going to be able to access the necessary information about plasma donors with suspected or diagnosed AIDS.

---

[47] ABRA was founded in 1971 to represent plasma collectors and manufacturers of plasma products. Its membership comprised 80 per cent of for-profit source plasma collectors and all for-profit plasma product manufacturers in the USA, as well as a majority worldwide; see Leveton *et al.*, *HIV and the Blood Supply*, p. 38.

[48] *Ibid.*, Appendix D, pp. 292–4.

[49] *Ibid.*, pp. 143–6.

[50] *Ibid.*, p. 104. In general, it was recognised that the US prison population was at high risk for infectious diseases, including HBV.

[51] *Ibid.*, p. 72. One of the plasma product companies, Alpha Therapeutics, took the decision in December 1982 to exclude all plasma donors who identified that they had been in Haiti, used intravenous drugs, or engaged in male-to-male sexual contact.

[52] *Ibid.*, p. 30.

Mention had also been made in the ABRA recommendations published in January 1983 concerning the use of surrogate testing (nonspecific laboratory marker testing) to identify potential AIDS high-risk donors. At the CDC meeting in January 1983, CDC staff had identified a 90 per cent correlation between persons who had HBV core antibodies and those most likely to be infected with AIDS. The CDC therefore recommended that a surrogate test which would identify HBV core antibody positive donors should be implemented by US blood services and the plasma products industry, so that this category of donors could then be excluded from blood and plasma donation.[53] Notwithstanding the CDC's recommendation, however, the plasma products industry was not in favour of introducing such surrogate testing and wanted further feasibility studies to be done.[54] Industry representatives maintained such position in the context of their advisory role on the FDA's BPAC, demanding that a taskforce be set up to evaluate the efficacy of introducing HBV core antibody surrogate testing.

The BPAC taskforce reported back in early 1984, with a majority opposing the introduction of HBV core antibody testing on plasma donations.[55] Notwithstanding BPAC's position, one company went on to implement the surrogate test with a view to obtaining an advantage over its competitors, although the majority of the industry opted to maintain its opposition to surrogate testing. Given the number of representatives from the industry on BPAC during this period, their position on surrogate testing proved influential with the FDA. As previously mentioned in Chapter 2, the FDA was receptive to adopting the advice it received from the committee in line with its longstanding consensus-driven approach to the formulation and implementation of expert advice in relation to the US blood system. A subsequent review of the FDA's role in the circumstances that led to the HIV blood contamination episode in the USA found that plasma product industry representatives on BPAC were able to exert undue influence on the FDA leadership in line with their own commercial interests and 'at the expense of the public interest'.[56]

The US-based industry was prepared to move much more quickly in relation to switching to heat treatment of factor concentrates. Although the research that had been done to date had primarily been undertaken with the aim of inactivating HBV, it was apparent by 1982 that whatever was causing AIDS was also affecting the same groups that were at high risk of contracting HBV. It was therefore likely that heat treatment to inactivate HBV would also inactivate this new infectious

---

[53] *Ibid.*, p. 112.   [54] *Ibid.*, p. 72.   [55] *Ibid.*, p. 119.   [56] *Ibid.*, p. 121.

agent. Between 1983 and 1984, most of the companies obtained licences from the FDA to market heat-treated factor concentrates based on research done to inactivate HBV. The discovery of the AIDS virus in 1984 enabled scientific researchers to confirm later that same year that heat treatment of factor concentrates also eliminated this new virus.[57] Such confirmation enabled the companies to subsequently obtain a variation in their FDA heat treatment licences to include the inactivation of HIV. Despite now having a licence to manufacture and market such products, however, many of the companies focused on eliminating existing inventories of non-heat-treated factor concentrates worldwide, rather than recalling such products. These practices persisted in the absence of any regulatory mandate from either the FDA or other national regulatory agencies that they supply only heat-treated factor concentrates and notwithstanding the companies' awareness that they were much more likely to be contaminated by HIV than were heat-treated products.[58]

An examination of the approach taken by the plasma products industry to address the risk posed by HIV to factor concentrates was included in a wide-ranging review conducted by the Institute of Medicine (IOM) in the mid 1990s. The IOM Report found that the industry had moved too slowly in relation to conducting research into methods of viral inactivation, particularly in relation to the use of heat treatment for factor concentrates. It concluded that such methods could have been successfully developed before the 1980s by the industry and this would have subsequently 'prevented many cases' of HIV in PWH.[59] The main reasons for the sluggishness identified on the part of the industry derived from the lack of strong incentives provided by US regulatory and public health authorities, as well as a prevailing complacency on the part of all relevant stakeholders about viral (i.e. HBV) contamination of factor concentrates.[60] In addition, the industry was able to act largely in line with its own commercial interests because the FDA had adopted a regulatory style that was primarily consensus-driven, as well as collegiate, in approach. This meant that the approach to risk governance involving the blood system which was adopted by the FDA was reactive and cautious, despite a range of regulatory powers at its disposal which could have led to a more proactive approach to dealing with the specific risk posed by HIV.[61]

---

[57] *Ibid.*, p. 78.
[58] Krever, *Commission of Inquiry on the Blood System*, pp. 415–84.
[59] Leveton *et al.*, *HIV and the Blood Supply*, p. 95.
[60] *Ibid.*, p. 96.   [61] *Ibid.*, pp. 7–10.

While the FDA's remit was limited to US-based companies, as well as plasma collections and manufacturing of factor concentrates that took place in the USA, the fact that there was a global market for factor concentrates meant that the approach taken by the FDA clearly had implications for the risk faced by PWH who used US-sourced products in other countries. Taking England by way of example,[62] well over 50 per cent of the factor concentrates used by PWH were imported from US-based manufacturers and sourced from American paid donors during this period.[63] This was against a background of long-term problems associated with meeting patient demand for factor concentrates, in the context of a wider failure to achieve national self-sufficiency in such products.[64] Although it was clear by mid 1983 that US-sourced factor concentrates were at risk of HIV contamination, the considered view of the UK government and its advisers at the time was that the level of risk was not sufficient to warrant the withdrawal of supply of such products. In any case, it was pointed out that efforts were already underway to achieve national self-sufficiency in the near future and therefore this potential risk would then be adequately addressed.[65] When HIV testing became available, it was apparent that such a view had been misplaced, with high rates of HIV infection among PWH who had used US-sourced products on a regular basis.[66]

The Medicines Division within the then Department of Health and Social Security, which had responsibility for overseeing quality and safety issues involving factor concentrates was under-resourced in terms of both administrative capacity and technical expertise. This made it susceptible to being 'captured' by pharmaceutical interests, such as the plasma products industry, in relation to claims made about the safety of their products.[67] Complicating the situation was the fact that

[62] Although what happened in England is set out by way of example, the approach taken in this country was mirrored in other developed countries that imported US-sourced factor concentrates for their haemophilia population. For an overview, see reports by government-sponsored inquiries in Ireland and Canada: Lindsay, *Report of the Tribunal of Inquiry*; Krever, *Commission of Inquiry on the Blood System*.

[63] Jones, 'Factor VIII: supply and demand'.

[64] For a detailed discussion of this issue, see Chapters 3 and 4; see also Archer *et al.*, *Independent Public Inquiry Report*, pp. 27–39, 44.

[65] Archer *et al.*, *Independent Public Inquiry Report*, pp. 40–1.

[66] The rates of HIV infection ranged between 50 and 76 per cent on a regional basis; see UK Haemophilia Centre Doctors' Organisation (UKHCDO) (AIDS Group), 'Prevalence of HIV antibody to HTLV-III in haemophiliacs in the UK', p. 176. The rate of infection among PWH with factor IX deficiency was only 10 per cent, which was attributable to their use of locally sourced products.

[67] Moran, *Governing the Health Care State*, pp. 155–6.

haemophilia doctors had traditionally been given a significant degree of clinical freedom in the relation to the choices they made regarding the ordering and prescribing of products for their patients. The availability of factor concentrates had transformed the treatment of haemophilia in the 1970s. Many treating doctors had witnessed this transformation in the lives of their patients and were very reluctant to accept withdrawal of treatment with the products in the 'absence of scientific proof' that there was a link between HIV and the use of US-sourced products.[68] Factors such as the strong professional commitment to the use of factor concentrates, longstanding problems with ensuring adequate supply to meeting growing demand, regulatory capture and a lack of coordination with other national regulators such as the FDA, all combined to create an environment in which US-sourced factor concentrates were marketed and supplied in countries such as England, in circumstances where there was a lack of sufficient and independent regulatory oversight of the safety of such products.

Innovation and product safety in the post-HIV blood contamination era

The political and legal fallout from national HIV blood contamination episodes involving PWH who had used US-sourced factor concentrates 'posed one of the biggest challenges' for the plasma products industry.[69] The industry recognised that there had been a failure to adequately deal with the risk posed by HIV,[70] and there was now an urgent need to focus on ensuring the safety of their products. It was also recognised that much stronger quality control over the sourcing of plasma used in the industry's products was needed, whilst at the same time ensuring that there was access to sufficient supplies of plasma. While independent providers of source plasma continued to exist, companies moved to acquire a range of source plasma collectors to ensure supply and quality control in line with the growing move towards vertical integration of the industry.[71] Currently, plasma collected in the USA, Germany, Austria

---

[68] Lindsay, *Report of the Tribunal of Inquiry*, pp. 156–7.

[69] C. Waller, 'Historical perspectives on blood and plasma products, the stakeholders and the issues', *Pharmaceuticals Policy and Law*, 7 (2006), 7–19 at 9; J. L. Valverde, 'The political dimension of blood and plasma derivatives', *Pharmaceuticals Policy and Law*, 7 (2006), 21–33 at 21.

[70] von Hoegen and Gustafson, 'The importance of greater regulatory harmonization', p. 172.

[71] Nauenberg and Sullivan, 'Firm behavior in the US market for Factor VIII', p. 1602; J. Penrod, 'PPTA leadership interview: Gordon Naylor', *The Source* (Spring 2009), 6–7 at 7.

and Sweden comprises approximately 75 per cent of plasma collected worldwide,[72] with more than 50 per cent being collected in the USA.[73] About 35 per cent of plasma used is recovered plasma, with the remaining 65 per cent being source plasma collected through plasmapheresis.[74] Between 23 and 28 million litres of human plasma are used in plasma products manufacture each year, in batches of several thousand litres in approximately seventy factories.[75]

Several steps were taken to improve the quality and safety of plasma collection, including the shift towards automated plasmapheresis technology and the adoption of voluntary standards for plasma collection under the industry's International Quality Plasma Program (IQPP).[76] Two such standards involve the concepts of the 'qualified donor' and 'inventory hold'. All potential donors in the USA, for example, are initially screened against the industry's National Donor Deferral Registry, which contains the names of individuals who have previously tested positive for HIV, HBV or HCV at plasma collection centres. If a first-time donor tests negative for a known virus, then the same procedure must be undertaken within a further six months. If the donor is again negative, then their plasma can be used and they are accepted as a 'qualified donor'. Holding the donor's initial plasma donation until this second procedure takes place is what is referred to as 'inventory hold'. In short, it means that plasma provided by a one-time donor is no longer accepted for plasma products manufacture.[77] More recently, the US-based industry has been working with the AABB and the FDA to develop a Donor History Questionnaire which provides a standardised set of tools for meeting donor eligibility requirements on the part of source plasma collection centres in the USA.[78]

---

[72] K. Krause, 'Integrate blood and plasma collections: a modern approach', *Pharmaceuticals Policy and Law*, 7 (2006), 49–54 at 49.

[73] J. M. Bult, 'Future trends', *Pharmaceuticals Policy and Law*, 7 (2006), 263–9 at 263.

[74] Burnouf, 'Modern plasma fractionation', pp. 102–3.

[75] *Ibid.*, p. 101.

[76] J. Penrod and M. Gustafson, 'The evolution of safety in source plasma collection', *The Source* (Spring 2009), 16–18 at 18; A. Farrugia, M. Gustafson and I. von Hoegen, 'Decades of safety measures', *The Source* (Spring 2009), 8–12 at 8. The Plasma Protein Therapeutics Association (PPTA) also operates an independent certification programme known as Quality Standards of Excellence, Assurance and Leadership (QSEAL) for its members covering adherence to voluntary standards in relation to collecting, processing and testing of source plasma; see Plasma Protein Therapeutics Association (PPTA), *Quality Standards of Excellence, Assurance and Leadership (QSEAL)* (www.pptaglobal.org).

[77] V. Grifols, 'Financing plasma proteins: unique challenges', *Pharmaceuticals Policy and Law*, 7 (2006), 187–98 at 189; Bult, 'Future trends', p. 265.

[78] At the time of writing, the FDA had given preliminary approval to the US-based industry's national donor questionnaire. Feedback was being sought on draft guidance that

While source plasma collection could be considered a mature industry with a record of 'steady innovation', the manufacturing part of the industry has engaged in a significant degree of both process and product innovation in the wake of national HIV blood contamination episodes, facilitated in large part by advances in biotechnology. This led to the development of what has become known as the 'gold standard' for viral inactivation of factor concentrates, as well as plasma products more generally. Achieving this standard involves two separate treatments which are designed to ensure inactivation of both enveloped and non-enveloped viruses (to the extent that this is possible).[79] The first treatment is designed to inactivate most enveloped viruses, including HIV, HBV and HCV, and usually involves the use of solvent detergents. This is then followed by the use of heat treatment processes, which are designed to inactivate both enveloped and non-enveloped viruses. Nanofiltration was also introduced in the early 1990s with the aim of reducing the risk of transmission of non-enveloped viruses.[80]

In addition, advances in viral DNA detection through the use of nucleic acid amplification technology (NAT) were also employed to significantly reduce the potential for 'window period' plasma donations to enter the manufacturing pool.[81] As a result of such innovation, it has been claimed that there has been no recorded transmission of HIV, HBV or HCV in US-licensed plasma products that have been subjected to such viral inactivation treatments since the end of the 1980s.[82] In the circumstances, it has been suggested that the country of origin of

had been prepared by the FDA in relation to this questionnaire. Such feedback was to be considered by the FDA before final approval was given to the questionnaire; see Plasma Protein Therapeutics Association (PPTA), *PPTA Donor History Questionnaire* (www.pptaglobal.org).

[79] Viruses which may be transmissible through plasma products are classified as either enveloped or non-enveloped viruses. The membrane of enveloped viruses contains lipid molecules, whereas the membrane of non-enveloped viruses contains mainly proteins. The difference is important in relation to the use of standard inactivation treatments as enveloped viruses respond well to such treatments, whereas non-enveloped viruses do not; see Grifols, 'Financing plasma proteins', pp. 189–90.

[80] Burnouf, 'Modern plasma fractionation', pp. 108–9.

[81] The 'window period' for TTIs, such as HIV or HCV, occurs where a person may have been infected with the virus, but has not as yet produced antibodies which can be detected under conventional testing technology. A person who has been infected with HIV or HCV but who has not produced antibodies can still transmit the virus through plasma and/or whole blood donation; see W. K. Roth, 'Quarantine plasma: quo vadis?', *Transfusion Medicine and Hemotherapy*, 37 (2010), 118–22.

[82] E. Tabor, 'The epidemiology of virus transmission by plasma derivatives: clinical studies verifying the lack of transmission of hepatitis B and C viruses and HIV type 1', *Transfusion*, 39 (1999), 1160–8; Burnouf, 'Modern plasma fractionation', p. 108.

plasma used in such products is no longer of importance, provided there is appropriate donor selection and screening.[83]

On a parallel front, advances in biotechnology led to innovation in the type of products that were manufactured and supplied by the industry to PWH. In 1988, a monoclonal antibody purification process was introduced which produced higher purity and safer factor concentrates. However, the most significant breakthrough in safety terms came with the development of factor VIII products manufactured through the use of recombinant DNA technology (rFVIII). While first and second generations of rFVIII contained some plasma and animal proteins, they were removed from the third generation of products, thus virtually eliminating the risk of transmission of blood-borne pathogens.[84] Product innovation has come at a high cost for both national health systems and third-party reimbursers that cover the cost of this type of product. Many developed countries, which have experienced adverse consequences resulting from HIV and other blood contamination episodes, have nevertheless opted to move towards the use of recombinant products in the treatment of haemophilia. In the USA and Europe, for example, between 50 and 80 per cent of people with the most common form of haemophilia now use factor VIII recombinant products.[85] In the UK, guidelines have also now been published on the circumstances in which rFVIII should be considered the treatment of choice for certain sub-groups within the national haemophilia population.[86]

Notwithstanding what seems to be an inexorable move towards ever greater market penetration of these products in developed countries, both PWH and their treating doctors remain wary of a wholesale move away from plasma products for a number of reasons. They wish to ensure that there is sufficient choice and availability of products available for the treatment of haemophilia, including both recombinant and plasma-based factor concentrates.[87] This is because not all patients respond

---

[83] J. Rautonen, 'Finland: national policy', *Pharmaceuticals Policy and Law*, 7 (2006), 221–4 at 222.

[84] M. Franchini and G. Lippi, 'Recombinant Factor VIII concentrates', *Seminars in Thrombosis and Hemostasis*, 36 (2010), 493–7.

[85] T. Burnouf, 'Plasma proteins: Unique biopharmaceuticals – unique economics', *Pharmaceuticals Policy and Law*, 7 (2006), 209–18 at 213. In France, over 80 per cent of the haemophilia population now use such products; see P. Rouger, 'France: national policy', *Pharmaceuticals Policy and Law*, 7 (2006), 255–9 at 258.

[86] D. Keeling, C. Tait and M. Makris, 'Guideline on the selection and use of therapeutic products to treat haemophilia and other hereditary bleeding disorders', *Haemophilia*, 14 (2008), 671–84.

[87] B. O'Mahony and A. Turner, 'The Dublin Consensus Statement on vital issues relating to the collection of blood and plasma and the manufacture of plasma products', *Vox Sanguinis*, 98 (2010), 447–50.

well to the use of recombinant products.[88] There have also been recurrent shortages over the years in relation to the range of products used by PWH. Therefore, ensuring ongoing supply across a range of products remains a priority.[89] While a symbiotic relationship exists between the industry and representative groups who act on behalf of PWH, there is an understanding about the fact that their priorities are different. As consumers, PWH (and their treating doctors) wish to ensure availability, choice, quality and safety at an affordable price. While the industry cultivates the relationship with their customer base, innovation in clotting factor therapies over the past twenty years in the wake of HIV blood contamination episodes has come at a high cost, which the industry wants to recover in line with a suitable profit margin.[90]

The potential for industry collusion on such issues may stem to some extent from the nature, structure and production costs associated with plasma products manufacture. First, the industry is essentially manufacturing and supplying products which deal in large part with what are known as 'orphan diseases'. Such a focus sets it apart from the larger pharmaceutical industry, which has a much wider potential customer base, depending on the drugs involved.[91] Second, the industry is highly integrated in terms of plasma collection, manufacture and supply and this has led to the emergence of a small number of major players with a diverse product portfolio and global market access.[92] Third, the manufacture of plasma products operates as a niche industry within the wider pharmaceutical sector. For the latter, direct manufacturing costs are low at approximately 19 per cent and this needs to be compared to such costs for the plasma products industry, which stand

---

[88] There are some PWH who may develop what are known as 'inhibitors' (or antibodies) as a result of using products to treat their bleeding episodes. This has occurred in relation to the use of both recombinant and plasma products. It means that the use of particular types of products may not be successful in treating bleeding episodes. For further details, see Keeling *et al.*, 'Guideline on the selection and use of therapeutic products to treat haemophilia', p. 681.

[89] F. von Auer, 'Germany: national policy', *Pharmaceuticals Policy and Law*, 7 (2006), 225–31 at 229; Betts, 'The United Kingdom: national policy', *Pharmaceuticals Policy and Law*, 7 (2006), 233–41 at 238.

[90] In this regard, it has been suggested that the costs associated with product innovation and viral inactivation treatment have led to industry collusion on pricing and product availability in the marketplace for products to treat haemophilia (see Nauenberg and Sullivan, 'Firm behavior in the US market for Factor VIII', pp. 1591–3; K. Garber, 'rFactor VIII deficit questioned', *Nature Biotechnology*, 18 (2000), 1133).

[91] Burnouf, 'Plasma proteins', p. 216.

[92] *Ibid.* In order to obtain suitable profit margins, a plasma products manufacturer would aim to have a balanced portfolio of products. This involves ensuring that the plasma collected can be used to manufacture several products, rather than focusing exclusively on one type of product.

at 70 per cent (covering the collection, testing, storing and manufacture of products). Fourth, unlike the pharmaceutical industry, the plasma products industry faces significant transaction costs with respect to ensuring regulatory compliance involving the quality and safety of the source material (e.g. plasma) used in product manufacture, an aspect which has become particularly important in the wake of HIV blood contamination episodes.[93] In light of such factors, industry representatives have argued that the products it manufactures should be viewed as a 'special case', both in terms of the costs charged for its products and in relation to the level of reimbursement received from third-party payers and/or state-funded health systems.[94]

Market access for the plasma products industry has also been complicated by the fact that there has long been involvement on the part of nation-states in determining the terms under which such national access will be granted. In large part this has turned on whether or not state-sponsored, not-for-profit manufacturers of plasma products operate in national contexts. Several European countries have sponsored the development of manufacturing facilities on a not-for-profit basis, including Belgium, Finland, France, Luxembourg, Netherlands, England (using US plasma) and Scotland (using imported plasma).[95] This type and level of state involvement has brought a potent mix of ethics, politics and economics into market access and supply issues for the industry, which it is suggested is not faced by other sectors of the pharmaceutical industry to the same degree.[96] While access to plasma products is urgently needed in developing countries, adequate reimbursement policies are for the most part not in place, thus making it an unattractive market option for the industry.[97] Given current global market conditions, the likelihood of plasma products such as factor concentrates being made available on a widespread basis to PWH in developing countries in the wake of the shift towards recombinant products in developed countries is likely to remain more aspirational than real.

In the wake of national HIV blood contamination episodes, the approach taken to the regulation of the collection, manufacture and supply practices of the plasma products industry has changed dramatically with a view to enhancing quality and safety. In terms of self-regulation, the industry has worked hard to enhance its image with respect to facilitating product safety. This has included the adoption of voluntary industry

[93] Grifols, 'Financing plasma proteins', pp. 196, 198.
[94] Waller, 'Historical perspectives on blood and plasma products', pp. 16–18.
[95] Ibid., p. 17.   [96] Ibid., p. 16.
[97] A. Farrugia, 'Product delivery in the developing world: options, opportunities and threats', Haemophilia, 10 (2004), 77–82.

standards, such as the IQPP, in relation to plasma collection. Most significantly for the industry has been the shift towards heightened and much more stringent regulatory oversight at both national and supranational levels. Government inquiries held in the wake of HIV blood contamination episodes found that the response of national regulators to the emerging risk of transmission of the virus in plasma products had been slow and largely ineffective, where there had been any response at all.[98]

Mention has already been made previously in this chapter regarding the findings contained in the IOM Report in the USA, which concluded that the response of the FDA had been inadequate and that it should have taken a more proactive leadership role in responding to the emerging risk of HIV to the national blood system. In the wake of such criticisms, the FDA has substantially changed its approach to engaging in regulatory oversight in the field and this has led to claims that the plasma products industry has become one of the most strictly regulated in the USA.[99] Steps taken by the FDA have included mandating the adoption of a range of viral inactivation and testing technologies to enhance product safety; the promotion of Good Manufacturing Practice (GMP) principles; and the pursuit of greater transparency in its risk decision-making processes involving the blood system. As mentioned in Chapter 2, this has involved revamping the membership and remit of BPAC, its chief blood advisory committee, so as to avoid the sort of regulatory capture by industry that was apparent during the time HIV posed a risk to the national blood system.[100] Given that over 50 per cent of the world's plasma is collected in the USA, in addition to the majority of the industry being US based, the change in the regulatory posture of the FDA has had a major impact on the approach taken by the industry to quality and safety issues both within the USA and beyond. Greater inter-regulatory communication and sharing of information between the FDA and other national regulators has also meant that the more proactive approach taken by the FDA has had a much stronger ripple effect beyond the USA.[101]

---

[98] See, for example, Lucas, *Transfusion sanguine et SIDA*; Krever, *Commission of Inquiry on the Blood System*; Lindsay, *Report of the Tribunal of Inquiry*.

[99] Valverde, 'The political dimension of blood and plasma derivatives', p. 24; Burnouf, 'Plasma proteins', p. 214.

[100] For further details, see www.fda.gov/AdvisoryCommittees/Committees MeetingMaterials/BloodVaccinesandOtherBiologics/BloodProductsAdvisory Committee/default.htm.

[101] See also Confidentiality Arrangements concluded between the EU (EC and EMEA) and the USA (FDA/DHHS), Implementation Plan for Medicinal Products for Human Use (updated June 2007), which aims to facilitate cooperation and sharing of relevant information with regard to medicinal products, including plasma products (www.emea.europa.eu/docs/en_GB/document_library/Other/2009/12/WC500017981.pdf).

Separate to enhanced regulatory oversight by the FDA in the field, there has also been significant regulatory activity at both national and supranational levels in Europe in response to HIV blood contamination episodes. The main driver for action has been the adoption of a series of governance initiatives over the past ten years that were designed to establish EU-wide regulatory regimes to enhance the quality and safety of blood components, as well as plasma products. Although these initiatives are examined in more detail in Chapter 8, it is important to note for present purposes that the plasma products industry must comply with quality and safety standards set out in the Blood Directive with regard to the source material (e.g. plasma) that they collect.[102] The industry is also subject to specific regulatory requirements for 'medicinal products derived from human blood and plasma', which are set out in the Directive for the Community code for medicinal products for human use.[103] One of the most important initiatives in the area has been the Plasma Master File (PMF) system.[104] The creation, maintenance and updating of the PMF is the responsibility of the manufacturers of plasma products. It must contain all the required scientific data on the quality and safety relating to the source material used in plasma products from the time of collection to manufacturing plasma pools.[105] Such developments have also contributed to enhanced regulatory oversight by the EMA of quality and safety issues involving plasma products more generally.[106]

Together, the USA and the EU comprise the largest and most financially lucrative markets for the plasma products industry. Ensuring regulatory compliance is therefore a necessary adjunct to doing business in these markets. The main industry criticisms associated with regulatory compliance between the two markets include significant additional costs due to a lack of harmonisation, as well as the fact that regulators on both sides of the Atlantic have become overly precautionary in their

---

[102] Article 31, Blood Directive.
[103] Directive 2001/83/EC of the European Parliament and of the Council of 6 November 2001 on the Community code relating to medicinal products for human use, OJ L 311, 28.11.2001.
[104] The PMF was created pursuant to Commission Directive 2003/63/EC of 25 June 2003 amending Directive 2001/83/EC of the European Parliament and of the Council on the Community code relating to medicinal products for human use, OJ L 149, 27.6.2003.
[105] European Medicines Agency, Plasma Master File (PMF) (www.ema.europa.eu).
[106] European Medicines Agency, Committee for Medicinal Products for Human Use (CHMP), Guideline on Plasma-Derived Medicinal Products, EMA/CHMP/BWP/706271/2010, 21 July 2011.

demands for enhanced product safety.[107] The industry has argued that this has resulted in the stifling of innovation, as well as an increase in costs, which could threaten the long-term viability of the industry and therefore patient access to their products.[108]

In relation to the issue of regulatory harmonisation between the USA and the EU, industry commentators have argued that although many of the concepts or principles guiding quality and safety are similar, regulators interpret them in different ways.[109] For example, there is currently no mutual recognition between the FDA and the EU regarding the use of source plasma. Therefore, products manufactured from US plasma can be accepted on the EU market following inspection approvals from EU inspectors under the PMF system. However, a separate independent licence is required for European source plasma to be used in products marketed in the USA. It has proved extremely cumbersome in practice for European source plasma collectors to obtain such licences from the FDA and most currently do not have them. Testing required on plasma also differs between the USA and the EU, thus adding to production costs which may make using European plasma for products marketed in the USA a non-economically viable proposition.[110] As a result of this regulatory variation, individual plasma product manufacturers need to make strategic economic decisions about whether to produce products that conform to the most stringent regulatory requirements, or to produce a range of products that meet the diverse national and/or supranational regulatory arrangements that currently exist.[111]

Although work has been undertaken by the FDA and the EMA, as well as through the ICH, to bring about greater regulatory harmonisation in the case of plasma products, the industry has argued that a lot more needs to be done.[112] Although it is supportive of greater cross-national and global harmonisation, the industry also recognises that one of the adverse consequences resulting from greater cooperation between national regulatory authorities may be that even more stringent

---

[107] Farrugia, 'The regulatory pendulum in transfusion medicine'.
[108] von Hoegen and Gustafson, 'The importance of greater regulatory harmonization', p. 171.
[109] Ibid., pp. 172, 175.
[110] Ibid., p. 175.
[111] N. M. Jacobson, 'The art of balanced production', Pharmaceuticals Policy and Law, 7 (2006), 81–7 at 86.
[112] Burnouf, 'Modern plasma fractionation', p. 115. The ICH brings together representatives from the global pharmaceutical industry, as well as regulatory authorities from Europe, Japan and the USA, to discuss scientific and technical aspects of product registration with a view to greater regulatory harmonisation; see www.ich.org.

requirements may be imposed upon it.[113] To that extent, it has sought to engage in dialogue on regulatory harmonisation in institutional environments which are expert-dominated, focused on technical issues and not subject to ongoing monitoring and evaluation by reference to democratically accountable institutions and mechanisms. It is for these reasons that the industry gravitates towards supranational organisations such as the ICH in the interests of promoting its own agenda for technical and/ or regulatory harmonisation.[114] It remains unclear whether this is likely to result in the enhanced safety of its products.

Conclusion

In the context of an overarching examination of the relationship between risk and innovation, this chapter analysed the commercial and industrial aspects involved in the sourcing and supply of factor concentrates used to treat haemophilia by the for-profit plasma products industry. In the 1960s, the industry emerged to address the growing demand for factor concentrates which had revolutionised the treatment of haemophilia. This occurred in circumstances where many national blood services in developed countries were unable to meet such demand through existing whole blood collection sourced through VNRBD. The fact that the industry collected much of the plasma used in its products through paid donation and operated in a dysfunctional regulatory environment at both national and supranational levels (where they existed at all) contributed to the development of exploitative and unsafe donor collection practices by the 1970s. Knowledge of such practices antagonised transfusionists working in national blood services and served to further polarise stakeholder views regarding whether blood should be seen as a either a gift or a commodity.

The dichotomous policy framing of blood as either a gift or a commodity proved to be problematic in terms of facilitating effective risk governance, particularly during the period in which HIV posed a risk to national blood systems in the 1980s. This was because it operated in practice to privilege VNRBD to the exclusion of taking account of how market processes facilitated by innovation in blood technology impacted on risk governance. This meant that the risk faced by PWH who used the industry's factor concentrates was not adequately addressed by those

---

[113] von Hoegen and Gustafson, 'The importance of greater regulatory harmonization', p. 176.
[114] J. Abraham and T. Reed, 'Trading risks for markets: the international harmonisation of pharmaceuticals regulation', *Health Risk and Society*, 3 (2001), 113–28.

with responsibility for national blood systems, resulting in high rates of HIV infection in PWH. This outcome highlighted the importance of recognising the relationship between the social and the economic in devising and implementing a holistic approach to governance processes where multi-valued human biological materials, such as blood and plasma products, are involved.

In the wake of HIV blood contamination episodes, the industry engaged in both process and product innovation with a view to enhancing product safety. While such innovation has currently significantly reduced, if not eliminated, the risk of contamination of such products by known transmissible agents, the promotion of innovation on its own should not be viewed as the great panacea for preventing or redressing failures in risk governance. The politicisation of risk that occurred in the wake of such contamination episodes now requires that innovation in this context, as well as markets in such products, be subject to stringent regulatory governance which takes account of the relationship between the social and the economic in order to enhance blood safety and facilitate the protection of patient-recipients. At a minimum, this requires regulatory cooperation and harmonisation at both national and supranational levels, involving the use of standard setting for quality and safety; the establishment of legally binding risk regulation regimes, where possible; and the monitoring of supranational regulatory governance and industry activity through democratically accountable institutions and mechanisms. Where this is not possible at supranational level, then this should take place on a periodic basis at national level.

In the wake of the loss of public trust that occurred as a result of national HIV blood contamination episodes, risk governance in the field has become politicised and this has implications for the approach taken to innovation by the industry. Although innovation involving plasma products, such as factor concentrates, has been driven primarily by the need to enhance quality and safety in the wake of such episodes, it operates as a dependent variable in the context of (regulatory) governance initiatives that have followed in the wake of the politicisation of risk in the field. While this may seem a less than satisfactory state of affairs for those involved in the industry, there is a need to accept that where there has been a loss of public trust, risk governance in the context of innovation involving multi-valued biological materials is likely to be more complex, less certain, and more prone to political and regulatory intervention.

6   The rise of the recipient

In *The Gift Relationship*, Titmuss largely focused on donors in the context of the donor–recipient relationship: their characteristics, recruitment and motivation. In contrast, the patient-recipient was minimally sketched and largely depicted as a passive and necessarily trusting individual, reliant on the goodwill of donors and national blood services.[1] He was writing at a time when those in charge of blood services, as well as the medical profession and national governments, were primarily focused on how best to organise the systematic collection of whole blood and its components to ensure that the growing demand for them was met. In this regard, ensuring that there were a sufficient number of individuals available to donate good quality and safe blood on an ongoing basis was a priority. This particular focus on donors necessarily filtered through into national and supranational blood policy and was informed in large part by the core professional beliefs of transfusionists in charge of national blood services, as has been previously discussed in Chapter 4.

In the 1980s, HIV blood contamination episodes in developed countries brought about a change in focus with regard to the donor–recipient relationship in the context of risk governance involving the blood system. One group of patient-recipients that was particularly affected by such episodes were people with haemophilia (PWH). High rates of HIV infection among this group provided the point of focus – the 'grievance'[2] – which acted as the catalyst for political mobilisation as they demanded financial redress for the harm they had suffered, as well as

---

[1] Titmuss, *The Gift Relationship*, pp. 143–4.
[2] Although I prefer to use the term 'grievance' as the descriptor which provides the impetus for mobilisation on the part of haemophilia groups, I do acknowledge that other concepts have been used to describe this phenomenon, including for example 'biographical disruption' (see G. Williams, 'The genesis of chronic illness', *Sociology of Health and Illness*, 6 (1984), 175–200); 'moral shock' (see J. Jasper and J. Poulsen, 'Recruiting strangers and friends: moral shocks and social networks in animal rights and anti-nuclear protests', *Social Problems*, 42 (1995), 104–26); and changing conceptions of 'patienthood' which has resulted in active contestation over health-related issues (see K. Landzelius, 'Introduction: Patient organization movements and new

accountability on the part of those with responsibility for blood safety with respect to the circumstances that had led to national HIV blood contamination episodes.

The aim of this chapter is to focus on how national haemophilia groups came to transform their grievances over HIV blood contamination episodes,[3] using legal tactics to realise their mobilisation goals.[4] Such tactics included the pursuit of legal action in the courts for financial compensation for the harm they had suffered; lobbying for the adoption of financial assistance legislation; and the use of legal or quasi-legal institutions, such as government-sponsored inquiries (whether judge-led or not), into the circumstances that led to the episodes.[5] What such examination reveals is the importance of a diverse range of legal tactics being available for use by aggrieved patient groups, such as those representing PWH, to realise political mobilisation goals. Notwithstanding such availability, their successful use in the present circumstances proved to be contingent upon the specific dynamics created by available 'windows of opportunity' in national legal and political contexts.[6] Although the contingent nature involved in the use of legal tactics meant that some haemophilia groups enjoyed more success than others, their use

metamorphoses in patienthood', *Social Science and Medicine*, 62 (2006), 529–37 at 529–33).

[3] I accept that other recipient groups, in particular those who contracted HIV through blood transfusion, also mounted political campaigns for redress in a number of countries. However, campaigns run by haemophilia groups tended to be much more organised with respect to the use of legal strategies to achieve campaign objectives. This accounts for the focus on haemophilia groups in this chapter.

[4] There is an extensive literature on the issue of dispute processing, particularly within US socio-legal studies. Here I am drawing in particular on the seminal paper of Felstiner *et al.* on the emergence of grievances and their transformation into disputes; see W. L. F. Felstiner, R. L. Abel and A. Sarat, 'The emergence and transformation of disputes: naming, blaming and claiming...', *Law and Society Review*, 15 (1980–81), 631–54.

[5] As mentioned in the introductory chapter, the use of the term 'law' in this book is broad and includes regulatory governance, as well as the use of private law mechanisms and legal institutions by individuals, such as PWH, who were infected with HIV through the use of plasma products.

[6] This draws on the academic literature which examines the dynamics of legal mobilisation in the context of social movements or other organised interest groups; see, for example, M. McCann, *Rights at Work: Pay Equity Reform and the Politics of Legal Mobilization* (Chicago University Press, 1994); L. Mather, 'Theorizing about trial courts: lawyers, policymaking and tobacco litigation', *Law and Social Inquiry*, 23 (1998), 897–940; A.-M. Marshall, 'Injustice frames, legality and the everyday construction of sexual harassment', *Law and Social Inquiry*, 28 (2003), 659–89; M. Pieterse, 'Health, social movements and rights-based litigation in South Africa', *Journal of Law and Society*, 35 (2008), 364–88. In using the term 'windows of opportunity', I am drawing on its use in J. W. Kingdon, *Agendas, Alternatives and Public Policies*, 1st edn (Boston: Little Brown, 1984).

nevertheless contributed to the creation of a governance environment in which those with institutional, professional and political responsibilities for the blood system were incentivised to adopt a more proactive approach to managing risk in the field.

In the post-HIV blood contamination era, such an approach included greater recourse to the use of the precautionary principle and risk regulation, both of which will be examined in more detail in the following chapters. In order to examine these arguments in detail, the political mobilisation of haemophilia groups is situated in the context of the general rise in patient activism in recent years. Thereafter, the political campaigns run by PWH groups in the wake of HIV blood contamination episodes are examined, drawing on those that took place in the USA, England and France by way of example. This is followed by an analysis of the role of legal tactics in such campaigns. The penultimate section of the chapter considers how and why the political mobilisation of haemophilia groups contributed to the politicisation of risk involving the blood system.

Contextualising the political mobilisation of haemophilia groups

The mobilisation of PWH in the wake of national HIV blood contamination episodes coincided with a general upsurge in health-related activism by patient groups.[7] Over the past thirty years, it has been argued that there has been a change in patient expectations regarding access to information, choice of treatment and quality of care.[8] In recent years, this trend has been accelerated by the opportunity to access multiple independent sources of medical and health-related information and like-minded groups via the internet.[9] This has been accompanied by a more critical analysis of the role of the medical profession in the provision of healthcare, with a particular focus on re-evaluating the profession's relationship with the state, as well as patients.[10] Patient-related activism has taken different forms, including

---

[7] J. Allsop, K. Jones and R. Baggott, 'Health consumer groups in the UK: a new social movement?', *Sociology, of Health and Illness*, 26 (2004), 737–56 at 741.

[8] R. Baggott, J. Allsop and K. Jones, *Speaking for Patients and Carers: Health Consumer Groups and the Policy Process* (Basingstoke: Palgrave, 2005), p. 9.

[9] P. Radin, '"To me, it's my life": medical communication, trust and activism in cyberspace', *Social Science and Medicine*, 62 (2006), 591–601 at 592–3; C. Ganchoff, 'Speaking for stem cells: biomedical activism and emerging forms of patienthood', *Advances in Medical Sociology*, 10 (2008), 225–45 at 229.

[10] J. Gabe, D. Kelleher and G. Williams (eds.), *Challenging Medicine* (London: Routledge, 1994); Moran, *Governing the Health Care State*, pp. 10–16; Baggott *et al.*, *Speaking for Patients and Carers*, p. 9.

facilitating access to healthcare treatments, promoting relevant scientific research, challenging established biomedical knowledge based on lay expertise, greater participation in health policy-making processes, and facilitating the accountability of health decision-makers and institutions.[11]

It has been suggested that patients' awareness and experience of illness is a key factor which leads them to identify with others and to form representative groups.[12] This was certainly the case with the formation of groups at local and national level by PWH and their families in the latter half of the twentieth century, the founding and promotion of which was often underpinned by their treating doctors. The rationale for their formation was the shared and often stigmatised experience of living with haemophilia and its consequences, particularly in circumstances where there was little or no effective medical treatment for the disease up until the 1960s. Haemophilia groups would have been traditionally characterised as 'inner-focused', insular and deferential to the medical profession and predominantly concerned with

[11] There has been a proliferation of research in this area, as well as a good deal of variation in the use of terms to describe the phenomenon: 'patient empowerment' (see J. M. Anderson, 'Empowering patients: issues and strategies', *Social Science and Medicine*, 43 (1996), 697–705); 'active patients' (see J. Barbot, 'How to build an "active patient"? The work of AIDS associations in France', *Social Science and Medicine*, 62 (2006), 538–51); 'patient emancipation' (see C. Williamson, 'The patient movement as an emancipation movement', *Health Expectations*, 11 (2008), 102–12); 'biological citizenship' (see A. Petryna, *Life Exposed: Biological Citizens after Chernobyl* (Princeton University Press, 2002); N. Rose and C. Novas, 'Biological citizenship', in A. Ong and S. Collier (eds.), *Global Assemblages: Technology, Politics and Ethics as Anthropological Problems* (Malden, MA: Blackwell Publishing, 2005), pp. 439–63); and 'therapeutic citizenship' (see V. Nguyen, 'Antiretroviral globalism: biopolitics and therapeutic citizenship', in A. Ong and S. Collier (eds.), *Global Assemblages: Technology, Politics and Ethics as Anthropological Problems* (Malden, MA: Blackwell Publishing, 2005), pp. 124–44). Various terms have also been used to describe different types of patient activist groups such as 'health social movements' (see P. Brown and S. Zavestoski, 'Social movements in health: an introduction', *Sociology of Health and Illness*, 26 (2004), 679–94) and 'health consumer groups' (see Baggott *et al.*, *Speaking for Patients and Carers*). This is in addition to research which has examined how patients' experience of illness informs the way in which they interact and challenge established biomedical knowledge (see S. Epstein, *Impure Science: AIDS, Activism and the Politics of Knowledge* (Berkeley, CA: University of California Press, 1996); K. Kielmann and F. Cataldo, 'Tracking the rise of the "expert patient" in evolving paradigms of HIV care', *AIDS Care*, 22 (2010), 21–8).

[12] P. Brown, S. Zavestoski, S. McCornick *et al.*, 'Embodied health movements: new approaches to social movements in health', *Sociology of Health and Illness*, 26 (2004), 50–80 at 55; Allsop *et al.*, 'Health consumer groups in the UK', p. 737. It has been suggested that it should not be assumed that simply sharing a patient experience will lead to the formation of a collective identity. This may turn on the field of biomedicine at issue and there may in any case be different kinds of identity formed leading to action; see Ganchoff, 'Speaking for stem cells', p. 227.

providing self-help and support for members who shared a common experience of illness.[13] Medical deference was fostered by the fact that many of their treating doctors had been involved in the management of their disease, as well as that of other family members for most, if not all, of their lives.[14] This led to the acceptance of the prevailing biomedical knowledge model, which favoured the use of factor concentrates for both preventive and treatment purposes, from the 1970s onwards. This was also accompanied by medical complacency in relation to the contraction of infectious diseases, such as HBV, which came to be viewed as an acceptable risk for PWH, given the benefits of treatment with such products.

While their shared experience of haemophilia provided the basis of a collective identity for haemophilia groups,[15] it was the sense of grievance generated in the wake of high rates of HIV infection among PWH that would provide the basis for collective action in the political and legal spheres from the late 1980s onwards.[16] Collective action in health-related areas has been conceptualised in different ways within the relevant academic literature. Some commentators have drawn on insights gained from social movement theory to explain the formation and mobilisation of different types of 'health social movements'. Such movements are said to be centrally organised around health and address issues such as access to, or the provision of, health services; health inequality and inequity based on race, ethnicity, gender, class or sexuality; and the experience of illness, disability and contested illness.[17] Other commentators have identified the phenomenon of 'protest groups' which are formed in the wake of 'adverse events'. In the UK, for example, data collected on such groups showed that more than half had been formed

[13] D. Kelleher, 'Self-help groups and medicine', in J. Gabe, D. Kelleher and G. Williams (eds.), *Challenging Medicine* (London: Routledge, 1994), pp. 104–17.

[14] Barbot, 'How to build an "active patient"?', p. 539.

[15] 'Collective identity' has been defined as an 'individual's moral and emotional connection with a broader community, category, practice or institution. It is a perception of shared status of relation which may be imagined rather than experienced directly, and it is distinct from personal identities, although it may form part of a personal identity'; see F. Polletta and J. Jasper, 'Collective identity and social movements', *Annual Review of Sociology*, 27 (2001), 283–305 at 285. Collective action is said to occur 'when people affected by a particular condition seek to alter the terms of engagement with healthcare providers and thus gain greater control over their own bodies'; see Allsop *et al.*, 'Health consumer groups in the UK', p. 737.

[16] It has been suggested that a sense of 'grievance' in the wake of the experience of illness provides the impetus for identity formation and political mobilisation; see Brown *et al.*, 'Embodied health movements', p. 58.

[17] *Ibid.*, 52; see also D. Hess, 'Technology- and product-oriented movements: approximating social movement studies and science and technology studies', *Science Technology and Human Values*, 30 (2005), 515–35.

from the early 1990s onwards.[18] Many such groups referred to them-selves as 'victims'; they tended to view medical practices as paternal-istic and oppressive; and were distrustful of healthcare professionals. The longevity of such groups varied and some ceased to exist once the period of protest was over and/or redress was (or was not) achieved.[19]

The political mobilisation of haemophilia groups in the wake of HIV blood contamination episodes does not fit easily within the typ-ology of patient activist groups referred to within the relevant academic literature. They were initially established as self-help groups for PWH and their families, as well as being firmly aligned with prevailing models of biomedical knowledge and clinical practice in relation to the treat-ment of their condition. Against this background, it could be hypoth-esised that these types of groups would tend to be 'poorly mobilised' due to their acceptance of the prevailing biomedical model and their failure to make links with and learn from other patient activist groups.[20] Although the consequences of high rates of HIV infection among PWH provided the central point of grievance which acted as a catalyst for political mobilisation, such response was not uniform amongst mem-bers of such groups, with some preferring to engage in more strident activism than others.[21] Whether mobilised through breakaway group activity or not, haemophilia groups nevertheless adopted many of the tactics described as being part of the repertoire of 'health social move-ments' and/or 'protest groups'.[22] In the final analysis, it is perhaps best to view the political mobilisation of haemophilia groups in the wake of HIV blood contamination episodes as a hybrid form of the type of patient activism identified within the relevant academic literature.

People with haemophilia and HIV blood contamination episodes

Many haemophilia groups in developed countries were formed in the latter half of the twentieth century, offering self-help and support for PWH and their families.[23] Some were more locally focused than others, but there tended to be a national office for administration, dissemination

---

[18] Allsop et al., 'Health consumer groups in the UK', p. 749.

[19] Ibid., pp. 750–1.

[20] P. Brown and S. Zavetovski, Social Movements in Health (Blackwood, NJ: Blackwell Publishing, 2005), p. 274.

[21] D. Kirp, 'The politics of blood: haemophilia activism in the AIDS crisis', in Feldman and Bayer (eds.), Blood Feuds, pp. 293–322 at 302.

[22] Allsop et al., 'Health consumer groups in the UK', pp. 750–1; Kirp, 'The politics of blood', p. 296.

[23] Resnik, Blood Saga, pp. 20–35.

and advocacy purposes. Difficulties in ensuring adequate financial support for their activities led some national groups to rely (to a greater or lesser degree) on various stakeholders in national blood systems. In the USA, for example, the for-profit plasma products industry had long provided financial support to the National Hemophilia Foundation (NHF), in addition to professional support being offered by prominent haemophilia doctors and research scientists.[24] In the UK, the association between haemophilia and the Royal Family led to elite and political support for the work of the UK Haemophilia Society.[25] In France, l'Association française des hémophiles (AFH) was situated within the National Centre for Blood Transfusion based in Paris and received ongoing financial and other support for its work from blood services.[26] In the early 1960s, the World Federation of Hemophilia (WFH) was formed to represent PWH and their families on an international basis. Over time, it created a global network of national haemophilia groups and haemophilia doctors, as well as inviting participation from other relevant stakeholder groups, through a series of regular meetings, including the holding of biannual Congresses. The WFH became a forum for exchanging ideas on research and best practice regarding the treatment of haemophilia, including issues relating to the management of risk.[27]

The relationship between PWH and their treating doctors was both paternalistic and protective, with many doctors having known their patients for most of their lives. PWH and their families placed absolute trust in their treating doctors and the medical advice they provided to them in relation to the treatment they received, the risks involved and the products used for their condition.[28] As a result of the dynamics of this relationship, doctors who were involved in the treatment of haemophilia were more often than not influential in the formation and development of national haemophilia groups. In the USA,

---

[24] The NHF was forced to declare bankruptcy in the late 1970s due to ongoing financial problems. This contributed to its reliance on financial support from the plasma products industry; see Leveton *et al.*, *HIV and the Blood Supply*, p. 173. In any case, there had long been support on the part of many US haemophilia doctors for collaboration with the plasma products industry. Kenneth Brinkhous, the scientist who had been responsible for initial breakthroughs in haemophilia research, had been the first chair of the NHF's internal medical advisory committee, known as MASAC. Brinkhous had also been responsible for the collaborative partnership with Hyland (Baxter) that had led to the trialling and marketing of factor concentrates in the 1960s; see Resnik, *Blood Saga*, p. 40.

[25] Berridge, *AIDS in the UK*.   [26] Starr, *Blood*, p. 310.

[27] World Federation of Hemophilia (www.wfh.org).

[28] Leveton *et al.*, *HIV and the Blood Supply*, p. 171.

the NHF formed an internal expert advisory committee, known as the Medical and Scientific Advisory Council (MASAC), which was comprised of scientists involved in researching haemophilia, as well as haemophilia doctors.[29] In France, the traditionally close and paternalistic relationship between PWH and their treating doctors was further strengthened by the notion of *la médicine liberale*, which saw the doctor placed in a position of ultimate authority by the patient, as well as the state.[30] In England, haemophilia doctors organised themselves on an independent basis through the UK Haemophilia Centre Doctors' Organisation (UKHCDO). The organisation collected and coordinated data on haemophilia, as well as on the treatment received by PWH. The work of haemophilia doctors in England was embedded within the overarching structure of the NHS. Therefore, treatment, product and funding decisions were often influenced by the preferences of individual senior haemophilia doctors, in line with local and/ or regional health budgets. The nature of the doctor–patient relationship reflected the paternalistic approach taken in other developed countries as well.[31]

Up until the 1980s, there were a number of issues that were of common concern to national haemophilia groups in developed countries: promoting scientific research and advances in technology in relation to the treatment of haemophilia, as well as ensuring that PWH received appropriate treatment for their condition. In the USA, for example, the NHF became politicised, engaging in advocacy and lobbying on behalf of its membership. Its preferred approach was to operate separately from other groups representing those with other chronic conditions, viewing haemophilia and the problems associated with it as requiring particular attention.[32] Their advocacy efforts were successful, resulting in greater political recognition being given to haemophilia. This included funding for Haemophilia Treatment Centres and the delivery of what became known as the comprehensive care model to the national haemophilia population.[33] When combined with the use of

---

[29] Resnik, *Blood Saga*, p. 36.
[30] Casteret, *L'Affaire du sang contaminé*, p. 113.
[31] Archer *et al.*, *Independent Public Inquiry Report*, pp. 11, 60–2.
[32] Resnik, *Blood Saga*, p. 57.
[33] The comprehensive care model employs a multi-disciplinary approach to dealing with the medical, rehabilitative and psychosocial effects of having haemophilia. It is particularly focused on the anticipation and/or prevention of illness, injury and death associated with the condition. It is usually delivered by a dedicated team of healthcare professionals in a specialised haemophilia treatment centre; see B. L. Evatt, 'The natural evolution of haemophilia care: developing and sustaining comprehensive care globally', *Haemophilia*, 12 (2006), 13–21 at 13–14.

factor concentrates and home therapy,[34] it provided independence and near normal life expectancy for PWH.[35] It was a model that would gain broad acceptance internationally and was subsequently implemented in a number of other countries in the 1970s and 1980s,[36] although the extent to which sufficient supplies of factor concentrates were available to implement successful comprehensive care regimes varied between countries.[37]

Prior to the emergence of HIV, the availability of cryoprecipitate and then factor concentrates had transformed the lives of many PWH and their families.[38] In relation to cryoprecipitate, the product could be prepared and distributed by local blood services. For many PWH, treatment with the product could still involve attendance at, and/or admission to, a local hospital as it took time for cryoprecipitate to thaw from frozen before it could be administered. However, the donor exposure from using the product was relatively low, usually ranging between five and fifteen donors in order to treat a bleeding episode.[39] In contrast, vials of the white powder that made up the industrially produced factor concentrates could be stored in the home refrigerator and once a person with haemophilia (or a member of their family) had received the appropriate training, they could then self-treat bleeds at home or wherever they were based. The donor exposure resulting from the use of factor concentrates presented a much higher risk of transmission of blood-borne infectious agents, as anywhere between 1,000 and 50,000 plasma donations could be used in the manufacture of a single lot of the product.[40] The revolutionary effect which factor concentrates had on the lives of PWH structured how their treating doctors viewed the risk of transmissible diseases in such products. There was a strong professional belief held by haemophilia doctors in the efficacy of factor concentrates, which it was argued bordered on 'unwarranted dogmatism'.[41]

---

[34] 'Home therapy' involves PWH treating their bleeding episodes themselves, whether at home or elsewhere. The advantage of home therapy is that bleeding episodes can be treated quickly and usually without the need to attend the hospital for treatment. This assists in preventing the more debilitating effects of such episodes and also gives PWH more control over their condition, as well as their lives more generally.

[35] Resnik, *Blood Saga*, p. 110.

[36] Evatt, 'The natural evolution of haemophilia care', p. 13; Rizza *et al.*, 'Treatment of haemophilia in the UK', p. 349.

[37] There were significant problems in meeting the growing demand for factor concentrates in countries such as England during the 1970s and 1980s; see Archer *et al.*, *Independent Public Inquiry Report*, pp. 23–40.

[38] *Ibid.*, pp. 90–5.

[39] Resnik, *Blood Saga*, p. 41.

[40] Krever, *Commission of Inquiry on the Blood System*, p. 22.

[41] Archer *et al.*, *Independent Public Inquiry Report*, p. 63.

This in turn led to a professional complacency about the transmission of viruses, such as HBV. This came to be viewed as an 'acceptable risk' for PWH in the 1970s, given what were seen as the immense benefits of treatment with factor concentrates.[42]

There was a remarkable degree of commonality in the way in which the risk faced by PWH was dealt with in the early to mid 1980s in countries such as the USA, England and France. In the context of uncertainty over the aetiology and consequences of infection with AIDS, many haemophilia doctors opted to maintain the status quo, recommending that those with the severe form of haemophilia continue treatment with factor concentrates. They only sought to minimise exposure to factor concentrates in relation to PWH who required treatment on an irregular basis or those who were newly diagnosed with the condition.[43] As mentioned previously, a strongly paternalistic doctor–patient relationship existed in the context of treatment of haemophilia during this period. This resulted in an approach to risk communication with patients about HIV that was based on reassurance, rather than one which engaged in a full and frank discussion of patient concerns or a consideration of alternative treatment options. One of the more troubling aspects of such paternalism during this period was that it led haemophilia doctors to expose their patients to HIV testing and other studies, often without their knowledge or consent.[44]

---

[42] Leveton et al., HIV and the Blood Supply, pp. 171–2. A notable exception to this view was held by a then leading US haemophilia physician, Dr Oscar Ratnoff. He had long advocated the use of cryoprecipitate, given the greater risk of contracting HBV (and thereafter HIV) from the use of high donor exposure products, such as factor concentrates; see Resnik, Blood Saga, p. 132.

[43] The guidelines issued by the NHF in the USA in January 1983 were subsequently adopted (with some variation) in many other countries as well. Key guidelines included that PWH with the severe form of the disease should continue to use factor concentrates or cryoprecipitate as prescribed by their physicians; those with little or no exposure to factor concentrates should be treated with cryoprecipitate, including children under the age of four years, those newly diagnosed with haemophilia and those with the mild form of the disease who required infrequent treatment (National Hemophilia Foundation, Medical and Scientific Advisory Council, Recommendations to Prevent AIDS in Patients with Hemophilia, 14 January 1983; see Leveton et al., HIV and the Blood Supply, Appendix D, p. 279). For the guidelines adopted in the UK and Ireland, see Lindsay, Report of the Tribunal of Inquiry, pp. 154–5.

[44] In France, for example, a well-known transfusionist and haemophilia doctor, Jean-Pierre Allain along with a number of colleagues, undertook research between 1983 and 1985 which involved monitoring PWH at various treatment centres to assess the relative safety of US- versus locally-sourced factor concentrates. The PWH who were the subject of the research were not informed about the study or its results. At the time, in March 1984, Allain reported that 45 per cent of blood samples collected from PWH were positive for HIV. A year later, he reported that a further 45 per cent of PWH who were previously negative for HIV were now positive for the virus (see Casteret, L'Affaire du sang contaminé, pp. 93–4, 116, 140).

With a paternalistic approach to the treatment of their patients, a professional commitment to the ongoing use of factor concentrates and continuing complacency over the risk of disease transmission in such products, haemophilia doctors (as well as transfusionists) failed to consider sufficiently robust risk reduction strategies in relation to the emerging risk posed by HIV to national haemophilia populations in the early to mid 1980s.[45] This was evidenced by the refusal to countenance a switch back, even on an interim basis, to the use of the less risky cryoprecipitate by those PWH who were treated with factor concentrates on a regular basis. Instead, the focus of concern remained primarily on the adverse logistical, cost and human resource problems associated with such a switch, rather than due consideration being given to the potential for PWH to enjoy a higher level of safety as a result of such a decision being made.[46]

An important risk reduction strategy would have included a timely changeover to the use of heat-treated factor concentrates by PWH. As was previously mentioned in Chapter 5, research into the use of heat treatment of such products by the plasma products industry had been underway since the 1970s.[47] Individual companies had eventually obtained licences from the FDA to make use of the process to inactivate HBV in the early 1980s. It was also considered likely that the process would be effective in inactivating HIV,[48] which was subsequently confirmed in late 1984.[49] Notwithstanding such developments, it would take a further year or even longer in some countries to ensure that heat-treated products were made available to their national haemophilia populations.[50] It has been argued that the relative slowness of such a move was attributable to a number of factors: there was a need to seek governmental and/or regulatory approval for the use of such products;

[45] Leveton et al., HIV and the Blood Supply, pp. 193–204; Archer et al., Independent Public Inquiry Report, pp. 42, 62–3.

[46] For the approach taken in the USA, see Leveton et al., HIV and the Blood Supply, pp. 175, 177–8; Resnik, Blood Saga, p. 130. For the approach taken in France, see Casteret, L'Affaire du sang contaminé, pp. 15, 82–3; Soulier, Transfusion et sida, p. 41.

[47] See Chapter 5, pp. 106–7.

[48] Resnik, Blood Saga, pp. 91–2.

[49] J. A. Levy, G. Mitra and M. M. Mozen, 'Recovery and inactivation of infectious retroviruses from factor VIII concentration', Lancet, ii (1984), 722–3.

[50] The NHF in the USA recommended a changeover to the use of heat-treated factor concentrates in October 1984 (see Leveton et al., HIV and the Blood Supply, p. 174). In England, calls were made for the introduction of heat-treated factor concentrates in December 1984 and products were imported from the USA from January 1985 onwards (see Editorial, 'Blood transfusion, haemophilia and AIDS', Lancet, ii (1984), 1433–5). In France, the changeover to heat-treated products did not take place until October 1985 (see Casteret, L'Affaire du sang contaminé, pp. 170–3).

additional financial resources had to be made available by national governments for the ordering of the products; and there needed to be an orderly changeover in industrial facilities to accommodate the manufacture of the products and to deal with the existing inventory of non-heat-treated products.[51] This was compounded by concerns about the clinical efficacy of such products. On this point, some haemophilia doctors were reluctant about prescribing heat-treated products for their patients given concerns about their contribution to inhibitor development, as well as the fact that the products were only officially licensed to inactivate HBV and many PWH had already been infected with this virus.[52]

Although mention has been made in previous chapters regarding the rates of HIV infection involving PWH in countries such as the USA, England and France, it is worth restating such findings here for the purposes of what is examined in subsequent sections of this chapter. Once HIV testing became available in 1985, it became apparent that there was a very high rate of HIV infection amongst the US haemophilia community. The overall infection rate was 63 per cent, with 96 per cent of those with the severe form of factor VIII deficiency becoming infected with the virus. Retrospective studies of blood samples collected on PWH showed that the first case of HIV involving a person with haemophilia had probably occurred in 1978 in the USA. The peak time for infection occurred around October 1982, declining significantly by July 1984.[53] In England, the overall rate of HIV infection for the national haemophilia population was 34 per cent, with the rate rising to 75 per cent for those who used US-sourced factor concentrates on a regular basis.[54] In France, the overall rate of HIV infection among

---

[51] Dealing with the existing inventory of non-heat-treated factor concentrates seemed to be uppermost in the mind of Dr Michel Garetta, then head of the Paris blood service and plasma products manufacturing facility. Although he was recorded as admitting that all lots of such products were likely to be contaminated with HIV in May 1985, he nevertheless ordered that such products continue to be distributed to unsuspecting PWH until the government approved the changeover to the use of heat-treated products, which took place later in 1985 (see Lucas, *Transfusion sanguine et SIDA*, pp. 40, 52; Casteret, *L'Affaire du sang contaminé*, pp. 149–50).

[52] It has been suggested that the high cost associated with using heat-treated factor concentrates in the USA may in fact have been the prime motivation for the delay in the NHF endorsing the move towards their widespread use before October 1984; see Resnik, *Blood Saga*, p. 130. In the 1983–84 period, leading haemophilia doctors in France were not convinced about the clinical efficacy of heat-treated factor concentrates; see Lucas, *Transfusion sanguine et SIDA*, p. 21.

[53] Kroner *et al.*, 'HIV-1 infection incidence among persons with hemophilia in the United States and Europe', pp. 280–1; Leveton *et al.*, *HIV and the Blood Supply*, p. 21.

[54] Cheingsong-Popov *et al.*, 'Prevalence of antibody to human T-lymphotropic virus type III'; Rizza *et al.*, 'Treatment of haemophilia in the UK'.

the national haemophilia population was 38 per cent, the highest in Europe. As with England, both US and locally sourced factor concentrates were implicated in the HIV infections of PWH.

Haemophilia groups, political mobilisation and the use of law

From the late 1980s onwards, haemophilia groups began to mobilise and undertake political campaigns demanding financial redress, as well as for those responsible for national HIV blood contamination episodes to be held to account. The initial catalyst for such mobilisation was the increasing ill-health of HIV-infected members and the consequent deterioration in their financial and personal situations. It marked the transition from such groups being constituted primarily as insular, self-help groups to being openly engaged in political activism, employing a range of strategies to realise their campaign goals. In this section, the focus is on the mobilisation of haemophilia groups in England, France and the USA, reflecting the chronological order in which mobilisation occurred. While there were several common strategies employed by these groups, there were also some significant differences reflecting the peculiarities of specific national political and legal contexts, as well as the nature and extent of opportunities that presented themselves. While haemophilia groups employed a range of tactics as part of their political campaigns, the focus of examination is on the use of legal tactics and the extent to which they influenced the realisation of campaign goals, as well as the political response to the fallout from national HIV blood contamination episodes.

England

The UK Haemophilia Society launched its first political campaign on behalf of HIV-infected members in 1987.[55] They demanded that the government establish a trust fund to provide financial assistance to its HIV-infected membership and their families. The Society framed this campaign in terms of the government having a moral responsibility to provide financial assistance, initially downplaying any potential legal responsibility that it might have as well. The Society emphasised that a failure to achieve national self-sufficiency in factor concentrates had

---

[55] The Society's political campaign was brought on behalf of its HIV-infected members throughout the UK. For the purposes of comparative analysis, however, the focus of examination in this section is predominantly on what took place in England.

resulted in a high level of dependency upon US-sourced products and it was these products that had been responsible for the vast majority of HIV infections among the national haemophilia population.[56] It viewed payment of adequate financial redress as an acceptance of political responsibility on the part of the government for what had happened to its HIV-infected members.

In terms of tactics, the Society preferred to focus on attracting media and parliamentary support for its campaign. In relation to media support, a leading UK newspaper, *The Sunday Times*, launched a campaign to force the government to meet the Society's demands. In addition, the Society focused on the political lobbying of Members of Parliament (MPs) in order to generate cross-party support for its campaign. In the mid to late 1980s, AIDS-related issues were viewed by many MPs in morally pejorative terms, with PWH being viewed as 'innocent victims' of the HIV blood contamination episode, as opposed to other groups that had been affected by the disease, such as gay men or intravenous drug users.[57] The Haemophilia Society was able to make use of this favourable political climate to garner parliamentary support for having PWH with HIV recognised as a special group which deserved particular recognition through the payment of financial redress.[58] The Society had long enjoyed political (as well as royal) patronage.[59] It played on these connections in order to attract support for its campaign, as well as taking advantage of the particular moral framing accorded to its HIV-infected membership in the political sphere.[60]

Although the government's initial response to the Society's campaign was to suggest that it was 'up to the courts to decide whether to attribute blame' and to argue that it did not want to set either a legal or political precedent for the payment of financial compensation to one particular group affected by the AIDS epidemic in the UK,[61] it eventually relented in the face of cross-party parliamentary support on the issue. In November 1987, the government agreed to make an ex-gratia payment of £10 million to provide financial assistance to PWH with HIV. Payment of such monies would be facilitated through the establishment of what became known as the Macfarlane Trust, to which

---

[56] J. Sherman, 'AIDS payment call for haemophiliacs', *The Times* (13/4/87).
[57] House of Commons, Parliamentary Debates, Vol. 105, 832–58.
[58] House of Commons, Social Services Committee, *Problems Associated with AIDS* (Paper 192–1), Vol. 1 (London: HMSO, 1987).
[59] Berridge, *AIDS in the UK*, p. 44.
[60] A. Pike, 'Plea by the haemophiliacs who have AIDS', *Financial Times* (10/11/87).
[61] Medical Correspondent, 'Blood victims need state relief fund of £2million a year', *The Guardian* (16/5/87).

applications could be made for financial assistance.[62] Disillusionment amongst PWH with HIV quickly set in, as delays in establishing the Trust lengthened and administrative and other obstacles were created to prevent easy access to much needed financial assistance.

The Society had initially been reluctant to support legal action by individual HIV-infected members, because it considered that such action had limited prospects for success. Growing disillusionment with the way in which the Macfarlane Trust operated led the Society to change its position to one of support for such litigation. In the next stage of its campaign, the Society again attracted cross-party parliamentary support. MPs began a letter-writing campaign to newspapers, the Prime Minister and other members of government, as well as tabling motions for debate on the matter in Parliament.[63] Although the government responded with a further payment of £19 million into the Macfarlane Trust, this did not satisfy the Society or its HIV-infected members. They wanted the flexibility provided by direct lump sum payments without the need to go through the Trust and considered that the successful settlement of group litigation offered them the best chance of achieving this result.[64] As a result, pre-trial applications and procedures in the group litigation continued throughout 1989 and 1990, with the first 'test case' being listed for trial in early 1991.[65]

Pre-trial litigation revealed that the government was most anxious to keep its policy documentation on the management of the blood system in the 1970s and 1980s from becoming available to the plaintiffs. It claimed public interest immunity on all such documentation on the grounds that 'public exposure of how policy is formed damages the decision-making process'.[66] In contrast, plaintiffs and their legal representatives saw it as a cynical attempt at covering up why national self-sufficiency had not been achieved during this period. In September 1990, the Court of Appeal ruled that the plaintiffs were entitled to see the documentation.[67] This ruling changed the dynamics of the litigation, as well as the wider political campaign on the part of the Society and its HIV-infected members. With a trial date for the first 'test case'

---

[62] M. Fletcher, 'Haemophiliacs with AIDS to get cash help', *The Times* (11/11/87); House of Commons, Parliamentary Debates, Vol. 122, 767 (16/11/87).

[63] M. Driscoll, '200 MPs join compensation battle', *The Sunday Times* (5/11/89).

[64] C. Brown, '£19 million for victims of HIV blood', *The Independent* (24/11/89).

[65] *Re HIV Haemophiliac Litigation* (1990) 41 BMLR 171 (Court of Appeal, Civ. Div). Details of the litigation, as well as settlement documentation, can be accessed at www.taintedblood.info/evidence.php.

[66] J. Davison and M. Driscoll, 'Compensation fight delayed by secrecy', *The Sunday Times* (29/7/90).

[67] *Re HIV Haemophiliac Litigation*.

pending, a range of institutional, political, professional and legal interests began to put pressure on the government to bring about a settlement of the litigation.[68] At the same time, senior civil servants also expressed their disquiet about the ongoing litigation and were particularly concerned that the government's policy of heavy reliance on the importation of US-sourced factor concentrates should not be subject to cross-examination at trial.[69] Finally, Mr Justice Ognall, the judge in charge of managing the group litigation, wrote a private letter to the parties to the litigation urging settlement. In the letter, which was subsequently leaked to the media, he argued that the government had a 'moral duty' to compensate the plaintiffs.[70]

Notwithstanding such appeals, however, the government remained firm in its opposition to the settlement of the litigation, having received legal advice that it had a good defence.[71] However, the position of the government was soon to change, with the removal of Margaret Thatcher as Prime Minister by her party. John Major became the new Prime Minister and moved to settle the group haemophilia litigation, seeing it as a political opportunity to present himself as a compassionate leader and therefore to distinguish himself from his predecessor.[72] In December 1990, he announced that an out-of-court settlement of £42 million had been agreed in respect of 1,200 legal claims that had now been brought by PWH with HIV. Cases in which there was a reasonable chance of proving negligence were to be settled separately.[73] Although the Society remained unhappy with the overall amount offered by the government, it was nevertheless prepared to recommend that its HIV-infected members accept the deal to end the litigation, particularly in view of their ill-health and limited life expectancy.[74] It took until

---

[68] F. Gibb, 'AIDS victims back in Court to urge release of papers', *The Times* (11/09/90); J. Davison and M. Driscoll, 'Doctors back haemophiliacs', *The Sunday Times* (11/11/90).

[69] C. Dyer, 'Clarke urged to settle AIDS claims', *The Guardian* (3/08/90).

[70] A copy of the letter sent by Mr Justice Ognall can be accessed at www.taintedblood. info/files/Harry%20Ognall.pdf.

[71] C. Dyer, 'Judge urges haemophilia settlement', *The Guardian* (1/10/90).

[72] Unknown author, 'Of cash and care and simple sense', *The Guardian* (2/12/90); R. Oakley and J. Sherman, 'Major pledges another £42million for haemophiliacs', *The Times* (12/12/90).

[73] A scale of payment was established depending on the type of plaintiff: a single man was to receive £23,500; married men with no children £32,500; married men with children £60,500; and HIV-infected partners £23,500. See *Re HIV Haemophilia Litigation*, The Main Settlement Agreement, 24/4/91 (www.taintedblood.info/files/ Settlement%20Agreement.pdf).

[74] A. Travis and C. Dyer, 'Government offers extra £42 million to blood victims', *The Guardian* (12/12/90).

June 1991 before the settlement was approved by the High Court and compensation was paid.[75]

In the mid to late 1990s, the Society turned its attention to campaigning for compensation for those of its members who had been infected with HCV. Similar tactics that had been employed during the earlier HIV campaign were also used in this campaign, including political lobbying of MPs, as well as the government.[76] The Society presented a revised financial compensation plan to the government in 2002.[77] In 2004, the government announced that it would provide limited financial compensation to PWH infected with HCV through what would become known as the Skipton Fund.[78] For the Society, as well as independent campaign groups of PWH that had emerged, such as Manor House and the Tainted Blood group,[79] the ongoing campaign for financial redress and political accountability had now been reframed as the contaminated blood disaster incorporating blood contamination episodes involving both HIV and HCV.[80] It was recognised that the HIV campaign of the late 1980s and early 1990s had failed to secure adequate long-term financial compensation and ongoing support for PWH. PWH and their families considered that they had been forced into a litigation settlement because of their anticipated limited life expectancy at the time. With improvements in the treatment of HIV, a significant number of PWH were still alive and in severe financial difficulties, often dealing with medical complications and treatment arising from infection with both viruses.[81]

Another noticeable aspect of the newly reframed contaminated blood disaster campaign was the demand for a government-sponsored inquiry into the circumstances that had led to PWH becoming infected with HIV and HCV. Galvanised by similar inquiries that had taken place in countries such as Canada and Ireland, the Society and associated independent campaign groups clearly saw the value in making use of

---

[75] Home News, '£42 million AIDS case finishes', *The Guardian* (11/06/91).

[76] A. Barnett, 'Blood blunder killed over 100 patients', *The Guardian* (7/11/99).

[77] J. Meikle, 'Haemophiliacs demand £522m payout', *The Guardian* (19/06/02).

[78] D. Batty, 'Reid agrees compensation over contaminated blood', *The Guardian* (23/01/04).

[79] The Manor House group is described as a 'group campaigning for justice for people with bleeding disorders who have been infected with deadly viruses through contaminated NHS treatment'. The Tainted Blood group is described as an 'independent campaigning and support group for those affected by the contaminated blood disaster'; see www.haemophilia.org.uk/get_involved/Contaminated+Blood+Campaign.

[80] For details of the Contaminated Blood campaign objectives as coordinated by the UK Haemophilia Society, see www.haemophilia.org.uk/get_involved/Contaminated+Blood+Campaign/The+Campaign/Campaign+Objectives.

[81] L. Martin, 'Aids scandal survivors demand new payout', *The Guardian* (16/04/06).

this legal tactic as a mechanism for facilitating political and institutional accountability for the contamination episodes. In light of the government's ongoing refusal to establish such an inquiry, a privately funded inquiry was established under the chairmanship of Lord Archer of Sandwell QC, which ran from 2007 to 2009.[82] The Archer Report, which was published in 2009, argued that a full public inquiry should have been held much earlier to address the issues raised by the haemophilia community. It found that there had been 'procrastination' on the part of the government with respect to achieving national self-sufficiency in the 1970s and 1980s, which had disastrous consequences in view of the significant reliance that was then placed on US-sourced factor concentrates which were highly contaminated with HIV and HCV. In the circumstances, it was found that a 'significant burden of responsibility' lay with US-based plasma product manufacturers. The Report concluded that 'commercial interests' had taken precedence over public health concerns and this should not be allowed to happen again. A series of recommendations was made regarding the improvement of financial redress arrangements for PWH and their families, as well as how best to improve patient involvement in decision-making about the treatment of haemophilia in England.[83]

The initial government response to the Archer Report was lukewarm, with the then Labour government refusing to accept the need for further compensation to be made available on an equivalent basis to the more generous payments that had been paid to PWH in Ireland in respect of their HIV and HCV infections.[84] In order to force the government to respond in a more positive way to the Report, Lord Morris of Manchester, a member of the House of Lords and President of the UK Haemophilia Society, tabled a Private Members' Bill which required full implementation of the recommendations set out in the Archer Report.[85] In addition, Andrew March, a person with haemophilia infected with

---

[82] Although the focus of examination is on what has taken place in England, it is important to note that there have been separate arrangements made for the payment of financial compensation in Scotland. In addition, a Scottish government-sponsored inquiry (the Penrose Inquiry) was established in 2008 to examine the circumstances in which PWH became infected with HIV and HCV through the use of NHS blood and blood products. A preliminary report was published in October 2010 and the inquiry is ongoing at the time of writing. For further details, see www.penroseinquiry.org.uk.

[83] Archer *et al.*, *Independent Public Inquiry Report*, pp. 105–10.

[84] Department of Health, Government response to Lord Archer's independent report on NHS supplied contaminated blood and blood products (London: Department of Health, 2009).

[85] The Contaminated Blood (Support for Infected and Bereaved Persons) Bill [HL] 2009–10. The Bill was the subject of a parliamentary debate in October 2010. In the absence of government support for the Bill, it is unlikely to ever be adopted as legislation.

HCV and a leading member of the independent campaign group Tainted Blood, brought an application for judicial review in the High Court challenging the reasoning set out in the government's decision not to offer further compensation in light of the Report. In April 2010, the High Court quashed the government's decision, thus requiring it to revisit the matter.[86] The incoming Conservative–Liberal Democrat coalition government then promised to review the matter. In January 2011, the government announced that further compensation payments would be made available to those infected with HIV and HCV, as well as family members in certain circumstances.[87] Many PWH remained unhappy with the amount offered by the government, viewing the criteria for eligibility and payment as overly restrictive. More broadly, the government's response was seen by many within the haemophilia community as simply 'a gesture rather than a settlement' and was therefore unlikely to bring 'closure' to the victims of the contaminated blood disaster in England.[88]

France

In the late 1980s, many PWH began to suffer from AIDS-related illnesses and the death toll began to rise in France. Their representative organisation, the AFH, found itself in a difficult position. It had long received institutional and professional support and was wary of antagonising those who provided such support. As a result, it initially preferred to pursue a campaign which adopted an 'accommodationist' strategy with the government, pursuing negotiations with a view to establishing a financial assistance fund for its HIV-infected members.[89]

---

[86] *The Queen (on the application of Andrew Michael March)* v. *The Secretary of State for Health* [2010] EWHC 765 (Admin) Case No. CO/9344/09.

[87] The additional compensation made payable includes an increase in payments from £25,000 to £50,000 for those who have progressed to more serious disease associated with HCV; there is to be an ongoing, index-linked payment of £12,800 per annum for those infected with HCV; all payments are to be exempted from means testing for social care service; there will be access to further payments by those infected with HCV on a discretionary basis in relation to particular needs; and the exclusion of families who lost a family member to HCV before 2003 is to be removed (see House of Commons, Parliamentary Debates (Hansard), Statement by the Honourable Mr Andrew Lansley, Secretary of State for Health, Contaminated Blood, Vol. 521, No. 95, Cols. 33–35 (10/01/2011)). The devolved administrations in Wales, Northern Ireland and Scotland have also announced their support for these additional payments (www.haemophilia.org.uk).

[88] S. Boseley, 'Increased offer for NHS patients infected with hepatitis C "disappointing"', *The Guardian* (10/1/11).

[89] Casteret, *L'Affaire du sang contaminé*, pp. 195, 111–12; Steffen, 'The nation's blood', pp. 110–11.

Initially, the AFH's campaign appeared to have little influence within government and bureaucratic circles, with concerns being expressed that if the AFH's demands were met, it would set an unwelcome precedent for compensating specific groups who had suffered injury through medical treatment.[90] The government eventually shifted its position on this matter, however, and offered to make ex-gratia payments to PWH with HIV in what was then described as an act of national solidarity.

In 1989, an initial agreement was reached between the AFH, the state, national social insurance funds and insurers for regional blood services to establish a compensation fund for PWH with HIV. It was to be funded through a tax on national social insurance funds. The proposed agreement was never in fact implemented, in the wake of a significant media and public backlash over the proposed funding mechanism for the ex-gratia payments. In the circumstances, it was felt that the government itself should accept responsibility for funding the payments, rather than its citizens.[91] At the same as this agreement was falling apart, fault-lines emerged within the AFH over the way in which it was conducting its campaign. Some of its more militant HIV-infected members wanted it to take more decisive action in demanding justice for what had happened to them. This eventually led one person with haemophilia with HIV, Jean-Pierre Garvanoff, to break away from the AFH and form *l'Association des polytransfusés* (AP) in 1989. The AP adopted a more militant approach than the AFH, using direct action tactics against those they considered responsible for their HIV infection. The tactics were similar to the ones being used by other AIDS activist groups, such as ACT-UP.[92] In addition, legal action was pursued in both criminal and civil jurisdictions against their treating doctors and various state entities.[93]

In the early 1990s, the situation changed again in the wake of damaging media revelations about the circumstances which had led to the HIV blood contamination episode in France. Leaked documents showed that Dr Michel Garetta, the head of the Paris blood service, was aware that all the lots of factor concentrates being distributed in 1985 were contaminated with HIV. In addition, Garetta and other senior political and administrative figures had established a series of corporate

---

[90] Casteret, *L'Affaire du sang contaminé*, p. 211.
[91] Steffen, 'The nation's blood', 113–14.
[92] ACT-UP (AIDS Coalition to Unleash Power) is a direct action advocacy group which acts on behalf of people with AIDS (PWA). Such advocacy is conducted in a range of social, political and medical arenas with a view to improving treatment and recognition of the needs of PWA.
[93] Feldman, 'Blood justice', p. 689.

structures to facilitate the commercial development of plasma products on the international blood market, which came very close to infringing the not-for-profit principle upon which the French national blood service had been based since the 1950s.[94] The public reaction to such media revelations was one of 'general stupefaction' that the French state and its administration could have knowingly engaged in such activity in relation to vulnerable French citizens. There was also a degree of shock that the much lauded French blood system had now been exposed as tainted.[95] The damaging revelations led to the resignation of Garetta as head of the Paris blood service in 1991.

In response to such revelations in the media, the Minister for Health commissioned a report by Michel Lucas, the Inspector-Général for Social Affairs, into the factual circumstances of what had now become known as *l'affaire du sang contaminé*. Published in September 1991, the Lucas Report concluded that transfusionists had failed to adequately manage the risk posed by HIV to the blood system and that the government had been primarily driven by economic and industrial, rather than safety, concerns in relation to the introduction of HIV testing in 1985.[96] In the wake of such findings and with increased media pressure on the government, the AFH began to press for a renegotiated compensation package for its HIV-infected members. It abandoned its 'accommodationist strategy' with the state, supporting its members, as well as the AP, in pursuing their legal action in the courts.[97]

By now, there were over 400 cases brought by PWH with HIV that were pending in administrative and criminal courts. Following a lengthy debate in the French Parliament, legislation was adopted to provide further and better financial compensation to PWH with HIV in early 1992. This was to be paid separately to any financial compensation that they received through legal action in the courts.[98] In addition, the government committed itself to widespread institutional reform of the French blood system, which was designed to ensure centralised policy and regulatory control over blood quality and safety.[99] Plasma

---

[94] M. Laronche, 'La Fondation nationale de transfusion sanguine justifie ses comptes', *Le Monde* (8/06/91).

[95] Casteret, *L'Affaire du sang contaminé*, p. 222.

[96] Lucas, *Transfusion sanguine et SIDA*, pp. 27–30, 42.

[97] J.-Y. Nau, 'L'association française des hémophiles réclame des indemnisations immédiates', *Le Monde* (16/09/91).

[98] Art. 47, Loi n° 91–1406 du 31 décembre 1991 portant diverses dispositions d'ordre social (1), JORF n° 3 du 4 janvier 1992, p. 178; see also Steffen, 'The nation's blood', pp. 114–15.

[99] J.-Y. Nau and F. Nouchi, 'La réforme du système de transfusion visera à garantir "la plus grande sécurité possible"', *Le Monde* (5/11/91).

products manufacture was reorganised and the earlier monopoly on the importation of plasma products by the Paris blood service was removed. Importation of plasma products would now be permitted, subject to centralised regulatory control. New training and professional review programmes for transfusionists involved in the French blood service were instituted, to be situated within the University hospital system.[100]

Notwithstanding such government reforms, the political fallout and negative public reaction to the HIV blood contamination episode was given further momentum as a result of three sets of legal proceedings that lasted throughout the 1990s and only came to an end in 2003.[101] In the first set of legal proceedings, it was announced in late 1991 that Michel Garetta and Professor Jean-Pierre Allain, formerly a senior clinician and researcher who had also been based at the Paris blood service in the 1980s, were to be indicted on criminal charges in relation to merchandising fraud under a 1905 law. Professor Jacques Roux, the former Minister for Health, and Dr Robert Netter, the director of the national agency for regulating pharmaceuticals, were also indicted on the criminal charge of failing to provide assistance to persons in danger.[102] Joined to these proceedings were claims for financial compensation that had been brought by individual PWH with HIV, which had by now been consolidated together in Paris.[103] The proceedings were framed in such a way that the trial judge was only required to consider what had happened between 21 March and 1 October 1985, and then only what had happened in relation to the manufacture and supply of products that were used in the treatment of PWH who were subsequently infected with HIV. It was suggested that the framing of the

---

[100] Starr, *Blood*, pp. 347, 351; Steffen, 'The nation's blood', pp. 121–2.
[101] It was agreed that all pending cases in the administrative, civil and criminal jurisdictions in various provinces arising out of the HIV blood contamination episode should be consolidated in Paris as far as possible. While there was no consistency of approach within the administrative court cases, the investigating judge in the civil cases held consultations with the public prosecutor, plaintiffs' advocates and government actors. In this way, they agreed on the charges that would be brought in the 1992 proceedings; see Feldman, 'Blood justice', p. 689.
[102] Unknown author, 'Le professeur Jacques Roux et les docteurs Robert Netter et Michel Garetta ont été inculpés', *Le Monde* (23/10/91).
[103] It is open to plaintiffs under French criminal law procedure to join a civil claim for financial compensation to a criminal complaint. Pursuing this approach can be advantageous for plaintiffs in that investigation of their claims is undertaken primarily by the investigating judge and therefore the costs of the investigation are not borne by the plaintiffs themselves. The disadvantages are that being a party to criminal proceedings means they cannot be heard as witnesses. In addition, once a plaintiff commences a prosecution, it is up to the Public Prosecutor's Office to decide on whether or not to continue the prosecution (see C. Elliot, *French Criminal Law* (Devon: Willan Publishing, 2001), pp. 32–4).

charges in this way had an underlying political rationale: it meant that there was unlikely to be any adverse findings on the course and direction of government policy-making regarding the timing and implementation of HIV testing, as well as on the issue of prison collections, both of which had led to France having the most HIV-contaminated blood supply in Europe during the early to mid 1980s.[104]

The trial took place in 1992 and Garetta was found guilty and given a four-year prison sentence. Allain was also found guilty and given a four-year sentence, with two years suspended. Roux was found guilty and given a two-year suspended sentence, whereas Netter was acquitted.[105] The judgment was appealed and, in 1994, the Court of Criminal Appeal confirmed the convictions and sentences of both Garetta and Allain.[106] The reaction of the national as well as the international medical and scientific community was one of shock and disbelief at the conviction of Allain, in particular. Senior international colleagues signed a petition demanding a presidential pardon for Allain, in addition to expressing their outrage at his conviction in the international scientific press.[107] They argued that it was unjust to single out individuals for what was considered a collective failure to address the risk posed by HIV to national blood systems.[108]

The next set of legal proceedings had its roots firmly in the political domain. The publication of the Lucas Report in 1991 had revealed the extent of involvement of three former Ministers in the Socialist government of the 1980s in crucial decisions about the management of the risk posed by HIV to the blood system. The three Ministers involved were Laurent Fabius, the former Prime Minister; Georgina Dufoix, the former Minister of Social Affairs; and Edmond Hervé, the former Minister for Health.[109] Both the AFH and the AP lobbied parliamentary representatives demanding that these former Ministers be held to account for their role in the HIV blood contamination

---

[104] J. Kramer, 'Bad blood', *The New Yorker* (11/10/93), 74–95 at 80. Kramer argued that the influence the government had long exercised over the judiciary in France could be seen in the choice of who was to be charged and how such charges were to be framed in relation to the first set of legal proceedings in the early 1990s. From the government's point of view, it was always a question of who was politically expendable and how the charges could be framed so as to avoid senior members of government being held to account for what had happened.

[105] L. Greilsamer, *Le procès du sang contaminé* (Paris: Éditions Le Monde, 1992).

[106] Cour de cassation, Chambre criminelle, 22 juin 1994 (Bull. crim, n° 248, p. 604).

[107] Editorial, 'Palais d'injustice', *Lancet*, 342 (1993), 188; D. Brahams, 'Trial and tribulations of J-P. Allain', *Lancet*, 342 (1993), 232–3.

[108] Soulier, *Tranfusion et sida*, p. 129; L. Greilsamer, 'Notre carence collective...', *Le Monde* (24/07/92).

[109] J.-Y. Nau and F. Nouchi, 'Affaire d'etat', *Le Monde* (16/09/91).

episode.[110] Following a lengthy process of constitutional reform, the newly created Cour de justice de la république was convened in February 1999 to try the three former Ministers, who had been charged with involuntary homicide, as well as involuntary assault.[111]

The trial of the three former Ministers raised a number of wider issues that became the subject of much public discussion, including the role of law in the political process, the criminalisation of public life and how responsibility should be assigned between those with expert knowledge and those who are politically accountable.[112] The Court handed down its judgment in March 1999, acquitting both Fabius and Dufoix, but finding Hervé guilty of failing to assist a person in danger. While the Court found that both Fabius and Dufoix had moved quickly to address the risk posed by HIV to the blood supply once they became aware of it, Hervé was found to be 'imprudent, inattentive and negligent' in the performance of his duties as Minister for Health. Although Hervé was found guilty on these grounds, he was not in fact given a penalty or a sentence. The Court considered that what he had been through as a result of the trial was punishment enough.[113] The findings of the Court did not satisfy the AFH and the AP, as well as other groups who represented those infected with HIV through blood transfusion. Together, they publicly denounced the trial as a farce and its findings as politically motivated. They declared that they now intended to shift their attention to the outstanding set of legal proceedings, which involved charges of poisoning against thirty persons arising out of the contamination episode.[114]

This outstanding set of legal proceedings had its origin in a prosecutorial submission that had been made during the appeal by Allain arising out of his original conviction at trial in 1992. During the course of such submission, the prosecutor had informed the court that poisoning was in fact a more appropriate charge to have been laid against those involved in the HIV blood contamination episode. Although concerns were raised by the legal representatives of Garetta and Allain at the time about the appropriateness of bringing this second set of proceedings,[115] a further judicial investigation was subsequently

---

[110] J.-Y. Nau, 'Entretien avec le president de l'Association des hémophiles', *Le Monde* (28/08/92).

[111] R. Bacqué, 'Douze parlementaires pour juger l'affaire du sang contaminé', *Le Monde* (14/01/99).

[112] J.-M. Colombani, 'Pour une justice équitable', *Le Monde* (9/02/99).

[113] Various authors, 'Sang: Fabius et Dufoix relaxés, Hervé condamné', *Le Monde* (10/03/99).

[114] S. Gelblat, 'Les victims dénoncent un "procès truqué"', *Le Figaro* (10/03/99).

[115] A. Dorozynski, 'French doctors face second trial', *British Medical Journal*, 309 (1994), 427.

opened. The investigation went on to examine the potential culpability for poisoning under French law of thirty people (including Garetta and Allain), who had been identified by the investigating judge as having been involved in decision-making processes which led to the contamination episode.

Following a lengthy investigation, it was announced in May 1999 that criminal charges were to be laid against a number of persons. Among those named were Garetta, who was charged with the crime of poisoning, with Allain and several other haemophilia doctors being charged with involuntary homicide and assault.[116] After a series of appeals by Garetta, the Criminal Appeal Court in Paris finally ruled in 2003 that the entire legal proceedings should be dismissed. In its judgment, the Court held that the standard required to satisfy a charge of poisoning under French law meant that it was necessary to have evidence of an intention to kill and this standard had not been met in these proceedings.[117] The court's ruling brought to an end thirteen years of judicial investigations, as well as a series of criminal, administrative and political trials arising out of the HIV blood contamination episode in France. Despite the legal dimension of the affair coming to an end, the fallout from the political scandal was to leave a lasting imprint on French public and political life for some time to come.

United States

Despite the high rate of HIV infection among PWH in the USA, their political mobilisation lagged well behind campaigns run by haemophilia groups in other developed countries. In both England and France, it was the deteriorating health of PWH with HIV that proved to be the initial catalyst for the launching of campaigns in the late 1980s. While this also occurred in the USA, the reaction was the opposite: PWH with HIV, as well as their representative organisation, the NHF, became closed and insular, fearful of public stigma being attached to them for having the disease. In a sense, this was understandable given the negative public reaction to a number of PWH with HIV going public with the difficulties they were experiencing. This was particularly highlighted in the case of Ryan White, a person with haemophilia from Indiana who was HIV positive, as well as the three Ray boys from Florida, who were all

[116] F. Nouchi, 'Vers un procès en assises de l'affaire du sang contaminé', *Le Monde* (22/05/99).
[117] Cour de cassation, Chambre criminelle, 18 juin 2003 (Bull. n° 127); see also N. Guibert, 'La Cour de cassation clôt définitivement l'affaire du sang contaminé', *Le Monde* (20/06/03).

banned from attending school. When the Ray family took legal action over the ban, their house was burnt down and they were forced to leave the town where they lived.[118]

Quite apart from the negative media and public reaction to PWH with HIV in the USA at the time, there were a number of other reasons why the NHF was not prepared to mount a political campaign on behalf of its HIV-infected members. Its then leadership viewed itself as primarily engaged in advocacy to generate increased research funding and better treatment options for its membership. It framed the HIV blood contamination episode involving their members as a tragedy, rather than one that should involve accusation and blame.[119] As a result, it did not see its role as advocating for, or supporting litigation on behalf of, PWH with HIV.[120] The NHF leadership also claimed that its membership had shown little, if any, interest in pursuing such a campaign. Between 1988 and 1992, this began to change in the wake of a groundswell of opposition from many PWH with HIV to the passive position adopted by the NHF in this regard.[121] It was during this time that two break-away groups were formed: the Hemophilia/HIV Peer Association and the Committee of Ten Thousand (COTT). The former group had been founded by Michael Rosenberg, who sought to challenge the legitimacy of the NHF as the body representing PWH with HIV. He argued that the NHF had systematically lied to its HIV-infected members and he abhorred the fact that some haemophilia doctors, including those who had been members of MASAC, had testified in litigation on behalf of the plasma product industry and against their own patients. He advocated the use of direct action tactics in line with those adopted by groups such as ACT-UP.[122] He framed what had happened to the haemophilia community as 'genocide', describing one leading haemophilia doctor, Professor Louis Aledort, as the 'Josef Mengele of the Hemophilia AIDS Holocaust'.[123]

The other influential breakaway group, COTT, had been founded originally as a peer support group in 1989. The choice of name reflected the estimated number of PWH with HIV in the USA. One of the founders

---

[118] Starr, *Blood*, p. 316; P. Siplon, *AIDS and the Policy Struggle in the United States* (Washington, DC: Georgetown University Press, 2002), pp. 54–5.

[119] Bayer, 'Blood and AIDS in America', p. 40; Siplon, *AIDS and the Policy Struggle*, pp. 55–6.

[120] J. Saul, *The Tainted Gift: A Comparative Study of the Culture and Politics of the Contamination of the Blood Supply with the AIDS Virus in France and the United States* (Cornell University, unpublished PhD thesis, 2005), p. 168.

[121] Resnik, *Blood Saga*, p. 154.

[122] Starr, *Blood*, pp. 325–6; Bayer, 'Blood and AIDS in America', p. 38.

[123] Bayer, 'Blood and AIDS in America', pp. 38–9.

of the group, Jonathan Wadleigh, was involved in ACT-UP, as well as having a background in civil rights activism.[124] Another founder, Corey Dubin, had previous experience with class actions and was therefore well positioned to devise and pursue a legal strategy for the group.[125] COTT was happy to align itself with other AIDS activist groups, as well as the gay community more generally. They disliked the 'innocent victim' label assigned to PWH with HIV, seeing it as unhelpful and divisive.[126] Unlike Rosenberg's group, COTT was more focused on pursuing litigation and political lobbying for financial compensation, as well as demanding accountability on the part of key decision-makers for what had happened to PWH with HIV. Both groups made increasing use of the internet, including chat rooms and other e-resources, to facilitate more immediate contact and information exchange with their membership.[127]

Relations between the NHF and its HIV-infected members reached a turning point at the NHF Annual Conference in 1992. The breakaway groups staged pickets and demonstrations, as well as producing a shame list of haemophilia doctors who had testified in litigation on behalf of the plasma products industry. Many such doctors were members of the NHF's MASAC. The breakaway groups argued that the NHF was now compromised and indeed complicit in the circumstances that had led to the HIV blood contamination episode.[128] In the wake of the fallout from the 1992 conference, several individual state and regional chapters of the NHF broke away from the national organisation in order to establish the Hemophilia Federation of America. This new organisation emphasised that it neither sought funding support from the plasma products industry, nor did it want its members to derive financial benefit from the manufacture or supply of plasma products. The organisation also wanted to foster more equal relationships with treating haemophilia doctors and other healthcare professionals, rather than the more paternalistic approach that had long been entrenched within the NHF.[129]

In an attempt to respond to the concerns of PWH with HIV, the NHF established a Special Assistance Council (SAC) in the early 1990s, in order to engage in direct negotiations with the plasma products industry regarding the payment of financial compensation to PWH with HIV. As part of negotiations, SAC had put forward a proposal for

[124] Siplon, *AIDS and the Policy Struggle*, p. 56.
[125] Saul, *The Tainted Gift*, p. 108.
[126] Siplon, *AIDS and the Policy Struggle*, pp. 56–7.
[127] Resnik, *Blood Saga*, p. 186.
[128] Bayer, 'Blood and AIDS in America', p. 40.
[129] Siplon, *AIDS and the Policy Struggle*, p. 56.

the payment of US$1.5 billion in financial compensation by the industry. Representatives from the breakaway groups found the negotiations with the industry to be 'humiliating' and the industry baulked at having to pay what they considered to be a very high sum. At the NHF Annual Conference in 1993, disagreements arose between the NHF executive and the breakaway groups over the SAC negotiations, with the latter objecting to the 'charity approach' adopted by the NHF. They also wanted payments to be made directly to the PWH with HIV, rather than trust arrangements being established which would have required applications for the release of monies on a piecemeal basis. By the end of 1993, the SAC campaign had collapsed.[130]

With the NHF in turmoil over its position towards its HIV-infected members in the early to mid 1990s, the leaders of COTT began to focus in earnest on realising its political campaign mobilisation goals which included justice through investigation, compensation and representation. Although they endeavoured to attract support from the media for the campaign, they struggled to interest either a core group of journalists who were prepared to follow the issue or the national agenda-setting newspapers more generally.[131] This reflected the ongoing problem they experienced in presenting what had happened to the haemophilia community as a national scandal,[132] rather than it being perceived as a limited failure in risk governance for which there was diffuse institutional, professional and political responsibility.

The breakaway groups had more success with political lobbying, although the NHF was involved in this process as well. Lobbying centred upon demands for financial compensation from the government, as well as for a Congressional investigation to be established into the circumstances that had led to the HIV blood contamination episode in the USA. In relation to the former, PWH with HIV were viewed by those in political leadership as the 'innocent victims' of the AIDS epidemic and so attracted 'sympathy and support' for their demands.[133] Such support was utilised in the adoption of the Ryan White CARE Act in 1990, which provided funding for medical and social services for people with HIV. Although the funding was to be provided to people living with HIV regardless of how they had acquired their infection, Ryan White, a person with haemophilia who was HIV positive, became

---

[130] Bayer, 'Blood and AIDS in America', pp. 46–7; Siplon, *AIDS and the Policy Struggle*, p. 60; Saul, *The Tainted Gift*, pp. 171–2.
[131] Feldman, 'Blood justice', p. 675; Saul, *The Tainted Gift*, p. 44.
[132] Saul, *The Tainted Gift*, p. 3.
[133] Resnik, *Blood Saga*, p. 142.

the politically acceptable face of the campaign which led to the adoption of the legislation.[134]

In 1995, the Ricky Ray Hemophilia Relief Bill was introduced into Congress. It aimed to establish a US$1 billion fund to provide US$125,000 to each PWH with HIV. The Bill had been named after one of the Ray brothers from Florida who had suffered significant discrimination in the wake of disclosing his HIV-positive status. The Bill was reintroduced in 1997 as the Ricky Ray Hemophilia Relief Fund, as it had not passed the necessary legislative hurdles in the previous Congress. This Bill asked for US$100,000 per PWH with HIV, with total funding of US$750 million. COTT enlisted professional lobbyists to press their case, held specific lobbying days in Washington and made use of e-resources to gather support from its membership.[135] Although the Bill was eventually passed in 1998, it only authorised the monies to be paid and a further piece of legislation was needed to appropriate the monies for payment.[136] This resulted in a further round of political lobbying and the relevant appropriation was finally made in 2000 to allow for the full payment of US$750 million.[137]

The leadership of COTT was unsuccessful in its demand for a Congressional investigation into the circumstances that led to the HIV blood contamination episode. Donna Shalala, the then Secretary of Health and Human Services, instead recommended that an investigation be conducted by a committee established under the auspices of the Institute of Medicine (IOM).[138] Although it lacked the legal powers and reach of a Congressional investigation, the IOM Committee to study HIV transmission through blood and blood products comprised an eminent, independent group of interdisciplinary experts. It operated as a type of government-sponsored inquiry, providing a mechanism by which members of the haemophilia community were able to have their voices heard and tell their stories of injustice and suffering.[139] The IOM Report, published in 1995, set out what would become the official narrative of the HIV blood contamination episode in the USA.[140]

---

[134] Ryan White Comprehensive AIDS Resources Emergency (CARE) Act of 1990 (Ryan White Care Act, Ryan White, Pub. L. 101–381, 104 Stat. 576, enacted August 18, 1990); see also Siplon, *AIDS and the Policy Struggle*, pp. 94–8.

[135] Siplon, *AIDS and the Policy Struggle*, pp. 62–3.

[136] Ricky Ray Hemophilia Relief Fund of 1998, Secs. 101–108 of Pub. L. 105–369, 112 Stat. 3368.

[137] Siplon, *AIDS and the Policy Struggle*, p. 64.

[138] Bayer, 'Blood and AIDS in America', pp. 40–1; Saul, *The Tainted Gift*, pp. 108–9.

[139] S. Keshavjee, S. Weiser and A. Kleinman, 'Medicine betrayed: hemophilia patients and HIV in the US', *Social Science and Medicine*, 53 (2001), 1081–94 at 1087.

[140] Bayer, 'Blood and AIDS in America', p. 45.

It was emphasised in the Report that the intention was not to assign blame. Instead, the aim was to understand the decision-making processes that had led to the contamination episode, with a view to informing the approach taken to enhancing blood safety in the future. Perhaps one of the unintended consequences resulting from the Report's failure to create a narrative of moral culpability and blame was that it may have contributed to the piecemeal and restricted approach taken to providing financial compensation to PWH with HIV, both by Congress and by the courts.[141] Having said that, the Report nevertheless did identify that much more could have been done to limit or avoid the HIV blood contamination episode, including its devastating impact on the national haemophilia community. It placed stress on regulatory and industry shortcomings in risk governance, particularly those of the FDA, blood services and the plasma industry.[142] The response of the CDC to the risk posed by HIV to the national blood system was looked upon more favourably in the Report. In the wake of its findings, the CDC became much more involved in dealing with the haemophilia community, particularly in relation to surveillance and safety issues.[143] The reaction of the haemophilia community was mixed: some viewed it as a 'partial vindication'; others saw it as a 'poor substitute' for the sort of justice they wanted in response to what had happened to them.[144] In the wake of the findings of the IOM Report, institutional structures to enhance blood safety were reorganised, particularly within the FDA. This included facilitating consumer representation on advisory committees which dealt with blood quality, availability and safety for the first time.[145]

Litigation by individuals infected with HIV through blood transfusion, as well as PWH with HIV, had met with limited success in the USA throughout the 1980s and into the 1990s.[146] One of the main reasons for the lack of success was that plaintiffs could only bring claims

---

[141] Keshavjee et al., 'Medicine betrayed', p. 1090.
[142] Leveton et al., HIV and the Blood Supply.
[143] Resnik, Blood Saga, p. 186.
[144] Siplon, AIDS and the Policy Struggle, pp. 58–9.
[145] Ibid., p. 65. These reforms will be discussed in more detail in Chapter 7.
[146] W. R. Janowitz, 'Safety of the blood supply – liability for transfusion associated AIDS', Journal of Legal Medicine, 9 (1988), 611–22; D. J. Russo, 'Blood bank liability to recipients of HIV contaminated blood', University of Dayton Law Review, 87 (1992–1993), 87–107; J. M. Kern and B. B. Croy, 'A review of transfusion-associated AIDS litigation: 1984 through 1993', Transfusion, 34 (1994), 484–91; D. Hensler, N. M. Pace, B. Dombey-Moore et al., 'Blood clotting products for haemophiliacs: in re Factor VIII or IX Concentrate Blood Products', in Class Action Dilemmas: Pursuing Public Goals for Private Gain (Rand Corporation Publications, 2000), pp. 293–317 at 295–6.

in negligence. Claims in negligence proved difficult to establish on a number of grounds. Plaintiffs were required to show that there had been a breach of a duty of care towards them by healthcare professionals, blood services and/or plasma product manufacturers. In many state jurisdictions, it was a professional standard of care that was applied to determine whether there had been a breach of duty. What this meant in practice was that if defendants had all approached the risk posed by HIV in the same way and, for example, did not respond in a proactive or timely manner to such risk, they would be most unlikely to be found to be negligent for the harm suffered by plaintiffs.[147] Another key element in establishing a claim in negligence is that it is necessary for plaintiffs to show that the breach of the duty of care caused the harm suffered. In the case of PWH with HIV who had regularly used factor concentrates, pinpointing when they had been infected with the virus was often extremely difficult, thus making it next to impossible to establish the period of time in which the breach could have caused them to become infected with HIV.[148]

The legal difficulties faced by PWH with HIV were compounded by the existence of what are known as 'blood shield' laws in the vast majority of states in the USA. These laws specifically exclude strict liability and implied warranty claims where a person has suffered harm through the administration of blood and/or plasma products.[149] The underlying rationale behind the introduction of such laws was that the

---

[147] J. Kelly, 'The liability of blood banks and manufacturers of clotting products to recipients of HIV-infected blood: a comparison of the law and reaction in the United States, Canada, Great Britain, Ireland and Australia', *John Marshall Law Review*, 27 (1994) 465–91 at 468–73. In the context of this litigation, it is interesting to note the case of *United Blood Services* v. *Quintana* 827 P. 2d 509 (Colorado, 1992), which involved a case of transfusion-transmitted AIDS. It was held on appeal that adherence to the professional standard of care was a rebuttable presumption of due care. A new trial was ordered and the plaintiff was awarded US$8.15 million by the jury. As the plaintiff died before verdict, the defendant appealed the jury verdict and the case was eventually settled for an undisclosed amount in 1993.

[148] A notable exception was the case of *Christopher* v. *Cutter Laboratories*, 53 F. 3d 1184 (11th Cir. 1995). In this case, it had been possible to identify specifically when the plaintiff had been infected with HIV and by which product. Although the jury initially awarded the plaintiff US$12 million, this was successfully appealed. The family of the plaintiff eventually received US$2 million; see Hensler *et al.*, 'Blood clotting products for haemophiliacs', p. 296.

[149] The blood shield laws appear in one of three forms: (1) declaration that transfusion is a service; (2) blanket exclusion from liability barring negligence; and (3) liability is limited only if the contamination is undetectable; see F. Shu-Acquaye and L. Innet, 'Human blood and its transfusion: the twists and turns of legal thinking', *Quinnipiac Health Law Journal*, 9 (2005–2006), 33–67, fn. 5 at 34–5. A key California case in 1977 confirmed that the state blood shield law applied to plasma product manufacturers; see *Fogo* v. *Cutter Laboratories*, 68 Cal. App. 3d 744, 137 Cal. Rptr. 417 (1977).

transfusion of blood was an inherently risky, albeit necessary, activity. If blood services faced the prospect of strict liability claims being made against them, then this would act as a significant disincentive against providing an important public service.[150] Even in those states which had not adopted specific legislation to this effect, there was existing case law to support the exemption in any case.[151] Most of these laws had been adopted at state level and/or confirmed by the courts by the end of the 1970s, following heavy political lobbying on the part of those involved in blood services in response to the threat of litigation based on strict liability claims.[152]

Notwithstanding the difficulties experienced by individual PWH with HIV in relation to successfully litigating their claims through the courts, senior members of COTT were of the view that embarking upon a national class action suit would prove to be a valuable legal tactic for obtaining financial compensation, as well as in providing a focus for examining the circumstances that had led to the HIV blood contamination episode involving PWH.[153] In September 1993, a class action suit was filed in Chicago in the name of Jonathan Wadleigh, one of the founders of COTT. The NHF executive had not received prior notification of the planned lawsuit and had been in the midst of ongoing negotiations with the plasma products industry over a financial assistance package. Relations between the NHF and COTT became further embittered as a result, with members of the NHF viewing the legal action by COTT as 'unethical' in the circumstances.[154]

---

[150] Hensler *et al.*, 'Blood clotting products for haemophiliacs', p. 295.

[151] In particular, the early case of *Perlmutter* v. *Beth David Hospital*, 308 NT 100, 123 NE 2d 192 (1954) found that blood is a service, not a product. This interpretation was adopted in case law in many other state jurisdictions.

[152] P. Siplon and B. Hoag, 'Protection for whom? Blood policy creation and interest representation', *Policy Studies Review*, 18 (2001), 193–224 at 207–14. Although it is outside the scope of what is being examined in this chapter, the merits or otherwise of maintaining US blood shield laws on both justice and safety grounds have been much debated within the relevant academic literature. For example, see P. T. Westfall, 'Hepatitis, AIDS and the blood product exemption from strict products liability in California: a reassessment', *Hastings Law Journal*, 37 (1986), 1101–32; M. J. Miller, 'Strict liability, negligence and the standard of care for transfusion-transmitted disease', *Arizona Law Review*, 36 (1994), 473–513; Shu-Acquaye and Innet, 'Human blood and its transfusion'; C. C. Havighurst, 'Trafficking in human blood: Titmuss (1970) and products liability', *Law and Contemporary Problems*, 72 (2009), 1–15.

[153] Members of COTT produced a booklet entitled *The Trail of AIDS in the Hemophilia Community* that contained hundreds of pages of documents which had been 'discovered' or otherwise disclosed over the years as a result of litigation on behalf of PWH with HIV; see Bayer, 'Blood and AIDS in America', pp. 39–40.

[154] Resnik, *Blood Saga*, p. 181.

What was even more surprising to the NHF was that it was named as a defendant in the class action suit, in addition to major plasma products manufacturers, namely Rhone-Poulenc Rorer Inc, Armour Pharmaceutical Company Inc, Miles Inc, Baxter Healthcare Corporation and Alpha Therapeutic Corporation.[155] Judge Grady, who had been placed in charge of case management of the class action suit, made an order in December 1993 that all existing claims issued in federal courts should be transferred to his court under the auspices of the Multi-District Litigation (MDL) procedure.[156] While the use of MDL was supported on the grounds that it was best to pool plaintiffs' resources in terms of pre-trial discovery and litigation, it was also a useful tactical move in the broader sense in that it made it much more likely that the litigation would attract media attention and political interest, therefore providing the necessary impetus for the defendants to negotiate a national settlement of the claims.[157]

In 1994, an application was made by the plaintiffs' legal representatives for class certification and this was subsequently granted in order to consider two key issues applicable to the whole class: first, whether the plasma products industry had been negligent in the collection of plasma, as well as in the manufacture and sale of factor concentrates; and second, whether the NHF had breached its fiduciary duty to the class of litigants as a result of advocating the use of factor concentrates.[158] In the meantime, settlement negotiations continued between the parties. Two defendants, Armour and Baxter, offered to pay US$30,000 per claim but this was subsequently withdrawn once class certification took place. The defendants appealed the class certification and this was reversed in a majority judgment. In the leading judgment of the majority, Judge Richard A. Posner took what was considered to be the unusual decision of reversing class certification on the grounds that Judge Grady had exceeded the grounds of permissible discretion in the management of federal litigation. Although differing views have been expressed as to

---

[155] *Wadleigh* v. *Rhone Poulenc Rorer Inc.* No. 93 C 5969 (N.D. Ill, filed Sept 30, 1993).
[156] *In re Factor VIII or IX Concentrate Blood Products Litigation*, MDL 986, No. 93 C 7452. The Multi-District Litigation (MDL) procedure is to be found at 28 U.S.C.§1407. The MDL procedure provides for civil actions pending in a range of federal courts to be transferred to one nominated federal court for the purposes of managing all pre-trial proceedings and discovery in the interests of promoting the 'just and efficient conduct of such actions'. Where cases are not settled or dismissed during this process, they are transferred back to the original courts of issue for trial. A Judicial Panel on Multi-District Litigation is convened to decide whether there should be a consolidation of cases under the MDL procedure and to which court all cases should be transferred for pre-trial management.
[157] Hensler *et al.*, 'Blood clotting products for haemophiliacs', pp. 298–9.
[158] *Ibid.*, p. 300.

the underlying rationale for the Appeal Court judgment, it appears that the majority gave great weight to the effect any class action might have on the ongoing financial viability of the plasma products industry.[159]

In the wake of the Appeal Court judgment, fault-lines began to appear between the plaintiffs and their legal representatives. The lawyers wanted to proceed with cases on an individual basis, running a number of 'test cases' in the first instance. Members of COTT wanted to preserve the class action and considered that an appeal to the Supreme Court against the judgment offered the best opportunity to do so. In the end, an appeal was lodged although it was subsequently denied by the Supreme Court.[160] Differences on how best to proceed became entrenched and members of COTT made application for their lawyers to be dismissed, which was rejected by Judge Grady. The then president of COTT, Corey Dubin, subsequently entered into secret, albeit unsuccessful, negotiations with one of the defendants, Baxter International, to settle the group of claims.[161]

In the end, formal settlement negotiations resumed between the legal representatives of the parties to the litigation in 1996 with the defendants having now taken the view that it wished to settle the group action. This eventually led them to make an offer of US$100,000 per plaintiff in respect of their HIV infection only, with families to be bound by the settlement. In August 1996, the Walker class action was filed for the purposes of facilitating the settlement of the claims, which eventually comprised 6,200 class members. The final settlement was approved in May 1997.[162] There were a number of plaintiffs who opted out of the Walker class action settlement in order to pursue their cases on an individual basis. The opt-outs included most of the COTT leadership, who remained unhappy with the terms of the settlement. By the end of 2000, a settlement for an undisclosed amount was reached in relation to most of the opt-out plaintiffs, bringing this episode of litigation on behalf of the PWH with HIV to a close in the USA.[163]

---

[159] *In the matter of Rhone-Poulenc Rorer Inc.*, 51 F 3d 1293 (7th Circ 1995); for analyses of the Appeal Court judgment, see Hensler *et al.*, 'Blood clotting products for haemophiliacs', p. 302; unknown author, 'Class actions. Class certification of mass torts. Seventh circuit overturns rule 23(b) certification of a plaintiff class of haemophiliacs. In re Rhone-Poulenc Rorer Inc., 51 F.3d 1293 (7th Circ), Cert Denied, 116 S. Ct. 1984 (1995)', *Harvard Law Review*, 109 (1996), 870–5.

[160] *In the matter of Rhone-Poulenc Rorer Inc.*, 51 F 3d 1293 (7th Circ 1995), *cert. denied*, *Grady* v. *Rhone-Poulenc Rorer Inc.*, 516 U.S. 867 (1995).

[161] Hensler *et al.*, 'Blood clotting products for haemophiliacs', pp. 302–3.

[162] *In re Factor VIII or IX Concentrate Blood Products Litigation*, No. 96 C 5024 (*Walker* settlement).

[163] Siplon, *AIDS and the Policy Struggle*, p. 62.

Analysing political mobilisation and the use of law

The examination of the political mobilisation of haemophilia groups in England, France and the USA in the wake of HIV blood contamination episodes revealed some striking similarities, as well as some important differences. Across all three countries, the established haemophilia groups initially pursued campaigns for financial assistance that were largely framed in terms of a narrative based on the moral culpability of those in political leadership, as well as other key professional, regulatory and institutional stakeholders. HIV-infected members were framed as innocent or unwitting victims of the contamination episode.[164] PWH with HIV were identified as a special group and there was no promotion of solidarity between other groups similarly affected with the virus.[165] What learning did take place with regard to the pursuit of these campaigns was clearly derived from the experiences of other national haemophilia groups. They engaged in traditional interest group activity, focusing on attracting media attention and exerting pressure in the political arena. These initial campaigns for financial assistance revealed the historical legacy of haemophilia groups as inward-looking self-help groups, dependent upon the goodwill and support of medical and political elites in relation to addressing the needs of their members.

It was the formation of breakaway groups, which were unhappy with the accommodationist strategy pursued in the political campaigns of established haemophilia groups, that represented an important shift on the part of PWH groups. This shift involved collective action which sought to combine both identity formation and traditional interest group activity.[166] Central to identity formation was the construction of a narrative based on a reframing of their grievances as rooted in accusation and blame. This was in addition to the use of a more diverse campaign repertoire, which incorporated the use of direct action tactics of the type used by activist groups such as ACT-UP. In relation to the first point, the reframing incorporated not only the need for adequate financial redress but also a demand for institutional, professional and political accountability for the circumstances that had led to the high rates of HIV infection among national haemophilia populations.

In relation to the second point, there was a growing appreciation on the part of the established haemophilia groups in England and France

---

[164] Kirp, 'The politics of blood', p. 310; Keshavjee *et al.*, 'Medicine betrayed', pp. 1083–4.
[165] Saul, *The Tainted Gift*, p. 103.
[166] See Kirp, 'The politics of blood', pp. 296–7.

of the importance of taking a more proactive and supportive approach to litigation in the courts on behalf of PWH with HIV. This became clear in the wake of the problems experienced in obtaining financial compensation for their HIV-infected members through their financial assistance campaigns. The preference was to support the activities of the breakaway groups in their more proactive approach. This change in approach was much less apparent in the USA. While the NHF claimed that its HIV-infected membership was not supportive of a proactive approach to attracting media interest and pursuing litigation in the courts, it is also clear that the NHF opted to maintain close ties with leading haemophilia doctors and the plasma products industry. It is likely that the NHF did not wish to pursue legal tactics which would have led to the development of an antagonistic environment with such parties, in circumstances where the NHF was dependent upon their professional and/or financial support.[167]

A more proactive approach to the use of a diverse range of legal tactics was also a key aspect of the campaigns run by the breakaway groups, with or without the support of the more established haemophilia groups. Legal tactics included the pursuit of litigation in the courts, lobbying for the adoption of financial assistance legislation and the establishment of tribunals of inquiry into the circumstances that had led to high rates of HIV infection involving PWH. The extent to which reliance was placed on one or more legal tactics over others turned on the way in which grievances were framed, as well as the ability of such groups to take advantage of windows of opportunity that presented themselves in the political and public spheres to realise mobilisation goals.

In its initial campaign in the late 1980s, the UK Haemophilia Society took advantage of its established parliamentary support base, as well as the preference of the then Thatcher government to adopt a mor-ally pejorative narrative of innocent versus guilty victims of AIDS, which fitted with its overall conservative ideology. It pressed home such advantage, which led to successive payments of financial assistance. The Society initially linked the acceptance of financial responsibility by the government to an acceptance of political responsibility for what had happened to their HIV-infected members, but this did not take place even when it eventually gave its support to ongoing litigation in the courts by a large group of PWH with HIV and their families. Under the English common law system, personal injury actions in the court take place within a rule-bound adversarial context, which has as its ultimate aim the payment of adequate financial redress for what has happened

---

[167] *Ibid.*, p. 302; see Leveton *et al.*, *HIV and the Blood Supply*, pp. 193–204.

to the injured plaintiff. Given this ultimate aim, defendants to such litigation may negotiate to end proceedings at any time prior to trial or verdict through the payment of what the plaintiffs and their legal representatives accept is adequate financial redress in the circumstances, taking account of any risks faced with regard to establishing liability. The failure to accept an offer made in such circumstances would have put plaintiffs at risk of having to pay for their own legal costs, as well as those of the defendants if they lost, or otherwise receiving an amount that was less than what was originally offered by the defendants.

Bargaining in the shadow of the law with a test case pending and costs mounting,[168] plaintiffs were faced with making difficult decisions once the government made what their legal representatives considered to be an adequate offer of financial redress. In the end, this provided the government with a great deal of control over bringing such legal action to an end. Because of this control mechanism, the government had the capacity to prevent the release of potentially damaging information at trial about the circumstances that had led to such high rates of HIV infection among PWH, thus obviating the need to deal with the messy and potentially politically damaging issue of being held to account for the HIV blood contamination episode. While a successful financial settlement of the legal action was eventually received, it was a legal tactic that did not necessarily facilitate political accountability with respect to the perceived failure to manage the risk posed to the collective public health as a result of HIV contamination of the blood supply.

It is therefore interesting to observe the shift in the approach taken by the Society in the years following the settlement of this legal action. Successive campaigns have been brought that have included a successful demand for financial assistance to be paid by the government in relation to the HCV infection of PWH. This has been in addition to a more expansive reframing of grievance which saw their ongoing political campaigns rebranded as one involving the contaminated blood disaster affecting PWH, rather than one just focused on a specific virus. The Society also appears to have embraced the campaigns pursued by breakaway groups, such as Tainted Blood and Manor House, adopting a coordinating role where possible. This led to a belated campaign for a government-sponsored inquiry to be established to examine the circumstances that led to the contaminated blood disaster, as well as

---

[168] It is important to take account of the (potential) impact of legal tactics that take place in the 'shadow' of more formal legal structures and processes; see R. H. Mnookin and L. Kornhauser, 'Bargaining in the shadow of the law: the case of divorce', *Yale Law Journal*, 88 (1979), 950–97 at 997.

a review of existing financial redress arrangements for PWH infected with HCV.

While the Scottish government has proved more receptive to the demands of haemophilia groups in this regard and has established the Penrose Inquiry, this has not been the case in England. In the absence of government support for such an inquiry in England, the Society and breakaway groups campaigned to establish a privately funded inquiry under the chairmanship of Lord Archer of Sandwell QC. Despite having no specific legal powers to subpoena relevant documentation or witnesses, the Archer Report was moderately successful in that it established a chronology and analysis of the circumstances that led to the HIV blood contamination episode in England, as well as in making a series of recommendations to deal with the longstanding grievances of the haemophilia community. It also served to refocus media and political attention on such grievances, forcing the government into making (limited) concessions regarding the payment of further financial redress. It has been a long drawn-out battle for the haemophilia community in England to realise their campaign goals. While the use of a diverse range of legal tactics has been helpful in this regard, a more strategic approach to the use of law would have been more advantageous in the early days of campaigning, particularly when the Society was clearly enjoying a strong groundswell of political and public support. Instead, the campaign was rebranded and persisted as a marginal issue for many years, underlining the importance of understanding the contingent relationship between political opportunity and the use of legal tactics in realising mobilisation goals for those engaged in patient activism.

In contrast, French PWH with HIV enjoyed more success with respect to realising mobilisation goals through the use of legal tactics than did their counterparts in England.[169] The established national haemophilia group, the AFH, as well as the breakaway group, the AP, did not initially have the sort of political access and support provided to their counterparts in England, which in turn influenced their campaigns and their use of legal and other tactics.[170] They were also successful in

---

[169] For a different view on the lack of effectiveness of national legal systems in dealing with 'tainted blood cases', see Feldman, 'Blood justice', p. 659.

[170] The lack of 'windows of opportunity' for groups deemed to have outsider status in established public policy-making processes in France was a reflection of longstanding problems within the political system in accommodating the demands of these sorts of groups. This often led such groups to engage in a form of 'protest politics', which included large-scale street demonstrations, civil disobedience and violent direct action. French governments had shown themselves to be vulnerable to such action, responding to such protests with a change in policy direction to take account of the concerns of such groups (see J. Keeler and P. Hall, 'Interest representation and the

attracting the support of a number of investigative journalists who were prepared to regularly report on the circumstances that had led to the HIV blood contamination episode in France, thus bringing it to public and political attention on an ongoing basis. Most importantly, the AP was very clear from an early stage in its campaign about the need to obtain not only adequate financial redress, but also recognition of political responsibility for what had happened to PWH as a result of the HIV blood contamination episode.

The option available under the French legal system for plaintiffs to bring legal proceedings in the criminal jurisdiction was a particularly successful legal tactic for realising this latter demand. The initiation of such proceedings led to the appointment of a judge who was required to investigate the circumstances that had led to the HIV contamination episode involving PWH. Although issue may be taken with the choice of criminal charges and how they were framed, the outcome of the trial, the convictions of key healthcare professionals who had responsibility for risk governance involving PWH with HIV in the 1980s and the subsequent criminal investigations that lasted throughout the 1990s nevertheless led to sustained political and public attention on the serious consequences resulting from the HIV blood contamination episode for the collective public health. Not only did it lead to widespread institutional reform of the national blood system, but it was also influential in bringing about significant improvements in public health risk governance in France more generally.

Haemophilia groups lobbied for the parliamentary trial of the three former Ministers who had political responsibility for managing the risk posed by HIV to the national blood system in the 1980s. Their success in having the constitutional court established was necessarily contingent upon ongoing political support within the French Parliament and the fluctuating battles for control and point scoring between the left and right political parties. Although differing views were held as to whether or not this court was effective in trying the Ministers, it nevertheless highlighted that those in political leadership were not immune in either political or legal terms from the need to account for their actions in relation to managing risks to public health. What it also highlighted was that the successful use of legal tactics by haemophilia groups in realising mobilisation goals also reflected their ability to take advantage of existing and new political and legal opportunities which arose in the national context.

politics of protest', in A. Guyomarch, H. Machin, P. Hall *et al.* (eds.), *Developments in French Politics 2* (Houndmills: Palgrave, 2001), pp. 50–67 at 63).

In the USA, the use of legal tactics as part of realising mobilisation goals was driven primarily by the breakaway group COTT, rather than the more established haemophilia organisation, the NHF. While the NHF preferred to focus on achieving financial assistance packages for HIV-infected members (either from the plasma products industry or Congress), COTT focused on the use of legal tactics in order to create an environment in which PWH with HIV and their families would achieve their campaign goals. These goals included both obtaining adequate financial redress as a group, as well as the holding of a Congressional inquiry that would (hopefully) result in a recognition of political and institutional responsibility for the circumstances that had led to high rates of HIV infection among PWH. Although there had been a series of individual court cases in various US states from the mid 1980s onwards on behalf of PWH with HIV, they had proved largely unsuccessful. Such individual litigation had been hampered by the inability to bring strict liability claims due to exclusion under state blood shield statutes and/or case law. As a result, haemophilia plaintiffs were forced to pursue claims in negligence only, in circumstances where the evidentiary and liability burdens proved to be formidable obstacles to success. While the rationale for the adoption of blood shield laws has by and large rested on the perceived need to protect a vital public service, the singling out of blood services and the plasma products industry to receive the benefit of such specialised treatment under US law is troubling, as it significantly limited the legal options of PWH with HIV in circumstances where an important matter of national public health, such as blood safety, was at issue.[171]

Notwithstanding such legal restrictions, COTT and their legal representatives recognised the importance of bringing a class action lawsuit against the plasma products industry. The large number of plaintiffs involved, as well as the costs related to defending such lawsuits, operated as pressure points for the industry in terms of facilitating settlement negotiations, notwithstanding class decertification on appeal. The use of the class action tactic was to be contrasted with the approach taken by the NHF leadership at the time, which preferred direct negotiations with the industry in circumstances where there was no threat of litigation or the transactional costs associated with it. While such negotiations petered out, the class action tactic eventually proved successful in terms of bringing about a financial settlement of the claims. Having

---

[171] The situation in the USA in this regard is to be contrasted with that in England where strict liability claims have been successfully brought by plaintiffs who received (HCV) contaminated blood; see *A* v. *National Blood Authority* [2001] 3 All ER 289.

said that, the amount available in the settlement deal for individual PWH (and their families) was not substantial in view of what they had suffered as a result of being infected with HIV. This contributed to conflict with the plaintiffs' legal representatives, particularly by the COTT leadership. In addition, the class action lawsuit never became the focus of sustained national media or political attention, but rather continued on as a rather technical legal affair which eventually resulted in the payment of limited financial compensation.[172] The use of this legal tactic met with limited success for groups such as COTT, whose leadership were focused on promoting a wider narrative of grievance and blame arising from the HIV blood contamination episode involving PWH in the USA.

While haemophilia groups were all involved in the political lobbying process that resulted in Congress adopting a financial assistance package through the passing of the Ricky Ray Hemophilia Fund Act, it was the COTT leadership that actively lobbied for a formal inquiry into the circumstances that had led to the HIV blood contamination episode. Although they were unsuccessful in obtaining a Congressional investigation with far-reaching legal powers to investigate the matter, the IOM Inquiry nevertheless proved to be an effective mechanism for the airing of grievances by individual PWH with HIV and their families; for establishing an official narrative of decision-making processes involving the risk posed by HIV to the national blood system in the 1980s; and for recommending improvements to enhance governance processes dealing with blood safety.

Although the IOM inquiry was not formally engaged in apportioning blame for what had happened, its findings regarding regulatory and industry failures in risk governance were fairly damning, particularly for the FDA. As will become apparent in the following chapter, the adverse findings from the IOM inquiry have clearly influenced the current approach taken by the FDA to managing risk involving the blood system. Rather like the class action lawsuit, the IOM inquiry and report also failed to capture widespread media and public attention. The use of legal tactics by COTT was shown to be only partially effective in terms of realising campaign goals. This partial success reflected the limited availability of windows of opportunity in what is a complex and diverse national political and legal environment, set against a background of longstanding diffusion of responsibility for the blood system.

---

[172] Feldman, 'Blood justice', p. 676.

Conclusion

This chapter examined the circumstances in which haemophilia groups in England, France and the USA became politically mobilised in the wake of national HIV blood contamination episodes, with a particular focus on the use of legal tactics to realise their campaign goals. In this regard, it was shown that the peculiarities of national socio-political and legal contexts influenced the availability and success of such tactics. It was also clear that the successful use of legal tactics to realise campaign goals was also contingent upon the availability of windows of opportunity in the political arena. While legislation for financial assistance packages, as well as individual or group litigation in the courts, were the preferred legal tactics for achieving financial redress, it was not clear that success in this regard led to satisfaction on the part of PWH with HIV with regard to the amount that was made available to them. Given what they had suffered through HIV infection, the expectations of PWH regarding what constituted adequate financial redress in the circumstances were not met for the most part.

The use of government-sponsored inquiries with full legal powers to investigate the circumstances that had led to national HIV blood contamination episodes was clearly the preferred legal tactic for facilitating transparency, as well as political and institutional accountability, for what had happened to PWH. This met with only limited success in the USA and England, in contrast to the situation in France where it led to inquisitorial legal proceedings in the criminal jurisdiction, as well as in Parliament. The use of a diverse range of legal tactics was clearly important to haemophilia groups in their political campaigns. Having said that, the extent to which such legal tactics proved to be successful varied across the three countries examined and was often politically contingent, as well as limited, by the particular dynamics of national legal systems. Although the primary focus of this chapter has been on examining the political mobilisation of haemophilia groups in the wake of national HIV blood contamination episodes, it also provided important background information on the political fallout from such episodes ahead of the examination of the use of the precautionary principle and risk regulation in Chapters 7 and 8. It is only with knowledge of this background that it is possible to understand how and why a much more proactive and precautionary approach is now taken with respect to risk governance involving the blood system.

7   The politics of precaution

The political fallout from HIV blood contamination episodes in countries such as the USA, England and France has led to heightened sensitivity on the part of political leaders and regulators with respect to managing perceived new risks to the blood system. One of the consequences of this heightened sensitivity has been to employ the precautionary principle in dealing with (potential) risks to blood safety. There has been considerable stakeholder debate and critique about whether and, if so, in what circumstances the principle should be used. In this regard, it has been suggested that the use of the principle is grounded in the pursuit of the desired political objective of a zero-risk blood supply, notwithstanding the fact that it is not realistically achievable in scientific, technological or economic terms.[1] The aim of this chapter is to examine the growing influence and impact of the precautionary principle in relation to risk governance involving the blood system. As such, it affords a relatively rare opportunity to examine a concrete example of how the principle has been interpreted and applied in the public health context.

In undertaking this examination, a number of arguments are made. First, the fallout from national HIV blood contamination episodes in developed countries has afforded primacy to the politics of precaution in relation to issues affecting blood safety. The politicisation of risk that occurred in the wake of such episodes largely accounts for this change. It served to create path dependencies which have led to heightened sensitivity on the part of governing entities to the potential for adverse public reaction resulting from any perceived failure to manage risks to the blood system.[2] There is variation in how such sensitivity has manifested itself in different countries, reflecting the peculiarities of national socio-cultural, institutional and political contexts. Any claim to universality in the interpretation and/or application of the precautionary

[1] Klein, 'Will blood transfusion ever be safe enough?', p. 238.
[2] See Chapter 1, p. 18, fn.65, for further details on the concept of path dependency.

principle in relation to managing risks to blood safety therefore needs to be viewed with caution.

Second, the use of the precautionary principle is likely to dominate risk governance in the field until it can be established that public trust in the safety of the blood system has been regained. This may take place to the detriment of applying traditional scientific risk-assessment techniques, as well as cost-effectiveness and proportionality criteria, in relation to the management of risks to public health. Although they are clearly relevant factors to be taken into account where appropriate, the fallout from HIV blood contamination episodes has created a highly politicised environment in which decisions about risks to the blood system must be taken, particularly those involving TTIs. This now structures concerns about reputational risk management on the part of regulators, as well as resulting in the polarisation and entrenchment of stakeholder positions regarding the interpretation and application of precautionary strategies.

Notwithstanding such political dynamics, what is now needed is greater clarity and transparency about where the line should be drawn regarding risk acceptability and therefore what the threshold for intervention should be for dealing with emerging risks to the blood system. This needs to be followed up by a more rigorous approach to evaluating the effectiveness of any measures implemented in line with the principle. In order to examine these arguments, the chapter first proceeds with a general overview of the role of the precautionary principle in risk governance, with particular reference to its application in the public health context. Thereafter, the way in which the principle has been applied to risk governance involving the blood system is examined. The chapter concludes with an analysis of the advantages and disadvantages of employing the principle in the field and assesses whether it is likely to contribute to enhanced blood safety.

The use of the precautionary principle
in the public health context

Historically speaking, the use of the precautionary principle has been most closely associated with environmental policy and regulation,[3] whereas its use in the public health context is of relatively recent origin. Although various definitions of the principle have been put forward, it

---

[3] In Europe, for example, its growing prominence has been associated with the German principle of *Vorsorgeprinzip*, which has been applied in the context of environmental policy from the 1970s onwards; see J. Steele, *Risks and Legal Theory* (Oxford: Hart Publishing, 2004), pp. 196–7.

may be summarised as requiring proactive action to be taken to prevent or minimise threats to human health or the environment, notwithstanding the absence of full scientific certainty about the nature and scope of such threats.[4] It is important to note that some interpretations of the principle suggest that cost–benefit analysis should be undertaken in determining whether or not precautionary measures should be adopted, whereas others do not.[5] It has been argued that there are a number of key aspects that need to be taken into account with regard to its application in managing risks to public health: the taking of preventive action in the face of uncertainty; the shifting of the burden of proof to the proponents of a particular activity to show that it is not harmful; the exploration of a wide range of alternatives to possibly harmful actions; and the need to increase public participation in decision-making about the use of precautionary strategies.[6]

At the heart of its application lies an attempt to deal with the problem of scientific uncertainty.[7] How to define, quantify and qualify the nature and extent of such uncertainty in a given set of circumstances has proved to be an enduring problem in risk governance in any case, but has nevertheless been brought into sharp focus with the prominence given to the use of the principle in dealing with this type of situation.[8] In some national and supranational polities, such as the EU for example, the principle has recognised legal status and is used in policy-making processes, regulation, as well as being interpreted and applied in case law.[9] How it is applied seems to vary at times between policy sectors,

---

[4] The definition provided is drawn from a number of sources: Principle 15, Rio Declaration on Environment and Development (1992) (www.unep.org/Documents. Multilingual/Default.asp?documentid=78&articleid=1163); Wingspread Consensus Statement on the Precautionary Principle (1998) (www.sehn.org/wing.html); Commission of the European Communities, Communication from the Commission on the Precautionary Principle (2.2.2000) COM (2000) 1.

[5] Principle 15, Rio Declaration on Environment and Development states that 'a lack of full scientific certainty should not be used as a reason for postponing cost-effective measures to prevent environmental degradation'. In contrast, the definition of the precautionary principle provided in the Wingspread Consensus Statement referred to in the previous footnote focuses on the need to take account of cost–benefit analysis in determining whether precautionary action should be taken; see www.sehn.org/wing. html.

[6] D. Kriebel and J. Tickner, 'Reenergizing public health through precaution', *American Journal of Public Health*, 91 (2001), 1351–55 at 1351.

[7] P. O'Malley, *Risk, Uncertainty and Government* (London: Glasshouse Press, 2004), p. 3.

[8] Steele, *Risks and Legal Theory*, p. 193.

[9] Fisher, *Risk Regulation*, pp. 208–11. For an examination of its application in EU case law, see de Sadeleer, 'The precautionary principle in EC environmental and health law'; J. Corkin, 'Science, legitimacy and the law: regulating risk regulation judiciously in the European Community', *European Law Review*, 33 (2008), 359–84.

as well as between different political and legal orders, thus making any claim to universality in approach a tenuous one.[10]

It is this variability in its (legal) status, as well as exactly how and when it should be applied in a given set of circumstances, which has made the use of the principle the subject of enduring controversy and ongoing criticism. It has been argued that it operates more as a 'state of mind', rather than offering any clear or consistent way forward in risk governance processes; it is more often than not used as cover for protectionism on the part of nation-states;[11] and it operates in practice to paralyse effective decision-making with respect to risk management, adopting an all or nothing approach, which is grounded in the emotion of fear and not in quantifiable risk assessment.[12] In the circumstances, it has been suggested that its use should be limited to dealing with risks which pose a serious and irreversible loss or damage.[13] This has led to calls for it to be rebranded as the 'anti-catastrophic principle': to be used only in special circumstances where it is not possible to make probabilistic calculations in relation to potentially catastrophic risks.[14]

In response to such criticisms, it has been argued that the principle is in fact grounded in the use, rather than the marginalisation, of science and that it serves to highlight its limits in dealing with potentiality and possibility, rather than probability.[15] Calling for its application in this context simply acknowledges that there may be a need for political leadership and responsibility for taking action in the face of science's limitations in quantifying risk. How best to reconcile the relationship between science and politics in applying the precautionary principle is the issue that lies at the heart of much of the controversy over its use. Critics of the use of the principle have called for a much clearer distinction between the two, and indeed for a political acceptance of scientific risk assessment on its own merits to deal with the problem of uncertainty. Other commentators have argued that any claim to a binary distinction being made between technocratic (scientific) and democratic (political) models of precautionary decision-making is too simplistic to describe

---

[10] G. Majone, 'What price safety? The precautionary principle and its policy implications', *Journal of Common Market Studies*, 40 (2002), 89–109 at 101; K. R. Foster, P. Vecchia and M. J. Repacholi, 'Science and the precautionary principle', *Science*, 288 (2000), 979–81 at 979.

[11] S. Funtowicz, I. Shepherd, D. Wilkinson *et al.*, 'Science and governance in the European Union: a contribution to the debate', *Science and Public Policy*, 27 (2000), 327–36 at 330; Majone, 'What price safety?', p. 106.

[12] Sunstein, *Laws of Fear*, p. 5.

[13] Majone, 'What price safety?', p. 104.

[14] Sunstein, *Laws of Fear*, p. 9.

[15] Steele, *Risks and Legal Theory*, p. 199.

the reciprocity that operates between science and politics, particularly in the context of uncertainty.[16] What has been recognised, however, is that the failure to define more clearly the parameters of the science–politics relationship in relation to the use of the precautionary principle may result in prolonged periods of indecision, as well as the stifling of innovation.

There has been much debate between the EU and the USA over how best to interpret the precautionary principle in relation to decision-making regarding (potential) risks to public health. In response to ongoing political and regulatory skirmishes with the USA, as well as disputation within the World Trade Organization (WTO),[17] the European Commission (Commission) sought to clarify the EU's position on the matter in a policy document published in 2000. It argued that the principle should be considered within a structured approach to the analysis of risk which comprises three elements, namely risk assessment, risk communication and risk management. The application of the principle was particularly important in relation to decision-making regarding the third and final element, as this dealt with risk acceptability which was recognised as being ultimately a political decision.[18] The Commission then elaborated on the factors to be taken into account where precautionary action is considered necessary: there must be proportionality to the chosen level of protection; the measures must be non-discriminatory in their application and consistent with similar measures already taken; there should be an examination of the potential benefits and costs of action or lack of action and this could include – where feasible – a more formal cost–benefit analysis which should take account of both economic and social factors; it should be subject to review in the light of new scientific data; and it should be capable of assigning responsibility for producing the type of scientific evidence that would enable a more comprehensive risk assessment, as and when appropriate.[19]

Notwithstanding the attempt at EU level to clarify the use of the precautionary principle, its application in practice has continued to attract

---

[16] Jasanoff, *The Fifth Branch*, p. viii; P. Weingart, 'Scientific expertise and political accountability: paradoxes of science in politics', *Science and Public Policy*, 26 (1999), 151–61 at 155–7; M. Everson and E. Vos, 'The scientification of politics and the politicisation of science', in M. Everson and E. Vos (eds.), *Uncertain Risks Regulated* (London: Routledge-Cavendish, 2009), pp. 1–17 at 3.

[17] See for example, R. Howse, 'Democracy, science and free trade: risk regulation on trial at the World Trade Organization', *Michigan Law Review*, 98 (2000), 2329–57; Jasanoff, *Designs on Nature*, p. 266.

[18] Commission of the European Communities, Communication from the Commission on the Precautionary Principle, pp. 3–4.

[19] *Ibid.*, pp. 4–5.

criticism. Although the EU has claimed that its approach is generally applicable in the fields of environmental protection, as well as human, animal and plant health,[20] it is not clear that this is in fact the case. Instead, it has been suggested that the principle operates in different ways across several different legal and policy contexts at EU and Member State levels.[21] The most evolved use of the principle in policy-making processes at EU level has occurred in relation to the authorisation of genetically modified (GM) products. Despite the attempt at EU level to delineate a principled approach to the use of the precautionary principle, the shifting political dynamics structuring the debate on the use (or otherwise) of GM products on the part of Member States has resulted in a less than clear and coherent approach to risk decision-making processes. An analysis of such processes suggests that the EU's approach appears to vacillate at times between a strict scientific assessment of risk and a highly precautionary approach. The principal reason for such vacillation is said to derive from the lack of political consensus on the part of Member States regarding the approach to be taken by the EU to risk governance in the field.[22] Against this background, it has been suggested that if the principle is to have enduring credibility, then there is a need for risk decision-making processes to be made more transparent. This includes making explicit which factors influence such processes.[23]

While political, institutional and scientific tensions persist in relation to the application of the precautionary principle within the EU itself, a broader tension exists between the EU and the USA over its application as well. This has been highlighted by US concerns over the EU's reluctance to authorise the use of GM products. The USA has a well-established approach to risk assessment grounded in the use of 'sound science' to inform regulatory judgments about the use of new products derived from innovation in biotechnology.[24] In order to protect scientific advice from overt politicisation, a strict demarcation is drawn between risk assessment and risk management, as well as between facts and values.[25] In the USA, the predominant focus is on risk assessment

[20] *Ibid.*, p. 10.
[21] Fisher, *Risk Regulation*, p. 208.
[22] M. Weimer, 'Applying precaution in EU authorization of genetically modified products – challenges and suggestions for reform', *European Law Journal*, 16 (2010), 624–57 at 626–7. For further details on the European Commission's revised approach to GMO cultivation, see http://ec.europa.eu/food/food/biotechnology/index_en.htm
[23] *Ibid.*, pp. 650–3.
[24] The basis for this approach is to be found in the National Research Council, *Risk Assessment in the Federal Government: Managing the Process* (Washington, DC: National Academy Process, 1983). This is colloquially known as the 'Red Book'.
[25] Jasanoff, *Designs on Nature*, pp. 265–6.

based on quantifiable evidence, supported by cost–benefit analysis and modelling. This is then used to justify claims to objectivity in the pursuit of a product-, rather than a process-, based approach to managing emerging public health risks.[26] Against this background, the attempt by the EU to make greater use of the precautionary principle in relation to the use of GM products, for example, has been viewed with 'suspicion' in the USA on the grounds that it is too vague and in fact operates as a cover for protectionist activities on the part of the EU's Member States.[27]

Within the published academic literature on the use of the precautionary principle (and the approach taken to risk regulation), there has been considerable debate on the extent to which it could be argued that either the USA or Europe could be considered more precautionary than the other in their approach to managing risks to public health. It has been suggested that the EU has historically adopted a more laissez-faire approach to risk governance than has been the case in the USA. In the wake of the political fallout from the bovine spongiform encephalopathy (BSE) scandal in the late 1990s, however, the EU suffered a loss of public trust and political legitimacy. This resulted in the adoption of policy-making and regulatory processes that has made it much more risk-averse in relation to ensuring human health protection than would be the case in the USA.[28] It was therefore argued that this loss of public trust had resulted in a 'flip-flop' in the approach taken to risk governance in this area between the EU and the USA.[29] This view has been challenged by other academic commentators for being far too generalised and that an examination of specific policy sectors is warranted before drawing such a conclusion. When specific policy sectors are examined, it is argued that in certain instances the USA is in fact more precautionary in its approach than the EU, and vice versa. In

---

[26] *Ibid.*, p. 83. It has been suggested that such an approach tends to downplay ambiguity and uncertainty, ignoring social constructions of risk in other political cultures; see Jasanoff, 'Citizens at risk', pp. 374–5.

[27] Jasanoff, 'Citizens at risk', p. 375.

[28] The BSE crisis at EU level arose in the wake of a perceived failure on the part of EU decision-makers and institutions to manage the risk to EU citizens posed by cases of BSE in cattle, an infectious disease which could be transmitted to humans through the food chain, with fatal consequences. The human form of the virus is known as vCJD. One of the consequences of this crisis was a loss of public confidence in the provision and use of scientific advice, as well as risk management generally, at EU level. For an overview of the BSE crisis and its consequences at EU level, see E. Vos, 'EU food safety regulation in the aftermath of the BSE crisis', *Journal of Consumer Policy*, 23 (2000), 227–55.

[29] R. E. Lofstedt and D. Vogel, 'The changing character of regulation: a comparison of Europe and the United States', *Risk Analysis*, 21 (2001), 399–405 at 401–4.

the circumstances, it has been suggested that there is a need to adopt a more nuanced approach to examining how the principle has been applied in specific policy contexts between the USA and the EU.[30]

The relationship between the precautionary principle and risk regulation has also been highlighted as problematic in the context of managing risks to public health. Although it has been suggested that the principle is central to risk regulation, there has been little systematic examination of the relationship between the two.[31] Commentators such as Fisher have suggested that this under-researched aspect of risk governance reflects a broader tension between whether the principle should be regarded as having universal application or whether a more nuanced approach is required to take account of context, both in its interpretation and application, across various policy sectors.[32] Fisher's observation rings true in the context of seeking to understand the relationship between precaution and risk regulation with respect to blood safety. As is highlighted in Chapter 8, which examines EU risk regulation involving blood quality and safety, the inter-relationship between the two for the purposes of dealing with emerging risks to blood safety is not necessarily made explicit in EU policy-making processes. Instead, it appears to be dealt with on an ad hoc basis as and when new risks appear, creating the potential for stakeholder disgruntlement and confusion, as well as problems with ensuring a clear and coherent approach to risk governance in the field.

The purpose of this section of the chapter was to provide a brief overview of the origins, controversy and current tensions that exist with respect to applying the precautionary principle to managing risks to public health, before examining how it has been specifically applied in the context of blood safety in recent years. Such overview highlighted a number of concerns about the use of the principle: it has been difficult to separate out science from politics in applying the principle; problems have arisen in identifying the factors that should

---

[30] Wiener and Rogers, 'Comparing precaution in the United States and Europe', p. 319; J. K. Hammitt, J. B Weiner, B. Swedlow *et al.*, 'Precautionary regulation in Europe and the United States: a quantitative comparison', *Risk Analysis*, 25 (2005), 1215–28.

[31] Fisher, *Risk Regulation*, pp. 210–11. Hutter has suggested that while the precautionary principle has affinities with risk-based regulation, it does not on its own constitute evidence of such regulation; see B. Hutter, 'The attractions of risk-based regulation: accounting for the emergence of risk ideas in regulation', *CARR Discussion Paper*, No. 33 (March 2005), pp. 1–18 at 4.

[32] E. Fisher, 'Opening Pandora's box: contextualising the precautionary principle in the European Union', in M. Everson and E. Vos (eds.), *Uncertain Risks Regulated* (London: Routledge-Cavendish, 2009), pp. 21–45 at 38.

trigger its use; it inappropriately blurs the line between risk assessment and management; and there is too wide a variation in interpretation and application across different policy sectors, as well as within national and supranational polities. In the circumstances, claims to any generalised interpretation and application of the principle in the public health context must be viewed with caution. With this in mind, the next section of the chapter examines the emergence and application of the principle in the context of risk governance involving the blood system.

The politics of precaution and risk governance involving the blood system

The political and legal fallout from HIV blood contamination episodes in countries such as the USA, England and France led to the implementation of institutional and regulatory reforms with a view to enhancing blood safety. In some cases, the course and direction of such reforms were informed by the findings of government-sponsored inquiries, whereas in other countries the adverse public and political reaction from the episodes themselves provided sufficient impetus for reform.[33] One of the main consequences which flowed from what is now a highly politically sensitive policy sector was the promotion of the precautionary principle as a key decision-making tool for managing emerging risks to blood safety.[34] The principle was seen as an important technique of legitimation for those with political and regulatory responsibility for the blood system, given the catastrophic loss of public trust that had occurred as a result of such contamination episodes.[35]

---

[33] Government-sponsored inquiries took place in a number of countries, including the USA, Canada and Ireland. While some focused exclusively on HIV, others also included an examination of HCV blood contamination episodes. For example, see Leveton et al., *HIV and the Blood Supply* (USA); Krever, *Commission of Inquiry on the Blood System* (Canada); and Lindsay, *Report of the Tribunal of Inquiry* (Ireland). In France, three separate sets of legal proceedings provided the impetus for reform over time. In the UK, there has been legal action in the courts, as well as a number of inquiries. In England, a privately funded inquiry took place; see Archer et al., *Independent Public Inquiry Report*. In Scotland, a government-sponsored inquiry is still ongoing at the time of writing; see the Penrose Inquiry (www.penroseinquiry.org.uk). For a detailed examination of the issue, see Chapter 6.

[34] Farrugia, 'The regulatory pendulum in transfusion medicine', p. 277; Wilson and Ricketts, 'The success of precaution?', p. 1475; Wilson, 'A framework for applying the precautionary principle to transfusion safety', p. 177.

[35] In France, for example, this was made explicit in the wake of the fallout from the HIV blood contamination scandal; see Hergon et al., 'Risk management in transfusion after the HIV blood contamination crisis in France', pp. 273–5.

Public trust has long been perceived as central to the functioning and success of national blood systems. Such trust has its origins in the enduring socio-cultural resonance of blood as a community and national resource; the emphasis placed by national blood services on the notion of the gift in donating and receiving blood as an act of social solidarity; and the fact that blood collection and supply is viewed as a valued public service.[36] Revelations concerning the circumstances that led to national HIV blood contamination episodes, as well as significant levels of HIV infection among recipients of blood and plasma products, saw such trust 'plummet' rapidly.[37] This was accompanied by public perceptions that there had been a serious breach of the social contract around which blood donation had been based,[38] leading to a sense of public betrayal by those with political, professional and institutional responsibility for blood safety. It was acknowledged that once lost, public trust would be difficult to regain and that a substantial period of time would need to elapse before the situation could be rectified.[39]

Defining the precautionary principle in the context of blood safety

Differing interpretations have been given to the precautionary principle in the context of risk governance involving the blood system. In what is considered to be a strict interpretation,[40] it has been suggested that preventive action should be taken where there is evidence that a potential disease-causing agent is or may be blood borne, even where there is no evidence that patient-recipients have been affected. If there is potential for harm to occur, then it should be assumed it will occur. If there are no measures that will entirely prevent harm, then measures that may only partially prevent transmission should be taken. In contrast, it has been argued that a more moderate approach is warranted which involves the principle being applied in situations of scientific uncertainty where there is a possibility of risk, but an absence of proof of harm. When this occurs, measures should be taken to deal with potentially serious risks.[41] A more structured approach has also been suggested which proposes a

---

[36] C. Galarneau, 'Blood donation, deferral and discrimination: FDA donor deferral policy for men who have sex with men', *American Journal of Bioethics*, 10 (2010), 29–39 at 29.

[37] D. Starr, 'Medicine, money, and myth: an epic history of blood', *Transfusion Medicine*, 11 (2001), 119–21 at 121.

[38] Titmuss, *The Gift Relationship*, pp. 88–9, 157, 224–6.

[39] Starr, 'Medicine, money, and myth', p. 121.

[40] Krever, *Commission of Inquiry on the Blood System*, p. 1049.

[41] H. Alter and H. Klein, 'The hazards of blood transfusion in historical perspective', *Blood*, 112 (2008), 2617–26 at 2620.

non- to a highly precautionary approach based on an assessment as to whether there is evidence of the risk being low, intermediate or high.[42]

It has been suggested that whether or not the precautionary principle should be applied in the absence of sound scientific evidence of risk may turn on public perceptions or expectations about blood safety. This is much more likely to be the case where there is a serious or catastrophic risk involving the blood system, such as the one previously posed by HIV. In all other cases, an in-depth risk assessment based on available medico-scientific evidence is much more likely to be possible.[43] While some have argued that this new precautionary paradigm has served those responsible for blood safety well in dealing with emerging risks,[44] others have criticised its use by politicians and regulators as being arbitrary and over-reaching in an operational context. How and why this has come about is explored in more detail below.

Most of the criticism has focused on what is perceived to be the political objective of achieving a zero-risk blood supply,[45] against a background where key decision-makers have become highly sensitised to potential adverse public perceptions and concerns over blood safety. One commentator has suggested that zero-risk can be 'simplistically measured' as the 'sum of the level of hazard and the level of outrage' resulting from negative public reaction in the wake of HIV blood contamination episodes, which in turn has led to a low tolerance for risk, particularly with respect to TTIs.[46] As a result, fear on the part of decision-makers of being held responsible for even a single case of TTI through the use of blood or plasma products has provided the underlying rationale for the current political and regulatory zero-risk mindset.[47] What is particularly problematic about this mindset is

---

[42] Wilson, 'A framework for applying the precautionary principle to transfusion safety', p. 181.

[43] E. C. Vamvakas, 'Evidence-based practice of transfusion medicine: is it possible and what do the words mean?', *Transfusion Medicine Reviews*, 18 (2004), 267–78 at 275.

[44] Alter and Klein, 'The hazards of blood transfusion in historical perspective', p. 2620.

[45] M. Germain, 'Application of a risk modelling technique to blood donor deferral issues', in J. A. Chiavetta, S. Deeks, M. Goldman *et al.* (eds.), 'Proceedings of consensus conference: blood-borne HIV and hepatitis – optimizing the donor selection process', *Transfusion Medicine Reviews*, 17 (2003), 1–30 at 6.

[46] L. Katz, 'Risk modeling in the health care environment: an overview', in J. A. Chiavetta, S. Deeks, M. Goldman *et al.* (eds.), 'Proceedings of consensus conference: blood-borne HIV and hepatitis – optimizing the donor selection process', *Transfusion Medicine Reviews*, 17 (2003), 1–30 at 5; cf. R. Dodd, 'Editorial: Prions and precautions: be careful for what you ask', *Transfusion*, 50 (2010), 956–8 at 956.

[47] Klein, 'Will blood transfusion ever be safe enough?', p. 238; Starr, 'Medicine, money, and myth', p. 121; J. P. AuBuchon, 'Managing change to improve transfusion safety', *Transfusion*, 44 (2004), 1377–83 at 1377.

that it has become difficult to ascertain exactly where the line should be drawn regarding what constitutes an acceptable risk in the context of blood safety.[48] The problems that have been encountered in this regard are highlighted by decision-makers' focus on what has been described as the 'safety tripod' in decision-making about blood safety. The application of this approach involves taking account of blood donor selection criteria, screening tests for pathogens and the use of pathogen reduction technologies.[49] Drawing on this approach, the next section examines how the use of the precautionary principle has impacted on the management of risks to blood safety in recent years.

Blood donor selection criteria

Blood services in developed countries employ a range of donor selection criteria with a view to minimising the risk of transmission of disease to patient-recipients. For the purposes of analysing how the precautionary principle has impacted upon this aspect of managing blood safety, a choice has been made in this section to limit examination to donor deferral policies that have been implemented to restrict or exclude blood donations by men who have sex with men (MSM), with a particular focus on the approach that has been taken in the USA and the UK. Such examination is also restricted to the risk of minimising HIV transmission through blood donation, although it is acknowledged that a number of TTIs have been mentioned in connection with MSM donor deferral policies.[50] Before proceeding to examine the current approach taken to the MSM donor deferral policy in countries such as the USA and the UK, it is important to take account of the historical legacy of the approach taken to excluding identified high-risk groups, such as gay men, during the time that HIV posed a risk to the blood system in the early to mid 1980s. The findings from a number of national inquiries into the circumstances that led to HIV blood contamination episodes revealed that donor screening of groups considered to be at high risk of transmitting the virus was not conducted in an effective manner, where it took place at all.[51]

---

[48] Germain, 'Application of a risk modelling technique to blood donor deferral issues', p. 6; Klein, 'Will blood transfusion ever be safe enough?', p. 239.

[49] A. Farrugia, 'The mantra of blood safety: time for a new tune?', *Vox Sanguinis*, 86 (2004), 1–7 at 2.

[50] For example, hepatitis C (HCV), hepatitis B (HBV) and human herpesvirus-8 (HHV-8).

[51] See fn. 33 above for details of such inquiries.

Numerous problems were encountered with implementing donor selection criteria during this period. In the first instance, transfusionists in charge of blood services had long struggled to cultivate a sufficient donor base to meet local and/or national needs and were therefore very concerned about being asked to exclude specific donor groups, as well as how this would impact upon supply.[52] Second, language drawn from epidemiological research was used by those with institutional and regulatory responsibility for blood safety to identify AIDS high-risk groups. For example, national blood services employed terminology such as 'homosexual men who had multiple (or many) partners' to exclude a certain group of gay men from blood donation,[53] although exactly how words such as 'multiple' or 'many' were to be interpreted was not made clear. In contrast, plasma collectors moved quickly to exclude 'homosexual men' as donors, without such qualifying language.[54] Third, transfusionists found themselves caught in the crossfire between an increasingly politically active gay rights movement which was concerned that AIDS donor exclusion policies were essentially homophobic and operated in practice to stigmatise gay men as a group on the one hand; and patient-recipient groups such as those with PWH who were concerned about identified high-risk groups, such as gay men, continuing to donate on the other hand. In the latter case, such concerns were grounded in PWH's dependence on plasma products in the treatment of their condition, as well as their vulnerability to contracting TTIs, given that such products were often sourced from the plasma of thousands of donors.[55]

Once HIV testing became available in the mid 1980s, national blood services amended their donor deferral policies to defer MSM from blood donation. Over time, differing national approaches have been taken with regard to this deferral policy. In the USA and Canada, MSM since 1977 are deferred and this operates in practice as a lifetime deferral. Other countries, such as South Africa, have adopted a

---

[52] For an historical overview, see Starr, *Blood*, pp. 174–274.

[53] US Department of Health and Human Services, Food and Drug Administration, Memorandum to All Establishments Collecting Human Blood for Transfusion, 24 March 1983, reproduced in Leveton *et al.*, *HIV and the Blood Supply*, Appendix D, pp. 290–1; for a comparative overview of AIDS donor exclusion criteria adopted in the early to mid 1980s in other developed countries, see Krever, *Commission of Inquiry on the Blood System*, Vol. 3, Part IV, pp. 721–954.

[54] Leveton *et al.*, *HIV and the Blood Supply*, p. 72; see also Appendix D, pp. 269–72. Excluding homosexual men without the qualifying phrase 'multiple' or 'many partners' was also supported by the NHF (see NHF MASAC, *Recommendations to Prevent AIDS in Patients with Hemophilia*, 14 January 1983, reproduced in Leveton *et al.*, *HIV and the Blood Supply*, Appendix D, pp. 279–80).

[55] Shilts, *And the Band Played On*, pp. 220–3.

six-month deferral, with Argentina, Australia, Hungary, Japan and the UK operating a twelve-month deferral.[56] In contrast to the adoption of a deferral policy based on the sexual orientation of a particular group, countries such as Italy and Spain have focused instead on particular high-risk behaviours. In Italy, donors are deferred for a period of four months following sexual activity involving multiple partners or a change of regular partner. In Spain, a six-month donor deferral exists following a change of partner (whether heterosexual or MSM) with permanent exclusion for those who disclose more than one sexual partner.[57] Such diversity in approach with regard to dealing with this issue appears to be largely attributable to differing national political and regulatory preferences regarding the appropriate level of precaution to be taken on the issue, underpinned by reliance on the screening of blood donations through the use of (mini-pool) NAT. The use of such technology has meant that HIV infection can now be identified approximately nine days after exposure by the donor to the virus.[58]

The extent to which the various policies adopted have been (or are likely to be) effective in screening out MSM donors at risk of transmitting HIV through blood donation has been the subject of evaluation in a number of national settings. In Australia, for example, a before and after study was undertaken which examined the implementation of the twelve-month deferral policy for MSM donors. It was found that there was no evidence of increased risk of HIV transmission in patient-recipients. This proved to be so despite concerns about a national increase in the rate of HIV infection among MSM.[59] In the case of donor deferral policies based on sexual behaviour, such as those adopted in Italy and Spain, questions have been raised about whether

---

[56] C. Seed, P. Kiely, M. Law et al., 'No evidence of a significantly increased risk of transfusion-transmitted human immunodeficiency virus infection in Australia subsequent to implementing a 12 month deferral for men who have had sex with men', Transfusion, 50 (2010), 2722–30 at 2723.

[57] National Health Service (NHS) Blood and Transplant, Current issues: deferral of men who have sex with men from blood donation: questions and answers: what are the donor selection criteria for men who have sex with men in other countries? (November 2011) (www.nhsbt.nhs.uk/current_issues/mhsm_faq/question_022.html).

[58] Seed et al., No evidence of a significantly increased risk of transfusion-transmitted human immunodeficiency virus infection in Australia', p. 2727; K. L. Davison, L. J. Brant, A. M. Presanis et al., 'A re-evaluation of the risk of transfusion-transmitted HIV prevented by the exclusion of men who have sex with men from blood donation in England and Wales, 2005–2007', Vox Sanguinis 101 (2011) 291–302 at 293.

[59] Seed et al., 'No evidence of a significantly increased risk of transfusion-transmitted human immunodeficiency virus infection in Australia', p. 2728.

they have actually been effective in screening out high-risk donors.[60] Other problems which have been identified in relation to implementing such an approach in other national settings include a lack of relevant expertise; limited institutional and personnel resources to undertake the type of detailed individual risk behaviour assessments that would be required prior to donation; the impact upon maintaining existing donor pools in the event that a series of questions were added to already detailed donor questionnaires; and the fact that its broad remit has the potential to exclude too many 'safe donors'.[61]

A key issue which has informed the precautionary approach taken to the issue of MSM donor deferral has been that of non-compliance with the policy by both existing and new donors.[62] Ensuring compliance with, rather than the length of, the deferral policy has been considered vital to maintaining high levels of blood safety, particularly involving TTIs such as HIV.[63] Based on current data, it is not clear how blood services should deal with the issue of non-compliance, particularly in circumstances where a donor does not identify themselves through their sexual behaviour.[64] Although there have been calls for the adoption of more nuanced questioning of donors regarding high-risk sexual behaviours within the MSM category to address this problem, this has not

---

[60] It has been reported that there has been a gradual increase in HIV positive donations over a ten-year period in Spain since the implementation of its donor deferral policy based on high-risk sexual behaviours. The increase has been concentrated in the MSM donor group. The donations in question have included those in the window period, as well as ones from repeat donors; see E. C. Vamvakas, 'Relative risk of reducing the lifetime blood donation deferral for men who have had sex with men versus currently tolerated transfusion risks', *Transfusion Medicine Reviews*, 25 (2011), 47–60 at 48.

[61] M. Goldman, Q.-L. Yi, X. Ye *et al.*, 'Donor understanding about current and potential deferral criteria for high-risk sexual behavior', *Transfusion* 51 (2011) 1829–34 at 1833.

[62] J. Pillonel, V. Heraud-Bousquet, B. Pelletier *et al.*, 'Deferral from donating blood of men who have sex with men: impact on the risk of HIV transmission by transfusion in France', *Vox Sanguinis* 102 (2012) 13–21 at 17; L. Byrne, L. J. Brant, K. Davison *et al.*, 'Transfusion-transmitted human immunodeficiency virus (HIV) from seroconverting donors is rare in England and Wales: results from HIV lookback, October 1995 through December 2008', *Transfusion*, 51 (2011), 1339–45 at 1341–3.

[63] Seed *et al.*, 'No evidence of a significantly increased risk of transfusion-transmitted human immunodeficiency virus infection in Australia', pp. 2727–8. Non-compliance with the existing lifetime MSM donor deferral policy was also noted to be a major problem in France; see Pillonel *et al.*, 'Deferral from donating blood of men who have sex with men', p. 5.

[64] J. Martucci, 'Negotiating exclusion: MSM, identity and blood policy in an age of AIDS', *Social Studies of Science*, 40 (2010), 215–41 at 217, 223, relying on A. Preda, *AIDS, Rhetoric and Medical Knowledge* (Cambridge University Press, 2004), pp. 230–2.

been seen as either generally feasible or appropriate by many national blood services.

Recently published research, which involved interviewing MSM donors in the UK, found that a sizeable minority of the sample had donated despite ineligibility to do so under what was then the UK's permanent MSM deferral policy. Reasons for non-compliance included the following: self-categorisation as low risk; discounting the sexual experience that barred donation; the need for discretion around sexual identity or practice; misconceptions relating to procedures safeguarding blood; misunderstanding of the exclusion criterion; and resentment over its perceived inequity vis-à-vis other deferred groups. Key findings from the study included a general lack of awareness among those interviewed about the permanent MSM donor deferral policy, as well as the fact that some non-compliant donors did not identify past male sexual experience as coming within the terms of such policy. In the circumstances, it was suggested that the rate of non-compliance could be improved through better communication about the fallibility of blood screening, as well as ensuring that both the details and (scientific) rationale for the MSM donor deferral policy were more effectively conveyed to donors. It was also recommended that particular attention be paid to how best to deal with the category of donors who did not identify themselves as gay or bisexual in order to inform them about risk behaviours associated with MSM activity.[65]

Recent challenges to the MSM donor deferral policy in countries such as the USA and the UK have highlighted the difficulties experienced by decision-makers in deciding whether or not to amend or remove the policy, in the context of a zero-risk mindset towards achieving blood safety. In the USA, for example, representative organisations for blood services have argued that the current MSM deferral policy no longer remains scientifically or technologically justifiable, particularly in the light of advances brought about by NAT screening of blood donations. In the circumstances, they have argued that the policy should be changed to a twelve-month deferral, bringing it into line with deferrals based on other high-risk behaviours.[66] Given the sensitivity of NAT

---

[65] P. Grenfell, W. Nutland, S. McManus *et al.*, 'Views and experiences of men who have sex with men on the ban on blood donation: a cross sectional survey with qualitative interviews', *British Medical Journal*, 343 (2011), d5604.

[66] In the USA, the AABB has supported a change in policy since 1997 and was joined in this position by both the ARC and ABC in 2006; see American Association of Blood Banks (AABB), America's Blood Centers (ABC) and American Red Cross (ARC), Joint Statement Before BPAC on Behavior-Based Blood Donors Deferrals in the Era of Nucleic Acid Testing (NAT), 9 March 2006 (www.aabb.org/pressroom/statements/Pages/bpacdefernat030906.aspx). In the USA, intravenous drug users

testing, it has been suggested all that remains is the residual risk of transmission of HIV posed by MSM donors which may arise after all other safeguards have been followed.[67] Such risk predominantly relates to donations made during the window period between exposure to HIV and the development of antibodies to the virus.[68] Based on a series of assumptions,[69] the nature of this residual risk is such that it needs to be based on statistical modelling.

On the basis of the latest modelling undertaken in the USA, it has been estimated that if the current permanent MSM donor deferral policy was to be amended to a twelve-month deferral, then this would result in one additional HIV positive unit of blood being released for transfusion every five and a half years. Conversely, if a five-year deferral was adopted, then it would be likely that an additional such unit would be released for transfusion on average every thirty-three years. In the event that either a one- or five-year deferral policy was adopted, it would be likely to result in a minimal to a small increase in the pool of donors eligible to donate.[70] It was also considered that the higher prevalence

and female sex workers are currently permitted to donate twelve months after their last risky contact/activity. Black women are also not deferred even though there is a high HIV prevalence amongst this group. One commentator has suggested that one of the underlying reasons for such inconsistency derives from the fact that in the USA, 'we are more sensitised to racism than homophobia'; see B. Roehr, 'Should men who have ever had sex with men be allowed to give blood? Yes', *British Medical Journal*, 338 (2009), b311.

[67] Comments made by J. Epstein, US FDA Workshop on Behavior-Based Donor Deferrals in the NAT Era, 8 March 2006, referred to in W. Leiss, M. Tyshenko and D. Krewski, 'Men having sex with men donor deferral risk assessment: an analysis using risk management principles', *Transfusion Medicine Reviews*, 22 (2008), 35–57 at 36.

[68] The current residual risk for HIV in the USA is estimated to be of the order of 1 in 2.3 million units of blood; see S. Anderson, H. Yang, L. M. Gallagher *et al.*, 'Quantitative estimate of the risks and benefits of possible alternative blood donor strategies for men who have had sex with men', *Transfusion*, 49 (2009), 1102–14 at 1103.

[69] The assumptions and estimates that have been made in order to produce current statistical modelling regarding the current MSM deferral policy in the USA have been criticised on the grounds that they have 'grossly overestimated the risk of HIV infectious donations entering the [US] blood supply'; see E. C. Vamvakas, 'Scientific background on the risk engendered by reducing the lifetime blood donation deferral period for men who have sex with men', *Transfusion Medicine Reviews*, 23 (2009), 85–102 at 92.

[70] If a twelve-month deferral policy was adopted in the USA, it has been estimated that it would result in a 0.88% mean annual increase in donors infected with neither HIV nor HBV (75,190 donors); or 0.17% mean annual increase (14,730 donors) if a five-year donor deferral policy was adopted; see Anderson *et al.*, 'Quantitative estimate of the risks and benefits of possible alternative blood donor strategies for men who have had sex with men', p. 1109. Earlier studies showed a higher estimate of risk of HIV transmission if the current MSM donor deferral policy was changed to one year or five years in the USA; see M. Germain, R. S. Remis and G. Delage, 'The risks and benefits of accepting men who have had sex with men as blood donors', *Transfusion*,

of HIV in the MSM population when compared to the general donor population would result in a 'disproportionate increase' in the number of donations testing positive for the virus in the first year following the implementation of either a twelve-month or five-year deferral policy.[71]

The FDA has considered whether its current MSM donor deferral policy should be amended on a number of occasions, based on receipt of expert advice. At meetings held in both 1997 and 2000, BPAC voted by narrow majorities to reject any moves to amend the policy, primarily on the grounds of uncertainty about the relationship between the scientific data presented regarding the relationship between MSM, sexual identity/behaviour and the risk of HIV. In 2000, this was further complicated by the emergence of concerns about another virus, known as human herpesvirus-8 (HHV-8), which was identified as being prevalent in the gay community. Although concern was expressed by committee members on both occasions about the prima facie discriminatory approach of the MSM donor deferral policy, it recommended that further investigations be undertaken regarding identity and sexual behaviour issues in the MSM donor population before a decision could be made to relax the policy.[72] In 2006, the FDA revisited the matter, holding a stakeholder workshop to consider the impact of developments in NAT testing on current blood donor deferral policies.[73] Although this meeting resulted in the American Red Cross (ARC) taking the decision to reverse its earlier opposition to relaxing the MSM donor deferral policy, the FDA's position remained unchanged.

In June 2010, the US Department of Health and Human Services Advisory Committee on Blood Safety and Availability (ACBSA) again considered whether the MSM donor deferral policy should be relaxed or removed.[74] Having heard evidence over a number of days from

---

43 (2003), 25–33; A. M. Sanchez, G. B. Schreiber, C. C. Nass et al., 'The impact of male to male sexual experience on risk profiles of blood donors', Transfusion, 45 (2005), 404–13.

[71] Anderson et al., 'Quantitative estimate of the risks and benefits of possible alternative blood donor strategies for men who have had sex with men', p. 1105.

[72] Martucci, 'Negotiating exclusion', pp. 223–31.

[73] Food and Drug Administration, Workshop on Behavior-Based Donor Deferrals in the NAT Era, 8 March 2006.

[74] In the wake of the findings of the IOM Report published in 1995 (see Leveton et al., HIV and the Blood Supply), the Advisory Committee on Blood Safety and Availability (ACBSA) was established in 1997. ACBSA provides advice to the US Secretary of Health and Human Services on a range of issues including the definition of public health parameters around safety and availability of the blood and blood products; broad public health, ethical and legal issues related to transfusion and transplantation safety; and the implications for safety and availability of various economic factors affecting product cost and supply (see www.hhs.gov/ash/bloodsafety/advisorycommittee/index.html).

groups with various positions on the matter, it came to a majority decision that the existing policy should remain in place for the time being. However, it was unanimous that the current policy was 'suboptimal' in that it permitted some potentially high-risk donations while excluding some low-risk donations. It recommended that further scientific and other research be undertaken in a number of key areas in order to provide the basis for considering an alternative approach to the current policy. In 2011, the Public Health Service Blood, Organ and Tissue Safety Working Group (BOTS WG) was commissioned by the US Assistant Secretary for Health to review the MSM donor deferral policy in light of ACBSA's recommendations. The Working Group has been requested to prioritise action and/or studies in order to produce data that would provide the basis for reconsidering the policy. Pending sufficient funding to undertake such studies, it may take up to three years before the data is collected and analysed and further action can be taken.[75]

The ultimate decision on whether the MSM donor deferral policy should be amended or removed rests with the FDA. The FDA has stated that its position on the issue is multi-factorial, taking account of both scientific and public health considerations. It argues that the current policy is based on scientific and epidemiological data which identifies that the 'HIV prevalence in potential donors with [a] history of male sex with males is 200 times higher than first time blood donors and 2000 times higher than repeat blood donors'.[76] In addition, MSM continue to account for the largest number of people newly infected with HIV in the USA. In the circumstances, the FDA has rejected the allegation that the current policy is based on any pejorative judgments concerning donors' sexual orientation.[77]

While accepting that the FDA's position on the MSM donor deferral policy is in line with a strict adherence to the 'safety tripod' previously referred to,[78] there is a need to acknowledge the complex

---

[75] US Department of Health and Human Services, Advisory Committee on Blood Safety and Availability, Recommendations (www.hhs.gov/ash/bloodsafety/advisory-committee/recommendations/resolutions.html). For a transfusionist perspective on the decision to retain the existing MSM donor deferral policy in the USA, see A. F. Eder and J. E. Menitove, 'Blood donations past, present and future', *Transfusion*, 50 (2010), 1870–7 at 1873.

[76] Food and Drug Administration, Blood Donations from Men Who Have Sex with Other Men Questions and Answers (www.fda.gov/biologicsbloodvaccines/blood-bloodproducts/questionsaboutblood/ucm108186.htm).

[77] *Ibid.*

[78] While the FDA's position on the MSM donor deferral policy has been described as a 'classic case of archaism in donor questioning', it is accepted that it is in line with a

inter-relationship of social, scientific and institutional factors that have fostered the politicised environment in which risk decision-making on this issue has taken place in the USA. Blood donation has long been associated with social solidarity and therefore to exclude gay men from engaging in such an act is not only to stigmatise them by association with a deadly disease, but also to perpetuate discrimination against gay men as a group.[79] Such discrimination has been justified to date largely on the grounds of advice generated and received from scientific and other experts regarding epidemiological data concerning the higher prevalence of HIV in MSM; empirical research showing that the majority of HIV-positive donors who are non-compliant with the current donor deferral policy are MSM; and assumptions about the likelihood of an HIV infectious unit from an MSM donor being released for transfusion based on statistical modelling. Although it has been claimed that any relaxation of the current MSM donor deferral policy should be based on science,[80] it is patently clear that the scientific basis for such change is the subject of contestation and challenge by experts and other stakeholders both within the USA, and beyond.[81]

In addition, the FDA is dealing with the historical legacy of criticism it suffered as a result of the influential IOM Report published in the mid 1990s on the circumstances that led to the HIV blood contamination episode in the USA. The Report found that the FDA had failed to show leadership in adopting a proactive approach in dealing with the risk posed by HIV to the US blood supply in the 1980s and made a series of recommendations for reform of the FDA's approach to managing

---

'strict adherence to the safety tripod'; see Farrugia, 'The mantra of blood safety: time for a new tune?', p. 2.

[79] It has been suggested that advocating for a change in the existing MSM donor deferral policy in the USA has been difficult for many in the gay community because maintaining the association between HIV and gay men has proved highly useful in terms of accessing political power and realising social legitimacy in the fight for research into, as well as treatment for, HIV; see Martucci, 'Negotiating exclusion', p. 232, drawing on Epstein, *Impure Science*, p. 53. It is important to note that the framing of gay men donating blood as a symbol of social inclusion and citizenship may not be universal. In the circumstances, account needs to be taken of particular approaches taken in different national settings; see B. Berner, 'The making of a risk object: AIDS, gay citizenship and the meaning of blood donation in Sweden in the early 1980s', *Sociology of Health and Illness*, 33 (2011), 384–98 at 395.

[80] Vamvakas, 'Scientific background on the risk engendered by reducing the lifetime blood donation deferral period for men who have sex with men', p. 99.

[81] See earlier in this chapter for differing positions adopted by scientific and other experts in relation to dealing with MSM as a high-risk group for transmitting HIV through blood donation. For a nuanced analysis of how the current MSM donor deferral policy is discriminatory in its effect, see C. Galarneau, 'Blood donation, deferral and discrimination'.

risks to blood safety.[82] Such legacy has created path dependencies in policy and regulatory processes which have led to the FDA adopting a highly precautionary approach in relation to blood safety, as well as being highly sensitised to any potential loss of credibility that might result from public and/or political criticism of its leadership role in this regard. The environment in which regulatory governance involving blood safety now takes place in the USA means that any perceived increase in the risk of transmission of TTIs through the blood supply, however minimal it may be, may currently not be a viable option for the FDA in political or reputational terms.[83]

There have also been a number of challenges to, as well as scientific reviews of, the UK's permanent MSM donor deferral policy in recent years.[84] Those who supported a relaxation of the policy argued that it was discriminatory and homophobic, as well as being based on scientific data that was not up-to-date.[85] It also operated in circumstances where blood services had not effectively communicated the rationale for maintaining the policy to either donors or the wider public.[86] Other commentators argued to the contrary, suggesting that it was ultimately a public health issue rather than one of homophobic discrimination but that support for the exclusion should be evidence-based, drawing on the most up-to-date data on the issue.[87] While UK blood services accepted the need for regular reviews of scientific data on the issue, their position was that any transmission of TTIs through blood transfusion was one too many. It therefore supported the maintenance of the permanent MSM deferral policy on the grounds of the higher risk

---

[82] Leveton *et al.*, *HIV and the Blood Supply*, pp. 209–16.

[83] E. C. Vamvakas, 'Relative risk of reducing the lifetime blood donation deferral for men who have had sex with men', p. 58.

[84] See SaBTO (Advisory Committee on the Safety of Blood, Tissues and Organs), Evidence-base for the exclusion of potential donors due to sexual behaviours associated with an increased risk of transfusion-transmissible infections – a report to the Advisory Committee on the Safety of Blood, Tissues and Organs (SaBTO), SaBTO 9–27 January 2009, Agenda Item 5, p. 4 (www.dh.gov.uk/prod_consum_dh/groups/dh_digitalassets/@dh/@ab/documents/digitalasset/dh_111629.pdf).

[85] The epidemiological data that had been relied upon in an earlier review of the MSM blood donor deferral policy in the UK had been collected in the late 1990s prior to the introduction of NAT testing; see K. Soldan and K. Sinka, 'Evaluation of the de-selection of men who have had sex with men from blood donation in England', *Vox Sanguinis*, 84 (2003), 265–73.

[86] R. Hurley, 'Bad blood: gay men and blood donation', *British Medical Journal*, 338 (2009), b779.

[87] This is the position adopted by the Terrence Higgins Trust, the UK's largest HIV and sexual charity. For further details regarding the charity's position on the issue, see Terrence Higgins Trust, Blood donations regulations changes – THT's response and guide (www.tht.org.uk/informationresources/policy/healthpolicy/blooddonations).

posed by MSM donors for the transmission of infectious diseases, such as HIV.[88]

In response to the most recent challenge to UK policy on the issue, the government's independent Advisory Committee on the Safety of Blood, Tissues and Organs (SaBTO) convened the Blood Donor Selection Steering Group, composed of scientific experts and stakeholder repre-sentatives, to review the current evidence base for the permanent MSM donor deferral policy. In undertaking the review, it was emphasised that any proposed change in the policy would be based on the effective-ness of blood donation screening technology, patient-recipient safety, the reasonable treatment of donors and current levels of compliance with the policy.[89] Since the last review in 2006, it had been noted that HIV infection could now be detected nine days after donors had been exposed to the virus. This had resulted from the introduction of mini-pool NAT testing in UK blood services in 2009.[90] Given such advances in testing technology, it was estimated that the residual risk of an HIV infectious unit entering the UK blood supply through a window period donation was now 1 in 5.8 million donations.[91]

The review identified non-compliance by MSM donors as potentially one of the most problematic factors that would arise in the event of any relaxation of the policy. Non-compliance with the permanent MSM donor deferral policy had been observed in a look back programme conducted by the UK blood services,[92] as well as in published research which had involved interviewing non-compliant MSM donors. While a number of reasons were identified as contributing to non-compliance (see earlier), it was found that such donors would be more likely to be compliant with a twelve-month deferral policy provided that its (scien-tific) rationale was explained to them.[93]

---

[88] National Health Service (NHS) Blood and Transplant, Exclusion of Men who have Sex with Men, Position Statement, 11 April 2011. This should be contrasted with its updated position following the government's decision to change to a twelve-month deferral policy; see National Health Service (NHS) Blood and Transplant, Position Statement – November 2011: Deferral of men who have sex with men from blood donation (www.blood.co.uk/can-i-give-blood/exclusion).

[89] SaBTO (Advisory Committee on the Safety of Blood, Tissues and Organs), Donor Selection Criteria Review (April 2011) (www.dh.gov.uk/en/Publicationsandstatistics/Publications/PublicationsPolicyAndGuidance/DH_129796?ssSourceSiteId=ab), p. 9.

[90] *Ibid.*, p. 19.

[91] Even prior to the introduction of mini-pool NAT testing in 2009, there had been no reported cases of HIV transmission to a recipient in the UK since 2003; *ibid.*, pp. 40–1.

[92] See Byrne *et al.*, 'Transfusion-transmitted human immunodeficiency virus (HIV) from seroconverting donors is rare in England and Wales'.

[93] Grenfell *et al.*, 'Views and experiences of men who have sex with men on the ban on blood donation'.

It was also noted by the Blood Donor Selection Steering Group that consideration of whether to maintain or relax the policy now had to take account of recent changes to national equality legislation, which prohibited discrimination on the grounds of sexual orientation by a public service provider. A blood service would only be exempt from such provision if it could show that it had reliable evidence that either the public or the donor would be put at risk by any refusal to accept a blood donation based on their sexual orientation.[94] The Group suggested that such legal developments needed to be situated within the broader socio-cultural context of greater societal acceptance and equality for the lesbian, gay, bisexual and transgender community. It concluded that the combination of scientific, technological, legal and social factors examined in the review meant that a change to a twelve-month MSM donor deferral policy could now be viewed as both feasible and reasonable in the circumstances.[95]

There were a number of noticeable gaps in the evidence base assembled as part of the review. This included a lack of data on the estimated likely gains in terms of any increase in the pool of eligible donors and consequent availability of blood for transfusion which would result from a change in policy.[96] Although the Group clearly viewed any increase in the eligible donor pool and consequent availability of more blood as relevant factors to take into account, it did not have any current data available to inform its assessment of the issue.[97] The Group also failed to offer any insights into how best to deal with men who do not self-identify as gay or bisexual in the context of blood donation. This is particularly problematic given that published research in the area had identified compliance, rather than length of deferral, as a key factor in ensuring the effectiveness of the policy.

In addition, a number of assertions were made by the Group concerning risk acceptability on the part of patient-recipients regarding any change in permanent deferral of MSM donors. In the review, reference is made to the fact that patients were more likely to focus on the risks posed by TTIs, as well as having a lower risk tolerance than donors.[98] However, such assertions were not backed up by any up-to-

---

[94] Section 29; Schedule 3, Part 3, paragraph 13, Equality Act 2010, c. 15.
[95] SaBTO, Donor Selection Criteria Review, pp. 40–3.
[96] This was in contrast to the position in the USA where modelling data was made available in this regard; see Anderson *et al.*, 'Quantitative estimate of the risks and benefits of possible alternative blood donor strategies for men who have had sex with men', p. 1109.
[97] SaBTO, Donor Selection Criteria Review, p. 51.
[98] *Ibid.*, pp. 51–2.

date qualitative research concerning the views of patient-recipients regarding any potential change in blood donor deferral policies. Such research may have provided more insight into questions such as what level of risk, if any, would be acceptable. Their (and by extension public) perception of risk is crucial in the context of facilitating public trust in blood safety, particularly given the historical legacy of HIV blood contamination episodes. What evidence has been assembled in other national settings on this issue has identified the fallout from such episodes as having altered the 'set point' for risk tolerance in relation to blood safety. This has resulted in zero tolerance for any change in policies that might increase the risk of transmission of TTIs through the blood supply, however minimal that was likely to be.[99] In the circumstances, the failure to gather a stronger evidence base with regard to the views of patient-recipients arising out of change to the MSM donor deferral policy, as well as the absence of a more detailed analysis of risk perception in this context, represent significant omissions in the Group's review.

The findings from the review were presented at a SaBTO meeting held in May 2011. In the one-page document that minutes this meeting, it simply states without further elaboration that there was now sufficient evidence available for SaBTO to make a recommendation regarding the MSM blood donor deferral policy to the government.[100] Four months later, the UK government announced that there would be a change to a twelve-month deferral for MSM blood donors.[101] From the documentation that has been made publicly available to date, there is little, if any, insight to be gained into how SaBTO or those in political leadership assessed the strengths and/or weaknesses of the assembled evidence base.[102] Notwithstanding the obvious political sensitivity of the issue, the historical legacy of blood contamination episodes in the UK meant that there should have been much greater transparency about how those with responsibility for blood safety determined where the line would be drawn with regard to risk acceptability in sanctioning the change to a twelve-month MSM donor deferral policy.

[99] Leiss et al., 'Men having sex with men donor deferral risk assessment', pp. 37–8.
[100] SaBTO, Summary of the Fourteenth Meeting, 3 May 2011 (www.dh.gov.uk/prod_consum_dh/groups/dh_digitalassets/@dh/@ab/documents/digitalasset/dh_129855.pdf).
[101] Department of Health, Lifetime blood donation ban lifted for men who have had sex with men, Press Release – 8 September 2011 (http://mediacentre.dh.gov.uk).
[102] A relevant factor in this regard may have been the longstanding political and institutional disposition towards maintaining secrecy in public policy deliberations in the UK; see M. J. Smith, The Core Executive in Britain (Basingstoke: Macmillan, 1999), p. 111.

Pathogen screening and reduction technologies

Another important component of the safety tripod for the blood system has been the adoption of a diverse range of pathogen screening technologies, designed to reduce and/or remove the risk of TTIs through the use of blood and plasma products. The adoption of such technologies could be seen by decision-makers as a neutral, scientifically validated way of potentially reducing and/or removing such risks without the need to confront the socio-cultural conflict that has arisen in the case of certain donor deferral policies (such as those involving MSM). Indeed, pathogen screening technologies, such as NAT, have proved remarkably successful in recent years in virtually eliminating the risk of TTIs through the use of blood and plasma products.[103] In the years following national HIV blood contamination episodes, stakeholder concerns have nevertheless grown about the alacrity with which regulators and political leaders have mandated the introduction of successive pathogen screening technologies. Such implementation has come at high cost and, at times, with what has been seen by such stakeholders as insufficient techno-scientific evidence of their efficacy or cost-effectiveness in reducing risk.[104] As one critic of this current state of affairs has somewhat acerbically commented, it appears that the zero-risk mindset panders to what is 'important in political and media terms', with the natural extension appearing to be that 'technology has only to be available for it to be introduced into the blood safety environment'.[105]

In terms of risk assessment as a prelude to decision-making over the adoption of particular technologies, serious questions have been raised over whether an approach based on sound science has underpinned such assessment.[106] For example, in the case of the adoption of leukodepletion to remove white cells from blood components to reduce the risk of vCJD transmission, stakeholders have questioned the scientific efficacy of adopting this technology in the absence of definitive serological test to

[103] R. Dodd, W. K. Roth, P. Ashford *et al.*, 'Transfusion medicine and safety', *Biologicals*, 37 (2009), 62–70 at 70; J.-P. Allain, S. L. Stramer, A. B. F. Carneiro-Proietti *et al.*, 'Transfusion-transmitted infectious diseases', *Biologicals*, 37 (2009), 71–7 at 71.

[104] Blajchman and Klein, 'Looking back in anger', p. 2.

[105] Farrugia, 'The regulatory pendulum in transfusion medicine', p. 280.

[106] D. Voak, E. A. Caffrey, J. A. J. Barbara *et al.*, 'Affordable safety for the blood supply in developed and developing countries', *Transfusion Medicine*, 8 (1998), 73–6 at 75; Kirp, 'The politics of blood', p. 314; B. Custer, 'Economic analyses of blood safety and transfusion medicine interventions: a systematic review', *Transfusion Medicine Reviews*, 18 (2004), 127–43 at 127.

detect the presence of the disease.[107] However, much of the adverse commentary on this issue has been linked to whether or not the proposed technology is likely to be cost-effective,[108] particularly when measured against the substantial rising costs associated with the supply of blood components in recent years. In the UK, for example, such costs were estimated to have grown from UK£250 million in 1995 to UK£500 million in 2005.[109] In other developed countries, the increased costs of supply are estimated to range between 26 per cent and 170 per cent.[110]

In the circumstances, it has been suggested that there is little evidence that the drive towards zero-risk has been matched by an equal emphasis on whether interventions associated with such rising costs are effective. Against this background, it has been argued that there is a need on the part of those making decisions with regard to the adoption of pathogen screening technologies to engage in a more systematic, quantifiable approach to determining their cost-effectiveness. Commentators who favour such an approach seek to draw comparisons with cost-effectiveness criteria adopted in relation to general healthcare interventions. In countries such as the USA, for example, this is generally estimated at US$55,000 per quality-adjusted life year (QALY).[111] The WHO has suggested that up to three times the gross domestic product (GDP) per person is an appropriate threshold for what should be considered cost-effective. Drawing on such figures, a comparison is then made with the cost of adopting each successive pathogen screening technology to be performed on blood donations in developed countries.

[107] S. Dzik, J. Aubuchon, L. Jeffries et al., 'Leukocyte reduction of blood components: public policy and new technology', Transfusion Medicine Reviews, 14 (2000), 34–52 at 49; M. Busch and B. Custer, 'Health outcomes research using large donor-recipient databases: a new frontier for assessing transfusion safety and contributing to public health', Vox Sanguinis, 91 (2006), 282–4 at 282; N. Graves, G. Clare, M. Haines et al., 'A policy case study of blood in Australia', Social Science and Medicine, 71 (2010), 1677–82.

[108] Cost-effectiveness analysis involves the quantification of benefits and costs associated with the adoption of a particular technology or intervention. It is a framework for evaluating specific public health choices or interventions compared to current practice. Risk assessment and cost-effectiveness analysis share certain techniques and approaches. The risks are characterised in a similar way, but cost-effectiveness analysis examines costs and long-term outcomes of the disease unlike risk assessment; see M. Busch, M. Walderhaug, B. Custer et al., 'Risk assessment and cost-effectiveness/utility analysis', Biologicals, 37 (2009), 78–87 at 81.

[109] R. Smith, 'Doctors question whether all blood transfusions are effective and necessary', British Medical Journal, 330 (2005), 558.

[110] B. Custer and J. S. Hoch, 'Cost-effectiveness analysis: what it really means for transfusion medicine decision making', Transfusion Medicine Reviews, 23 (2009), 1–12 at 3.

[111] Custer, 'Economic analyses of blood safety', pp. 138, 141.

In the quest for enhanced blood safety, it was recognised that the adoption of HIV testing in the 1980s in the USA was extremely cost-effective at US$3,600 per QALY, given the overall prevalence of the disease in the population.[112] However, each successive screening technology that has been introduced has proved less cost-effective, with the introduction of NAT screening of blood donations, for example, costing between US$1 million and US$2 million per QALY.[113] In France, a review of the use of NAT screening on blood donations over a four-year period showed that NAT screening had prevented only one case of post-transfusion chronic hepatitis. The introduction of such technology was nevertheless viewed as inevitable and indeed now 'irreversible', because of the perceived need to adopt all reasonable precautionary measures to increase blood safety.[114] Drawing on such data, it has been argued that regulators need to revisit their use of the precautionary principle in the context of blood safety as it has resulted in the adoption of successive pathogen screening technologies which show only 'marginal benefit',[115] in the absence of any – or any sufficiently detailed – assessment of their cost-effectiveness. What appears to be missing from arguments put forward in favour of the use of cost-effectiveness analyses, however, is the extent to which other important ethical and socio-political values may necessarily impact on risk decision-making with regard to the adoption of new blood-related technologies, as well as healthcare interventions more generally.[116]

In recent years, questions of scientific efficacy and cost-effectiveness have also been raised in relation to the use of pathogen reduction (or

---

[112] Busch *et al.*, 'Risk assessment and cost-effectiveness/utility analysis', p. 82.

[113] K. E. Berman, 'Expensive blood safety technologies: understanding and managing cost and access-to-care issues', *Transfusion Medicine Reviews*, 18 (2004), 1–10 at 2; Custer and Hoch, 'Cost-effectiveness analysis', p. 5.

[114] S. Laperche, P. Rouger, W. Smilovici *et al.*, 'Alternatives to nucleic acid testing in the blood transfusion service', *Lancet*, 360 (2002), 1519.

[115] Berman, 'Expensive blood safety technologies', p. 2.

[116] It is important to take note of ongoing academic and policy debates in the UK over the use of QALYs and cost-effectiveness analyses in relation to decision-making about healthcare interventions. It presents a more complex picture of the values and issues at stake than is elaborated upon in the literature published to date by US commentators who propose the use of cost-effectiveness analyses in the case of blood safety interventions. For an overview of some of the issues raised in the UK context, see the following: K. Syrett, 'Nice work? Rationing, review and the "legitimacy problem" in the new NHS', *Medical Law Review*, 10 (2002), 1–27; J. Harris, 'NICE is not cost-effective', *Journal of Medical Ethics*, 32 (2006), 378–80; K. Claxton and A. J. Culyer, 'Wickedness or folly? The ethics of NICE's decisions', *Journal of Medical Ethics*, 32 (2006), 373–7; and M. Quigley, 'A NICE fallacy', *Journal of Medical Ethics*, 33 (2007), 465–6.

inactivation) technologies (PRT).[117] This technology is able to target a broad range of nucleic acid containing pathogens. It has already been implemented for the purposes of screening blood components, such as platelets, in various European blood services.[118] For some commentators, however, questions remain over whether it is completely safe for end use by patient-recipients.[119] Pathogen screening technology currently only deals with the emergence of pathogens in the blood supply on a case-by-case basis, thus ensuring a reactive approach to risk governance. For those in favour of the adoption of PRT, it represents a 'new approach or paradigm in transfusion safety, namely the transition from a reactive to a proactive and pre-emptive strategy' for dealing with (infectious) pathogens that exist within the blood supply.[120] Although it is conceded that the initial implementation of PRT may be costly, it is argued that it represents a 'magic bullet' for achieving maximum blood safety, with the prospect of saving costs in the long term.[121]

If one accepts the magic bullet thesis, then the question then becomes whether PRT should replace some or all of the pathogen screening technologies that are currently used by blood services. Based on current modelling, it is not clear that PRT is likely to bring about significant cost savings at the present time.[122] However, there is a more important issue to consider, namely, whether or not there is a political or regulatory consensus that PRT should replace current pathogen screening technologies.[123] While it could be argued that the concept of PRT represents a new precautionary paradigm in technological terms,[124] the

[117] Two well-known types of PRT 'use a photoactive compound (riboflavin or amotosalen) and ultraviolet light treatment to prevent DNA or RNA replication'; see B. Custer, M. Agapova and R. Havlir Martinez, 'The cost-effectiveness of pathogen reduction technology as assessed using a multiple risk reduction model', *Transfusion*, 50 (2010), 2461–73 at 2461.

[118] J.-P. Allain, C. Bianco, M. A. Blajchman *et al.*, 'Protecting the blood supply from emerging pathogens: the role of pathogen inactivation', *Transfusion Medicine Reviews*, 19 (2005), 110–26 at 123.

[119] Dodd *et al.*, 'Transfusion medicine and safety', p. 63; R. Goodrich, 'A balanced approach to blood safety: a possible role for PRT', in C. Areya, H. Nakhasi, P. Mied *et al.*, 'FDA workshop on emerging infectious diseases: evaluating emerging infectious diseases (EIDs) for transfusion safety', *Transfusion* 51 (2011) 1863–4 at 1864.

[120] H. J. Alter, 'Pathogen reduction: a precautionary principle paradigm', *Transfusion Medicine Reviews*, 22 (2008), 97–102 at 97.

[121] *Ibid.*, pp. 100–2.

[122] Custer *et al.*, 'The cost-effectiveness of pathogen reduction technology'.

[123] Farrugia, 'The mantra of blood safety: time for a new tune?', p. 5.

[124] Alter, 'Pathogen reduction: a precautionary principle paradigm'; H. A. Perkins and M. P. Busch, 'Transfusion-associated infections: 50 years of relentless challenges and remarkable progress', *Transfusion*, 50 (2010), 2080–99 at 2094.

current zero-risk mindset of those with political and regulatory responsibility for blood safety means that there would need to be a high degree of certainty about the safety (and cost) benefits of PRT before it was likely that a decision would be taken to adopt them instead of, rather than in addition to, current pathogen screening technologies.

Conclusion

This chapter examined the influence and use of the precautionary principle in risk governance involving the blood system. The first section of the chapter provided a general overview of the way in which the precautionary principle has evolved and been used in the public health context. Such overview revealed that there is ongoing conflict and debate among stakeholders, politicians and regulators over how it should be defined and in what circumstances it should be applied; how scientific data should be used in the context of assessing uncertainty about risk; and to what extent political objectives should influence public health risk governance processes more generally.

The second section of the chapter examined the application of the precautionary principle in the context of blood safety. As has been observed in other policy sectors, this revealed similar problems with regard to its interpretation and application, following its increased use in the wake of national HIV blood contamination episodes. While differing interpretations have been offered as to how it should be applied in order to enhance blood safety, it is clear that it is much more likely to be used where there is a perceived serious or catastrophic risk to the blood system in circumstances where there remains a degree of uncertainty about the nature and scope of such a risk, as well as its impact on public health. Where confusion and conflict have arisen between stakeholders, regulators and politicians both within and across national settings is in relation to when the principle should be used in decision-making processes about risk acceptability. This was particularly apparent in the way in which those with responsibility for blood safety sought to deal with the implementation of restrictive donor selection criteria, such as the MSM blood donor deferral policy. An examination of how challenges to this policy were addressed in countries such as the USA and the UK revealed that where the line is to be drawn in terms of adopting a precautionary approach to blood safety is a complex undertaking in which scientific data, as well as a range of socio-cultural, political and legal factors, all need to be factored into the risk decision-making process.

Another area of contention has involved the extent of reliance on scientific and other evidence to ground the use of the precautionary principle in the context of managing risks to the blood system. For some stakeholders, decision-making with regard to risk assessment is not sufficiently grounded in sound science, whereas for others the focus is predominantly on the development and use of technology to enhance safety and bring about greater certainty. Yet still for others, there has been a failure to take account of the need for sufficiently rigorous risk–benefit and/or cost-effectiveness analyses to justify the use of the precautionary principle in the context of blood safety. Each of these strategies could be considered to have limitations and should not be viewed in isolation from other factors impacting upon risk governance in the field. While there is no doubt that scientific data and modelling may be vital in seeking to determine the nature of the risk, there may be gaps or omissions in scientific knowledge when dealing with uncertainty about the scope and impact of such risk on public health. In any case, those with medico-scientific expertise bring their own training, professional beliefs and practical experience to bear not only on how they construct risk, but also in how they engage in risk assessment. This necessarily impacts upon how they perceive the use, or conversely the inappropriate use, of precautionary strategies adopted in relation to risk governance involving the blood system.

The idea that innovation in technology can provide the magic bullet for dealing effectively with risks to blood safety should also be viewed with caution. Although a high degree of safety has now been achieved in developed countries as a result of the introduction of a range of pathogen screening technologies in recent years, it is important to keep in mind that each new innovation comes with questions about efficacy, safety and cost, as well as a need for regulatory oversight against a background of finite public health, financial or other resources. In the circumstances, innovation in technology needs to be considered alongside a range of other socio-cultural and political factors and should not be viewed on its own as either neutral in its application, or as offering a magic bullet in the context of blood safety.

Against a background of finite institutional and financial resources, the question of the costs involved in adopting a precautionary approach to dealing with risks to the blood system is a salient one. There is clearly a need to undertake risk–benefit analyses in relation to technological or other interventions and to factor the problem of competing risks into decision-making processes, such as blood or plasma product shortages, which may result from such interventions. It is debatable whether cost-effectiveness analysis offers a useful way forward in this regard, since its limitations are acknowledged even by those who see it as a useful aid in such decision-making processes. Cost-effectiveness analysis often draws on models and makes costs comparisons with other health interventions, but cannot account either for the complexities of dealing with a biological substance, such as blood, or for the uncertainties that accompany the emergence of a (new) pathogen that may pose a risk to the blood system.

Moreover, such analysis cannot address how best to deal with the loss of public trust that occurred in the wake of national HIV blood contamination episodes. This is not to say that cost considerations should not play a role but they are unlikely to be determinative given the political fallout from such episodes, at least for the foreseeable future. Indeed, it is the enduring legacy of such episodes in which the use of the precautionary principle in risk governance involving the blood system must be situated. While there does not appear to be any particular scientific or regulatory expectation that public expectations of a zero-risk blood supply are in fact realistically achievable, the fallout from such episodes clearly resulted in a catastrophic loss of public trust in a highly valued public health service. For those with political and regulatory responsibility for the blood system, this has necessitated constant vigilance with respect to regaining and then maintaining that trust. What it may also mean is that no increase in risk, however minimal, is currently publicly or politically acceptable in particular national settings.

Such legacy has also served to create path dependencies in institutional and political decision-making processes about blood safety issues, in which the politics of precaution now dominate risk governance involving the blood system. It has resulted in risk decision-making where its parameters may be influenced by credibility and reputational concerns on the part of those with responsibility for blood safety; where considerations such as cost-effectiveness or scientific risk assessment may be disregarded; where technology that offers a margin (however small) of increased safety may be quickly adopted; and where institutional decision-making processes regarding risk management over issues such as restrictive blood donor deferral policies may be undermined by the highly politicised environment in which it takes place.

Notwithstanding the fact that greater recourse to the use of the precautionary principle has clearly contributed to a proactive approach towards ensuring patient-recipient safety, what would be welcomed in this changed environment is greater clarity and transparency regarding the elements involved in risk decision-making processes in which the use of the precautionary principle is being considered. This is in addition to regulators and politicians paying greater attention to whether or not the aims and objectives of such processes have been effective in dealing with emerging risks to the blood system, as well as whether an appropriate balance has been struck between any competing risks and harms to public health that may arise as a result of the adoption of precautionary strategies. There is little publicly available evidence that this type of evaluation is taking place and this needs to change.

Stakeholders in the blood system, such as those in national blood services and the plasma products industry, may question and even resist the zero-risk mindset on the part of both regulators and politicians which is underpinned by the use of the precautionary principle in relation to blood safety. However, there is a need to accept that this now represents the current and future direction of risk governance in the field. The loss of public trust that occurred in the wake of national HIV blood contamination episodes has meant that the benchmark for public, political and regulatory expectations involving blood safety has now been set and it is high. This is likely to involve continuing (over-) reliance on technology at high cost, as well as maintaining adherence to restrictive donor selection criteria which may have unfortunate consequences, including the continuing stigmatisation of certain donor groups and the potential for blood shortages. This is now the brave new world of blood safety, in which the use of the precautionary principle is likely to remain an integral tool in risk governance for the foreseeable future.

8   Regulating risk

The politicisation of risk that occurred in the wake of national HIV blood contamination episodes led to heightened sensitivity on the part of key decision-makers in dealing with blood safety issues. Alongside the use of the precautionary principle, which was examined in detail in Chapter 7, the use of risk regulation has also become one of the preferred techniques of legitimation employed by those with responsibility for blood safety to enhance political credibility and restore public trust in the wake of such episodes. The aim of this chapter is to examine the design and effectiveness of risk regulation in the post-HIV blood contamination era. Drawing on a case study of EU risk regulation of blood and plasma products, a number of key arguments are made. First, the multi-valuing of human biological materials, such as blood, brings complexity to risk governance and it is argued that this cannot be accommodated by the dichotomous framing of blood as either a gift or a commodity. Given that how policy is framed may substantially impact upon how issues or problems are perceived,[1] it is important that achieving optimum patient-recipient safety operates as the predominant policy frame structuring the design and implementation of risk regulation in the field.

Second, how risk is defined determines the extent to which regulatory design is likely to be comprehensive. This requires an expansive definition to be adopted in relation to what constitutes risk for the purposes of regulation in the field.[2] Ideally, such definition should encompass a vein-to-vein approach with respect to facilitating blood safety, as well as ensuring that both the social and economic aspects involved in blood sourcing and supply are taken account of in the design of a holistic approach to risk regulation. Finally, determining whether risk

---

[1] Jasanoff, *Designs on Nature*, p. 23.
[2] On the importance of adopting an expansive approach to defining and interpreting risk so as to take account of ethical and social commitments involved in the regulation of technologies, see Lee, 'Beyond safety?', pp. 242–3.

regulation is effective needs to take account of whether the regime in question meets its stated aims and objectives; its comprehensiveness in dealing with risk-based issues; the degree of support for, or conversely resistance to, the regime by those entities subject to its remit; and the availability of accountability mechanisms for monitoring the regime.[3]

On this final point, the availability of informational and deliberative accountability mechanisms are important for facilitating transparency with regard to decision-making processes affecting risk regulation.[4] However, the politicisation of risk that occurred in the wake of national HIV blood contamination episodes makes it imperative for the purposes of maintaining public trust that the monitoring of regulation to enhance blood safety is also undertaken by institutions and/or individuals subject to electoral mandate. Such an approach is vital if risk regulation is to operate successfully as a technique of legitimation in the wake of such episodes. For present purposes, it is suggested that this should involve monitoring by the European Parliament (Parliament) of the totality of EU risk regulation involving blood and plasma products,[5] as well as periodic review by Member State parliaments where possible. In order to examine these arguments, the chapter first provides an overview of risk regulation in the EU context. Thereafter, key aspects of the separate regulatory regimes that operate at EU level in relation to blood and plasma products are examined. This is followed by an assessment of the effectiveness of such regimes by reference to the criteria identified above.

The EU and risk regulation

From the latter half of the twentieth century onwards, there has been a huge growth in the use of state-sponsored regulation over a wide range of social and economic activities. This has led to claims that we are

---

[3] I am here drawing on and adapting Brownsword's arguments regarding regulatory effectiveness and its relationship to regulatory legitimacy, as well as the legitimation of regulatory purposes (see Brownsword, *Rights, Regulation, and the Technological Revolution*, pp. 9–11).

[4] As mentioned in Chapter 1, regulatory theorists have identified a range of mechanisms that are important for facilitating accountability in the context of regulatory governance; see Black, 'Proceduralizing regulation', pp. 597–9; Prosser, *The Regulatory Enterprise*, p. 7.

[5] While it was argued in the mid 1990s that the use of non-majoritarian mechanisms of accountability would be more appropriate in the context of the EU regulatory state (see G. Majone, 'Regulatory legitimacy', in G. Majone (ed.), *Regulating Europe* (London: Routledge, 1996), pp. 284–301 at 285–7), the Parliament's role and oversight powers are now much more developed due to successive treaty amendments.

living in an era of the regulatory state,[6] engaged in steering rather than rowing.[7] More recent scholarship has emphasised the greater diversity of agencies, actors and organisations involved in regulation apart from the state, particularly at supranational level.[8] This has resulted in calls for the adoption of a broader, more decentred definition of regulation that acknowledges complexity, fragmentation and interdependencies, whilst at the same time rejecting any clear distinction between the public and private in understanding the regulatory process.[9] This is taking place in the context of 'post-regulatory state' politics,[10] as well as the rise of 'regulatory capitalism'.[11]

The EU has been described as having many of the hallmarks of the regulatory state, although it should be seen as operating in a different way to that seen at national level. The EU as a political and legal entity has some, but not all, of the features of statehood, with its main state-like activity residing in its power to engage in social and economic regulation. Regulation has been used to expand the EU's range of activities and level of control, as well as to enhance its legitimacy.[12] EU regulatory activity takes place against a background of limited resources and weak control mechanisms with regard to implementation and evaluation. Regulation is largely designed and monitored in the context of non-majoritarian decision-making processes which are informed by the provision of expert advice and deliberative stakeholder participation,

---

[6] G. Majone, 'The rise of the regulatory state in Europe', *West European Politics*, 17 (1994), 77–101 at 81; Moran, *The British Regulatory State*, p. 5.

[7] D. Osborne and T. Gaebler, *Reinventing Government: How the Entrepreneurial Spirit Is Transforming the Public Sector* (Reading, MA: Addison-Wesley, 1992).

[8] S. Picciotto, 'Introduction: reconceptualizing regulation in an era of globalization' *Journal of Law and Society*, 29 (2005) 1–11 at 1.

[9] See Black, 'What is regulatory innovation?', p. 11; Black, 'Constructing and contesting legitimacy and accountability in polycentric regulatory regimes', p. 140.

[10] It has been suggested that the term 'post-regulatory state' should be used to inform a different way of thinking about a 'wider range of norms, institutions and processes' involved in the process of regulatory governance; see C. Scott, 'Regulation in the age of governance: the rise of the post-regulatory state', in J. Jordana and D. Levi-Faur (eds.), *The Politics of Regulation: Institutions and Regulatory Reforms for the Age of Governance* (Cheltenham: Edward Elgar, 2004), pp. 145–74 at 146.

[11] 'Regulatory capitalism' has been defined as the privatisation, as well as the proliferation of new technologies of regulation and meta regulation, increased delegation to business and professional self-regulation, international networks of regulatory experts and increased regulation of state by state, in order to promote competition; see J. Braithwaite, 'Neoliberalism and regulatory capitalism', *Occasional Paper No. 5, Regulatory Institutions Network* (Canberra: ANU, 2005), pp. 1–43 at 12; D. Levi-Faur, 'Foreword', in J. Braithwaite, *Regulatory Capitalism: How it Works, Ideas for Making it Work Better* (Cheltenham: Edward Elgar Publishing, 2008), pp. vii–x at viii.

[12] Majone, 'The rise of the regulatory state', pp. 93–4.

where appropriate.[13] It has been suggested that such an approach is more suitable for complex and plural polities such as the EU, rather than relying on mechanisms of 'direct political accountability'.[14]

One of the main drivers of regulatory growth at EU level in recent years has been the perceived need to engage in more effective risk governance.[15] Although risk regulation was originally grounded primarily in the need to promote better functioning of the single market,[16] the political fallout from the failure to manage the BSE crisis in the late 1990s led to a much greater expansion in the use of this particular type of regulatory regime.[17] This was accompanied by a more sophisticated and detailed approach to the use of the precautionary principle in the context of risk assessment, management and communication.[18] This was done to facilitate more effective risk governance across a number of politically sensitive policy sectors, such as food safety, as well as to enhance the EU's battered credibility in the wake of the BSE crisis.[19] In the EU context, it has been suggested that there is a particular approach taken to risk regulation which reflects ongoing concerns about how best to promote the effective operation of the single market. In particular, this applies to the manufacture, supply and movement of goods within the EU market where there may be issues regarding health, environmental or technological risks associated with their use.[20] In institutional terms, the Commission dominates the approach taken to risk governance across a range of policy sectors where it pursues a structured approach to separating out risk assessment and management, underpinned by a strong reliance on scientific advice.[21]

[13] M. Lodge, 'Regulation, the regulatory state and European politics', *West European Politics*, 31 (2009), 280–301 at 288–9; C. Skelcher and J. Torfing, 'Improving democratic governance through institutional design: civic participation and democratic ownership in Europe', *Regulation & Governance*, 4 (2010), 71–91 at 75.

[14] Majone, 'Regulatory legitimacy', p. 286.

[15] Hood *et al.*, *The Government of Risk*, p. 4. Regulating risk has also come to be seen as a key activity of the regulatory state more generally; see M. Moran, 'Understanding the regulatory state', *British Journal of Political Science*, 32 (2002), 391–413 at 407.

[16] Fisher, *Risk Regulation*, p. 210.

[17] E. Vos, 'Overcoming the crisis of confidence: risk regulation in an enlarged European Union', Inaugural Lecture (University of Maastricht, 2004), 1–27; Vos, 'EU food safety regulation in the aftermath of the BSE crisis'.

[18] Commission of the European Communities, Communication from the Commission on the Precautionary Principle.

[19] Everson and Vos, 'The scientification of politics', p. 1.

[20] V. Heyvaert, 'Europe in a climate of risk: three paradigms at play', *LSE Law, Society and Economy Working Papers*, 06/2010, pp. 1–27 at 12, 16.

[21] Commission of the European Communities, Communication from the Commission on the Precautionary Principle, pp. 13–19; Corkin, 'Science, legitimacy and the law', p. 371; M. Kritikos, 'Traditional risk analysis and releases of GMOs into the European Union: space for non-scientific factors?', *European Law Review*, 34 (2009), 405–32 at 428.

The recognition of the need to take account of broader ethical, social and cultural values in risk governance involving areas such as bio-technology at EU level has manifested itself in practice through the adoption of a range of what have been described as 'new governance' mechanisms.[22] This has included increased recourse to the use of ethics expertise to represent such values in advisory terms, as well as attempts to increase stakeholder involvement through more participative forms of consultation and decision-making.[23] Such attempts have been criticised on a number of grounds. While there is a recognition that a more delib-erative approach to decision-making has great potential at EU level,[24] the adoption of such an approach appears to have operated more on a procedural, rather than a substantive, level in practice.[25] The attempt to separate out risk assessment and risk management in institutional terms has been viewed as 'artificial',[26] given that it is rather blurred in practice.[27] Scientific advice continues to strongly influence the approach taken by the Commission to risk governance in practice and it is debat-able whether the inclusion of additional ethics expertise has done much either to broaden the scope of decision-making or to take account of non-scientific values.[28] Either way, it has been suggested that the use of such expertise is no 'panacea' for the need to ensure greater political accountability in sensitive areas of risk governance at EU level.[29]

The Commission's expanded repertoire of (new) governance mecha-nisms in politically sensitive areas of governance is also grounded in more general concerns about the EU's perceived legitimacy, given that

[22] Commission of the European Communities, *European Governance: A White Paper* (2001) 428 final, 25.7.2001. 'New governance' has been defined in various ways. Broadly speaking, it is said to permit a more flexible and participatory approach to the formation of policy involving a range of stakeholders through shared learning, benchmarking and the development of best practice models. This may include the use of peer pressure to facilitate a shift towards mutually beneficial and agreed upon objectives; see G. de Búrca and J. Scott, 'Introduction: new governance, law and con-stitutionalism', in G. de Búrca and J. Scott (eds.), *Law and New Governance in the EU and the US* (Oxford: Hart Publishing, 2006), pp. 1–14 at 2.

[23] Jasanoff, *Designs on Nature*, p. 89.

[24] Skelcher and Torfing, 'Improving democratic governance through institutional design', p. 76.

[25] Borrás, 'Legitimate governance of risk at the EU level?', p. 71; Kritikos, 'Traditional risk analysis and releases of GMOs', p. 428; Weimer, 'Applying precaution in EU authorization of genetically modified products', p. 655; cf. Black, who argues that there is a need to be clear about what sort of democratic vision is at stake in relation to promoting deliberative processes in regulatory governance, as this will affect pro-cedural norms and outcomes; see Black, 'Proceduralizing regulation', p. 599.

[26] Heyvaert, 'Europe in a climate of risk', pp. 14–15.

[27] Kritikos, 'Traditional risk analysis and releases of GMOs', p. 428.

[28] *Ibid.*, p. 425.

[29] Corkin, 'Science, legitimacy and the law', p. 371.

its activities are not subject to the usual oversight and controls which operate in the context of democratic politics at Member State level.[30] In terms of claims to institutional legitimacy, there has been a 'longstanding tension' between the more technocratic approach to governance by non-majoritarian institutions such as the Commission on the one hand, and the democratically accountable Parliament and inter-governmental Council on the other hand.[31] Notwithstanding such internal tensions, the EU has traditionally relied on regulation as the preferred governance technique for enhancing its legitimacy,[32] usually in order to address issues pertaining to the single market, such as market failure or the need to promote innovation.[33] Rather than relying on new governance mechanisms, the use of regulation has been the preferred mode of legitimation in the blood policy sector. This is so, notwithstanding the fact that it is acknowledged to be a politically sensitive area of governance at EU level.

Regulating blood

The political fallout from HIV blood contamination episodes at Member State level provided the catalyst for action at EU level in relation to blood quality and safety.[34] In the 1990s, this led to the Commission proposing a programme of action in the field,[35] which was backed up by calls for action by both the European Parliament and the Council.[36] In

---

[30] How to address the EU's legitimacy problems arising out of the 'democratic deficit' has been the subject of substantial academic commentary; see, for example, F. Scharpf, *Governing in Europe: Effective and Democratic?* (Oxford University Press, 1999), p. 6; J. P. Magnette, 'European governance and civic participation: beyond elitist citizenship?', *Political Studies*, 51 (2003), 144–60; J. Thomassen and H. Schmitt, 'Democracy and legitimacy in the European Union' (2004) (www.mzes. unimannheim.de/publications/papers/Schmitt_26_1_04.pdf), p. 1.

[31] C. Scott, 'Governing without law or governing without government? New-ish governance and legitimacy of the EU', *European Law Journal*, 15 (2009), 160–73 at 170–1.

[32] A. Føllesdal, 'Legitimacy theories of the European Union', *ARENA Working Papers*, WP 04/15 (2004) (www.arena.uio.no/publications/working-papers2004/papers/ wp04_15.pdf), pp. 1–38 at 7–9.

[33] Market failure has long been considered one of the main rationales for regulatory intervention; see Hood *et al.*, *The Government of Risk*, pp. 61–5.

[34] Farrell, 'The emergence of EU governance in public health', p. 135.

[35] See, for example, Commission of the European Communities, Communication on Blood Safety and Self-Sufficiency in the Community.

[36] The European Parliament passed a series of resolutions on blood safety and Community self-sufficiency through voluntary, unpaid donations; see Resolution on self-sufficiency in and safety of blood and its derivatives in the European Community, OJ C 268, 4.10.1993; Resolution on safe blood transfusions and use of blood derivatives, OJ C 329, 6.12.1993; Resolution on blood safety in the European Union, OJ C 249, 25.9.1995; Resolution on blood safety in the European Union,

1999, a specific treaty power was created to enable the adoption of minimum harmonisation measures setting standards for blood quality and safety. This was accompanied by a proviso that Member States were not prevented from maintaining or introducing more stringent measures in line with national prerogatives.[37] EU treaty competence in the field was limited, however, with the power to adopt measures involving the donation and medical use of blood being specifically excluded.[38] In late 2000, the Commission published a legislative proposal for the adoption of a framework Blood Directive.[39] It was eventually adopted at EU level on 27 January 2003,[40] with Member States being required to transpose it into national law by 8 February 2005.[41] Once adopted,

OJ C 141, 13.5.1996. The Council set out its position in Council Conclusions of 13 December 1993 on self-sufficiency in blood in the European Community, OJ C 15, 18.1.1994; Council Resolution of 2 June 1995 on blood safety and self-sufficiency in the Community, OJ C 164, 30.6.1995; Council Resolution of 11 December 1996 on a strategy towards blood safety and self-sufficiency in the European Community, OJ C 374, 11.12.1996; 98/463/EC Council Recommendation of 29 June 1998 on the suitability of blood and plasma donors and the screening of donated blood in the European Community, OJ C 203, 21.7.1998.

[37] Article 168(4)(a) TFEU, ex Article 152(4)(a) EC. This legal competence also provides for the adoption of risk regulation regimes involving human biological materials, such as tissues/cells and organs, as well as blood. An examination of the regimes involving tissues/cells and organs is outside the scope of this chapter, but for an overview see Farrell, 'The politics of risk'. For a detailed overview of the regime adopted in relation to organ transplantation, see A. M. Farrell, 'Addressing organ shortage in the European Union: getting the balance right', in A. M. Farrell, D. Price and M. Quigley (eds.), *Organ Shortage: Ethics Law and Pragmatism* (Cambridge University Press, 2011), pp. 227–44.

[38] Article 168(7) TFEU, ex Article 152(5) EC.

[39] Commission of the European Communities, Proposal for a Directive of the European Parliament and of the Council setting standards of quality and safety for the collection, testing, processing, storage and distribution of human blood and blood components and amending Council Directive 89/381/EEC, COM (2000) 816 final, 13.12.2000.

[40] J.-C. Faber, 'The European Blood Directive: a new era of blood regulation has begun', *Transfusion Medicine*, 14 (2004), 257–73 at 258.

[41] Directive 2002/98/EC of the European Parliament and of the Council of 27 January 2003 setting standards of quality and safety for the collection, testing, processing, storage and distribution of human blood and blood components and amending Directive 2001/83/EC, OJ L 33, 8.2.2003. A series of Directives were subsequently adopted by the Commission to flesh out technical and other aspects of the framework Blood Directive: Commission Directive 2004/33/EC of 22 March 2004 implementing Directive 2002/98/EC of the European Parliament and of the Council as regards certain technical requirements for blood and blood components, OJ L 91, 30.3.2004; Commission Directive 2005/61/EC having regard to Directive 2002/98/EC of the European Parliament and of the Council of 27 January 2003 setting standards of quality and safety for the collection, testing, processing, storage and distribution of human blood and blood components and amending Directive 2001/83/EC, OJ L 256, 1.10.2005; Commission Directive 2005/62/EC of 30 September 2005 implementing Directive 2002/98/EC of the European Parliament and of the Council as regards Community standards and specifications relating to a quality system

the Commission was responsible for overseeing the implementation of the Directive, as well as monitoring levels of compliance, by Member States.[42]

The aim of the risk regulation regime established through the Blood Directive was to set minimum standards of blood quality and safety to address the regulatory vacuum that had existed for many years in relation to important aspects of blood quality and safety at Member State level, as well as on an EU-wide basis. In addition, it was designed to enhance political credibility and restore public trust in the wake of the fallout from national HIV blood contamination episodes. Against a background of longstanding concerns about the need to limit EU encroachment into health-related matters, the aims and objectives of the regime were narrowly defined, as was made clear in the circumscribed treaty competence. This was done to ensure that Member States retained a significant degree of flexibility and discretion with regard to pursuing preferred sourcing arrangements for the supply of blood and plasma products, as well as being able to adopt more stringent national measures to enhance blood safety, if required.

In broad terms, the Blood Directive deals with the collection and testing of human blood and blood components (blood), as well as to their processing, storage, and distribution when intended for transfusion.[43] It is directed primarily towards 'blood establishments' which include any structure or body that is responsible for any aspect of blood collection and testing.[44] The Directive comprises what is known as a Recital (or preamble) where the general aims and objectives of the regulatory regime are set out in general non-legally binding terms. This is followed by the legally binding substantive section of the Directive where a framework approach has been adopted in relation to the setting of blood quality and safety standards. Key standards which must be met include the appointment of a designated 'competent authority' to ensure the implementation of the Directive at national level,[45] as well as the appointment of a 'responsible person' to ensure its implementation

---

for blood establishments, OJ L 256, 1.10.2005; Commission Directive 2009/135/EC allowing temporary derogations to certain eligibility criteria for whole blood and blood components laid down in Annex III to Directive 2004/33/EC in the context of a risk of shortage caused by the Influenza A(H1N1) pandemic, OJ L 288, 4.11.2009.

[42] Articles 26–28, 32–33, Blood Directive.
[43] Article 2(1), Blood Directive.
[44] Hospital blood banks are excluded from this definition of blood establishments under Article 3(e) and Article 6 states that only Articles 7, 10, 11(1), 14, 15, 22 and 24 of the Directive apply to hospital blood banks.
[45] Article 4(1), Blood Directive.

within designated blood establishments.[46] To meet appropriate quality control standards, blood establishments must maintain appropriate
documentation in relation to their operational, training and reporting
procedures,[47] as well as ensuring that there is a suitable level of data
protection and confidentiality.[48] This is in addition to Member States
being required to design and implement a haemovigilance system in
order to track adverse reactions and events arising out of the use of
blood.[49]

Of particular note are the requirements set out in the Directive
regarding quality and safety standards in respect of blood donation
which cover storage, transport and distribution;[50] the need for specified
testing;[51] and those related to donor information, examination and eligibility.[52] Standard setting in relation to donor eligibility, such as those
involving epidemiological profiling, screening and testing, is seen as
crucial to the management of risks to the blood system,[53] particularly
in the case of emerging infectious diseases where no testing is likely to
be available. Although over 50 per cent of the source material used in
plasma products circulating within the EU are sourced from American
paid donors,[54] there is no explicit reference to this current market reality in the Directive. Indeed, there is only one explicit reference to what
is described as third country source material and this refers to the need

---

[46] Article 9, Blood Directive.
[47] Articles 11 and 12, Blood Directive.
[48] Article 24, Blood Directive.
[49] Articles 14–15, Blood Directive. For further details in relation to technical requirements, specifications and standards to be met in relation to traceability requirements
and notification of serious adverse events and reactions, see Commission Directive
2005/61/EC, OJ L 256, 1.10.2005; in relation to a quality system for blood establishments, see Commission Directive 2005/62/EC, OJ L 256, 1.10.2005. Full citation
details for these Directives are provided at fn. 41.
[50] Article 22, Blood Directive.
[51] Article 21, Blood Directive.
[52] Articles 16–19, Blood Directive.
[53] For a more detailed overview of the technical requirements now required in relation
to donor information, donor eligibility, storage, transport and distribution, quality
and safety requirements, and autologous transfusions, see Commission Directive
2004/33/EC, OJ L 91, 30.3.2004. Full citation details for this Directive are provided
at fn. 41.
[54] Lewis, 'EC Commission and blood self-sufficiency', p. 1228. This was an estimate
provided in the early 1990s. Accurate, up-to-date data on current levels relating to the
shortfall in plasma are difficult to obtain, as is the extent of Member State dependency
on US-sourced plasma products. Indeed, the last time the Commission published
any data on the issue was in 1994; see Commission of the European Communities,
Communication on Blood Safety and Self-Sufficiency in the Community.

to ensure that such material can be traced through Member State donor identification systems.[55]

Given the longstanding stakeholder conflict over what should be recognised as the preferred method for blood donation, it is also important to note how this was dealt with in the Blood Directive. References to the commitment to VNRBD and its putative link with enhanced blood safety are couched in the form of aspirational, non-legally binding, statements in the Recital to the Directive. In this regard, VNRBD is referred to as simply a factor which has the potential to contribute to high safety standards, therefore facilitating a high level of human health protection.[56] This is to be contrasted with the approach taken to VNRBD in the legally binding part of the Directive, where Member States are simply encouraged rather than required to take all necessary measures to ensure that blood is provided through this method of donation.[57] In the pursuit of the goal of a national blood supply sourced solely through VNRBD, the Directive also permits Member States to restrict or otherwise prohibit the importation of blood, provided it is in line with treaty obligations.[58] Nowhere in the Directive is VNRBD defined, although the definition provided by the Council of Europe may be taken into account.[59] The absence of any binding definition of VNRBD in the Directive no doubt provides for flexibility in interpretation, particularly with regard to what constitutes either financial compensation for, or reimbursement of expenses associated with, blood donation.[60]

Assessing effectiveness

It is clear that a comprehensive vein-to-vein approach to risk regulation in relation to blood was not on the political agenda at EU level at the

---

[55] Article 14(1), Blood Directive. In Commission Directives 2005/61/EC and 2006/62/EC, which were adopted to set out more detailed technical requirements in relation to the standards in the Blood Directive, Member States are required to ensure that blood establishments in third countries have both a quality system and a notification system in place for adverse events which are equivalent to what would be found in Member States or otherwise meet the requirements for such systems as set out in these Directives. Full citations for such Directives can be found at fn. 41.

[56] Paragraph 23, Recital, Blood Directive.

[57] Article 20(1), Blood Directive.

[58] Article 4(2), Blood Directive.

[59] Paragraph 23, Recital, Blood Directive.

[60] At a meeting of Member State competent authorities held to examine blood quality and safety issues in 2011, it was noted that the Blood Directive reflected the differing points of view between Member States regarding preferred methods for blood donation; see European Commission, Meeting of the Competent Authorities on Blood and Blood Components, Summary Report, 16–17 May 2011, SANCO D4/SV/hp ARES(2011), Brussels.

time when treaty powers were adopted in the field. Instead, the legacy of HIV blood contamination episodes at Member State level ensured that risk management was focused primarily on issues relating to blood sourcing and supply, rather than on risks faced by those who received blood in clinical settings. What was regrettable about such a focus was that it ignored a growing body of haemovigilance and other data that identified the clinical setting in which blood transfusion took place as posing as great, if not a greater, risk to patient-recipients.[61] In the circumstances, a golden opportunity was missed to devise appropriate standards and/or guidance for good clinical practice in the field,[62] in addition to promoting a more active partnership between blood services, clinicians and patient-recipients with regard to determining risk acceptability involving blood transfusion.[63]

In addition, the protracted political conflict that erupted during the course of inter-institutional negotiations over the adoption of the Blood Directive led to a series of compromises that further eroded any claim to comprehensive coverage in the regulatory regime.[64] One important omission from the Directive includes the failure to require that hospital blood services be subject to accreditation and licensing procedures. For Member States which operate such services, the imposition of such procedures was considered to be too onerous, given that such services tend to provide a limited range of blood-banking type assistance. While such exclusion may be understandable from the point of view of administrative capacity, it remains troubling from the point of view of blood safety. Despite their limited remit, such services nevertheless do engage in the core activity of supplying blood components for transfusion to patients. Therefore, the circumstances and environment in which such components are supplied should be subject to regulatory oversight with respect to licensing and inspection measures in order to ensure that appropriate quality and safety standards are met.[65]

---

[61] M. F. Murphy, S. J. Stanworth and M. Yazer, 'Transfusion practice and safety: current status and possibilities for improvement', *Vox Sanguinis*, 100 (2011), 46–59 at 46–52.

[62] Faber, 'The European Blood Directive', pp. 257, 271.

[63] Davis *et al.*, 'Blood transfusion safety: the potential role of the patient'. Developing EU guidance/standards with regard to blood risk management in clinical settings would have raised the profile of the issue and would have (hopefully) led to a greater focus on the need to obtain consent from patients concerning the independent risks associated with blood transfusion as part of medical treatment received. For an examination of this issue, see A. M. Farrell and M. Brazier, 'Consent to blood transfusion', *British Medical Journal*, 341 (2010), c4336.

[64] Faber, 'The European Blood Directive', p. 270.

[65] Robinson, 'The European Union Blood Safety Directive', p. 123.

However, the most important omission from the Directive relates to the failure to acknowledge the current market reality for the sourcing and supply of blood and plasma products within the EU. This omission has its origins in the political conflict that erupted between stakeholders, institutions and Member States about what should be recognised as the preferred method for blood donation in the EU. In the end, the need to achieve a political compromise that would allow for the adoption of the Directive resulted in a significant degree of ambiguity over the extent of Member States' legal commitment to realising VNRBD at national level. The nature of the compromise reached can be gleaned from the carefully crafted wording used in the Directive. As mentioned previously, Member States are simply encouraged rather than required to adopt measures to facilitate VNRBD.[66] It is made clear through the use of aspirational and open-ended terminology that the embedding of VNRBD as the preferred method for sourcing the EU blood supply had little political appeal for Member States in terms of its inclusion in a legally binding regulatory regime to be established under the terms of the Blood Directive.

One of the main underlying reasons for this position was the diversity of sourcing arrangements in place at national level. For example, Germany and Austria permit plasma collections from paid donors, as well as for-profit programmes for manufacturing plasma products. In contrast, the Netherlands and Finland only permit not-for-profit, state-funded programmes for manufacturing such products, sourced from VNRBD.[67] In Member States such as the UK, the risk posed by the transmission of vCJD in the blood supply in the late 1990s forced a rethink regarding the policy commitment to VNRBD. Faced with large sections of the British donor population being at risk of transmitting or contracting the disease, the government took the decision to import US-sourced plasma from paid donors for use in the manufacture of plasma products.[68] Making VNRBD a legally binding commitment in the Blood Directive would have been problematic for a number of Member States given their reliance on plasma products sourced from US paid donors manufactured and supplied by the for-profit sector of

[66] Article 20(1), Blood Directive.
[67] Hagen, *Blood: Gift or Merchandise?*, pp. 63–84.
[68] S. Boseley, 'NHS imports all plasma to avoid risk of CJD', *The Guardian* (14/5/98). Due to the risk of vCJD, only US-sourced plasma from paid donors has been used in the manufacture of blood products by BPL (Bio Products Laboratory, formerly known as the Blood Products Laboratory) since 1998. In 2002, the Department of Health purchased Life Resources Inc., the largest independent plasma supplier based in the USA, in order to ensure the long-term supply of plasma for the UK. A US holding company, DCI Biologicals, was established to manage the business. Both BPL and DCI Biologicals are now part of Plasma Resources UK Ltd (http://bpl.co.uk).

the industry. In practical terms, it would have led to a substantial short-fall in availability and choice of plasma products for citizens in such Member States.[69]

Notwithstanding the fact that VNRBD was shown to be an inadequate and ineffective frame of reference on its own for dealing with the risk posed by HIV to the blood system,[70] the ethico-social commitment to this method of donation continues to attract significant political, stakeholder and citizen support within the EU.[71] In the circumstances, this forced EU decision-makers to find a way forward which took account of support for such commitment, whilst at the same time achieving an acceptable political compromise that would allow for the adoption of the Directive. The result was a privileging of this commitment in the Blood Directive to the exclusion of transparency regarding the operation of the EU blood market. As was made clear in the wake of the fallout from national HIV blood contamination episodes, being transparent about this market should be seen as a necessary precondition to facilitating effective risk regulation in the field.

Since the Blood Directive was adopted at EU level, the Commission has been responsible for overseeing its implementation at Member State level. Much of its work in this regard has been focused on information gathering relating to the implementation phase.[72] What this has revealed is that while the majority of Member States have been able to transpose the Blood Directive in full into national law within the specified time limit,[73] others have experienced particular difficulties in meeting their obligations in this regard. This has been primarily attributable to the underdeveloped state of their national services, as well as

---

[69] Valverde, 'The political dimension of blood and plasma derivatives', p. 26.
[70] See Chapter 3. Other social science commentators who support such a view include Waldby and Mitchell, *Tissue Economies*, p. 49.
[71] Farrell, 'The politics of risk', pp. 49–50. Strong public support for the gift relationship in blood donation was evidenced in the following EU-wide surveys: INRA Europe, *Europeans and Blood*; European Opinion Research Group (EEIG), *Le don de sang*. Transfusionists who run Member State blood services, as well as those involved in the not-for-profit plasma products industry, are also strong supporters of VNRBD; see Chapter 3 for further details.
[72] For an overview of information gathering conducted by the Commission in the field, see http://ec.europa.eu/health/blood_tissues_organs/blood/index_en.htm.
[73] Commission of the European Communities, Report from the Commission to the Council, the European Parliament, the European Economic and Social Committee and the Committee of the Regions: First Report on the Application of the Blood Directive COM (2006) 313 final, 19.6.2006, Brussels; Commission of the European Communities, Meeting of the competent authorities on blood and blood components: summary report – 13 September 2006 (Art. 25 Dir.2002/98/EC): Brussels SANCO C/6 TB/ges D (2006) 360346.

their quality and safety systems.[74] In its most recent published report on the implementation of the Blood Directive, the Commission noted that its transposition at Member State level was satisfactory overall. However, further improvement was required in particular areas, such as accreditation, licensing and inspection of blood establishments, as well as in relation to the provision of information to the Commission regarding adverse events and reactions associated with the use of blood at Member State level.[75]

Interpreting how the standards set out in the Blood Directive should be implemented in practice has also proved to be an ongoing problem.[76] This has been acknowledged as a matter of concern by stakeholders,[77] as well as by national competent authorities,[78] particularly in relation to issues involving haemovigilance and inspections. Other areas of concern include the time it takes for the Commission to organise the updating and/or amending of standards set out in the Directive for the purposes of clarification or to address emerging risks to the blood system. Any delay at EU level has a knock-on effect at Member State level, as adopting new regulations can take an extended period of time. Some stakeholders have also argued that there has been a tendency towards 'overprescription' on the part of the Commission in relation to technical requirements, which has resulted in a lack of flexibility at Member State level with regard to meeting their regulatory obligations in the field. This has been compounded by the fact that much of the interpretation of such requirements on a day-to-day basis has been undertaken by transfusionists who previously worked within a governance environment largely shaped by non-legally binding standards and guidance developed under the auspices of the Council of Europe.[79]

The Commission is responsible for providing regular reports to key institutional bodies at EU level, such as the Parliament, the Economic

[74] Faber, 'The European Blood Directive', p. 269; M. H. Goncalves, M. C. Muon and J. d'Almeida Goncalves, 'Transposition of the blood directive – perspective of Portugal', *Transfusion Clinique et Biologique*, 12 (2005), 18–20 at 20.

[75] European Commission, Communication from the Commission to the Council, the European Parliament, the Economic and Social Committee and the Committee of the Regions on the application of Directive 2002/98/EC setting standards of quality and safety for the collection, testing, processing, storage and distribution of human blood and blood components and amending Directive 2001/83/EC, COM (2010) 3 final, 19.1.2010, Brussels, p. 9.

[76] European Commission, Meeting of the Competent Authorities on Blood and Blood Components.

[77] Faber, 'The European Blood Directive', pp. 262–3; Robinson, 'The European Union Blood Safety Directive', pp. 123–4.

[78] Commission of the European Communities, Meeting of the competent authorities on blood and blood components, pp. 2–5.

[79] Robinson, 'The European Union Blood Safety Directive', pp. 125–9.

and Social Committee and the Committee of the Regions, regarding Member States' experiences in implementing the Directive.[80] The Commission is also required to inform the Parliament and the Council of measures taken by Member States regarding the promotion of VNRBD, as well as any action it proposes to be taken in this regard.[81] In relation to this second reporting requirement, the Commission has now submitted two reports to date examining what measures Member States have taken to encourage VNRBD since the Blood Directive came into force. Although the majority of Member States have adopted measures in this regard, some continue to support mixed donation systems for sourcing blood and plasma products. There are also some important differences with regard to both the interpretation and application of VNRBD. In some Member States, donors are given time off work as a result of making blood donations but in others they are not. Expenses paid for blood donation differ in amount and type. Several Member States acknowledge the act of blood donation in different ways. Promotion of VNRBD differs between national settings and ranges from publication of guidance and practical materials on the one hand, to advertising to specific target groups on the other hand.[82]

The problems encountered with such diversity in approach to VNRBD within the EU were highlighted in the Court of Justice judgment in *Humanplasma GmbH* v. *Republik Österreich*.[83] In this case, the court was required to consider whether Austrian legislation, which banned the importation of blood products for direct transfusion where they had been sourced as a result of 'any payment whatsoever having been made', contravened EU law on the free movement of goods. Although the Austrian government accepted that the legislation in question contravened EU law, it nevertheless argued that it was justified on the grounds of the protection of public health, as well as being in accordance with the discretion provided to Member States to adopt measures to encourage VNRBD under the terms of the Blood Directive. The court did not accept such arguments. Given the requirements for post donation testing under the terms of the Directive, it found that paying for some of the donors' costs did not necessarily detract from the quality and safety

---

[80] Articles 26(1) and (3), Blood Directive.
[81] Article 20(2), Blood Directive.
[82] Commission of the European Communities, Report on the promotion by Member States of voluntary unpaid blood donations; European Commission, Report from the Commission to the European Parliament, the Council, the European Economic and Social Committee and the Committee of the Regions. 2nd Report on Voluntary and Unpaid Donation of Blood and Blood Components. COM (2011) 138 final.
[83] Case C-421/09, *Humanplasma GmbH* v. *Republik Österreich*, (2011) OJC 55/13, 9 December 2010.

of the donation. In the circumstances, reimbursement of expenses, such as small tokens, refreshments, as well as reimbursements of travel costs connected with the donation, were compatible with VNRBD. The court concluded that the legislation in question was neither necessary nor proportionate with respect to achieving the protection of human health.

While it may be argued that this judgment turns on its own facts, it nevertheless raises a number of important issues that need to be addressed at EU level. These include whether there should be greater consistency in the approach taken by Member States regarding the interpretation of VNRBD in the EU context, as well as in relation to (any) reimbursement of expenses. More broadly speaking, the Court of Justice clearly questioned the evidentiary basis regarding the link between VNRBD and enhanced blood quality and safety.[84] In the circumstances, more detailed consideration by the Commission of the issues raised by the Court of Justice judgment would be welcomed, particularly with regard to how best to deal with the current diversity in approach to VNRBD between Member States and what its potential impact might be, if any, on blood safety.

Drawing on the criteria identified at the start of the chapter, a complicated picture is presented with regard to assessing the effectiveness of the EU-wide risk regulation regime for blood. In a way, this is to be expected given the complex political dynamics operating in a multi-level governance environment such as the EU. Further complexity is added by virtue of the fact that blood safety has become a politically sensitive area of EU governance in the wake of HIV blood contamination episodes at Member State level. This political context has clearly resulted in a narrow, rather than an expansive, conception of risk which has impacted upon the design of regulation in the field. While this has meant that the narrowly drawn aims and objectives of the regulatory regime have largely been met, it has been done at the expense of pursuing a comprehensive vein-to-vein approach to facilitating blood safety. The focus on donor and supply issues necessarily lessens its effectiveness as a tool for managing risks to the blood system, particularly in clinical settings. An approach to regulatory design based on the use of minimum harmonisation measures has also resulted in a lack of uniformity in the approach by Member States in key areas likely to be vital to facilitating blood safety, such as those involving sourcing issues.

---

[84] For an industry perspective on the potential implications resulting from the Court of Justice's findings on this point, see J. Delacourt, 'European Court of Justice weighs in on donor compensation debate', *The Source* (Summer 2011), 16–17 at 17.

While such a result may be acceptable in political and practical terms, its implications for managing risk involving the blood system on an EU-wide basis is less clear. This is particularly so in circumstances where there is a lack of regulatory transparency about the current reality of the EU blood market and how this impacts upon the management of risks to blood safety.

Overall, it appears that the record of implementation of the terms of the Directive has been good, given the significant diversity in organisational, regulatory and systems capacity between Member States. Institutional monitoring and evaluation by the Commission has also contributed to the identification of problem areas with regard to interpreting and applying standards, although there has been stakeholder criticism over the extent to which the Commission has addressed such problems in a timely and effective manner. The fact that both Member States and the Commission are required to provide information about the workings of the regulatory regime to key institutional bodies such as the Parliament is particularly useful with regard to facilitating transparency and accountability. While not failsafe, it nevertheless provides a mechanism by which particular problems involved in risk regulation in the field can be identified and examined, as well as contributing to the success of the regulatory regime as a technique of legitimation in both political and public spheres.

Regulating plasma products

For many years, supranational regulatory governance in relation to plasma products was managed under the auspices of the Council of Europe and the WHO.[85] It was driven primarily by the need to promote technical harmonisation and, for the most part, was not legally binding. The absence of any legally binding supranational regulatory regime to facilitate blood quality and safety in the European context proved to be particularly problematic during the time when HIV posed a risk to the blood supply in the 1980s. However, the European regulatory landscape with regard to plasma products began to change from the late 1980s onwards. As part of the drive towards the creation of the single market, the EU adopted specific regulation relating to plasma products in 1989.[86] This legislation was subsequently incorporated into the EU regulatory

[85] See Chapter 2 for further details about the role of the Council of Europe and the WHO in this area.
[86] Council Directive 89/381/EEC of 14 June 1989 extending the scope of Directives 65/65/EEC and 75/319/EEC on the approximation of provisions laid down by law,

regime for pharmaceuticals in 2001 (see Directive (2001/83/EC)).[87] In addition, what is now known as the European Medicines Agency (EMA) was created in the mid 1990s to oversee the day-to-day regulation of pharmaceuticals within the EU, including plasma products.

Although it is outside the scope of this chapter to examine in detail the provisions of Directive 2001/83/EC as it applies to plasma products, it is important to highlight a number of key issues which are relevant for the purposes of the key arguments made in this chapter. First, the quality and safety standards that need to be met with regard to the source material used in plasma products must comply with the Blood Directive.[88] In order to understand the totality of the EU's regulatory regime in relation to blood quality and safety, therefore, the Blood Directive needs to be read in conjunction with Directive 2001/83/EC, as well as other supporting technical legislation and guidelines.[89] Second, Member States are encouraged to promote the sourcing and manufacture of plasma products through VNRBD.[90] As is the case with the Blood Directive, the use of such aspirational language offers Member States a significant degree of flexibility with regard to pursuing their preferred arrangements for the sourcing and supply of plasma products, notwithstanding any failure to fully source such products through VNRBD. In addition, no overt references are made to the sourcing of plasma products through paid donors in Directive 2001/83/EC. Instead, the focus is on ensuring that technical and scientific requirements, as well as quality and safety standards, are met in relation to the source material used in plasma products.

Third, detailed scientific and technical requirements which must be met when submitting an application dossier to the EMA to obtain an

regulation or administrative action relating to medicinal products and laying down special provisions for proprietary medicinal products derived from human blood or human plasma (repealed).

[87] Directive 2001/83/EC of the European Parliament and of the Council of 6 November 2001 on the Community code relating to medicinal products for human use, OJ L 311, 28.11.2001.

[88] Article 31, Blood Directive; Article 109, Title X, Directive 2001/83/EC.

[89] Please note that the plasma products industry takes account of Directive 2001/83/EC; other legislation dealing with good manufacturing practice (GMP), such as Commission Directive 2003/94/EC of 8 October 2003 laying down the principles and guidelines of good manufacturing practice in respect of medicinal products for human use and investigational products for human use, OJ L 262, 14.10.2003; guidelines published by the Biologics Working Party (BWP) of the Committee for Proprietary Medicinal Products (CPMP) based within the EMA; and relevant monographs of the European Pharmacopoeia; see G. Silvester, 'Regulatory overview – stable products background, current state of the art and future challenges', *Pharmaceuticals Policy and Law*, 7 (2006), 151–69 at 158.

[90] Article 110, Title X, Directive 2001/83/EC.

authorisation to market plasma products within the EU are set out in Annex I to Directive 2001/83/EC. By virtue of an amendment made to the Directive in 2003,[91] plasma product manufacturers now have the option of creating a Plasma Master File (PMF) in relation to the sourcing of their plasma products.[92] The PMF aims to provide for the harmonised control of relevant information regarding the source material used in the manufacture of plasma products within the EU. The PMF must contain a description of the overall safety strategy employed by the applicant. Such description should include reference to epidemiological data on blood transmissible diseases known in the donor population, the system of donor selection, methods of donor screening, whether donors are paid or unpaid, testing on plasma pools, products put on hold in inventory and what procedures are in place to track any potentially contaminated products.[93] Following a satisfactory evaluation, the EMA can issue a PMF certificate of compliance with EU legislation, which is valid throughout the EU. Summaries setting out details of the quality and safety of the source material used in plasma products that have been evaluated and authorised under the centralised procedure are published by the EMA in its European Public Assessment Reports (EPARs).[94]

Assessing effectiveness

It is difficult to undertake a detailed assessment of the effectiveness of EU risk regulation of plasma products by reference to the criteria identified at the start of the chapter. As mentioned previously, the EMA is responsible for regulatory oversight of quality and safety aspects associated with the licensing and marketing of plasma products, as part of a broader remit regarding EU regulation of pharmaceuticals. In the

---

[91] See Commission Directive 2003/63/EC of 25 June 2003 amending Directive 2001/83/EC of the European Parliament and of the Council on the Community code relating to medicinal products for human use, OJ L 159, 27.6.2003.

[92] The plasma products industry had been advocating for the creation of the PMF system since the 1990s; see I. von Hoegen, 'Epidemiology regulatory landscape', *The Source* (Fall 2011), 22–3 at 22; see also Chapter 5 for a discussion of the relationship between the PMF system and innovation in the case of plasma products manufacture.

[93] European Agency for the Evaluation of Medicinal Products, Committee for Proprietary Medicinal Products (CPMP), Guideline on the Scientific Data Requirements for a Plasma Master File (PMF), EMEA/CPMP/BWP/3704/03, 26 February 2004; see also European Medicines Agency, Committee for Medicinal Products for Human Use (CHMP), Guideline on Epidemiological Data on Blood Transmissible Infections, EMA/CHMP/BWP/548524/2008, 22 April 2010.

[94] For further details, see European Medicines Agency, Plasma Master File (PMF) (www.ema.europa.eu).

context of such oversight, emphasis is placed on devising and ensuring compliance with appropriate technical specifications and updates in order to meet licensing requirements with respect to marketing such products on an EU-wide basis. In the case of plasma products, harmonisation across Member States, as well as between the EU and third countries such as the USA, is seen as a desirable goal in order to facilitate both innovation and the (cost-) effective functioning of the EU market for such products.[95] The assessment and management of risks to plasma products takes place in an institutional decision-making environment which is largely insulated from the vagaries of political contestation and ongoing political monitoring which the regulation for blood is subject to under the terms of the Blood Directive. Such monitoring has facilitated a degree of transparency and provision of information in relation to blood quality and safety issues, which is not currently made available by the EMA in relation to plasma products.

Notwithstanding such limitations, a number of relevant points can be made with respect to assessing the effectiveness of EU risk regulation involving plasma products. It is clear that the fallout from HIV blood contamination episodes at Member State level has impacted upon the management of risk in relation to the sourcing and supply of plasma products in the EU context. What such episodes highlighted was the dysfunctional and fragmented nature of regulatory governance at Member State level regarding the quality and safety of the source material used in such products, a significant proportion of which was drawn from US paid donors. In the absence of appropriate regulatory oversight, too much reliance had been placed on US-based plasma products manufacturers vouchsafing for the safety of such source material, with disastrous results for national haemophilia populations who used such products. All this occurred against the backdrop of a failure on the part of those with responsibility for blood safety in the European context to acknowledge the extent of, as well as the potential adverse safety implications resulting from, the continued importation of such products to meet growing consumer demand.

In the wake of the fallout from such episodes, there has clearly been a concerted effort made at EU level to address quality and safety issues in relation to the source material used in plasma products. This has been done through applying the quality and safety standards set out in the Blood Directive to such source material, which in turn fed into the creation of the PMF. Although such reforms should be acknowledged as a welcome harmonisation tool for setting quality and safety standards

[95] Silvester, 'Regulatory overview', p. 167.

in relation to the use of the source material in plasma products,[96] it is important to keep in mind that the PMF remains optional rather than mandatory. This potentially lessens its effectiveness as a strategy for enhancing blood safety, particularly in relation to US-sourced plasma products which comprise well over half of the EU market for such products.

Although the EMA publishes summary details concerning plasma quality and safety for medicinal products licensed under its centralised procedure,[97] there appears to be little information published on an ongoing basis about the extent to which those subject to the regulatory regime are compliant with the Blood Directive with respect to the use of the source material in plasma products or with the PMF system more generally. Information has been published by the plasma products industry where claims have been made about the absence of transmission of TTIs (such as HIV, HBV and HCV) in plasma products due to improved screening and manufacturing procedures.[98] However, it would be helpful in terms of transparency if such claims were independently evaluated by the EMA, with the results of such evaluation being made publicly available in an easily accessible manner. While it is to be hoped that the EMA's recent initiative with regard to enhancing oversight of quality and safety issues involving plasma products will lead to greater public transparency,[99] its record to date in this regard has not been good. It is a state of affairs that is aggravated by the fact that risk regulation involving plasma products is not subject to the type of political monitoring and reporting requirements which apply in the case of blood (as set out in the Blood Directive).

The disconnection between risk regulation regimes for blood and plasma products, as well as the persistence of bifurcated institutional and monitoring arrangements for managing such regimes, appears to have been justified in the past on the grounds that plasma products manufacture is a niche operation within the larger pharmaceutical industry, the governance of which has traditionally been situated within EU institutional structures which are focused on the promotion of

---

[96] von Hoegen and Gustafson, 'The importance of greater regulatory harmonization', p. 173.

[97] Such summaries are published through the EPAR mechanism, although the EMA's online search facility for EPARs involving plasma products is not easy to navigate for non-experts; see www.ema.europa.eu.

[98] Tabor, 'The epidemiology of virus transmission by plasma derivatives'; Burnouf, 'Modern plasma fractionation', p. 108.

[99] European Medicines Agency, Committee for Medicinal Products for Human Use (CHMP), Guideline on Plasma-Derived Medicinal Products.

enterprise and innovation.[100] With policy responsibility for both blood and plasma products (as part of pharmaceuticals) now under the control of the Directorate General for Health and Consumers (DG SANCO) within the Commission,[101] it is to be hoped that the initiative is taken to pursue a more holistic, transparent and accountable approach to regulatory governance in the field.

Conclusion

This chapter examined the design and effectiveness of risk regulation in the post-HIV blood contamination era, drawing on a case study of EU risk regulation involving blood and plasma products. In the wake of the political fallout from HIV blood contamination episodes in various Member States, the establishment of an EU-wide legally binding risk regulation regime setting minimum standards for blood quality and safety through the Blood Directive was to be welcomed, given previously inadequate or non-existent national regulation in the field. The extent to which EU risk regulation of blood and plasma products could be said to be effective was analysed by reference to identified criteria including whether it met its stated aims and objectives; its comprehensiveness in dealing with risk-based issues; the degree of support for, or conversely resistance to, the regime by those entities subject to its remit; and the availability of accountability mechanisms for its monitoring. Such analysis presented a complicated picture with respect to assessing the effectiveness of the totality of risk regulation in the field, particularly given the fact that two separate regimes operate in relation to blood and plasma products and there is some degree of overlap between the two.

Although it has been argued in this book that viewing blood as either a gift or a commodity is an inappropriate policy frame for managing the complexity that arises in risk governance involving the blood system, the political conflict that erupted between stakeholders, institutions and other actors during the course of inter-institutional negotiations over the adoption of the Blood Directive showed that it continued to have relevance as a framing device in policy and regulatory processes at EU level. In the search for a political compromise which would facilitate the adoption of the Directive, the ethico-social commitment to the gift relationship was privileged to the detriment of being transparent about the current market reality in which well over half of the

---

[100] Farrell, 'The politics of risk', p. 62.
[101] See http://ec.europa.eu/health/human-use/index_en.htm.

plasma products in circulation in the EU are sourced from paid donors in third countries, such as the USA. If risk regulation in the field is to be effective, then such market reality needs to be acknowledged in circumstances where ensuring optimum patient-recipient safety should operate as the main policy framing device informing regulatory design and implementation.

It was also found that an expansive, rather than a narrow, interpretation of what constituted risk was important for facilitating comprehensiveness in regulatory design. The extent to which an expansive interpretation was possible, however, was determined by the political and institutional dynamics affecting risk governance in the field more generally. In the case of the risk regulation regime involving blood, key dynamics included longstanding Member State concerns over perceived EU encroachment into health-related matters. This resulted in a very limited transfer of competence from Member States to EU level in order to facilitate the adoption of risk regulation in the field. What transfer of competence took place in this case was done for the specific purpose of restoring credibility and enhancing public trust in the wake of the fallout from national HIV blood contamination episodes. The legacy of such episodes resulted in a focus on donation and supply issues in the context of dealing with TTIs. This operated to the detriment of a more rounded and comprehensive vein-to-vein approach to risk management which would have included taking account of the particular risks faced by patient-recipients in the administration of blood in clinical settings.

In the case of the regulatory regime for plasma products, path dependencies created by its embedding within the broader regime for pharmaceuticals at EU level operated as a key dynamic structuring the approach taken to managing risk. In line with the longstanding approach taken to the regulation of pharmaceuticals at supranational level, the approach taken by the EMA to the assessment and management of risk takes place in a largely closed, expert-driven decision-making environment that has been dominated by an institutional mindset that has traditionally focused on promoting technical harmonisation, facilitating innovation and enhancing market competitiveness. Such institutional path dependencies have contributed to a lack of transparency about how the regulatory regime for plasma products operates, including levels of compliance or conversely resistance, with regard to meeting quality and safety standards in relation to such products. In turn, this has made it difficult to undertake any meaningful assessment of the effectiveness of the regime with regard to the management of risk involved in the sourcing and supply of plasma products.

This is to be contrasted with the risk regulation regime established under the Blood Directive which requires regular reporting on how the regime is operating in practice, as well as on specific issues such as the promotion of VNRBD at member state level. It facilitates ongoing monitoring of the regime's strengths and/or weaknesses as a tool for managing (emerging) risks to blood quality and safety by a range of EU institutions, including the Parliament. The fact that such monitoring is undertaken by a democratically accountable institution, such as the Parliament, is also particularly important if the regulatory regime is to operate successfully as a technique of legitimation in the post-HIV blood contamination era. Given the fact that two regimes for blood and plasma products are now under the overarching institutional control of DG SANCO, the effectiveness of risk regulation in the field would be enhanced if a more joined-up approach was taken to incorporating the social and economic aspects involved in blood sourcing and supply in the EU context. This would be in addition to ensuring that there was regular monitoring of risk governance involving blood *and* plasma products by key institutional bodies, such as the Parliament. Only time will tell if this turns out to be the case.

9   Conclusion

The overarching aim of this book was to examine the inter-relationship between politics, ethics and law in risk governance involving human biological materials, drawing on a case study involving the sourcing and supply of blood. The parameters of the case study were limited to an examination of governance processes involved in managing risks posed by transfusion-transmitted infections (TTIs) in blood and plasma products. HIV blood contamination episodes in countries such as the USA, England and France were used by way of example to highlight particular difficulties faced by those with responsibility for the blood system in dealing with the emergence of a serious risk to public health, as well as the adverse consequences resulting from the loss of political credibility and public trust that occurred in the wake of the perceived failure to manage such risk. There were a number of reasons for choosing this particular case study. First, blood has socio-cultural, scientific and commercial value in the wake of scientific and technological developments that have occurred over the last fifty years and it is this multi-valuing process that presents challenges in terms of facilitating effective risk governance. Findings from this case study are therefore also likely to have broader implications for the management of risk involving other multi-valued human biological materials, particularly given their increasingly diverse use in a range of (new) health technologies.

The politicisation of risk

For the purposes of the book, risk was conceptualised as a socio-cultural construct that is influenced by public perception, necessitating a political response where the protection of public health is at stake. One of the main features of the politicisation of risk is heightened sensitivity on the part of governing entities to the potential for adverse public reaction resulting from any perceived failure to manage risks to public health. This heightened sensitivity leads to responses to emerging risks that are focused primarily on enhancing political credibility and justifying the legitimacy of their preferred courses of action. In certain circumstances, this may lead to the subordination of traditional scientific risk assessment and cost–benefit analysis to political concerns, as well as increased recourse to precautionary and regulatory strategies to legitimate policy decisions, manage ethical concerns and enhance public trust.

Drawing on this perspective, the focus was on examining the construction of, as well as the consequences resulting from, the politicisation of risk involving multi-valued human biological materials, such as blood. National HIV blood contamination episodes, as well as their aftermath, provided a useful pivot point around which an examination of this phenomenon was undertaken. Key aspects involved in the construction phase that were examined in Chapters 2 to 5 included dysfunctional regulatory governance which promoted an exclusionary approach between the social and the economic in the context of blood sourcing and supply within and across national boundaries; and the ethico-social commitment to the gift relationship in blood donation which operated as a predominant factor underpinning risk governance involving the blood system. Key aspects involved in the consequences phase that were examined in Chapters 6 to 8 included the political dynamics that contributed to heightened sensitivity on the part of governing entities in responding to risks to the blood system; and the role of legitimating techniques, such as the precautionary principle and risk regulation, in redressing the loss of political credibility and public trust that occurred in the wake of national HIV blood contamination episodes. Findings resulting from this examination of key aspects are now explored in detail below.

Managing ethical concerns

Ethical concerns have loomed large in policy-making processes involving the use of multi-valued human biological materials and the ability to manage such concerns have become an important legitimising aspect of risk governance in the field. The focus of examination in this book was on how such concerns operated as important policy frames informing the approach taken to risk governance involving the blood system. With this focus in mind, two key arguments put forward by Titmuss regarding the ethical commitment to the gift relationship in blood donation were challenged. First, Titmuss linked the gift relationship in blood donation to the promotion of blood safety, arguing that the voluntary, altruistic and non-remunerated nature of the act made it much more likely that the donor would not transmit disease to the anonymous patient-recipient. This particular argument was explored in detail in Chapter 3 and was followed up by an examination of its adoption as a core professional belief by transfusionists involved in national blood services in Chapter 4. How this impacted on the assessment and management of the risk posed by HIV to selected national blood systems, as well as in relation to patient-recipient groups, such as people with haemophilia (PWH), was examined in Chapters 4 and 6, respectively. This examination revealed that reliance on the gift relationship had become an inadequate frame of reference on its own for assessing and managing risks to blood safety. Instead, it was found that it was one among a range of ethical, institutional, economic, techno-scientific and political factors that needed to be taken into account in risk governance involving the blood system.

Titmuss also argued that it was important for the dynamics of the marketplace to be excluded in favour of the gift relationship in blood donation as it promoted important social values and fostered good community relations. While Titmuss's argument in this regard was examined in detail in Chapter 3, its impact in national and supranational blood policy and regulation was explored in Chapters 2, 4 and 5. The examination of historical and current developments impacting on the governance of the blood system which was provided in Chapter 2 highlighted how past and current governance arrangements dealing with blood sourcing and supply arrangements at both national and supranational levels had served to perpetuate this exclusionary approach between the social and the economic. This had led to the development of a bifurcated approach (which was particularly pronounced at supranational level) to the governance of blood and its components which are collected and supplied by national blood services on the one hand; and the manufacture and supply of plasma products by industry on the other hand. The examination of the core professional beliefs of transfusion experts in Chapter 4 also revealed the importance the group attached to promoting this exclusionary approach between the social and the economic in the context of justifying their commitment to VNRBD and national self-sufficiency in blood and plasma products sourced through this method of donation.

Market dynamics affecting risk governance involving the blood system were the focus of examination in Chapter 5, with a particular emphasis placed on the role and impact of scientific and technological innovation on the development of the for-profit plasma products industry at both national and supranational levels. Such examination revealed that innovation should not be seen on its own as the great panacea for managing risk involving the blood system. Instead, the pursuit of innovation needed to be mediated by stringent regulatory governance at both national and supranational levels. It also revealed that the perpetuation of the exclusionary approach between the social and the economic, which structured governance processes involving the blood system, had adversely impacted upon the assessment and management of the risk posed by HIV transmission in plasma products.

A key finding across Chapters 2 to 5 was that this exclusionary approach was no longer appropriate for managing risks to blood safety, particularly given the increasing diversity of blood sourcing, supply and consumption arrangements both within and across national boundaries. Governing entities need to recognise the fact that the multi-valuing of human biological materials, such as blood, contributes to complexity in risk governance which cannot be successfully managed through a dichotomous policy framing of blood as either a gift or a commodity. Instead, what is needed is a more holistic and flexible approach to risk governance, where every link in the donor–recipient chain is focused on achieving the primary objective of patient-recipient safety. Such an approach is to be preferred to any rigidity in approach brought about by a priori ethical, professional or commercial commitments with respect to sourcing and supply issues.

The role of law

There was also a particular focus in the book on the role and impact of law in risk governance involving the blood system. The term 'law' was defined broadly to include soft and hard law, covering guidelines, recommendations, principles, case law and regulation, as well as legal institutions, such as tribunals and courts. The involvement of law in the construction of the politicisation of risk was highlighted in Chapters 5 and 6. Chapter 5 focused primarily on an examination of the interrelationship between risk and innovation in the context of the production and supply of plasma products, such as factor concentrates used by PWH in the treatment of their condition. This examination revealed the importance of both national and supranational regulatory regimes in mediating this relationship. The initial development of the for-profit plasma products industry was marked by dysfunctional regulation in relation to quality and safety aspects of collection, production and supply arrangements, where such regulation existed at all. Process and product innovation by the industry in the wake of HIV blood contamination episodes has significantly reduced the rate of TTIs in plasma products. However, the loss of public trust that occurred in the wake of such episodes now requires that innovation in this context, as well as markets in such products, are subject to stringent regulatory governance which takes account of the relationship between the social and the economic in order to enhance blood safety. At a minimum, this requires regulatory cooperation and harmonisation at both national and supranational levels, involving the use of standard setting for quality and safety, as well as the establishment of legally binding regulatory regimes, where possible.

The role of law in the political mobilisation of PWH groups in England, France and the USA was the subject of examination in Chapter 6. In political campaigns conducted by PWH groups in such countries, law operated as a key strategy through which such groups sought redress and accountability in relation to the perceived failure on the part of governing entities to manage the risk posed by HIV to national blood systems in the 1980s. An examination of such political campaigns revealed that although the degree of success such groups achieved was to some extent mediated by specific opportunities available in national political and legal contexts, it was important in terms of restorative justice for HIV-infected PWH that a range of legal mechanisms was made available for facilitating financial redress and accountability arising out of the contamination episodes. In the post-HIV blood contamination era, the outcomes of such campaigns also contributed to a much more proactive approach on the part of governing entities to dealing with emerging risks to blood safety.

A key aspect of this more proactive approach has been increased recourse to the use of the precautionary principle and risk regulation. An examination of their current role in risk governance in the field in Chapters 7 and 8 showed that they have operated as legitimating techniques to redress the loss of political credibility and public trust that occurred in the wake of national HIV blood contamination episodes, in addition to bringing about behaviour modification on the part of key stakeholders in order to enhance blood safety. However, it was found that greater clarity and transparency were needed in terms of assessing the extent to which these techniques have been effective in promoting blood safety. Ensuring effectiveness is vital for maintaining the ongoing legitimacy of such techniques as cornerstones of a proactive approach to risk governance involving the blood system.

In Chapter 7, the particular challenges faced by those with responsibility for blood safety in meeting public and political expectations of zero-risk were examined in the context of a broader evaluation of the use of the precautionary principle in risk governance in the field. It was clear that a precautionary approach to managing risks to blood safety was now prevalent, particularly in relation to the use of restrictive donor selection criteria and the implementation of technologies to reduce the rate of TTIs. What such examination also revealed was that the loss of public trust that occurred in the wake of national HIV blood contamination episodes meant that a precautionary approach now dominated risk governance in the field. This was likely to occur in circumstances where traditional scientific risk assessment and cost–benefit analysis were subordinated to overriding political concerns regarding the use of precautionary strategies to promote blood safety.

Chapter 8 examined the design and effectiveness of risk regulation as a preferred technique of legitimation, drawing on a case study of EU risk regulation of blood and plasma products. The effectiveness of risk regulation was analysed by reference to a number of identified criteria including whether it met its stated aims and objectives in both design and implementation; its degree of comprehensiveness in dealing with risk-based issues; the degree of support for, or conversely resistance to, the regime by those entities subject to its remit; and the availability of accountability mechanisms for its monitoring. Such analysis revealed the importance of adopting an expansive approach to interpreting risk in which regulatory design was focused on the setting of standards to achieve optimum patient-recipient safety, rather than on conceiving of blood as either a gift or a commodity. This offered the best way forward towards the realisation of a comprehensive vein-to-vein approach to managing risk, as well as ensuring that the social and economic aspects involved in blood sourcing and supply were made transparent and incorporated into a holistic approach to regulatory design and implementation. It was also shown that the politicisation of risk that occurred in the wake of national HIV blood contamination episodes now makes it imperative for the purposes of maintaining public trust that monitoring of regulation to enhance blood safety is undertaken by institutions and/or individuals that are subject to an electoral mandate. Such an approach is vital if risk regulation is to operate successfully as a technique of legitimation in the wake of such episodes.

A final word: multi-valued human biological materials and risk governance

A key objective of this book has been to examine what constitutes effective risk governance involving multi-valued human biological materials, such as blood. Drawing on the findings from the chosen case study, I now conclude with a final word on the key elements that should underpin risk governance involving such materials in order to achieve this objective.[1] First, an ethically principled approach to the use of multi-valued human biological materials needs to take full account of the various links in the donor–recipient chain, including donation, production, supply and consumption. Policy and regulatory framing should predominantly focus on how best to ensure the safety of patient-recipients. This should replace the current lopsided approach which focuses on the ethics of how such materials are donated or otherwise provided. In both national and supranational governance environments, this has led to an over-reliance on the merits of the gift relationship as providing the ethical underpinning for the use of human biological materials, as well as operating as a useful legitimising device for those in political leadership. As the findings from this book make clear, maintaining the commitment to the gift relationship on ethical and safety grounds has proved to be inadequate on its own for facilitating effective risk governance of multi-valued human biological materials, such as blood.

Second, risk governance involving the use of multi-valued human biological materials should involve both public and political participation in deliberative processes of decision-making about where the line should be drawn in terms of risk acceptability. Such participation needs to be informed by an understanding of the diverse and complex arrangements which currently operate in relation to blood sourcing, supply and consumption within and across national boundaries. In addition to such informed participation, there should be regular oversight of governance initiatives involving multi-valued human biological materials at both national and supranational levels by reference to democratically accountable institutions and mechanisms. It should be emphasised that it is only where multi-valuing is at stake that this approach should be seen as imperative. In practical terms, this means that risk governance may become politicised. It may also result in traditional scientific risk assessment and cost–benefit analysis becoming subordinated to overarching political concerns, particularly in relation to the interpretation and application of a precautionary approach to managing (perceived) risks. This is the price that needs to be paid in order to ensure that public trust in, as well as the political legitimacy of, governance initiatives involving multi-valued human biological materials are maintained.

---

[1] I recognise that there would need to be a nuanced application of these key elements in practice, depending on the type of human biological material involved, as well as the differing ethical, political and regulatory dynamics that might arise in particular national and supranational governance environments. I have already examined this issue in detail in the EU context; see Farrell, 'The politics of risk', pp. 49–63.

Third, national and supranational regulation, together with the availability of both private and public legal mechanisms for facilitating financial redress and accountability of governing entities, are vital for enhancing the quality and safety of multi-valued human biological materials, as well as public trust in the legitimacy of governance processes dealing with the use of such materials. The availability of financial redress and accountability for those individuals who have suffered harm through the use of such materials is also important not only in terms of restorative justice, but also because it should be seen as being a necessary part of the process of learning from failures in risk governance. Risk regulation should be viewed as a preferred technique of legitimation in the interests of promoting and maintaining public trust. A holistic approach to the design of such regulation, which takes account of the inter-relationship between the social and the economic, as well as adopting an expansive interpretation of risk, should also be viewed as imperative in this context. If legal competence is absent, then soft, incremental forms of regulatory governance should be supported, including the use of guidelines, recommendations and standard setting.

Moves towards greater regulatory cooperation and harmonisation have been complicated not only by the unique properties of multi-valued human biological materials, but also by increasingly diverse and complex sourcing and supply arrangements for such materials within and across national boundaries. Nevertheless, the search for regulatory consensus on how best to deal with risk in this context remains a laudable goal, provided it does not lead to a 'race to the bottom' in terms of determining risk acceptability and the setting of quality and safety standards. In the final analysis, facilitating effective risk governance of such materials is likely to involve complexity in decision-making and require ongoing institutional evaluation and political monitoring to ensure implementation and compliance. A principled approach is vital in the circumstances, but it is one that must ultimately be mediated by the pragmatics of ensuring that risks to public health are minimised and vulnerable groups or individuals are protected from harm as far as possible.

Bibliography

Abraham, J. and Reed, T., 'Progress, innovation and regulatory science in drug development: the politics of international standard-setting', *Social Studies of Science*, 32 (2002), 337–69.

'Trading risks for markets: the international harmonisation of pharmaceuticals regulation', *Health Risk and Society*, 3 (2001), 113–28.

Alessandrini, M., 'Community volunteerism and blood donation: altruism as a lifestyle choice', *Transfusion Medicine Reviews*, 21 (2007), 307–16.

Allain, J.-P., Bianco, C., Blajchman, M. A., Brecher, M. E., Busch, M., Leiby, D., Lin, L. and Stramer, S., 'Protecting the blood supply from emerging pathogens: the role of pathogen inactivation', *Transfusion Medicine Reviews*, 19 (2005), 110–26.

Allain, J.-P., Stramer, S. L., Carneiro-Proietti, A. B. F., Martins, M. L., Lopes da Silva, S. N., Ribeiro, M., Proietti, F. A., and Reesink, H. W., 'Transfusion-transmitted infectious diseases', *Biologicals*, 37 (2009), 71–7.

Allsop, J., Jones, K. and Baggott, R., 'Health consumer groups in the UK: a new social movement?', *Sociology of Health and Illness*, 26 (2004), 737–56.

Alter, H. J. 'Pathogen reduction: a precautionary principle paradigm', *Transfusion Medicine Reviews*, 22 (2008), 97–102.

Alter, H. and Klein, H., 'The hazards of blood transfusion in historical perspective', *Blood*, 112 (2008), 2617–26.

American Association of Blood Banks (AABB), America's Blood Centers (ABC) and American Red Cross (ARC), Joint Statement Before BPAC on Behavior-Based Blood Donors Deferrals in the Era of Nucleic Acid Testing (NAT), 9 March 2006 (www.aabb.org/pressroom/statements/Pages/bpacdefernat030906.aspx).

Anderson, J. M., 'Empowering patients: issues and strategies', *Social Science and Medicine*, 43 (1996), 697–705.

Anderson, S. A., Yang, H., Gallagher, L. M., O'Callagh, S., Forsheet, R. A., Busch, M. P., McKenna, M. T., Williams, I., Williams, A., Kuehnert, M. J., Stramer, S., Kleinman, S., Epstein, J. and Dayton, A. I., 'Quantitative estimate of the risks and benefits of possible alternative blood donor strategies for men who have had sex with men', *Transfusion*, 49 (2009), 1102–14.

Archard, D., 'Selling yourself: Titmuss's argument against a market in blood', *Journal of Ethics*, 6 (2002), 87–102.

Archer, the Right Honourable Lord Archer of Sandwell QC, Jones, N. and
  Willetts, J., *Independent Public Inquiry Report on NHS Supplied Contaminated
  Blood and Blood Products* (2009).
Arrow, K., 'Gifts and exchanges', *Philosophy and Public Affairs*, 4 (1972),
  343–62.
AuBuchon, J. P., 'Managing change to improve transfusion safety', *Transfusion*,
  44 (2004), 1377–83.
Ayres, I. and Braithwaite, J., *Responsive Regulation: Transcending the Deregulation
  Debate* (Oxford University Press, 1992).
Bacqué, R., 'Douze parlementaires pour juger l'affaire du sang contaminé', *Le
  Monde*, 14/01/99.
Baggott, R., Allsop, J. and Jones, K., *Speaking for Patients and Carers: Health
  Consumer Groups and the Policy Process* (Basingstoke: Palgrave, 2005).
Baldwin, R., Cave, M. and Lodge, M., 'Introduction: Regulation – the field and
  the developing agenda', in Baldwin, R., Cave, M. and Lodge, M. (eds.),
  The Oxford Handbook of Regulation (Oxford University Press, 2010).
Barbara, J., Contreras, M. and Hewitt, P., 'AIDS: a problem for the transfu-
  sion service?' *British Journal of Hospital Medicine*, 36 (1986), 178–84.
Barbara, J. and Flanagan, P., 'Blood transfusion risk: protecting against the
  unknown', *British Medical Journal*, 316 (1998), 717–18.
Barbot, J., 'How to build an "active patient"? The work of AIDS associations
  in France', *Social Science and Medicine*, 62 (2006), 538–51.
Barnett, A., 'Blood blunder killed over 100 patients', *The Guardian*, 7/11/99.
Batty, D., 'Reid agrees compensation over contaminated blood', *The Guardian*,
  23/01/04.
Bayer, R., 'Blood and AIDS in America: science, politics and the making of
  an iatrogenic catastrophe', in Feldman, E. A. and Bayer, R. (eds.), *Blood
  Feuds: AIDS, Blood, and the Politics of Medical Disaster* (New York: Oxford
  University Press, 1999), pp. 20–58.
Bayer, R. and Feldman, E. A., 'Understanding the blood feuds', in Feldman,
  E. A. and Bayer, R (eds.), *Blood Feuds: AIDS, Blood, and the Politics of
  Medical Disaster* (New York: Oxford University Press, 1999), pp. 2–16.
Beal, R., 'Titmuss revisited', *Transfusion Medicine*, 9 (1999), 352–9.
Beal, R. and van Aken, W., 'Gift or good? A contemporary examination of the
  voluntary and commercial aspects of blood donation', *Vox Sanguinis*, 63
  (1992), 1–5.
Beck, S., 'Blood centers and plasma centers: mutual benefit', *The Source*
  (Summer 2011), 12–15.
Beck, U., *Risk Society: Towards a New Modernity* (London: Sage, 1992).
Berger, K., Klein, H. G., Seitz, R., Schramm, W. and Spieser, J. M., 'The
  Wilbad Kreuth initiative: European current practices and recommenda-
  tions for optimal use of blood components', *Biologicals*, 39 (2011), 189–93.
Berman, K. E., 'Expensive blood safety technologies: understanding and
  managing cost and access-to-care issues', *Transfusion Medicine Reviews*,
  18 (2004), 1–10.
Berner, B., 'The making of a risk object: AIDS, gay citizenship and the mean-
  ing of blood donation in Sweden in the early 1980s', *Sociology of Health and
  Illness*, 33 (2011), 384–98.

Berridge, V., 'AIDS and the gift relationship in the UK', in Oakley, A. and Ashton, J. (eds.), R. M. Titmuss, *The Gift Relationship: From Human Blood to Social Policy* (London: LSE Books, 1997), pp. 15–40.

AIDS in the UK: The Making of Policy 1981–1994 (Oxford University Press, 1996).

Betts, J. P., 'The United Kingdom: national policy', *Pharmaceuticals Policy and Law*, 7 (2006), 233–41.

Black, J., 'Constructing and contesting legitimacy and accountability in polycentric regulatory regimes', *Regulation & Governance*, 2 (2008), 137–64.

'Decentring regulation: understanding the role of regulation and self-regulation in a "post-regulatory" world', *Current Legal Problems*, 54 (2001), 103–47.

'Proceduralizing regulation: part 1', *Oxford Journal of Legal Studies*, 20 (2000), 597–614.

'What is regulatory innovation?' in Black, J., Lodge, M. and Thatcher, M. (eds.), *Regulatory Innovation: A Comparative Analysis* (Cheltenham: Edward Elgar, 2005), pp. 1–15.

Blajchman, M. A., 'Transfusion medicine – the coming of age of a new specialty', *Transfusion Medicine Reviews*, 1 (1987), 1–3.

Blajchman, M. A. and Klein, H. G., 'Looking back in anger: retrospection in the face of a paradigm shift', *Transfusion Medicine Reviews*, 11 (1) (1997), 1–5.

Block, F., 'Introduction', in Block, F. (ed.), K. Polanyi, *The Great Transformation: The Political and Economic Origins of Our Time*, 2nd edn (Boston, MA: Beacon Press, 2001), pp. 1–16.

Borrás, S., 'Legitimate governance of risk at the EU level? The case of genetically modified organisms', *Technological Forecasting and Social Change*, 73 (2006), 61–75.

Borzini, P., Nembri, P. and Biffoni, F., 'The evolution of transfusion medicine as a stand alone discipline', *Transfusion Medicine Reviews*, 11 (1997), 200–8.

Boseley, S., 'Increased offer for NHS patients infected with hepatitis C "disappointing"', *The Guardian*, 10/1/11.

'NHS imports all plasma to avoid risk of CJD', *The Guardian*, 14/5/1998.

Bove, L. L., Bednall, T., Masser, B. and Buzza, M., 'Understanding the plasmapheresis donor in a voluntary, nonremunerated environment', *Transfusion* 51 (2011) 2411–24.

Bovens, M., Hart, P. and Peters, B. G. (eds.), *Success and Failure in Public Governance: A Comparative Analysis* (Cheltenham: Edward Elgar, 2001).

Brahams, D., 'Trial and tribulations of J-P. Allain', *Lancet*, 342 (1993), 232–3.

Braithwaite, J., 'Neoliberalism and regulatory capitalism', *Occasional Paper No. 5, Regulatory Institutions Network* (Canberra: ANU, 2005), pp. 1–43.

Restorative Justice and Responsive Regulation (Oxford University Press, 2002).

Brown, C., '£19 million for victims of HIV blood', *The Independent*, 24/11/89.

Brown, P. and Zavestoski, S., 'Social movements in health: an introduction', *Sociology of Health and Illness*, 26 (2004), 679–94.

Social Movements in Health (Blackwood, NJ: Blackwell Publishing, 2005).

Brown, P., Zavestoski, S., McCornick, S., Mayer, B., Morello-Frosch, R. and Gasior Altman, R., 'Embodied health movements: new approaches to social movements in health', *Sociology of Health and Illness*, 26 (2004), 50–80.

Brownsword, R., *Rights, Regulation, and the Technological Revolution* (Oxford University Press, 2008).

Brunsson, N. and Jacobsson, B., 'The contemporary expansion of standardization', in Brunsson, N., Jacobsson, B. and Associates (eds.), *A World of Standards* (Oxford University Press, 2000), pp. 1–17.

Bult, J. M., 'Future trends', *Pharmaceuticals Policy and Law*, 7 (2006), 263–9.

Burnouf, T., 'Modern plasma fractionation', *Transfusion Medicine Reviews*, 21 (2007), 101–17.

'Plasma proteins: Unique biopharmaceuticals – unique economics', *Pharmaceuticals Policy and Law*, 7 (2006), 209–18.

Busby, H., 'Biobanks, bioethics and concepts of donated blood in the UK', *Sociology of Health and Illness*, 28 (2006), 850–65.

'The meanings of consent to the donation of cord blood stem cells: perspectives from an interview-based study of a public cord blood bank in England', *Clinical Ethics*, 5 (2010), 22–7.

'Trust, nostalgia and narrative accounts of blood banking in England in the 21st century', *Health*, 14 (2010), 369–82.

Busch, M. and Custer, B., 'Health outcomes research using large donor-recipient databases: a new frontier for assessing transfusion safety and contributing to public health', *Vox Sanguinis*, 91 (2006), 282–4.

Busch, M., Walderhaug, M., Custer, B., Allain, J.-P., Reddy, R. and McDonough, B., 'Risk assessment and cost-effectiveness/utility analysis', *Biologicals*, 37 (2009), 78–87.

Byrne, L., Brant, L. J., Davison, K. and Hewitt, P., 'Transfusion-transmitted human immunodeficiency virus (HIV) from seroconverting donors is rare in England and Wales: results from HIV lookback, October 1995 through December 2008', *Transfusion*, 51 (2011), 1339–45.

Callum, J. L., Lon, Y., Lima, A. and Merkley, L., 'Transitioning from "blood" safety to "transfusion" safety: addressing the single biggest risk of transfusion', *ISBT Science Series*, 6 (2011), 96–104.

Camporesi, P., *The Juice of Life: The Symbolic and Magic Significance of Blood*, trans. R. R. Barr (New York: Continuum Publications, 1996).

Cash, J., 'The blood transfusion service and the National Health Service', *British Medical Journal*, 295 (1987), 617–19.

Casteret, A. M., *L'Affaire du sang contaminé* (Paris: Éditions La Decouverte, 1992).

Centers for Disease Control, *Morbidity and Mortality Weekly Report*, July 16, 1982.

Morbidity and Mortality Weekly Report, December 10, 1982.

Cervia, J. S., Sowemimo-Coker, S. O., Ortolano, G. O., Wilkins, K., Schaffer, S. and Wortham, S. T., 'An overview of prion biology and the role of blood filtration in reducing the risk of transfusion-transmitted variant

Creutzfeldt-Jakob Disease', *Transfusion Medicine Reviews*, 20 (2006), 190–206.

Cheingsong-Popov, R., Weiss, R., Dalgleish, R. A., Tedder, R. S., Shanson, D. C., Jeffries, D. J., Ferns, R. B., Briggs, E. M., Weller, I. V. and Mitton, S. *et al.*, 'Prevalence of antibody to human T-lymphotropic virus type III in AIDS and AIDS-risk patients in Britain', *Lancet*, ii (1984), 477–80.

Chotray, V. and Stoker, G., *Governance Theory: A Cross-Disciplinary Approach* (Basingstoke: Palgrave Macmillan, 2008).

Claxton, K. and Culyer, A. J., 'Wickedness or folly? The ethics of NICE's decisions', *Journal of Medical Ethics*, 32 (2006), 373–7.

Colombani, J.-M., 'Pour une justice équitable', *Le Monde*, 9/02/99.

Commission of the European Communities, Communication on Blood Safety and Self-Sufficiency in the Community, COM (94) 652 final, 21.12.1994.

Communication from the Commission on the Precautionary Principle, COM (2000) 1 final, 2.2.2000.

European Governance: A White Paper (2001) 428 final, 25.7.2001.

Implementing the Community Lisbon Programme: Communication from the Commission to the Council, the European Parliament, the European Social and Economic Council and the Committee of the Regions, More Research and Innovation – Investing for Growth and Employment: A Common Approach, COM (2005) 488 final, 12.10.2005.

Innovation Tomorrow: Innovation Policy and the Regulatory Framework (Brussels: DG Enterprise, 2002).

Meeting of the competent authorities on blood and blood components: summary report – 13 September 2006 (Art. 25 Dir.2002/98/EC): Brussels SANCO C/6 TB/ges D (2006) 360346.

Proposal for a Directive of the European Parliament and of the Council setting standards of quality and safety for the collection, testing, processing, storage and distribution of human blood and blood components and amending Council Directive 89/381/EEC, COM (2000) 816 final, 13.12.2000.

Report on the promotion by Member States of voluntary unpaid blood donations.

Report from the Commission to the Council and the European Parliament on the promotion by Member States of voluntary, unpaid blood donations, COM (2006) 217 final, 17.5.2006.

Report from the Commission to the Council, the European Parliament, the European Economic and Social Committee and the Committee of the Regions: First Report on the Application of the Blood Directive COM (2006) 313 final, 19.6.2006, Brussels.

Confidentiality Arrangements concluded between the EU (EC and EMEA) and the US (FDA/DHHS), Implementation Plan for Medicinal Products for Human Use (updated June 2007) (www.emea.europa.eu/docs/en_GB/document_library/Other/2009/12/WC500017981.pdf).

Cooper, M. H. and Culyer, A. J., *The Price of Blood* (London: Institute of Economic Affairs, 1968).

Corkin, J., 'Science, legitimacy and the law: regulating risk regulation judiciously in the European Community', *European Law Review*, 33 (2008), 359–84.

Council Conclusions of 13 December 1993 on self-sufficiency in blood in the European Community, OJ C 15, 18.1.1994.

Council of Europe, European Directorate for the Quality of Medicines and HealthCare (EDQM) (www.edqm.eu).

Council of Europe, European Directorate for the Quality of Medicines and HealthCare, *Guide to the Preparation, Use and Quality Assurance of Blood Components*, 16th edn (Strasbourg: Council of Europe, 2010) (www.edqm.eu).

Council of Europe, European Directorate for the Quality of Medicines and HealthCare, Pharmacopoeial Discussion Group. International Harmonisation: Statement of Harmonisation Policy (2003) (www.edqm.eu).

Council of Europe, European Directorate for the Quality of Medicines and HealthCare, Terms of Reference of the European Committee (Partial Agreement) on Blood Transfusion (CD-P-TS) Factsheet, 1076th Meeting, (3–4 February 2010) (www.edqm.eu).

Council of Europe, European Directorate for the Quality of Medicines and HealthCare, Working Procedures of the Pharmacopoeial Discussion Group (PDG), Revised Version (June 2010) (www.edqm.eu).

Council Resolution of 2 June 1995 on blood safety and self-sufficiency in the Community, OJ C 164, 30.6.1995.

Council Resolution of 11 December 1996 on a strategy towards blood safety and self-sufficiency in the European Community, OJ C 374, 11.12.1996.

Custer, B., 'Economic analyses of blood safety and transfusion medicine interventions: a systematic review', *Transfusion Medicine Reviews*, 18 (2004), 127–43.

Custer, B., Agapova, M. and Havlir Martinez, R., 'The cost-effectiveness of pathogen reduction technology as assessed using a multiple risk reduction model', *Transfusion*, 50 (2010), 2461–73.

Custer, B. and Hoch, J. S., 'Cost-effectiveness analysis: what it really means for transfusion medicine decision making', *Transfusion Medicine Reviews*, 23 (2009), 1–12.

Davies, S. C., 'Editorial: Reforming England's blood transfusion service', *British Medical Journal*, 311 (1995), 1383–4.

Davis, C. and Abraham, J., 'Rethinking innovation accounting in pharmaceutical regulation: a case study in the deconstruction of therapeutic advance and therapeutic breakthrough', *Science, Technology and Human Values*, 36 (2011), 791–815.

Davis, R. E., Vincent, C. A. and Murphy, M. F., 'Blood transfusion safety: the potential role of the patient', *Transfusion Medicine Reviews*, 25 (2011), 12–23.

Davison, J. and Driscoll, M., 'Compensation fight delayed by secrecy', *The Sunday Times*, 29/7/90.

'Doctors back haemophiliacs', *The Sunday Times*, 11/11/90.

Davison, K. L., Brant, L. J., Presanis, A. M. and Soldan, K., 'A re-evaluation of the risk of transfusion-transmitted HIV prevented by the exclusion of men who have sex with men from blood donation in England and Wales, 2005–2007', *Vox Sanguinis* 101 (2011) 291–302.

de Búrca, G. and Scott, J., 'Introduction: new governance, law and constitutionalism', in de Búrca, G. and Scott, J. (eds.), *Law and New Governance in the EU and the US* (Oxford: Hart Publishing, 2006), pp. 1–14.

Delacourt, J., 'European Court of Justice weighs in on donor compensation debate', *The Source* (Summer 2011), 16–17.

del Pozo, P. R., 'Paying donors and the ethics of blood supply', *Journal of Medical Ethics*, 20 (1994), 31–5.

de Sadeleer, N., 'The precautionary principle in EC environmental and health law', *European Law Journal*, 12 (2006), 139–72.

Department of Health, Government response to Lord Archer's independent report on NHS supplied contaminated blood and blood products (London: Department of Health, 2009).

Lifetime blood donation ban lifted for men who have had sex with men, Press Release – 8 September 2011 (http://mediacentre.dh.gov.uk).

Devine, K., 'Risky business? The risks and benefits of umbilical cord blood collection', *Medical Law Review*, 18 (2010), 330–62.

Dickenson, D., 'Consent, commodification and benefit-sharing in genetic research', *Developing World Bioethics*, 4 (2004), 109–24.

Djelic, M.-L. and Quack, S., 'Transnational communities and governance', in Djelic, M.-L. and Quack, S. (eds.), *Transnational Communities: Shaping Global Economic Governance* (Cambridge University Press, 2009), pp. 3–36.

Djelic, M.-L. and Sahlin-Andersson, K., 'Introduction: A world of governance: the rise of transnational regulation', in Djelic, M.-L. and Sahlin-Andersson, K. (eds.), *Transnational Governance: Institutional Dynamics of Regulation* (Cambridge University Press, 2006), pp. 1–28.

Dodd, R., 'Editorial: Prions and precautions: be careful for what you ask', *Transfusion*, 50 (2010), 956–8.

Dodd, R., Roth, W. K., Ashford, P., Dax, E. M. and Vyas, G., 'Transfusion medicine and safety', *Biologicals*, 37 (2009), 62–70.

Domen, R. E., 'Paid-versus-volunteer blood donation in the United States: a historical overview', *Transfusion Medicine Reviews*, 10 (1995), 53–9.

Dorozynski, A., 'French doctors face second trial', *British Medical Journal*, 309 (1994), 427.

Douglas, H., *Science, Policy and the Value-Free Ideal* (University of Pittsburgh Press, 2009).

Douglas, M., 'Foreword: No free gifts', in Mauss, M., *The Gift: The Form and Reason for Exchange in Archaic Societies* (London: Routledge, 1990), translated by W. D. Halls from M. Mauss, 'Essai sur le don', *Sociologie et Anthropologie* (Paris: Presses Universitaires de France, 1950), pp. vii–xviii.

Risk Acceptability According to the Social Sciences (London: Routledge, 1985).

Risk and Blame (London: Routledge, 1992).

Drake, A. W., Finkelstein, S. N. and Sapolsky, H. M., *The American Blood Supply* (Cambridge, MA: MIT Press, 1982).

Driscoll, M., '200 MPs join compensation battle', *The Sunday Times*, 5/11/89.

Dyer, C., 'Clarke urged to settle AIDS claims', *The Guardian*, 3/08/90.

'Judge urges haemophilia settlement', *The Guardian*, 1/10/90.

Dzik, S., Aubuchon, J., Jeffries, L., Kleinman, S., Manno, C., Murphy, M. F., Popovsky, M. A., Sayers, M., Silberstein, L. E., Slichter, S. J. and Vamvakas, E. C., 'Leukocyte reduction of blood components: public policy and new technology', *Transfusion Medicine Reviews*, 14 (2000), 34–52.

Ebner, A., 'Transnational markets and the Polanyi problem', in Joerges, C. and Falke, J. (eds.), *Karl Polanyi, Globalisation and the Potential of Law in Transnational Markets* (Oxford: Hart Publishing, 2011), pp. 19–40.

Eder, A., Goldman, M., Rossmann, S., Waxman, D. and Bianco, C., 'Selection criteria to protect the blood donor in North America and Europe: past (dogma), present (evidence) and future (hemovigilance)', *Transfusion Medicine Reviews*, 23 (2009), 205–20.

Eder, A. F. and Menitove, J. E., 'Blood donations past, present and future', *Transfusion*, 50 (2010), 1870–7.

Editorial, 'The national blood transfusion service today', *British Medical Journal*, 281 (1980), 405–6.

'Blood transfusion, haemophilia and AIDS', *Lancet*, ii (1984), 1433–5.

'Palais d'injustice', *Lancet*, 342 (1993), 188.

Elliot, C., *French Criminal Law* (Devon: Willan Publishing, 2001).

Emmanuel, E. J., 'Is health care a commodity?', *Lancet*, 350 (1997), 1713–14.

Epstein, S., *Impure Science: AIDS, Activism and the Politics of Knowledge* (Berkeley, CA: University of California Press, 1996).

Ertmann, M. M. and Williams, J. (eds.), *Rethinking Commodification: Cases and Readings in Law and Culture* (New York University Press, 2005).

European Agency for the Evaluation of Medicinal Products, Committee for Proprietary Medicinal Products (CPMP), Guideline on the Scientific Data Requirements for a Plasma Master File (PMF), EMEA/CPMP/BWP/3704/03, 26 February 2004.

European Commission, Communication from the Commission to the Council, the European Parliament, the Economic and Social Committee and the Committee of the Regions on the application of Directive 2002/98/EC setting standards of quality and safety for the collection, testing, processing, storage and distribution of human blood and blood components and amending Directive 2001/83/EC, COM (2010) 3 final, 19.1.2010, Brussels.

European Commission, Meeting of the Competent Authorities on Blood and Blood Components (Art. 25 Dir. 2002/98/EC), 12–13 April 2010, SANCO C6 TB/RP D(2010) 360180 Brussels.

European Commission, Meeting of the Competent Authorities on Blood and Blood Components, Summary Report, 16–17 May 2011, SANCO D4/SV/hp ARES(2011), Brussels.

European Commission, Report from the Commission to the European Parliament, the Council, the European Economic and Social Committee and the Committee of the Regions. 2nd Report on Voluntary and Unpaid Donation of Blood and Blood Components. COM (2011) 138 final.

European Haemophilia Consortium (EHC) (www.ehc.eu).

European Medicines Agency, Committee for Medicinal Products for Human Use (CHMP), Guideline on Epidemiological Data on Blood Transmissible Infections, EMA/CHMP/BWP/548524/2008, 22 April 2010.

European Medicines Agency, Committee for Medicinal Products for Human Use (CHMP), Guideline on Plasma-Derived Medicinal Products, EMA/CHMP/BWP/706271/2010, 21 July 2011.

European Medicines Agency, Committee for Medicinal Products for Human Use (CHMP) (www.ema.europa.eu).

European Medicines Agency, Plasma Master File (PMF) (www.ema.europa.eu).

European Opinion Research Group (EEIG), *Le don de sang*, Eurobaromètre spécial, 1883–4/Vague 58.2 (Brussels: European Commission, 2003).

European Parliament, Resolution on blood safety in the European Union, OJ C 249, 25.09.1995.

European Parliament, Resolution on the communication from the Commission on blood safety and self-sufficiency in the European Community, OJ C 141, 13.05.1996.

European Parliament, Resolution on safe blood transfusions and use of blood derivatives, OJ C 329, 6.12.1993.

European Parliament, Resolution on self-sufficiency in and safety of blood and its derivatives in the European Community, OJ C 268, 4.10.1993.

Evatt, B. L., 'The natural evolution of haemophilia care: developing and sustaining comprehensive care globally', *Haemophilia*, 12 (2006), 13–21.

Everson, M. and Vos, E., 'The scientification of politics and the politicisation of science', in Everson, M. and Vos, E. (eds.), *Uncertain Risks Regulated* (London: Routledge-Cavendish, 2009), pp. 1–17.

Faber, J.-C., 'The European Blood Directive: a new era of blood regulation has begun', *Transfusion Medicine*, 14 (2004), 257–73.

Farrell, A. M., 'Addressing organ shortage in the European Union: getting the balance right', in Farrell, A. M., Price, D. and Quigley, M. (eds.), *Organ Shortage: Ethics Law and Pragmatism* (Cambridge University Press, 2011), pp. 227–44.

'Is the gift still good? Examining the politics and regulation of blood safety in the European Union', *Medical Law Review*, 14 (2006), 155–79.

'The emergence of EU governance in public health: the case of blood policy and regulation', in Steffen, M. (ed.), *Health Governance in Europe* (London: Routledge, 2005), pp. 134–51.

'The politics of risk and EU governance of human material', *Maastricht Journal of European and Comparative Law*, 16 (2009), 41–64.

Farrell, A. M. and Brazier, M., 'Consent to blood transfusion', *British Medical Journal*, 341 (2010), c4336.

Farrugia, A., 'International movement of plasma and plasma contracting', in Vyas, G. N. and Williams, A. E. (eds.), *Advances in Transfusion Safety* (Basel: Karger, 2005), pp. 85–96.

'Product delivery in the developing world: options, opportunities and threats', *Haemophilia*, 10 (2004), 77–82.

'Safety and supply of haemophilia products: worldwide perspectives', *Haemophilia*, 10 (2004), 327–33.

'The mantra of blood safety: time for a new tune?', *Vox Sanguinis*, 86 (2004), 1–7.

'The regulatory pendulum in transfusion medicine', *Transfusion Medicine Reviews*, 16 (2002), 273–82.

Farrugia, A., Gustafson, M. and von Hoegen, I., 'Decades of safety measures', *The Source* (Spring 2009), 8–12.

Faulkner, A., *Medical Technology into Healthcare and Society: A Sociology of Devices, Innovation and Governance* (Houndmills: Palgrave Macmillan, 2009).

Feldman, E. A., 'Blood justice: courts, conflict and compensation in Japan, France and the United States', *Law and Society Review*, 34 (2000), 651–701.

Feldman, E. A. and Bayer, R. (eds.), *Blood Feuds: AIDS, Blood, and the Politics of Medical Disaster* (New York: Oxford University Press, 1999).

Felstiner, W. L. F., Abel, R. L. and Sarat, A., 'The emergence and transformation of disputes: naming, blaming and claiming...', *Law and Society Review*, 15 (1980–81), 631–54.

Fidler, D. P. and Gostin, L. O., 'The new International Health Regulations: an historic development for international law and public health', *Journal of Law, Medicine and Ethics*, 34 (2006), 85–94.

Fisher, E., 'Opening Pandora's box: contextualising the precautionary principle in the European Union', in Everson, M. and Vos, E. (eds.), *Uncertain Risks Regulated* (London: Routledge-Cavendish, 2009), pp. 21–45.

Risk Regulation and Administrative Constitutionalism (Oxford: Hart Publishing, 2007).

Flanagan, P., 'ISBT Board response to the Dublin consensus statement', *Vox Sanguinis*, 100 (2011), 250–1.

Fletcher, M., 'Haemophiliacs with AIDS to get cash help', *The Times*, 11/11/87.

Føllesdal, A., 'Legitimacy theories of the European Union', *ARENA Working Papers*, WP 04/15 (2004), 1–38.

Food and Drug Administration, Blood Donations from Men Who Have Sex with Other Men Questions and Answers (www.fda.gov/biologicsbloodvaccines/bloodbloodproducts/questionsaboutblood/ucm108186.htm).

Workshop on Behavior-Based Donor Deferrals in the NAT Era, 8 March 2006 (www.fda.gov).

Foster, K. R., Vecchia, P. and Repacholi, M. J., 'Science and the precautionary principle', *Science*, 288 (2000), 979–81.

Franceschi, S., Dal Maso, L. and La Vecchia, C., 'Trends in incidence of AIDS associated with transfusion of blood and blood products in Europe and the United States, 1985–93', *British Medical Journal*, 311 (1995), 1534–6.

Franchini, M. and Lippi, G., 'Recombinant Factor VIII concentrates', *Seminars in Thrombosis and Hemostasis*, 36 (2010), 493–7.

Fraser, B., 'Seeking a safer blood supply', *Lancet*, 365 (2005), 559–60.

Freeman, C., *The Economics of Industrial Innovation* (London: Pinter, 1982).

Freeman, R., 'HIV and the blood supply in the United Kingdom: professionalism and pragmatism', in Bovens, M., Hart, P. and Peters, B. G. (eds.), *Success and Failure in Public Governance: A Comparative Analysis* (Cheltenham: Edward Elgar, 2001), pp. 567–81.

Friedman, M.A., Lead Deputy Commissioner, Food and Drug Administration, Testimony on FDA's regulation of blood, blood products, and plasma, before the House Committee on Government Reform and Oversight, Subcommittee on Human Resources and Intergovernmental Relations, 5 June 1997 (www.hhs.gov/asl/testify/t970605a.html).

Funtowicz, S. O. and Ravetz, J. R., 'Risk management as a postnormal science', *Risk Analysis*, 12 (1992), 95–7.

Funtowicz, S., Shepherd, I., Wilkinson, D. and Ravetz, J. R., 'Science and governance in the European Union: a contribution to the debate', *Science and Public Policy*, 27 (2000), 327–36.

Gabe, J., Kelleher, D. and Williams, G. (eds.), *Challenging Medicine* (London: Routledge, 1994).

Galarneau, C., 'Blood donation, deferral and discrimination: FDA donor deferral policy for men who have sex with men', *American Journal of Bioethics*, 10 (2010), 29–39.

Ganchoff, C., 'Speaking for stem cells: biomedical activism and emerging forms of patienthood', *Advances in Medical Sociology*, 10 (2008), 225–45.

Garber, K., 'rFactor VIII deficit questioned', *Nature Biotechnology*, 18 (2000), 1133.

Gaul, G., 'The blood brokers: the loose way the FDA regulates blood industry', *Philadelphia Inquirer*, 25/9/89.

Gelblat, S., 'Les victims dénoncent un "procès truqué"', *Le Figaro*, 10/03/99.

Germain, M., 'Application of a risk modelling technique to blood donor deferral issues', in Chiavetta, J. A., Deeks, S., Goldman, M., Hannon, J., Leach-Bennett, J., Megann, H., O'Brien, S. and Webert, K. (eds.), 'Proceedings of consensus conference: blood-borne HIV and hepatitis – optimizing the donor selection process', *Transfusion Medicine Reviews*, 17 (2003), 1–30 at 6.

Germain, M., Remis, R. S. and Delage, G., 'The risks and benefits of accepting men who have had sex with men as blood donors', *Transfusion*, 43 (2003), 25–33.

Geronimi, J. P., Henry-Bonnot, F., Feltz, A., Morelle, A., Roquel, A. and Vernerey, M., *Les Collectes de sang en milieu pénitentiare* (Paris: Inspection Générale des services judiciaires ISGJ RMT 1392 IGAS Code Mission SA07 No. 92 119) (Novembre 1992).

Gibb, F., 'AIDS victims back in Court to urge release of papers', *The Times*, 11/09/90.

Giddens, A., *The Consequences of Modernity* (Stanford University Press, 1990).

Gieryn, T., 'Boundary-work and the demarcation of science from non-science: strains and interests in professional ideologies of scientists', *American Sociological Review*, 48 (1983), 781–95.

Gillespie, T. W. and Hillyer, C. D., 'Blood donors and factors impacting the blood donation decision', *Transfusion Medicine Reviews*, 16 (2002), 115–30.

Gold, R., *Body Parts: Property Rights and the Ownership of Human Biological Materials* (Washington, DC: Georgetown University Press, 1996).

Goldberg, R., 'Paying for bad blood: strict product liability after the Hepatitis C litigation', *Medical Law Review*, 10 (2002), 165–200.

Goldman, M., Yi, Q.-L., Ye, X., Tessier, L. and O'Brien, S. F., 'Donor understanding about current and potential deferral criteria for high-risk sexual behavior', *Transfusion* 51 (2011) 1829–34.

Goncalves, M. H., Muon, M. C. and d'Almeida Goncalves, J., 'Transposition of the blood directive – perspective of Portugal', *Transfusion Clinique et Biologique*, 12 (2005), 18–20.

Goodrich, R., 'A balanced approach to blood safety: a possible role for PRT', in Areya, C., Nakhasi, H., Mied, P., Epstein, J., Hughes, J. Gwinn, M., Kleinman, S., Dodd, R., Stramer, S., Walderhaug, M., Ganz, P., Goodrich, R., Tibbetts, C. and Asher, D., 'FDA workshop on emerging infectious diseases: evaluating emerging infectious diseases (EIDs) for transfusion safety', *Transfusion* 51 (2011) 1863–4.

Gostin, L. O., 'Meeting the survival needs of the world's least healthy people: a proposed model for global health governance', *Journal of the American Medical Association*, 298 (2007), 225–8.

Gottweis, H., Salter, B. and Walby, C., *The Global Politics of Human Embryonic Stem Cell Science: Regenerative Medicine in Transition* (Houndmills: Palgrave Macmillan, 2009).

Graves, N., Clare, G., Haines, M. and Bird, R., 'A policy case study of blood in Australia', *Social Science and Medicine*, 71 (2010), 1677–82.

Greilsamer, L., *Le procès du sang contaminé* (Paris: Éditions Le Monde, 1992). 'Notre carence collective...', *Le Monde*, 24/07/92.

Grenfell, P., Nutland, W., McManus, S., Datta, J., Soldan, K. and Wellings, K., 'Views and experiences of men who have sex with men on the ban on blood donation: a cross sectional survey with qualitative interviews', *British Medical Journal*, 343 (2011), d5604.

Grifols, V., 'Financing plasma proteins: unique challenges', *Pharmaceuticals Policy and Law*, 7 (2006), 187–98.

Grin, J. and van de Graaf, H., 'Technology assessment as learning', *Science, Technology and Human Values*, 21 (1996), 72–99.

Grippner, G., Granovetter, M., Block, F., Biggart, N., Beamish, T., Hsing, Y., Hart, G., Arrighi, G., Mendell, M., Hall, J., Burawoy, M., Vogel, S. and O'Riain, S., 'Polanyi symposium: a conversation on embeddedness', *Socio-Economic Review*, 2 (2007), 109–35.

Guibert, N., 'La Cour de cassation clôt définitivement l'affaire du sang contaminé', *Le Monde*, 20/06/2003.

Haas, P. M., 'Introduction: Epistemic communities and international policy coordination', *International Organization*, 46 (1992), 1–35.

Hagen, P., *Blood: Gift or Merchandise? Towards an International Blood Policy* (New York: Alan R. Liss Inc., 1982).
Blood Transfusion in Europe: A 'White Paper' (Strasbourg: Council of Europe, 1993).

Hammitt, J. K., Weiner, J. B., Swedlow, B., Kall, D. and Zhou, Z., 'Precautionary regulation in Europe and the United States: a quantitative comparison', *Risk Analysis*, 25 (2005), 1215–28.

Harris, J., 'NICE is not cost-effective', *Journal of Medical Ethics*, 32 (2006), 378–80.

Havighurst, C. C., 'Trafficking in human blood: Titmuss (1970) and products liability', *Law and Contemporary Problems*, 72 (2009), 1–15.

Healy, K., *Last Best Gifts: Altruism and the Market for Human Blood and Organs* (Chicago University Press, 2006).

Hensler, D., Pace, N. M., Dombey-Moore, B., Giddens, B., Gross, J. and Molker, K., 'Blood clotting products for haemophiliacs: in re Factor VIII or IX Concentrate Blood Products', in *Class Action Dilemmas: Pursuing Public Goals for Private Gain* (Rand Corporation Publications, 2000), pp. 293–317.

Hergon, E., Moutel, G., Duchange, N., Bellier, L., Rouger, P. and Hervé, C., 'Risk management in transfusion after the HIV blood contamination crisis in France: the impact of the precautionary principle', *Transfusion Medicine Reviews*, 19 (2005), 273–80.

Hermitte, M.-A., *Le sang et le droit* (Paris: Éditions du Seuil, 1996).

Hess, D., 'Technology- and product-oriented movements: approximating social movement studies and science and technology studies', *Science Technology and Human Values*, 30 (2005), 515–35.

Heyvaert, V., 'Europe in a climate of risk: three paradigms at play', *LSE Law, Society and Economy Working Papers*, 06/2010, 1–27.

Hillyer, C. D., Blumberg, N., Glynn, S. A. and Ness, P. M., 'Transfusion recipient epidemiology and outcomes research: possibilities for the future', *Transfusion*, 48 (2008), 1530–7.

Home News, '£42 million AIDS case finishes', *The Guardian*, 11/06/91.

Hood, C., Rothstein, H. and Baldwin, R., *The Government of Risk: Understanding Risk Regulation Regimes* (Oxford University Press, 2001).

House of Commons, Parliamentary Debates, Vol. 105, 832–58.

House of Commons, Parliamentary Debates, Vol. 122, 767, 16/11/87.

House of Commons, Parliamentary Debates (Hansard), Statement by the Honourable Mr Andrew Lansley, Secretary of State for Health, Contaminated Blood, Vol. 521, No. 95, Cols. 33–35, 10/01/2011.

House of Commons, Social Services Committee, *Problems Associated with AIDS* (Paper 192–1), Vol. 1 (London: HMSO, 1987).

Howse, R., 'Democracy, science and free trade: risk regulation on trial at the World Trade Organization', *Michigan Law Review*, 98 (2000), 2329–57.

Hurley, R., 'Bad blood: gay men and blood donation', *British Medical Journal*, 338 (2009), b779.

Hutt, E., 'Specialised plasma products', *Pharmaceuticals Policy and Law*, 7 (2006), 67–73.

Hutter, B., 'The attractions of risk-based regulation: accounting for the emergence of risk ideas in regulation', *CARR Discussion Paper*, No. 33 (March 2005), pp. 1–18.

INRA Europe, *Europeans and Blood, Eurobarometer 41.0* (Brussels: European Commission, 1995).

International Federation of Blood Donor Organizations (FIODS) (www.fiods. org).

International Federation of Red Cross and Red Crescent Societies (IFRC) (www.ifrc.org).

International Patient Organisation for Primary Immunodeficiencies (IPOPI) (www.ipopi.org).

International Plasma Fractionation Association (IPFA), *IPFA Position Statement: Towards a Safe, Secure and Sufficient and National Supply of Plasma Products*. Executive Summary. EB–2009–06.

Jacobson, N. M., 'The art of balanced production', *Pharmaceuticals Policy and Law*, 7 (2006), 81–7.

Jacobsson, B., 'Standardization and expert knowledge', in Brunsson, N., Jacobsson, B. and Associates (eds.), *A World of Standards* (Oxford University Press, 2000), pp. 40–9.

Janowitz, W. R., 'Safety of the blood supply – liability for transfusion associated AIDS', *Journal of Legal Medicine*, 9 (1988), 611–22.

Jasanoff, S., 'Citizens at risk: cultures of modernity in the US and EU', *Science as Culture*, 11 (2002), 363–80.

Designs on Nature: Science and Democracy in Europe and the United States. (Princeton University Press, 2005).

'Judgment under siege: the three-body problem of expert legitimacy', in Maasen, S. and Weingart, P. (eds.), *Democratization of Expertise? Exploring Novel Forms of Scientific Advice in Political Decision-Making – Sociology of the Sciences*, 24 (2005), 209–24.

The Fifth Branch: Science Advisers as Policymakers (Cambridge, MA: Cambridge University Press, 1990).

Jasper, J. and Poulsen, J., 'Recruiting strangers and friends: moral shocks and social networks in animal rights and anti-nuclear protests', *Social Problems*, 42 (1995), 104–26.

Jevons, F., 'Who wins from innovation?' *Technology Analysis & Strategic Management*, 4 (1992), 399–412.

Johnson, D. B., *Blood Policy: Issues and Alternatives*. Proceedings of a Conference sponsored by the Center for Health Policy Research of the American Enterprise Institute for Public Policy Research (Washington, DC: American Enterprise Institute, 1977).

Jones, P., 'Factor VIII: supply and demand', *British Medical Journal*, 280 (1980), 1531–2.

Jordana, J. and Levi-Faur, D., 'The politics of regulation in the age of governance', in Jordana, J. and Levi-Faur, D. (eds.), *The Politics of Regulation: Institutions and Regulatory Reforms for the Age of Governance* (Cheltenham: Edward Elgar, 2004), pp. 1–28.

Kasperson, R. E., Renn, O., Slovic, P., Brown, H., Emel, J., Goble, R., Kasperson, J. X. and Ratick, S., 'The social amplification of risk', *Risk Analysis*, 8 (1988), 177–87.

Katz, L., 'Risk modeling in the health care environment: an overview', in Chiavetta, J. A., Deeks, S., Goldman M. *et al.* (eds.), 'Proceedings of consensus conference: blood-borne HIV and hepatitis – optimizing the donor selection process', *Transfusion Medicine Reviews*, 17 (2003), 1–30.

Keeler, J. and Hall, P., 'Interest representation and the politics of protest', in Guyomarch, A., Machin, H., Hall, P. and Hayward, J. (eds.), *Developments in French Politics 2* (Houndmills: Palgrave, 2001), pp. 50–67.

Keeling, D., Tait, C. and Makris, M., 'Guideline on the selection and use of therapeutic products to treat haemophilia and other hereditary bleeding disorders', *Haemophilia*, 14 (2008), 671–84.

Kelleher, D., 'Self-help groups and medicine', in Gabe, J., Kelleher, D. and Williams, G. (eds.), *Challenging Medicine* (London: Routledge, 1994), 104–17.

Kelly, J., 'The liability of blood banks and manufacturers of clotting products to recipients of HIV-infected blood: a comparison of the law and reaction in the United States, Canada, Great Britain, Ireland and Australia', *John Marshall Law Review*, 27 (1994), 465–91.

Kent, J., Faulkner, A., Geesink, I. and FitzPatrick, D., 'Towards governance of human tissue engineered technologies in Europe: framing the case for a new regulatory regime', *Technological Forecasting and Social Change*, 73 (2006), 41–60.

Keohane, R. O., 'Governance in a partially globalized world', in Held, D. and McGrew, A. (eds.), *Governing Globalization: Power, Authority and Global Governance* (Cambridge: Polity Press, 2002), pp. 325–47.

Keohane, R. O. and Nye, J. S. Jr, 'Introduction', in Nye, J. S. Jr and Donahue, J. D. (eds.), *Governing in a Globalizing World* (Washington, DC: Brookings Institution, 2000), pp. 1–41.

Keown, J., 'The gift of blood in Europe: an ethical defence of EC Directive 89/381', *Journal of Medical Ethics*, 23 (1997), 96–100.

Kern, J. M. and Croy, B. B., 'A review of transfusion-associated AIDS litigation: 1984 through 1993', *Transfusion*, 34 (1994), 484–91.

Keshavjee, S., Weiser, S. and Kleinman, A., 'Medicine betrayed: hemophilia patients and HIV in the US', *Social Science and Medicine*, 53 (2001), 1081–94.

Kielmann, K. and Cataldo, F., 'Tracking the rise of the "expert patient" in evolving paradigms of HIV care', *AIDS Care*, 22 (2010), 21–8.

Kincaid, H., Dupré, J. and Wylie, A., *Value-Free Science?: Ideas and Illusions* (Oxford University Press, 2007).

Kingdon, J. W., *Agendas, Alternatives and Public Policies*, 1st edn (Boston: Little Brown, 1984).

Kirp, D., 'The politics of blood: hemophilia activism in the AIDS crisis', in Feldman, E. A. and Bayer, R. (eds.), *Blood Feuds: AIDS, Blood, and the Politics of Medical Disaster* (New York: Oxford University Press, 1999), pp. 293–322.

Kitcher, P., *Science, Truth and Democracy* (Oxford University Press, 2001).

Klein, H. G., 'Transfusion medicine: the evolution of a new discipline', *Journal of the American Medical Association*, 258 (1987), 2108–9.

Klein, H., 'Will blood transfusion ever be safe enough?', *Journal of the American Medical Association*, 284 (2000), 238–40.

Klein, H. G., Spahn, D. R. and Carson, J. L., 'Red blood cell transfusion in clinical practice', *Lancet*, 370 (2007), 415–26.

Kohler-Koch, B. and Rittberger, B., 'The governance turn in EU studies', *Journal of Common Market Studies*, 44 (2006), 27–49.

Kramer, J., 'Bad blood', *The New Yorker* (11/10/93), 74–95.

Krause, K., 'Integrate blood and plasma collections: a modern approach', *Pharmaceuticals Policy and Law*, 7 (2006), 49–54.

Kretschmer, V., Weippert-Kretschmer, M., Slonka, J., Karger, R. and Zeiler, T., 'Perspectives of paid whole and plasma donation', in Vyas, G. N. and Williams, A. E. (eds.), *Advances in Transfusion Safety* (Basel: Karger, 2005), pp. 101–11.

Krever, the Honourable Mr Justice H., *Commission of Inquiry on the Blood System in Canada*, 3 vols (Ottawa: Canadian Government Publishing, 1997).

Kriebel, D. and Tickner, J., 'Reenergizing public health through precaution', *American Journal of Public Health*, 91 (2001), 1351–55.

Krimsky, S. and Golding, D. (eds.), *Social Theories of Risk* (Westport, CT: Praeger Publishers, 1992).

Kritikos, M., 'Traditional risk analysis and releases of GMOs into the European Union: space for non-scientific factors?', *European Law Review*, 34 (2009), 405–32.

Kroner, B. K., Rosenberg, P. S., Aledort, L. M., Alvord, W. G. and Goedert, J. J., 'HIV-1 infection incidence among persons with hemophilia in the United States and Europe', *Journal of Acquired Immune Deficiency Syndromes*, 7 (1994), 279–86.

Kuhn, T. S., *The Structure of Scientific Revolutions*, 3rd edn (University of Chicago Press, 1998).

Landzelius, K., 'Introduction: Patient organization movements and new metamorphoses in patienthood', *Social Science and Medicine*, 62 (2006), 529–37.

Lane, R., 'Letter: Safety levels of blood for haemophiliacs', *The Independent*, 15/4/91.

Laperche, S., Rouger, P., Smilovici, W., Herve, P. and Lefrere, J.-J., 'Alternatives to nucleic acid testing in the blood transfusion service', *Lancet*, 360 (2002), 1519.

Larkin, M., 'WHO's blood-safety initiative: a vain effort?', *Lancet*, 355 (2000), 1245.

Laronche, M., 'La Fondation nationale de transfusion sanguine justifie ses comptes', *Le Monde*, 8/06/91.

Latour, B., *Science in Action: How to Follow Scientists and Engineers through Society* (Cambridge, MA: Harvard University Press, 1987).

Lee, M., 'Beyond safety? The broadening scope of risk regulation', *Current Legal Problems*, 62 (2009), 242–85.

Le Grand, J., 'Afterword', in Oakley, A. and Ashton, J. (eds.), R. M. Titmuss, *The Gift Relationship: From Human Blood to Social Policy* (London: LSE Books, 1997), pp. 333–9.

Leiss, W., Tyshenko, M. and Krewski, D., 'Men having sex with men donor deferral risk assessment: an analysis using risk management principles', *Transfusion Medicine Reviews*, 22 (2008), 35–57.

Leveton, L., Sox, H. C. and Stoto, M. A. (eds.), *HIV and the Blood Supply: An Analysis of Crisis Decisionmaking* (Committee to Study HIV Transmission through Blood and Blood Products, Division of Health Promotion and Disease Prevention) (Washington, DC: National Academy Press, 1995).

Levidow, L., 'Biotechnology regulation as symbolic normalization', *Technology Analysis & Strategic Management*, 6 (1994), 273–90.

Levi-Faur, D., 'Foreword', in Braithwaite, J., *Regulatory Capitalism: How it Works, Ideas for Making it Work Better* (Cheltenham: Edward Elgar Publishing, 2008), pp. vii–x.

Levy, J. A., Mitra, G. and Mozen, M. M., 'Recovery and inactivation of infectious retroviruses from factor VIII concentration', *Lancet*, ii (1984), 722–3.

Lewis, S., 'EC Commission and blood self-sufficiency', *Lancet*, 342 (1993), 1228.

Lindsay, A., *Report of the Tribunal of Inquiry into the Infection with HIV and Hepatitis C of Persons with Haemophilia and Related Matters* (Dublin: Government Publications, 2002).

Lodge, M., 'Regulation, the regulatory state and European politics', *West European Politics*, 31 (2009), 280–301.

Lofstedt, R. E. and Vogel, D., 'The changing character of regulation: a comparison of Europe and the United States', *Risk Analysis*, 21 (2001), 399–405.

Lucas, M., *Transfusion sanguine et SIDA en 1985: chronologie des faits et de decisions pour ce qui concern les hémophiles* (Paris: Inspections Générales des Affaires Sociales, 1991).

Maasen, S. and Weingart, P., 'What's new in scientific advice to politics?', in Maasen, S. and Weingart, P. (eds.), *Democratization of Expertise? Exploring Novel Forms of Scientific Advice in Political Decision-Making – Sociology of the Sciences*, 24 (2005), 1–19.

Magnette, J. P., 'European governance and civic participation: beyond elitist citizenship?', *Political Studies*, 51 (2003), 144–60.

Majone, G. (ed.), *Regulating Europe* (London: Routledge, 1996).

Majone, G., 'Regulatory legitimacy', in Majone, G. (ed)., *Regulating Europe* (London: Routledge, 1996), pp. 284–301.

'The rise of the regulatory state in Europe', *West European Politics*, 17 (1994), 77–101.

'What price safety? The precautionary principle and its policy implications', *Journal of Common Market Studies*, 40 (2002), 89–109.

Marshall, A.-M., 'Injustice frames, legality and the everyday construction of sexual harassment', *Law and Social Inquiry*, 28 (2003), 659–89.

Martin, L., 'Aids scandal survivors demand new payout', *The Guardian*, 16/4/06.

Martucci, J., 'Negotiating exclusion: MSM, identity and blood policy in an age of AIDS', *Social Studies of Science*, 40 (2010), 215–41.

Mather, L., 'Theorizing about trial courts: lawyers, policymaking and tobacco litigation', *Law and Social Inquiry*, 23 (1998), 897–940.

Mattli, W. and Woods, N., 'In whose benefit? Explaining regulatory change in global politics', in Mattli, W. and Woods, N. (eds.), *The Politics of Global Regulation* (Princeton University Press, 2009), pp. 1–43.

Mauss, M., *The Gift: The Form and Reason for Exchange in Archaic Societies* (London: Routledge, 1990), translated by W. D. Halls from M. Mauss, 'Essai sur le don', *Sociologie et Anthropologie* (Paris: Presses Universitaires de France, 1950).

McCann, M., *Rights at Work: Pay Equity Reform and the Politics of Legal Mobilization* (Chicago University Press, 1994).

McCarthy, M., 'What's going on at the World Health Organization?', *Lancet*, 360 (2002), 1108–10.

McCullough, J., 'Innovation in transfusion medicine and blood banking: documenting the record in 50 years of TRANSFUSION', *Transfusion*, 50 (2010), 2542–6.

Medical Correspondent, 'Blood victims need state relief fund of £2million a year', *The Guardian*, 16/5/87.

Meikle, J., 'Haemophiliacs demand £522m payout', *The Guardian*, 19/06/02.

Miller, M. J., 'Strict liability, negligence and the standard of care for transfusion-transmitted disease', *Arizona Law Review*, 36 (1994), 473–513.

Mnookin, R. H. and Kornhauser, L., 'Bargaining in the shadow of the law: the case of divorce', *Yale Law Journal*, 88 (1979), 950–97.

Moran, M., 'From command state to regulatory state', *Public Policy and Administration*, 15 (2000), 1–13.

Governing the Health Care State: A Comparative Study of the United Kingdom, the United States and Germany (Manchester University Press, 1999).

The British Regulatory State: High Modernism and Hyper-Innovation (Oxford University Press, 2003).

'Understanding the regulatory state', *British Journal of Political Science*, 32 (2002), 391–413.

Munzer, S., 'An uneasy case against property rights in body parts', *Social Philosophy and Policy*, 11 (1994), 259–86.

Murphy, M. F., Stanworth, S. J. and Yazer, M., 'Transfusion practice and safety: current status and possibilities for improvement', *Vox Sanguinis*, 100 (2011), 46–59.

Murray, T. H., 'Gifts of the body and the needs of strangers', *Hastings Center Report*, 17 (1987), 30–8.

National Health Service (NHS) Blood and Transplant, Current issues: deferral of men who have sex with men from blood donation: questions and answers: what are the donor selection criteria for men who have sex with men in other countries? (November 2011) (www.nhsbt.nhs.uk/current_issues/mhsm_faq/question_022.html).

Exclusion of Men who have Sex with Men, Position Statement, 11 April 2011.

Position Statement – November 2011: Deferral of men who have sex with men from blood donation (www.blood.co.uk/can-i-give-blood/exclusion).

National Hemophilia Foundation, Medical and Scientific Advisory Council, *Recommendations to Prevent AIDS in Patients with Hemophilia*, 14 January 1983.

National Research Council, *Risk Assessment in the Federal Government: Managing the Process* (Washington, DC: National Academy Press, 1983).

Nau, J.-Y., 'Entretien avec le president de l'Association des hémophiles', *Le Monde*, 28/08/92.

Nau, J.-Y., 'L'association française des hémophiles réclame des indemnisations immédiates', *Le Monde*, 16/09/91.

Nau, J.-Y. and Nouchi, F., 'Affaire d'etat', *Le Monde*, 16/09/91.

'Des produits sanguins ont été importés illégalement', *Le Monde*, 13/2/92.

'La réforme du système de transfusion visera à garantir "la plus grande sécurité possible"', *Le Monde*, 5/11/91.

Nauenberg, E. and Sullivan, S. D., 'Firm behavior in the US market for Factor VIII: a need for policy?', *Social Science and Medicine*, 39 (1994), 1591–603.

Nelkin, D., 'Cultural perspectives on blood', in Feldman, E. A. and Bayer, R. (eds.), *Blood Feuds: AIDS, Blood, and the Politics of Medical Disaster* (New York: Oxford University Press, 1999), pp. 274–92.

Nouchi, F., 'Vers un procès en assises de l'affaire du sang contaminé', *Le Monde*, 22/05/99.

Nyugen, V., 'Antiretroviral globalism: biopolitics and therapeutic citizenship', in Ong, A. and Collier, S. (eds.), *Global Assemblages: Technology, Politics and Ethics as Anthropological Problems* (Malden, MA: Blackwell Publishing, 2005), pp. 124–44.

Oakley, A. and Ashton, J., 'Introduction to the new edition', in Oakley, A. and Ashton, J., (eds.), R. M. Titmuss, *The Gift Relationship: From Human Blood to Social Policy* (London: LSE Books, 1997), pp. 3–13.

Oakley, A. and Ashton, J. (eds.), R. M. Titmuss, *The Gift Relationship: From Human Blood to Social Policy by Richard Titmuss* (London: LSE Books, 1997).

Oakley, R. and Sherman, J., 'Major pledges another £42million for haemophiliacs', *The Times*, 12/12/90.

Ogus, A. I., *Regulation: Legal Form and Economic Theory* (Oxford: Hart Publishing, 2004).

O'Mahony, B. and Turner, A., 'The Dublin Consensus Statement on vital issues relating to the collection of plasma and the manufacture of plasma products', *Vox Sanguinis*, 98 (2010), 447–50.

'The Dublin Consensus Statement 2011 on vital issues relating to the collection and provision of blood components and plasma-derived medicinal products', *Vox Sanguinis* 102 (2011) 140–3.

O'Malley, P., *Risk, Uncertainty and Government* (London: Glasshouse Press, 2004).

Organisation for Economic Co-operation and Development (OECD), *The OECD Innovation Strategy: Getting a Head Start on Tomorrow* (Paris: OECD, 2010).

Osborne, D. and Gaebler, T., *Reinventing Government: How the Entrepreneurial Spirit Is Transforming the Public Sector* (Reading, MA: Addison-Wesley, 1992).

Otway, H. and Winterfeldt, D., 'Expert judgment in risk analysis and management: process, context and pitfalls', *Risk Analysis*, 12 (1992), 83–93.

Penrod, J., 'PPTA leadership interview: Gordon Naylor', *The Source* (Spring 2009), 6–7.

Penrod, J. and Gustafson, M., 'The evolution of safety in source plasma collection', *The Source* (Spring 2009) 16–18.

Perkins, H. A. and Busch, M. P., 'Transfusion-associated infections: 50 years of relentless challenges and remarkable progress', *Transfusion*, 50 (2010), 2080–99.

Petryna, A., *Life Exposed: Biological Citizens after Chernobyl* (Princeton University Press, 2002).

Picciotto, S., 'Introduction: reconceptualizing regulation in an era of globalization', *Journal of Law and Society*, 29 (2005), 1–11.

Regulating Global Corporate Capitalism (Cambridge University Press, 2011).

Pierre, J. (ed.), *Debating Governance: Authority, Steering and Democracy* (Oxford University Press, 2000).

Pierre, J. and Peters, B. G., *Governance, Politics and the State* (Basingstoke: Palgrave Macmillan, 2000).

Pierson, P., 'The limits of design: explaining institutional origins and change', *Governance*, 13 (2000), 475–99.

Pieterse, M., 'Health, social movements and rights-based litigation in South Africa', *Journal of Law and Society*, 35 (2008), 364–88.

Pike, A., 'Plea by the haemophiliacs who have AIDS', *Financial Times*, 10/11/87.

Pillonel, J., Heraud-Bousquet, V., Pelletier, B., Semaille, C., Velter, A., Saura, C., Desenclos, J.-C., Dani, B. (and the blood donor epidemiological surveillance study group), 'Deferral from donating blood of men who have sex with men: impact on the risk of HIV transmission by transfusion in France', *Vox Sanguinis* 102 (2011) 13–21.

Pinch, T., 'The sun-set: the presentation of certainty in scientific life', *Social Studies of Science*, 11 (1981), 131–58.

Plant, R., 'Gifts, exchanges and the political economy of health care. Part 1: Should blood be bought and sold?', *Journal of Medical Ethics*, 3 (1977), 166–73.

Plasma Protein Therapeutics Association (PPTA) (www. pptaglobal.org).

Plasma Protein Therapeutics Association (PPTA), *PPTA Donor History Questionnaire* (www.pptaglobal.org).

Plasma Protein Therapeutics Association (PPTA), *Quality Standards of Excellence, Assurance and Leadership (QSEAL)* (www.pptaglobal.org).

Plasma Protein Therapeutics Association (PPTA), *The Facts about Plasma Collection* (www.pptaglobal.org).

Plasma Protein Therapeutics Association (PPTA), *The Facts about Plasma Used to Produce Life-Saving Therapies* (www.pptaglobal.org).

Polletta, F. and Jasper, J., 'Collective identity and social movements', *Annual Review of Sociology*, 27 (2001), 283–305.

Preda, A., *AIDS, Rhetoric and Medical Knowledge* (Cambridge University Press, 2004).

Prosser, T., *The Regulatory Enterprise: Government, Regulation and Legitimacy* (Oxford University Press, 2010).

Quigley, M., 'A NICE fallacy', *Journal of Medical Ethics*, 33 (2007), 465–6.

Rabinow, P., *French DNA – Trouble in Purgatory* (Chicago University Press, 1999).

Radin, M., *Contested Commodities: The Trouble with Trade in Sex, Children, Body Parts and Other Things* (Cambridge, MA: Harvard University Press, 1996).

Radin, P., '"To me, it's my life": medical communication, trust and activism in cyberspace', *Social Science and Medicine*, 62 (2006), 591–601.

Raffensperger, C. and Tickner, J. (eds.), *Protecting Public Health and the Environment: Implementing the Precautionary Principle* (Washington, DC: Island Press, 1999).

Rautonen, J., 'Finland: national policy', *Pharmaceuticals Policy and Law*, 7 (2006), 221–4.

Renn, O., 'Three decades of risk research: accomplishments and new challenges', *Journal of Risk Research*, 1 (1998), 49–71.

Resnik, S., *Blood Saga: Hemophilia, AIDS and the Survival of a Community* (Berkeley, CA: University of California Press, 1999).

Rio Declaration on Environment and Development (1992) (www.unep.org/Documents.Multi lingual/Default.asp?documentid=78&articleid=1163).

Rizza, C. R., Spooner, R. J. D., Giangrande, P. (on behalf of the UK Haemophilia Centre Doctors' Organisation), 'Treatment of haemophilia in the UK: 1981–1996', *Haemophilia*, 7 (2001), 349–59.

Roberts, D. J., Allain, J.-P., Kitchen, A. D., Field, S. and Bates, I., 'Blood transfusion in a global context', in Murphy, M. F. and Pamphilon, D. H. (eds.), *Practical Transfusion Medicine*, 3rd edn (Oxford: Wiley-Blackwell, 2009), pp. 251–65.

Robinson, E. A. E., 'The European Union Blood Safety Directive and its implications for blood services', *Vox Sanguinis*, 93 (2007), 122–30.

Roehr, B., 'Should men who have ever had sex with men be allowed to give blood? Yes', *British Medical Journal*, 338 (2009), b311.

Rose, N. and Novas, C., 'Biological citizenship', in Ong, A. and Collier, S. (eds.), *Global Assemblages: Technology, Politics and Ethics as Anthropological Problems* (Malden, MA: Blackwell Publishing, 2005), pp. 439–63.

Rosenau, J. N., 'Governance in a new global order', in Held, D. and McGrew, A. (eds.), *Governing Globalization: Power, Authority and Global Governance* (Cambridge: Polity Press, 2002), pp. 70–86.

Roth, W. K., 'Quarantine plasma: quo vadis?' *Transfusion Medicine and Hemotherapy*, 37 (2010), 118–22.

Rothstein, H., Huber, M. and Gaskell, G., 'A theory of risk colonization: the spiralling regulatory logics of institutional and societal risk', *Economy and Society*, 35 (2006), 91–112.

Rouger, P., 'France: national policy', *Pharmaceuticals Policy and Law*, 7 (2006), 255–9.

Rueda, A., 'Rethinking blood shield statutes in view of the hepatitis C pandemic and other emerging threats to the blood supply', *Journal of Health Law*, 34 (2001), 419–58.

Russo, D. J., 'Blood bank liability to recipients of HIV contaminated blood', *University of Dayton Law Review*, 87 (1992–1993), 87–107.

Sabatier, P. A., 'The advocacy coalition framework: revisions and relevance for Europe', *Journal of European Public Policy*, 5 (1998), 98–130.

SaBTO (Advisory Committee on the Safety of Blood, Tissues and Organs), Donor Selection Criteria Review (April 2011) (www.dh.gov.uk/en/Publicationsandstatistics/Publications/PublicationsPolicyAndGuidance/DH_129796?ssSourceSiteId=ab).

Evidence-base for the exclusion of potential donors due to sexual behaviours associated with an increased risk of transfusion-transmissible infections – a report to the Advisory Committee on the Safety of Blood, Tissues and Organs (SaBTO), SaBTO 9–27 January 2009, Agenda Item 5 (www.dh.gov.uk/prod_consum_dh/groups/dh_digitalassets/@dh/@ab/documents/digitalasset/dh_111629.pdf).

Summary of the Fourteenth Meeting, 3 May 2011 (www.dh.gov.uk/prod_consum_dh/groups/dh_digitalassets/@dh/@ab/documents/digitalasset/dh_129855.pdf).

Sanchez, A. M., Schreiber, G. B., Nass, C. C., Glynn, S., Kessler, D., Hirschler, N., Fridey, J., Bethel, J., Murphy, E. and Busch, M. P., 'The impact of male to male sexual experience on risk profiles of blood donors', *Transfusion*, 45 (2005), 404–13.

Sapolsky, H. M. and Finkelstein, S. N., 'Blood policy revisited: a new look at the "gift relationship"', *Public Interest*, 46 (1977), 15–27.

Saul, J., *The Tainted Gift: A Comparative Study of the Culture and Politics of the Contamination of the Blood Supply with the AIDS Virus in France and the United States* (Cornell University, unpublished PhD thesis, 2005).

Scharpf, F., *Governing in Europe: Effective and Democratic?* (Oxford University Press, 1999).

Schneider, D. M., 'What is kinship all about?', in Parkin, R. and Stone, L. (eds.), *Kinship and Family: An Anthropological Reader* (Oxford: Blackwell Publishing, 2003), pp. 257–74.

Schneider, W. H., 'Arnault Tzanck, MD (1886–1954)', *Transfusion Medicine Reviews*, 24 (2010), 147–50.

Scott, C., 'Governing without law or governing without government? New-ish governance and legitimacy of the EU', *European Law Journal*, 15 (2009), 160–73.

'Regulation in the age of governance: the rise of the post-regulatory state', in Jordana, J. and Levi-Faur, D. (eds.), *The Politics of Regulation: Institutions and Regulatory Reforms for the Age of Governance* (Cheltenham: Edward Elgar, 2004), pp. 145–74.

Seed, C., Kiely, P., Law, M. and Keller, A. J., 'No evidence of a significantly increased risk of transfusion-transmitted human immunodeficiency virus infection in Australia subsequent to implementing a 12-month deferral for men who have had sex with men', *Transfusion*, 50 (2010), 2722–30.

Setbon, M., *Pouvoirs contre sida: de la transfusion sanguine au dépistage: decisions et pratiques en France, Grande-Bretagne et Suède* (Paris: Éditions du Seuil, 1993).

Shaz, B. H. and Hillyer, C. D., 'Transfusion medicine as a profession: evolution over the past 50 years', *Transfusion*, 50 (2010), 2536–41.

Sherman, J., 'AIDS payment call for haemophiliacs', *The Times*, 13/4/87.

Shilts, R., *And the Band Played On: Politics, People and the AIDS Epidemic* (New York: Penguin Books, 1987).

Shu-Acquaye, F. and Innet, L., 'Human blood and its transfusion: the twists and turns of legal thinking', *Quinnipiac Health Law Journal*, 9 (2005–2006), 33–67.

Silvester, G., 'Regulatory overview – stable products background, current state of the art and future challenges', *Pharmaceuticals Policy and Law*, 7 (2006), 151–69.

Singer, P., 'Altruism and commerce: a defence of Titmuss against Arrow', *Philosophy and Public Affairs*, 2 (1973), 312–20.

Siplon, P., *AIDS and the Policy Struggle in the United States* (Washington, DC: Georgetown University Press, 2002).

Siplon, P. and Hoag, B., 'Protection for whom? Blood policy creation and interest representation', *Policy Studies Review*, 18 (2001), 193–224.

Skelcher, C. and Torfing, J., 'Improving democratic governance through institutional design: civic participation and democratic ownership in Europe', *Regulation & Governance*, 4 (2010), 71–91.

Skogstad, G., 'Legitimacy and/or policy effectiveness?: Network governance and GMO regulation in the European Union', *Journal of European Public Policy*, 10 (2003), 321–38.

Slovic, P., 'Perceived risk, trust, and democracy', *Risk Analysis*, 13 (1993), 675–82.

Smith, M. J., 'Mad cows and mad money: problems of risk in the marking and understanding of policy', *British Journal of Politics and International Relations*, 6 (2004), 312–32.

The Core Executive in Britain (Basingstoke: Macmillan, 1999).

Smith, R., 'Doctors question whether all blood transfusions are effective and necessary', *British Medical Journal*, 330 (2005), 558.

Snow, D. A., Rochford, E. B., Worden, S. K. and Benford, R. D., 'Frame alignment processes, micromobilization and movement participation', *American Sociological Review*, 51 (1986), 464–81.

Soldan, K. and Sinka, K., 'Evaluation of the de-selection of men who have had sex with men from blood donation in England', *Vox Sanguinis*, 84 (2003), 265–73.

Soulier, J.-P., *Transfusion et sida: le droit à la verité* (Paris: Éditions Frison-Roche, 1992).

Stainsby, D., Jones, H., Asher, D., Atterbury, C., Boncinelli, A., Brant, L., Chapman, C. E., Davison, K., Gerrard, R., Gray, A., Knowles, S., Love, E. M., Milkins, C., McClelland, D. B., Norfolk, D. R., Soldan, K., Taylor, C., Revill, J., Williamson, L. M. and Cohen, H. (SHOT Steering Group), 'Serious hazards of transfusion: a decade of haemovigilance in the UK', *Transfusion Medicine Reviews*, 20 (2006), 273–82.

Starr, D., *Blood: An Epic History of Medicine and Commerce* (New York: Alfred A. Knopf, 1998).

'Medicine, money, and myth: an epic history of blood', *Transfusion Medicine*, 11 (2001), 119–21.

Steele, J., *Risks and Legal Theory* (Oxford: Hart Publishing, 2004).

Steffen, M., 'The nation's blood: medicine, justice and the state', in Feldman, E. A. and Bayer, R. (eds.), *Blood Feuds: AIDS, Blood and the Politics of Medical Disaster* (New York: Oxford University Press, 1999), pp. 95–126.

Stein, J., Besley, J., Brook, C., Hamill, M., Klein, E., Krewski, D., Murphy, G., Richardson, M., Sirna, J., Skinner, M., Steiner, R., van Aken, P. and Devine, D., 'Risk-based decision-making for blood safety: preliminary report of a consensus conference', *Vox Sanguinis* (2011), doi: 10.111.j.1423-0410.2011.01526.x.

Stoker, G., 'Designing institutions for governance in complex environments: normative, rational choice and cultural institutional theories explored and contrasted', *ESRC Fellowship Paper No. 1* (University of Manchester, 2004).

Stoto, M. A., 'The precautionary principle and emerging biological risks: lessons from swine flu and HIV in blood products', *Public Health Reports*, 117 (2002), 546–52.

Strong, M., Farrugia, A. and Rebulla, P., 'Stem cell and cellular therapy developments', *Biologicals*, 27 (2009), 103–7.

Sullivan, P., 'Developing an administrative plan for transfusion medicine – a global perspective', *Transfusion*, 45 (2005), 224S–40S.

Sunstein, C., *Laws of Fear: Beyond the Precautionary Principle* (Cambridge University Press, 2005).

Syrett, K., 'Nice work? Rationing, review and the "legitimacy problem" in the new NHS', *Medical Law Review*, 10 (2002), 1–27.

Tabor, E., 'The epidemiology of virus transmission by plasma derivatives: clinical studies verifying the lack of transmission of hepatitis B and C viruses and HIV type 1', *Transfusion*, 39 (1999), 1160–8.

Terrence Higgins Trust, Blood donations regulations changes – THT's response and guide (www.tht.org.uk/informationresources/policy/healthpolicy/blooddonations).

The Contaminated Blood (Support for Infected and Bereaved Persons) Bill [HL] 2009–10.

Thelen, K. and Steinmo, S., 'Historical institutionalism in comparative politics', in Steinmo, S., Thelen, K. and Longstreth, F. (eds.), *Structuring Politics: Historical Institutionalism in Comparative Perspective* (Cambridge University Press, 1992), pp. 1–32.

Thomassen, J. and Schmitt, H., 'Democracy and legitimacy in the European Union' (2004) (www.mzes.unimannheim.de/publications/papers/Schmitt_26_1_04.pdf).

Titmuss, R. M., *The Gift Relationship: From Human Blood to Social Policy* (London: George Allen & Unwin, 1970).

Travis, A. and Dyer, C., 'Government offers extra £42 million to blood victims', *The Guardian*, 12/12/90.

Tutton, R., 'Gift relationships in genetics research', *Science as Culture*, 11 (2002), 524–42.

UK Haemophilia Centre Doctors' Organisation (UKHCDO) (AIDS Group), 'Prevalence of HIV antibody to HTLV-III in haemophiliacs in the UK', *British Medical Journal*, 293 (19/7/86), 175–6.

Unknown author, 'Class actions. Class certification of mass torts. Seventh circuit overturns rule 23(b) certification of a plaintiff class of haemophiliacs. In re Rhone-Poulenc Rorer Inc., 51 F.3d 1293 (7th Circ), Cert Denied, 116 S. Ct. 1984 (1995)', *Harvard Law Review*, 109 (1996), 870–5.

'Le professeur Jacques Roux et les docteurs Robert Netter et Michel Garetta ont été inculpés', *Le Monde*, 23/10/91.

'Of cash and care and simple sense', *The Guardian*, 2/12/90.

US Department of Health and Human Services, Advisory Committee on Blood Safety and Availability, Recommendations (www.hhs.gov/ash/bloodsafety/advisorycommittee/recommendations/resolutions.html).

Valverde, J. L., 'The political dimension of blood and plasma derivatives', *Pharmaceuticals Policy and Law*, 7 (2006), 21–33.

Vamvakas, E. C., 'Evidence-based practice of transfusion medicine: is it possible and what do the words mean?' *Transfusion Medicine Reviews*, 18 (2004), 267–78.

'Relative risk of reducing the lifetime blood donation deferral for men who have had sex with men versus currently tolerated transfusion risks', *Transfusion Medicine Reviews*, 25 (2011), 47–60.

'Scientific background on the risk engendered by reducing the lifetime blood donation deferral period for men who have sex with men', *Transfusion Medicine Reviews*, 23 (2009), 85–102.

van der Poel, C. L., Seifried, E. and Schaasberg, W. P., 'Paying for blood donations: still a risk?', *Vox Sanguinis*, 83 (2002), 285–93.

Various authors, 'Sang: Fabius et Dufoix relaxés, Hervé condamné', *Le Monde*, 10/03/99.

Vincent-Jones, P., 'Embedding economic relationships through social learning? The limits of patient and public involvement in healthcare governance in England', *Journal of Law and Society*, 38 (2011), 215–44.

Voak, D., Caffrey, E. A., Barbara, J. A. J., Pollock, A., Scott, M. and Contreras, M. C., 'Affordable safety for the blood supply in developed and developing countries', *Transfusion Medicine*, 8 (1998), 73–6.

Vogel, D., 'The globalization of pharmaceutical regulation', *Governance: An International Journal of Policy and Administration*, 11 (1998), 1–22.

'The hare and the tortoise revisited: the new politics of consumer and environmental regulation in Europe', *British Journal of Political Science*, 33 (2003), 557–80.

von Auer, F., 'Germany: national policy', *Pharmaceuticals Policy and Law*, 7 (2006), 225–31.

von Hoegen, I., 'Epidemiology regulatory landscape', *The Source* (Fall 2011), 22–3.

von Hoegen, I. and Gustafson, M., 'The importance of greater regulatory harmonization', *Pharmaceuticals Policy and Law*, 7 (2006), 171–6.

von Schubert, H., 'Donated blood – gift or commodity? Some economic and ethical considerations on voluntary vs commercial donation of blood', *Social Science and Medicine*, 39 (1994), 201–6.

Voo, T. C., 'The social rationale of the gift relationship', *Journal of Medical Ethics* 27 (2011) 663–7.

Vos, E., 'EU food safety regulation in the aftermath of the BSE crisis', *Journal of Consumer Policy*, 23 (2000), 227–55.

'Overcoming the crisis of confidence: risk regulation in an enlarged European Union', Inaugural Lecture, University of Maastricht (2004), 1–27.

Waldby, C. and Mitchell, R., *Tissue Economies: Blood, Organs, and Cell Lines in Late Capitalism* (Durham, NC: Duke University Press, 2006).

Waldby, C., Rosengarten, M., Treloar, C. and Fraser, S., 'Blood and bioidentity: ideas about self, boundaries and risk among blood donors and people living with Hepatitis C', *Social Science and Medicine*, 59 (2004), 1461–71.

Waller, C., 'Historical perspectives on blood and plasma products, the stakeholders and the issues', *Pharmaceuticals Policy and Law*, 7 (2006), 7–19.

Webster, A., *Health, Technology and Society: A Critique* (Houndmills: Palgrave Macmillan, 2007).

Webster, A. (ed.), *New Technologies in Health Care: Challenge, Change and Innovation* (Houndmills: Palgrave Macmillan, 2006).

Weimer, M., 'Applying precaution in EU authorization of genetically modified products – challenges and suggestions for reform', *European Law Journal*, 16 (2010), 624–57.

Weingart, P., 'Scientific expertise and political accountability: paradoxes of science in politics', *Science and Public Policy*, 26 (1999), 151–61.

Westfall, P. T., 'Hepatitis, AIDS and the blood product exemption from strict products liability in California: a reassessment', *Hastings Law Journal*, 37 (1986), 1101–32.

Wiener, J. B. and Rogers, M., 'Comparing precaution in the United States and Europe', *Journal of Risk Research*, 5 (2002), 317–49.

Williams, G., 'The genesis of chronic illness', *Sociology of Health and Illness*, 6 (1984), 175–200.

Williamson, C., 'The patient movement as an emancipation movement', *Health Expectations*, 11 (2008), 102–12.

Wilson, K., 'A framework for applying the precautionary principle to transfusion safety', *Transfusion Medicine Reviews*, 25 (2011), 177–83.

Wilson, K. and Ricketts, M. N., 'The success of precaution? Managing the risk of transfusion transmission of variant Creutzfeldt-Jakob disease', *Transfusion*, 44 (2004), 1475–8.

Wilson, K., Wilson, M., Hébert, P. C. and Graham, I., 'The application of the precautionary principle to the blood system: the Canadian blood system's vCJD donor deferral policy', *Transfusion Medicine Reviews*, 17 (2003), 89–94.

Wingspread Consensus Statement on the Precautionary Principle (1998) (www.sehn.org/wing.html).

World Federation of Hemophilia (WFH) (www.wfh.org).

World Health Organization (WHO), Blood Products and Related Biologicals, Blood Regulators Network (www.who.int/bloodproducts/brn/en).

Blood Transfusion Safety, Collaboration and Partnerships (www.who.int/bloodsafety/collaboration/en/index.html).

Blood Transfusion Safety, Global Collaboration for Blood Safety (2000–2010) (www.who.int/bloodsafety/gcbs/en).

Blood Transfusion Safety, Global Database on Blood Safety (www.who.int/bloodsafety/global_database/en).

Expert Committee on Biological Standardization (www.who.int/biologicals/expert_committee/en/index.html).

World Health Organisation (WHO), Expert Committee on Biological Standardization. Recommendations for the production, control and regulation of human plasma for fractionation (Technical Report Series – 941, Annex 4, 2006).

World Health Organization, *Global Blood Safety and Availability: Key Facts and Figures, 2010* (www.who.int/worldblooddonorday/media/en).

World Health Organization (WHO), *Global Consultation, 100% Voluntary Non-Remunerated Donation of Blood and Blood Components* (Geneva: WHO, 2009).

The Melbourne Declaration on 100% Voluntary Non-remunerated Donation of Blood and Blood Components (June 2009) (www.who.int).

Wynne, B., 'Creating public alienation: expert cultures of risk and ethics on GMOs', *Science as Culture*, 10 (2001), 445–81.

'May the sheep safely graze? A reflexive view of the expert-lay knowledge divide', in Lash, S., Szerszynski, B. and Wynne, B. (eds.), *Risk, Environment and Modernity: Towards a New Ecology* (London: Sage, 1996), pp. 44–83.

'Risk and social learning: reification to engagement', in Krimsky, S. and Golding, D. (eds.), *Social Theories of Risk* (Westport, CT: Praeger Publishers, 1992), pp. 275–300.

'Uncertainty and environmental learning: reconceiving science and policy in the preventative paradigm', *Global Environmental Change*, 2 (1992), 111–27.

Yeung, K., 'The regulatory state', in Baldwin, R., Cave, M. and Lodge, M. (eds.), *The Oxford Handbook of Regulation* (Oxford University Press, 2010), pp. 64–83.

Index

ABO blood groups, 77
acquired immune deficiency syndrome
    (AIDS), 2, 36
    case involving PWH, 90
    donor screening guidelines, 86, 89, 92
    as public health threat, 84
    risks posed by, 84, 89
    transmission through blood
        transmission, 84
Advisory Committee on Blood
    Safety and Availability (ACBSA),
    183, 184
Advisory Committee on the Safety
    of Blood, Tissues and Organs
    (SaBTO), 187, 189
AIDS capital of Europe, 68
AIDS Coalition to Unleash Power
    (ACT-UP), 143, 149, 158
AIDS donor screening guidelines, 93,
    108
albumin, 102
Aledort, Louis, 149
Allain, Jean-Pierre, 145–8
Alpha Therapeutic Corporation, 156
altruistic donation of blood, 58, 88
American Association of Blood Banks
    (AABB), 33, 80
American Blood Resources Association
    (ABRA), 108
    recommendations for plasma industry,
    109
American Red Cross (ARC), 33, 70, 80,
    183
Anti-haemophiliac Factor (AHF)
    product, 105
apheresis, 102
Archer Report, 141
Archer, Lord, 141, 161
Armour Pharmaceutical Company Inc,
    156
Arrow, Kenneth, 60
Article 168(4)(a) TFEU, 49

Baxter Healthcare Corporation, 156
Behringwerke, 107
Biologics Working Party (BWP), 215
blood banker, 81
blood banks
    AABB, 34
    ARC, 34
Blood Directive, 49–51, 120, 205
    aim and objective of, 205–7
    effectiveness of plasma products, 217
    related to plasma products, 215
blood donation, gift relationship in,
    12–15
    vs blood as commodity, 63–7
    economics in, 59–60
    ethics in, 58–9
    by prisoners, 90
    risk in, 60–3
blood donor selection criteria, 177–89
Blood Donor Selection Steering Group,
    187
Blood Products Advisory Committee
    (BPAC), 37, 109
    antibody testing on plasma donations,
    110
    deferral policy and, 183
Blood Products Laboratory (BPL), 85
Blood Regulators Network (BRN), 44
'blood shield' laws, 154
blood system, global governance of, 41–2
    Council of Europe, 45–9
    European Union (EU), 49–51
    key stakeholders, 51–4
    WHO, 42–5
blood transfusion, 4
    and AIDS risk, 84
    Council of Europe recommendations,
    45
    EDQM, role of, 46
    in England, 79
    evolution as transfusion medicine,
    79–83

blood transfusion (*cont.*)
  in France, 79–80
  as gift or commodity debate, 63–7
  HIV risk and, 83–94
  recognition as independent specialty,
    94–7
  risk categories, 89
blood, historical overview, 27–9
  ancient Greek, 27
  circulatory system, 28
  separation of albumin from
    blood, 29
  use in World War, 28–9
bloodletting, 27
blood-related disorders, 81
Brinkhous, Kenneth, 105
BSE crisis, at EU level, 172

Canada, PWH activism in, 140
cellular therapies, 4
Centers for Disease Control (CDC), 36,
    153
  on potential AIDS high-risk donors,
    110
  on transmissible agent, 108
centralized national blood service, 43
centrifugation method, 103
clotting disorders, treatment of, 38
clotting Factor VIII powder,
    purified, 38
clotting factors, 29, 38, 102, 105
coagulation Factors VIII and IX, 104
Cohn fractionation method, 29, 38, 102
Cohn, Dr Edwin, 29
collection and supply of blood, approach
    to, 79
  national blood services, 81
  organized, 82
  prison, 90, 104
  in US, 80
coloured donors, 61
commercialisation of blood, 61
Committee for Medicinal Products for
    Human Use (CHMP), 50
Committee of Ten Thousand (COTT),
    149, 155, 157, 163
Committee on Quality Assurance in
    Blood Transfusion Services, 45
Council of Europe, in regulating blood
    system, 45–9
  agreement with EDQM, 49
  Convention on European
    Pharmacopoeia, 47
  expert committees, 45
  in the field of blood transfusion, 46–9
  principle of VNRBD, 45

Public Health Committee, 48
  subject matter of recommendations, 45
Court of Justice, 212
cryoprecipitate, 38, 105, 132, 134
Cutter Laboratories, 105

Direction-Générale de la santé (DGS),
    87
Directive 2001/83/EC, 215
Directive for the Community code for
    medicinal products for human use,
    120
Directorate General for Health and
    Consumers (DG SANCO), 219
doctor–patient relationship, 131
  in the context of haemophilia
    treatment, 133
  transfusionist views, 82
donor deferral policies, 179
  for MSM, 181–9
Donor History Questionnaire, 114
donor screening guidelines, AIDS, 86,
    89, 93, 108
Dubin, Corey, 150, 157
Dufoix, Georgina, 146

Emergency Blood Transfusion Service,
    79
England
  AIDS epidemic in, 137
  Blood Products Laboratory (BPL), 85
  blood systems in, 57, 59
  blood transfusion regulation, 13, 32–3
  goal of national self-sufficiency in
    plasma products, 85
  proactive approach of governments and
    regulators, 94
  PWH activism in, 136–42
  source and method of blood donation,
    68–9
  transfusion service in, 79
  transfusionists' professional belief
    system, 85–7
  use of factor concentrates, 86
  work of haemophilia doctors in, 131
epistemic community, in governance
    processes, *see* transfusionists'
    professional belief system
ethical concerns, in using blood, 11–15,
    223–5
European Biological Standardisation
    Programme (BSP), 49
European Blood Alliance (EBA), 51
European Committee on Blood
    Transfusion (Steering Committee)
    (CD-P-TS), 45, 47

European Directorate for the Quality
of Medicines and HealthCare
(EDQM), 46–9
  agreement with Council of Europe, 49
  in biological standardisation
    programme, 49
  common sampling and testing
    programme, 49
  and EU regulation, 46
  issues involving medicines, role in, 47
  in quality assurance of blood
    components, role in, 47
  recommendations for blood
    components, 47
  responsibilities, 46
  role in promoting PhEur, 48
  trilateral agreement, 48
European Haemophilia Consortium
  (EHC), 53
European Medicines Agency (EMA), 49,
  50, 120, 215, 217, 218
European Pharmacopoeia (PhEur), 47
  at EU level, 48
  Commission, 47
European Public Assessment Reports
  (EPARs), 216
EU-wide regulatory regime, for blood,
  49–51, 199–203
  Blood Directive, 49–51
  direct political accountability, 201
  establishment of CHMP, 50
  precautionary principle, 170–3
Expert Committee on Biological
  Standardization (ECBS), 44
exploitative plasma collection
  practices, 82

Fabius, Laurent, 146
factor concentrates, 136, 156
  benefits of, 133
  commercialisation of, 105
  demand in Europe, 40
  donor exposure and, 132
  heat inactivation of, 104–6
  issues related to, 106–7
  limitations, 106
  usage in England, 86
  US-based companies, 40
Factor VIII concentrate, 103, 105, 106
Factor IX concentrate, 105, 106
Factor VIII deficiency, 135
failed haematologists, 81
FDA mandate, for blood and plasma
  products, 35–7
  automatic recall policy and, 109
  BPAC recommendations, 37
    vs CDC, 36, 84, 110
  decision-making processes, issues with,
    36
  for HIV high-risk donor groups, 40
  HIV risk and, 36, 109, 110, 112
  MSM donor deferral policy, 183,
    184–6
  for plasma collection centres and
    manufacturers, 109
  on quality and safety issues, 119
  viral inactivation testing, 119
Food Drug and Cosmetic Act., 35
for-profit plasma products industry,
    development of, 51, 101, see also risk
    regulation of blood and plasma
    products
  amount of blood collected from healthy
    donors, 103
  approach to plasma collection, 118–19
  collection of plasma and fractionation
    process, 96–7
  donor screening, 114
  factor concentrates and, 106–7
  financial support, 130
  harmonisation between US and EU on
    quality and safety, 121–2
  HIV risk and, 106–7
  industrial production, 102
  market access, 118
  plasma collection, 103, 113
  pooling of plasma donations, effect of,
    103
  post-war decades, in US, 103
  potential for industry collusion, 117–18
  research and innovation, 102–4
  viral inactivation research, 104–6
fractionation technology, 102
France
  blood transfusion regulation, 13, 32–3
  blood transfusion service in, 79–80
  financial reimbursement arrangements
    in, 88
  legal proceedings by PWH with HIV,
    145–8
  plasma products manufacturing in, 144
  PWH activism in, 142–8
  self-sufficiency in plasma products, 88
  source and method of donation, 68
  transfusionists' professional belief
    system in, 87–91
  VNRBD in, 63

Galen's theory of vitalism, 27
gamma globulin, 104
Garetta, Dr Michel, 91, 143, 145–8
Garvanoff, Jean-Pierre, 143

gay men, as plasma donors, 39
genetically modified (GM) products, 171
gift relationship, in blood donation,
    12–15, 31, 82
  vs blood as commodity, 63–7
  donor–recipient relationship, 61
  economics and, 59–60
  ethics and, 58–9
  importance of payment mechanism, 62
  Kenneth's views, 60
  risk and, 60–3
Gift Relationship, The, 57, 60, 63, 64, 82
Global Collaboration on Blood Safety
    (GCBS), 43
global plasma products industry,
    development of, 38–41
  cooperative arrangements, 41
  cryoprecipitate, 38
  in developing countries, 40
  harmonization measures on technical
    aspects, 41
  international spot market, 39
  OPEC of plasma, 40
  plasma donors, 39
  plasmapheresis technique, 38–9
  purified clotting Factor VIII powder, 38
  regulatory governance, 41–2
  safety and quality issues, 40
  short supply agreements, 39
  spot markets, 39
  strategies to obtain supplies of plasma,
    39–40
  in US border, 40
global regulatory governance, of blood
    system, 41–2
  Council of Europe, 45–9
  European Union (EU), 49–51
  key stakeholders, 51–4
  WHO, 42–5
good manufacturing practices (GMP),
    35, 119
Grady, Judge, 156, 157
Greater London Red Cross Blood
    Transfusion Service, 79
gross domestic product (GDP) and
    precautionary principle, 191

haematopoietic progenitor cells
    (HPCs), 4
haemophilia activism, 22, 126–9
Haemophilia Society, UK, 137
haemophilia treatment, 105, 131, 150
  haemophilia disorder, overview, 104
  options, 104–6
health social movements, 128

health-related activism, by PWH, 126–9
healthy adult donor, 103
heat inactivation method, for viral
    inactivation, 104–6
heat-treated products, 111, 134, 135
  factor concentrates, 104–6
Hemophilia AIDS Holocaust, 149
Hemophilia Federation of America, 150
Hemophilia/HIV Peer Association, 149
hepatitis, 60
hepatitis B virus (HBV) infection, 35,
    111, 134
  HBV vaccine for, 39
  risk of contracting, 110
  testing for, 106
  treatment to inactivate, 110
hepatitis non-A, non-B (NANB), 106
Hervé, Edmond, 146
high-risk donor categories, 89
HIV blood contamination episodes, 78,
    79, 117, 153, 164, 203
  approach to plasma collection, 118
  blood transfusion as gift or commodity
    debate and, 13
  in developed countries, 166
  development of transfusion medicine,
    role in, 94–7
  donor screening and, 177
  donor–recipient relationship, 124
  EU regulation and, 49
  FDA mandates and, 36, 37
  need for law, 17–20
  plasma product safety issues post,
    113–22
  political mobilisation of haemophilia
    group and, 126–9
  political scandals and, 2
  politization of risk and, 10
  PWH and, 129–36
  risk governance and, 4–8, 226
  as a risk to national blood systems,
    83–94
  in United States, 83–5, 150, 151
HIV high-risk donor groups, 40
human herpes virus–8 (HHV–8), 183
human immunodeficiency virus (HIV),
    2, *see also* HIV blood contamination
    episodes; transfusionists'
    professional belief system
  blood contamination, 2
  in France, 91
  testing, 2, 32, 40, 87, 91
  VNRBD and, 67–70
Hyland Laboratories, 105
hyper-immune plasma, 104

immunoglobulin, 102
innovation, product and process, 101
 automated processes, 102
 Cohn fractionation method, 102
 development of cryoprecipitate, 105
 factor concentrates, 105
 viral inactivation research, 106
Institute of Medicine (IOM), 152
 report on plasma products industry,
  111, 185
inter-connected transnational markets,
 development of, 73
international 'spot market', for plasma
 products, 39
International Conference on
 Harmonisation (ICH), 48
International Federation of Blood Donor
 Organizations (IFBDO/FIODS), 52
International Federation of Red Cross
 and Red Crescent Societies (IFRC),
 53
International Patient Organisation
 for Primary Immunodeficiencies
 (IPOPI), 53
International Plasma Fractionators
 Association (IPFA), 51–2
International Quality Plasma Program
 (IQPP), 114, 119
International Society of Blood
 Transfusion (ISBT), 51, 80
intravenous drug users, 89
Ireland, PWH activism in, 140

l'affaire du sang contaminé, 144
l'Association des polytransfusés (AP), 143
l'Association française des hémophiles
 (AFH), 130, 161
 compensation fund for PWH with
  HIV, 142
 against parliamentary representatives,
  146
 relation with AP, 143
la médicine liberale, notion of, 131
Landsteiner, Karl, 28
liquid plasma, shelf-life of, 29
Lucas Report, 144, 146
Lucas, Michel, 144

Macfarlane Trust, 137–8
Major, Prime Minister John, 139
malaria, 60
Manor House, 140, 160
March, Andrew, 141
market-based blood system, 57
Mauss, 58

Medical and Scientific Advisory Council
 (MASAC), 131, 149, 150
medico-scientific community, 81
medico-scientific professions, 92
Melbourne Declaration, 43
men who have sex with men
 (MSM), 86
 blood donations by, 177
 deferral policies for, 178, 181–9
 and HIV risk, 179
Mengele, Josef, 149
Miles Inc, 156
Montagnier, Dr Luc, 89
Multi-District Litigation (MDL)
 procedure, 156
multi-valued human biological materials,
 73, 101

nanofiltration, 115
national blood services
 approach to blood collection and
  supply, 81
 in England, 32–3
 FDA regulations in US, 35–7
 in France, 32–3
 as gift relationship, 31
 impact of institutional and regulatory
  dysfunction, 35
 in United States, 33–7
National Centre for Blood Transfusion,
 130
National Donor Deferral Registry, 114
national healthcare budgets, 43
National Hemophilia Foundation
 (NHF), 130, 131, 157
 approach to haemophilia doctors, 159
 legal proceedings on behalf of PWH,
  148–57
 relation with HIV-infected members,
  150
 relationhsip with COTT, 155, 163
 relationship with HIV-infected
  members, 151
 SAC negotiaitons and, 151
Netter, Dr Robert, 145
non-heat-treated products, 135
non-profit national blood services, 82
nucleic acid amplification technology
 (NAT), 115, 181, 190

Official Medicines Control Laboratories
 (OMCL), 48, 49
Ognall, Justice, 139
Oliver, Percy Lane, 79
OPEC of plasma, 40

organized blood collection, as a business, 82
orphan diseases, 117

paid donors, 42
  risk associated with, 35
Paris blood service, 88, 92
  transfusionists' views, 91
pathogen reduction (or inactivation) technologies (PRT), 193
pathogen screening technologies, 190–4
patient-recipient groups, 53
people with haemophilia (PWH), 33, 38, 53, 82, 86, 117, 118, 124
  acceptable risk, 133
  AIDS involving, 108
  cases of AIDS involving French PWH, 90
  demand for US-sourced plasma products, 88
  donor exposure and, 132
  England, activism in, 136–42
  factor concentrates for, 89
  financial compensation, 140, 144
  France, activism in, 142–8
  group litigations and, 138
  heat-treated factor, use of, 134
  HIV blood contamination episodes and, 129–36
  HIV in, 99, 111, 112, 135
  infected with HCV, 140
  legal difficulties in US, 154
  life expectancy of, 132
  mobilisation of, 126–9, 226
  Parisian blood service and, 91
  pneumocystis carinii pneumonia involving, 108
  relationship with treating doctors, 130
  sourcing of plasma products, 67
  treatment options, 104–6
  US, activism in, 148–57
  use of law and, 158–64
  with factor concentrates, 106
peripheral blood stem cell transplants, 4
Pharmacopoeial Discussion Group (PDG), 48
Plasma Master File (PMF) system, 120, 121, 216, 218
Plasma Protein Therapeutics Association (PPTA), 51–2
plasma-derived medicinal products, 1, 82, see also risk regulation of blood and plasma products
  in France, 88
  in treatment of haemophilia, see haemophilia treatment

  role and impact of law on, 15–17
  though VNRBD, 13
plasmapheresis centres, 40
plasmapheresis technique, 38–9, 102, 103, 114
platelets, 29
pneumocystis carinii pneumonia, 108
political context of risk governance, 10–11
Pool, Dr Judith Graham, 38, 105
Posner, Judge Richard A., 156
precautionary principle, 227
  blood donor selection criteria, 177–89
  blood safety and, 175–7
  cost-effectiveness criteria, 191
  at EU level, 170–3
  pathogen screening and reduction technologies, 190–4
  in public health context, 158–64
  in US, 172
prison inmates, as plasma donors, 39, 68
  transfusionists' views, 90
  as a valuable source, 104
professional recognition, as transfusionists, 81–2
public health and precautionary principle, 158–64
Public Health Service Blood, Organ and Tissue Safety Working Group (BOTS WG), 184

qualified donor, 114
quality-adjusted life years (QALY) and precautionary principle, 191

reciprocity in social relations, 58
recombinant DNA technology (rFVIII), 116
Red Cross, 40
  blood sourcing and supply, role in, 53
  British, work in blood transfusion service, 79
replacement donors, 42
Rhone-Poulenc Rorer Inc, 156
Ricky Ray Hemophilia Fund Act, 164
Ricky Ray Hemophilia Relief Bill, 152
Ricky Ray Hemophilia Relief Fund, 152
risk governance
  blood as a gift vs commodity debate, 12–15
  in the context of blood contamination, 4–8
  effective, 17–20
  ethical concerns of, 11–15
  of multi-valued human biological materials, 228–9

in political context, 10–11
politics of precaution and, 174–94
in public health, 2–8
role and impact of law on, 15–17,
    225–7
socio-economic context of sourcing
    and supply issues, 14–15
transfusionists' professional belief
    system and, 91–4
VNRBD and, 70–3
risk regulation of blood and plasma
    products, 227
    Blood Directive, aim and objective of,
        205–7
    blood quality and safety, 203–14
    context of governance, 214–19
    effectiveness of plasma products and,
        216–19
    in EU, 199–203
    risk assessment, 207–14
Rosenberg, Michael, 149
Ryan White CARE Act, 151

Select Committee of Experts on Quality
    Assurance in Blood Transfusion
    Services, 47
self-sufficiency, in control of plasma
    products, 85
serological testing, on blood donations,
    92–3
serum hepatitis, transmission via blood,
    60
Shalala, Donna, 152
Shanbrom, Dr Edward, 105, 106
short supply agreements, for plasma
    products, 39
'skid row' neighbourhoods, 39, 60
Skipton Fund, 140
social rehabilitation, blood donation as
    an act of, 68, 90
source plasma, 39
Special Assistance Council (SAC), 150
syphilis, 60

Tainted Blood group, 140, 142, 160
Thatcher, Prime Minister Margaret, 139
Titmuss, Richard, 82, see also gift
    relationship, in blood donation 31
    arguments in favour of VNRBD, 64
    comparison of blood systems in
        England and US, 59
    conceptualisation of blood donation as
        gift relationship, 58
    on coloured donors, 61
    criticism on his representation of US
        blood system, 62–3

on donor–patient/recipient
    relationship, 61
economic efficiency of blood donation,
    59–60
establishment of market-based blood
    system, 57
importance of gift-giving in social
    relations, 58
on financial reward for blood donation,
    59
on growth of paid donors in US, 61
on payment mechanism, 62
on risk involved in blood transfusion,
    60–3
on risk of serum hepatitis from
    transmission, 60
on selection of donors, 60
transfusion consultant, 94
transfusion medicine, development of,
    94–7
transfusionists' professional belief
    system, 64–5, 77–8, 82
    approach to scientific disciplines, 92
    development of serological testing,
        92–3
    in England, 85–7
    in France, 87–91
    goal of national self-sufficiency, 91
    of Parisian blood supply, 91
    prison inmates as blood donors, 90
    relationship with loyal donors, 92
    risk governance and, 91–4
    role in developing transfusion
        medicine, 94–7
    in United States, 83–5, 92
    in VNRBD, 71, 90
transfusion-transmitted infections
    (TTIs), 7, 12, 44, 71, 101, 166, 176,
        186, 188, 218, 226
Tzanck, Dr Arnault, 79–80

UK Haemophilia Centre Doctors'
    Organisation (UKHCDO), 131
UK Haemophilia Society, 159
umbilical cord blood, 4
United States
    blood collection in, 80
    blood system in, 59, 62, 83
    factor concentrates, issues with, 86, 87,
        112, 113, 135, 139, 141
    FDA regulations related to blood and
        plasma products, 35–7
    HIV risk in, 83–5
    HIV testing in, 87
    legal proceedings by PWH with HIV,
        148–57

United States (*cont.*)
national blood services in, 33–7
paid donors, growth of, 61, 89
plasma products industry, 38–41, 64,
107, 108, 110, 112, 115, 141
precautionary principle in, 172
PWH activism in, 148–57
risk of serum hepatitis from
transmission in, 60
source and method of blood donation,
69
threats posed by AIDS, 84

variant Creutzfeldt-Jakob disease (vCJD),
97
viral inactivation research, 104–6
gold standard, 115
voluntary non-remunerated blood
donation (VNRBD), 12, 39, 56, 78,
83
blood safety and, 65
Council of Europe and, 45
deleterious effect on blood system, 67
in France, 80, 88
goal of national self-sufficiency, 86
HIV risk and, 67–70
IFBDO and, 52
issues within EU, 211–13
merits of, 63
options of donor self-exclusion, 92
plasma products through, 13
as preferred sourcing method, 82
risk governance and, 70–3
stakeholders promoting, 53
transfusionists' support for, 64–5,
72–3, 92, 96–7

Tzanck's view, 79–80
WHO and, 42–3

Wadleigh, Jonathan, 155
White, Ryan, 148, 151
World Blood Donor Day, 42
World Federation of Hemophilia (WFH),
53, 130
World Health Organization (WHO), 40
and VNRBD, 42–3
basis for blood collection, 42
Blood Regulators Network
(BRN), 44
centralised blood collection systems,
43
criticism on optimum approach, 43
in developing norms, standards, and
guidance, 44
expert groups for plasma products, 44
global consultation meeting, 42
governance initiatives, 43
Melbourne Declaration, 43
optimum organisational approach, 43
prioritisation of global blood safety, 43
in regulating blood system, 42–5
specific constitutional functions, 44
testing technologies, 44
WHO Global Blood Safety Network,
44
WHO Global Forum for Blood Safety,
44
World Trade Organization (WTO), 170
World War Two, blood transfusion
service, 80, 82, 105

zero-risk blood supply, 176

Lightning Source UK Ltd.
Milton Keynes UK
UKOW07f1123031214

242585UK00001B/114/P